Lecture Notes in Computer Science 14402

Founding Editors

Gerhard Goos
Juris Hartmanis

Editorial Board Members

The series Lecture Notes in Computer Science (LNCS), including its subseries Lecture Notes in Artificial Intelligence (LNAI) and Lecture Notes in Bioinformatics (LNBI), has established itself as a medium for the publication of new developments in computer science and information technology research, teaching, and education.

LNCS enjoys close cooperation with the computer science R & D community, the series counts many renowned academics among its volume editors and paper authors, and collaborates with prestigious societies. Its mission is to serve this international community by providing an invaluable service, mainly focused on the publication of conference and workshop proceedings and postproceedings. LNCS commenced publication in 1973.

Howon Kim · Jonghee Youn
Editors

Information Security Applications

24th International Conference, WISA 2023
Jeju Island, South Korea, August 23–25, 2023
Revised Selected Papers

 Springer

Editors
Howon Kim ⓘ
Pusan National University
Busan, Korea (Republic of)

Jonghee Youn
Yeungnam University
Gyeongbuk, Korea (Republic of)

ISSN 0302-9743   ISSN 1611-3349 (electronic)
Lecture Notes in Computer Science
ISBN 978-981-99-8023-9   ISBN 978-981-99-8024-6 (eBook)
https://doi.org/10.1007/978-981-99-8024-6

This Springer imprint is published by the registered company Springer Nature Singapore Pte Ltd.
The registered company address is: 152 Beach Road, #21-01/04 Gateway East, Singapore 189721, Singapore

Paper in this product is recyclable.

Preface

In the modern digital landscape, progress in information technology has undoubtedly improved various facets of our daily lives. Nonetheless, as technology advances, so do the intricacies of safeguarding data, networks, and systems. Therefore, engaging in research, the dissemination of knowledge, and the creation of innovative techniques are of paramount importance, to ensure various aspects of information security.

The World Conference on Information Security Applications (WISA) is a premier security research event, hosted by the Korea Institute of Information Security and Cryptology (KIISC); sponsored by the Ministry of Science, ICT, and Future Planning (MSIP); and co-sponsored by the Electronics & Telecommunications Research Institute (ETRI), the Korea Internet & Security Agency (KISA), and the National Security Research Institute (NSR). We are open to participants coming from diverse backgrounds, including researchers and practitioners passionate about advancing the state of the art as well as addressing fundamental security challenges. In 2023, WISA explored the innovative possibilities of various technologies in enhancing (and threatening) cyber security: artificial intelligence (AI), blockchain-driven security, hardware cryptography, quantum and post-quantum cryptography, as well as other technical and practical aspects of security applications.

This volume is composed of the 25 selected papers presented at WISA during August 23–25, 2023, on Jeju Island, Republic of Korea, and one additional revised paper accepted from WISA 2022. Furthermore, we were honored to have an invited talk by SeongHan Shin from the National Institute of Advanced Industrial Science and Technology, Japan, entitled "5G-AKA and EAP-AKA from Cryptographic Perspectives". In addition, we especially welcomed valuable insights from our two keynote speakers: Bhasin Shivam from Nanyang Technological University, Singapore, who gave a talk on "Leaking AI: On Side-Channel Vulnerabilities (and More) on EdgeML Devices", and Bo-Yin Yang from Academia Sinica, Taiwan, whose presentation focused on "Post-Quantum Cryptography: Now and Onwards".

The great dedication and tireless work of the General Chairs, Organizing Committee, and reviewers; the generous support of our sponsors and co-sponsors; and the enthusiastic involvement of all attendees collectively resulted in yet another high-quality event. We extend our heartfelt appreciation to every Program Committee member for their invaluable contributions, and we sincerely thank reviewers, authors, and participants from across the globe for their unwavering support. Finally, we sincerely appreciate the assistance of the Springer team for the LNCS proceedings.

September 2023

Howon Kim
Jonghee Youn

Organization

General Chair

Yoojae Won — Chungnam National University,
Republic of Korea

Program Committee Chairs

Howon Kim — Pusan National University, Republic of Korea
Jonghee Youn — Yeungnam University, Republic of Korea

Organizing Committee Chairs

Kiwook Sohn — Seoul National University of Science and
Technology, Republic of Korea
Jong-Hyouk Lee — Sejong University, Republic of Korea

Program Committee

Joonsang Baek	University of Wollongong, Australia
Xiaofeng Chen	Xidian University, China
Jin-Hee Cho	Virginia Tech, USA
Yeongpil Cho	Hanyang University, Republic of Korea
Dooho Choi	Korea University, Republic of Korea
Hongjun Choi	DGIST, Republic of Korea
Swee-Huay Heng	Multimedia University, Malaysia
Jin Hong	University of Western Australia, Australia
Qiong Huang	South China Agricultural University, China
Eul-Gyu Im	Hanyang University, Republic of Korea
Yuseok Jeon	UNIST, Republic of Korea
YouSung Kang	ETRI, Republic of Korea
Dongseong Kim	The University of Queensland, Australia
Doowon Kim	University of Tennessee, USA
Jong Kim	POSTECH, Republic of Korea
Jongsung Kim	Kookmin University, Republic of Korea
Taeguen Kim	Soonchunhyang University, Republic of Korea

Hiroaki Kikuchi	Meiji University, Japan
Hyun Kwon	Korea Military Academy, Republic of Korea
Yonghwi Kwon	University of Virginia, USA
Young-Woo Kwon	Kyungpook National University, Republic of Korea
Changhoon Lee	Seoul National University of Science and Technology, Republic of Korea
Hyungon Moon	UNIST, Republic of Korea
Eueung Mulyana	Bandung Institute of Technology, Indonesia
Masakatsu Nishigaki	Shizuoka University, Japan
Marcus Peinado	Microsoft, USA
Junghwan Rhee	University of Central Oklahoma, USA
Ulrich Rührmair	Ruhr University Bochum, Germany
Kouichi Sakurai	Kyushu University, Japan
Hwajeong Seo	Hansung University, Republic of Korea
Seog Chung Seo	Kookmin University, Republic of Korea
Junji Shikata	Yokohama National University, Japan
Sang Uk Shin	Pukyong National University, Republic of Korea
SeongHan Shin	National Institute of Advanced Industrial Science and Technology (AIST), Japan
Amril Syalim	University of Indonesia, Indonesia
Naoto Yanai	Osaka University, Japan
Meng Yu	Roosevelt University, USA

Organizing Committee Members

Haehyun Cho	Soongsil University, Republic of Korea
Dong-Guk Han	Kookmin University, Republic of Korea
Misim Jung	Culture Makers, Republic of Korea
Bona Kim	SSNC, Republic of Korea
Eunyoung Kim	NSR, Republic of Korea
Jeong Nyeo Kim	ETRI, Republic of Korea
Kibom Kim	NSR, Republic of Korea
Hyun O Kwon	KISA, Republic of Korea
Yoonjung Kwon	NAONWORKS, Republic of Korea
Im-Yeong Lee	Soonchunhyang University, Republic of Korea
Jun Lee	KISTI, Republic of Korea
Daesung Moon	ETRI, Republic of Korea
Dong-Hwan Oh	KISA, Republic of Korea
Jung Taek Seo	Gachon University, Republic of Korea
Jungsuk Song	KISTI, Republic of Korea

Invited Talk and Keynotes

5G-AKA and EAP-AKA from Cryptographic Perspectives (Invited Talk)

Seonghan Shin

National Institute of Advanced Industrial Science
and Technology, Japan

Abstract: As widely known, 5G is an infrastructure technology essential for IoT, smart cities, AR/MR/VR, ultra-high-definition video services, etc. Currently, 3GPP has been standardizing the 5G-AKA and EAP-AKA' protocols for mutual authentication between UE (User Equipment) and HN (Home Network) and sharing anchor keys in 5G communications. In this talk, I will revisit the 5G-AKA and EAP-AKA' protocols from cryptographic perspectives.

Leaking AI: On Side-Channel Vulnerabilities (and more) on EdgeML Devices (Keynote)

Bhasin Shivam

Nanyang Technological University, Singapore

Abstract: EdgeML combines the power of machine (deep) learning and edge (IoT) devices. Owing to its capability of solving difficult problems in sensor nodes and other resource constrained devices, EdgeML has seen adoption in a variety of domains like smart manufacturing, remote monitoring, smart homes etc. However, deployment on edge devices exposes machine/deep learning algorithms to a range of new attacks, especially physical attacks. In this talk, we explore the landscape of practical physical attacks on EdgeML. First, we show how side-channel attacks can be used to reverse engineer architectures and parameters of deep learning models. These models are often proprietary with commercial value and contain information on sensitive training data. The feasibility of these attacks is shown both on standalone microcontrollers as well as commercial ML accelerators. Further, we demonstrate practical and low-cost cold boot-based model recovery attacks on Intel Neural Compute Sticks 2 (NCS2) to recover the model architecture and weights, loaded from the Raspberry Pi with high accuracy. The proposed attack remains unaffected by the model encryption features of the NCS2 framework.

Post-Quantum Cryptography: Now and Onwards (Keynote)

Bo-Yin Yang

Academia Sinica, Taiwan

Abstract: NIST has recently selected a first group of candidates for standardization in its PQC (Post-Quantum Cryptography) standardization process. However, we have not come close to achieving or even thoroughly preparing for the migration to PQC, yet. We will discuss what has transpired in PQC, what is the state-of-the-art in PQC, what topics do remain in PQC, and what needs to be done in the upcoming post-quantum migration. Finally, we will summarize what is happening around the world in regards to PQC, particularly to the ongoing standardization process(es).

Contents

Attacks and Defenses

Hardware and Software Security

Post-Quantum Cryptography and Quantum Cryptanalysis

Cryptography

A New Higher Order Differential of LCB

Naoki Shibayama$^{(\boxtimes)}$ and Yasutaka Igarashi

Tokyo University of Science, 2641 Yamazaki, Noda, Chiba 278-8510, Japan
7323703@ed.tus.ac.jp, yasutaka@rs.noda.tus.ac.jp

Abstract. LCB is a 32-bit block cipher proposed by Roy et al. in 2021. The designers evaluated its security against differential cryptanalysis, linear cryptanalysis, and so on. On the other hand, it has not been reported the security of LCB against higher order differential cryptanalysis, which is one of the algebraic attacks. In this paper, we applied higher order differential cryptanalysis to LCB. Consequently, we found a new full-round higher order differential characteristic of LCB using 1-st order differential. Exploiting this characteristic, it is possible to apply the distinguishing attack to full-round LCB with 2 chosen plaintexts. Then, we also show that LCB can be broken under the condition for known plaintext attacks. Furthermore, we tried to improve the round function of LCB to analysis this vulnerability.

Keywords: Cryptanalysis · Higher order differential · Saturation property · Block cipher · LCB

1 Introduction

LCB [1] is a 32-bit block cipher with a 64-bit secret key proposed by Roy et al. in 2021. The number of rounds is 10. The designers claim that LCB exploits the benefits of Feistel structure and Substitution Permutation Network to give more security. Then, they evaluated its security against typical attack, such as differential attack, linear attack, and impossible differential attack, and argued that LCB is secure enough against these attacks. So far, Chan et al. [2] reported the results of differential attack on LCB. On the other hand, it has not been reported the security of LCB against higher order differential attack. Higher order differential attack is a powerful and versatile attack on block cipher. It exploits the properties of higher order differential of functions, defined by Lai, and derive an attack equation to estimate the key, and then determines the key by solving a formula.

Our Contributions. This paper shows a new higher order differential of LCB. By focusing on the structure of LCB, we found the 10-round, i.e., full-round higher order differential characteristic of LCB using 1-st order differential. As far as we know, this is the first report which investigates the higher order differential of LCB. If we use it, it is possible to apply the distinguishing attack to full-round of LCB with 2 chosen plaintexts and encryption operations. Furthermore, we

H. Kim and J. Youn (Eds.): WISA 2023, LNCS 14402, pp. 3–15, 2024.
https://doi.org/10.1007/978-981-99-8024-6_1

also derive an equivalent LCB and show that the LCB is attackable by known plaintext attack with only 1 known plaintext. In order to overcome this weakness, we tried to improve the round function of LCB. As a result, the modified LCB reduced the length of the higher order differential characteristics to 5-round, and its algorithm is confirmed to be strengthened by our computer experiments.

Outline. The remainder of this paper is organized as follows. Section 2 explains the algorithm of LCB. Section 3 gives the general theory of the higher order differential attack. Section 4 shows the results of the higher order differential characteristics of LCB. Then, we perform the attack to full-round LCB in Sect. 5. Section 6 presents the modified LCB and describes its security against higher order differential attack. Section 7 finally concludes the paper.

2 The Algorithm of LCB

This section briefly describes the structure of LCB. It consists of the permutation, the key addition, and the swap. Figure 1 shows the data processing part of LCB. The function F Block consists of three permutations shown in Fig. 2. The symbol 'S', 'P', and 'L' denote the 4-bit, 8-bit, and 16-bit permutation as shown in Table 1, Table 2, and Table 3 respectively. We represent the MSB of these table as $i = 1$. The symbol '$\oplus$' represents an Exclusive-OR operation. Its input plaintext and output ciphertext are represented by $\mathbf{X}_1$ and $\mathbf{C}_{10}$ respectively. Let $\mathbf{X}_i = (X_i^{\mathrm{L}}, X_i^{\mathrm{R}})$, $X_i^{\mathrm{J}} = (x_{i,1}^{\mathrm{J}}, x_{i,2}^{\mathrm{J}}, x_{i,3}^{\mathrm{J}}, x_{i,4}^{\mathrm{J}})$, $x_{i,\ell}^{\mathrm{J}} \in \mathrm{GF}(2)^4$ and $\mathbf{C}_i = (C_i^{\mathrm{L}}, C_i^{\mathrm{R}})$, $C_i^{\mathrm{J}} = (c_{i,1}^{\mathrm{J}}, c_{i,2}^{\mathrm{J}}, c_{i,3}^{\mathrm{J}}, c_{i,4}^{\mathrm{J}})$, $c_{i,\ell}^{\mathrm{J}} \in \mathrm{GF}(2)^4$ be an i-th round input and output respectively, where $1 \leq i \leq 10$, $\mathrm{J} \in \{\mathrm{L}, \mathrm{R}\}$, $1 \leq \ell \leq 4$. $\mathbf{RK}_i = (RK_i^{\mathrm{L}}, RK_i^{\mathrm{R}})$, $RK_i^{\mathrm{J}} = (rk_{i,1}^{\mathrm{J}}, rk_{i,2}^{\mathrm{J}}, rk_{i,3}^{\mathrm{J}}, rk_{i,4}^{\mathrm{J}})$, $rk_{i,\ell}^{\mathrm{J}} \in \mathrm{GF}(2)^4$ are 32-bit round keys. The number of iterated rounds of data processing part is 10.

The key scheduling function divides a 64-bit secret key $\mathbf{K}$ into four 16-bit subkeys K_ℓ as follows.

$$\mathbf{K} = (K_1, K_2, K_3, K_4) \tag{1}$$

For i-th round of encryption, the round keys $\mathbf{RK}_i$ are given by Table 4.

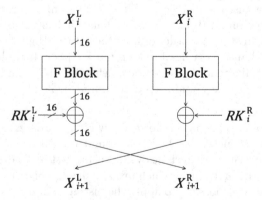

Fig. 1. Data processing part of LCB

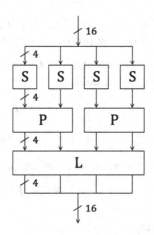

Fig. 2. F Block

Table 1. 4-bit permutation (S)

i	1	2	3	4
S	1	4	2	3

Table 2. 8-bit permutation (P)

i	1	2	3	4	5	6	7	8
P	1	5	4	8	2	6	3	7

Table 3. 16-bit permutation (L)

i	1	2	3	4	5	6	7	8
L	1	9	8	16	2	10	7	15
i	9	10	11	12	13	14	15	16
L	3	11	6	14	4	12	5	13

Table 4. $\mathbf{RK}_i$ ($1 \le i \le 10$)

i	Odd	Even
$\mathbf{RK}_i$	(K_1, K_2)	(K_3, K_4)

3 Higher Order Differential Attack

In this section, we describe the definition of higher order differential and some of its properties, and we also consider an attack equation using these properties.

3.1 Higher Order Differential [3]

Let $E(\cdot)$ be an encryption function as follows:

$$Y = E(X; K), \qquad (2)$$

where $X \in \mathrm{GF}(2)^n$, $Y \in \mathrm{GF}(2)^m$, and $K \in \mathrm{GF}(2)^s$. For a block cipher, X, K, and Y denote plaintext, key, and ciphertext respectively. Let $\{\mathbf{a}_1, \mathbf{a}_2, \cdots, \mathbf{a}_i\}$ be a set of linearly independent vectors in $\mathrm{GF}(2)^n$ and $V^{(i)}$ be a sub-space spanned by these vectors. The i-th order differential of $E(X; K)$ with respect to X is defined as follows.

$$\Delta_{V^{(i)}}^{(i)} E(X; K) = \bigoplus_{\alpha \in V^{(i)}} E(X \oplus \alpha; K) \qquad (3)$$

In the following, we abbreviate $\Delta_{V^{(i)}}^{(i)}$ as $\Delta^{(i)}$, when it is clearly understood.

In this paper, we use the following properties of the higher order differential.

Property 1. If the algebraic degree of $E(X;K)$ with respect to X equals to $N (\leq n)$, then the following equation holds.

$$deg_X\{E(X;K)\} = N \rightarrow \begin{cases} \Delta^{(N)}E(X;K) = const, \\ \\ \Delta^{(N+1)}E(X;K) = 0. \end{cases} \quad (4)$$

Property 2. Higher order differential has a linear property on $\oplus$ operation.

$$\Delta^{(N)}\{E_1(X;K_1) \oplus E_2(X;K_2)\} = \Delta^{(N)}E_1(X;K_1) \oplus \Delta^{(N)}E_2(X;K_2) \quad (5)$$

3.2 Saturation Properties

We describe some definitions of saturation properties related to this paper.

Let a set of 2^N elements of N-bit values be $\mathbf{X} = \{X_i|X_i \in \{0,1\}^N, 0 \leq i < 2^N\}$. Now we first categorize saturation properties of the set $\mathbf{X}$ into six types depending on conditions defined as follows.

– **Constant** (C): if $\forall_{i,j}, X_i = X_j$
– **All** (A): if $\forall_{i,j}, i \neq j \Leftrightarrow X_i \neq X_j$
– **Even** (E): if $\forall_i, Y_i \equiv 0 \,(\text{mod } 2)$
– **Mod2** (M): if $\forall_{i,j}, Y_i \equiv Y_j \,(\text{mod } 2)$
– **Balance** (B): $\bigoplus_i X_i = 0,$

– **Unknown** (U): Others,

where Y_i denotes the number of occurrences of $X = i$.

If the saturation property of 2^ℓ elements of ℓ-bit values is 'A', it is expressed as $A_{(\ell)}$. Further, when $A_{(\ell)}$ is divided into $m (\geq 2)$-nibble, it is written as follows.

$$A_{(\ell)} = (A^1 A^2 \cdots A^m),$$

where $\ell = 4m$. For example, 8-th order differential $A_{(8)}$ is written as $(A^1 A^2)$.

In the following, the symbol 'c' indicates the saturation property of 1-bit value which is 'C'. Then, if the saturation property of 1-nibble values $x_{i,\ell}^J$ is 'C', we express this as $\{x_{i,\ell}^J\} = C$. For multiple-nibble values, it is expressed as a similar manner. For example, if the saturation property of 4-nibble values $(x_{i,1}^J, x_{i,2}^J, x_{i,3}^J, x_{i,4}^J)$ is $(A^1 A^2 C C)$, we express this as $\{(x_{i,1}^J, x_{i,2}^J, x_{i,3}^J, x_{i,4}^J)\} = (A^1 A^2 C C)$. We also use the following abbreviation.

$$\{(x_{i,1}^J, x_{i,2}^J, x_{i,3}^J, x_{i,4}^J)\} = (C C C C) = \mathbf{C},$$

$$\{(x_{i,1}^J, x_{i,2}^J, x_{i,3}^J, x_{i,4}^J)\} = (A^1 A^2 A^2 A^3) = \mathbf{A}.$$

Property 3. If the saturation property of ciphertext Y is 'C', 'A', 'E', 'M', or 'B' using ℓ-th order differential, $\Delta^{(\ell)}Y = 0$. Then, if the saturation property of its 1-bit value y is '$A_{(1)}$' using 1-st order differential, $\Delta^{(1)}y = 1$.

3.3   Attack Equation

Consider an r-round iterative block cipher. Let $H_{r-1}(X) \in \mathrm{GF}(2)^m$ be a part of the $(r-1)$-th round output and $C(X) \in \mathrm{GF}(2)^n$ be the ciphertext corresponding to the plaintext $X \in \mathrm{GF}(2)^n$. $H_{r-1}(X)$ is expressed as follows.

$$H_{r-1}(X) = F_{r-1}(X; K_1, K_2, \cdots, K_{r-1}), \tag{6}$$

where $K_i \in \mathrm{GF}(2)^s$ be the i-th round key and $F_i(\cdot)$ be a function of $\mathrm{GF}(2)^n \times \mathrm{GF}(2)^{s \times i} \to \mathrm{GF}(2)^m$.

If the algebraic degree of $F_{r-1}(\cdot)$ with respect to X is less than N, we have the following from Property 1.

$$\Delta^{(N)} H_{r-1}(X) = 0 \tag{7}$$

Let $\widetilde{F}(\cdot)$ be a decoding function that calculates $H_{r-1}(X)$ from a ciphertext $C(X) \in \mathrm{GF}(2)^n$.

$$H_{r-1}(X) = \widetilde{F}(C(X); K_r), \tag{8}$$

where $K_r \in \mathrm{GF}(2)^s$ denotes the r-th round key to decode $H_{r-1}(X)$ from $C(X)$. From Eqs. (3), (7), and (8), we can derive following equation and can determine K_r by solving it.

$$\bigoplus_{\alpha \in V^{(N)}} \widetilde{F}(C(X \oplus \alpha); K_r) = 0 \tag{9}$$

In the following, we refer to Eq. (9) as an attack equation.

4   Higher Order Differential Characteristics of LCB

By the computer experiments, we searched for the higher order differential characteristics of LCB using a heuristic method. In our search, the secret keys K_ℓ were set randomly and the 1-st order differential characteristics were investigated comprehensively. As a result, we found that LCB has a 10-round, i.e., full-round characteristics. One of them is shown below.

$$(\text{A1}) \quad (((A_{(1)}ccc)\,C\,C\,C),\mathbf{C}) \xrightarrow{10r} (((A_{(1)}ccc)\,C\,C\,C),\mathbf{C})$$

In the above characteristic, the left-hand side of the formula expresses the input property and the right-hand side means the 10-th round output property, and the path is depicted in Fig. 3. We omit the input of the key in the figure, because they have no influence on the characteristic. Although we found many other characteristics easily by changing the position of $A_{(1)}$ in the input property, we omit the description of them.

In the structure of LCB, since there is no diffusion between the MSB 16-bit X_1^L and the LSB 16-bit X_1^R of the input plaintext, a fixed value is always propagated in X_i^L or X_i^R, in which 1-st order differential is not inputted. Furthermore, as LCB is composed of the permutation, for any number of rounds, the saturation property of 1-bit, 31-bit of its output are always $A_{(1)}$, c respectively.

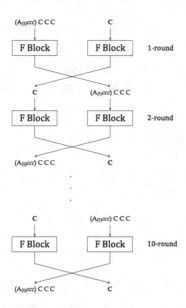

Fig. 3. 10-round characteristic using 1-st order differential

5   Attack on the Full-Round LCB

In this section, we present the distinguishing attack to full-round LCB by using the higher order differential characteristic shown in Sect. 4. Then, we also show an equivalent LCB and describe the key recovery attack under the condition for known plaintext attacks.

5.1   Distinguishing Attack

From the results of the above simulations, we found a new 10-round characteristic using 1-st order differential. Let $\mathbf{C}_i = (C_i^{\mathrm{L}}, C_i^{\mathrm{R}})$ be an i-th round ciphertext. By exploiting the characteristic (**A1**), we can derive the following attack equation from Property 2.

$$\bigoplus C_{10}^{\mathrm{R}} = 0. \tag{10}$$

We use Eq. (10) as a distinguisher and claim that the attack is successful if this equation is satisfied. Therefore, it is possible to apply the distinguishing attack to full-round LCB with 2 blocks for chosen plaintext and times of encryption operation.

5.2   Key Recovery Attack

Figure 4 shows the equivalent circuit which calculates ciphertext $(C_{10}^{\mathrm{L}}, C_{10}^{\mathrm{R}})$ from plaintext $(X_1^{\mathrm{L}}, X_1^{\mathrm{R}})$. Note that the swap of each round is equivalently transformed, and the round keys RK_i^{J} are expressed by the secret keys K_ℓ according

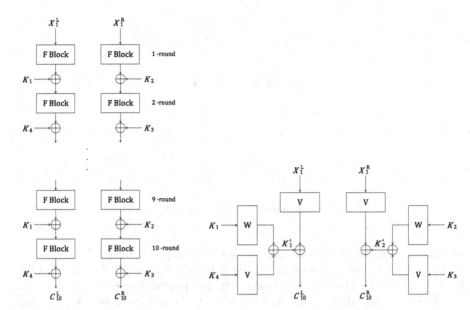

Fig. 4. Equivalent LCB   **Fig. 5.** Equivalent circuit of Fig. 4

Table 5. 16-bit permutation (V)

i	1	2	3	4	5	6	7	8
V	1	13	2	14	5	9	6	10
i	9	10	11	12	13	14	15	16
V	7	11	8	12	3	15	4	16

Table 6. 16-bit permutation (W)

i	1	2	3	4	5	6	7	8
W	1	7	9	15	5	3	13	11
i	9	10	11	12	13	14	15	16
W	2	8	10	16	6	4	14	12

to Table 4 in the figure. From the figure, it is clear that the MSB 16-bit data X_1^L is only influenced by keys K_1, K_4 and the LSB 16-bit data X_1^R by K_2, K_3 respectively.

In addition, because LCB does not have any non-linear function, we use an equivalent representation of Fig. 4 shown in Fig. 5 to simplify the attack algorithm. Here, the symbol 'V' and 'W' are the 16-bit permutation shown in Table 5 and Table 6 respectively. The permutation V is equivalent to transformation of the function F Block applied 10 times. Moreover, K_ℓ ($1 \le \ell \le 4$) are respectively

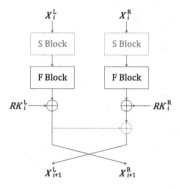

Fig. 6. Data processing part of modified LCB

replaced by equivalent keys K_1' and K_2' given by $K_1' = W[K_1] \oplus V[K_4]$, $K_2' = W[K_2] \oplus V[K_3]$. Then, these keys can be determined from $K_1' = V[X_1^L] \oplus C_{10}^L$, $K_2' = V[X_1^R] \oplus C_{10}^R$. Therefore, attackers prepare a pair of the ciphertexts $\mathbf{C}_{10}$ and its corresponding plaintexts $\mathbf{X}_1$, they can identify the two 16-bit keys K_1' and K_2'.

6 Modification of LCB

As mentioned above, since LCB is a vulnerable algorithm, we found a full-round characteristic of LCB using 1-st order differential. In this section, we try to strengthen the LCB algorithm. Then, we discuss its security against higher order differential attack.

6.1 The Algorithm

Figure 6 shows the data processing part of modified LCB. The modified LCB adds the following two components to the original one as improvements[1].

- The non-linear layer S Block which consists of four parallel PRINCE [4] 4-bit S-boxes is added before the linear function F Block to introduce nonlinearity.
- An $\oplus$ operation from the MSB 16-bit X_1^L to the LSB 16-bit X_1^R is added after the round keys addition in order to introduce diffusion between X_1^L and X_1^R.

6.2 Higher Order Differential Characteristics

If we use 16-th order differential in the same manner as in Sect. 4, the higher order differential characteristic of modified LCB from input to 5-round output can be written as follows.

---

[1] The improving LCB proposed in [2], which replaced only the S-box by a non-linear function, has full-round higher order differential characteristics since there is no diffusion between X_1^L and X_1^R.

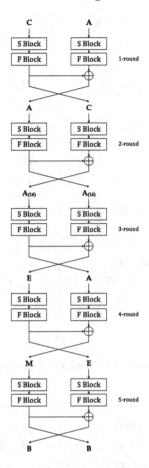

Fig. 7. 5-round characteristic of modified LCB using 16-th order differential

$$(\text{A16}) \quad (\mathbf{C}, \mathbf{A}) \xrightarrow{5r} (\mathbf{B}, \mathbf{B})$$

The path of the characteristic of (A16) is depicted in Fig. 7. We also found that the length of the higher order differential characteristics is the same using 31-st order differential. Thus, the length of the higher order differential characteristics is reduced to 5-round from full-round, so that the algorithm of modified LCB is confirmed to be stronger than the original one.

6.3   Higher Order Differential Attack

In this subsection, we estimate the number of chosen plaintexts and computational complexity for the 8-round modified LCB attack by using the 5-round characteristic of (A16).

Attack Equation. Figure 8 shows the equivalent circuit of modified LCB which calculates 5-th round output C_5^L from 8-th round ciphertext (C_8^L, C_8^R). Because

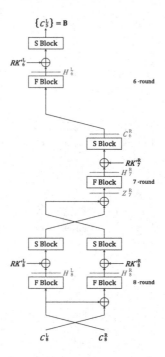

Fig. 8. Equivalent circuit of modified LCB which calculates 5-th round output C_5^L from 8-th round ciphertext (C_8^L, C_8^R)

F Block is a linear function, we can move the i-th round key RK_i^J as shown in Fig. 8. Note that RK_i^J is replaced by equivalent key $RK_i'^J = \text{F Block}^{-1}(RK_i^J)$, where F Block^{-1} denotes the inverse function of F Block, and $RK_i'^J = (rk_{i,1}'^J, rk_{i,2}'^J, rk_{i,3}'^J, rk_{i,4}'^J)$, $rk_{i,\ell}'^J \in \text{GF}(2)^4$, $1 \le i \le 10$, $J \in \{L, R\}$, $1 \le \ell \le 4$. Let $H_i^J = (h_{i,1}^J, h_{i,2}^J, h_{i,3}^J, h_{i,4}^J)$, $h_{i,\ell}^J \in \text{GF}(2)^4$ be the variable after the round key is added, and $Z_i^J = (z_{i,1}^J, z_{i,2}^J, z_{i,3}^J, z_{i,4}^J)$, $z_{i,\ell}^J \in \text{GF}(2)^4$ be an output of function F Block.

The attack equation for the key recovery attack on 8-round modified LCB using the characteristic of (A16) is allows.

$$\bigoplus c_{5,\ell}^L = 0, \tag{11}$$

$$c_{5,\ell}^L = \text{S}^{-1}(h_{6,\ell}^L \oplus rk_{6,\ell}'^L), H_6^L = \text{F Block}^{-1}(C_6^R),$$
$$C_6^R = \text{S Block}^{-1}(H_7^R \oplus RK_7'^R), H_7^R = \text{F Block}^{-1}(Z_7^R),$$
$$Z_7^R = \text{S Block}^{-1}(H_8^L \oplus RK_8'^L) \oplus \text{S Block}^{-1}(H_8^R \oplus RK_8'^R),$$
$$H_8^L = \text{F Block}^{-1}(C_8^R), H_8^R = \text{F Block}^{-1}(C_8^L \oplus C_8^R),$$

where S^{-1} and S Block^{-1} denote the inverse function of S-box and S Block respectively. Though there are four 16-bit unknown keys $RK_6'^L$, $RK_7'^R$, $RK_8'^L$, and RK'^{R}_{8}, we can efficiently recover these keys using the relation among the round keys. In the key schedule, from Table 4, since the 16-bit secret key K_3 is added as the 6-round key RK^{L}_{6} and the 8-round one RK^{L}_{8} respectively, so RK'^{L}_{6} is equivalent to RK'^{L}_{8}. Because of this relation, the number of bit of unknown can be reduced from 64-bit to 48-bit.

Attack Algorithm. We describe the derivation for the four 4-bit Mod 2 Frequency Distribution Table (MFDT) of $c^{L}_{5,\ell}$ in Eq. (11) using the partial sum technique [5]. Then, we calculate $\bigoplus c^{L}_{5,\ell}$ from the MFDT of $c^{L}_{5,\ell}$, and confirm if Eq. (11) holds.

Attackers execute the following procedure to recovery the 48-bit keys RK'^{R}_{7}, RK'^{L}_{8}, and RK'^{R}_{8}.

Step1. The 32-bit MFDT (MFDT(1)) of (C^{L}_{8}, C^{R}_{8}) derives from 2^{16} ciphertexts corresponding to the input a set of 2^{16} plaintexts.

Step2. The 32-bit MFDT (MFDT(2)) of (H^{L}_{8}, H^{R}_{8}) can derive from MFDT(1).

Step3. By assuming the 8-bit keys $rk'^{L}_{8,1}$ and $rk'^{R}_{8,1}$, the 28-bit MFDT (MFDT(3)) of $(z^{R}_{7,1}, h^{L}_{8,2}, h^{L}_{8,3}, h^{L}_{8,4}, h^{R}_{8,2}, h^{R}_{8,3}, h^{R}_{8,4})$ can calculate from MFDT(2).

Step4. By assuming the 8-bit keys $rk'^{L}_{8,2}$ and $rk'^{R}_{8,2}$, the 24-bit MFDT (MFDT(4)) of $(z^{R}_{7,1}, z^{R}_{7,2}, h^{L}_{8,3}, h^{L}_{8,4}, h^{R}_{8,3}, h^{R}_{8,4})$ can calculate from MFDT(3).

Step5. By assuming the 8-bit keys $rk'^{L}_{8,3}$ and $rk'^{R}_{8,3}$, the 20-bit MFDT (MFDT(5)) of $(z^{R}_{7,1}, z^{R}_{7,2}, z^{R}_{7,3}, h^{L}_{8,4}, h^{R}_{8,4})$ can calculate from MFDT(4).

Step6. By assuming the 8-bit keys $rk'^{L}_{8,4}$ and $rk'^{R}_{8,4}$, the 16-bit MFDT (MFDT(6)) of Z^{R}_{7} can calculate from MFDT(5).

Step7. The 16-bit MFDT (MFDT(7)) of H^{R}_{7} can derive from MFDT(6).

Step8. By assuming the 16-bit keys RK'^{R}_{7}, the 16-bit MFDT (MFDT(8)) of C^{R}_{6} can calculate from MFDT(7).

Step9. The four 4-bit MFDTs (MFDT(9,ℓ)) of $h^{L}_{6,\ell}$ $(1 \le \ell \le 4)$ can derive from MFDT(8).

Step10. By inputting the four 4-bit keys $rk'^{L}_{8,\ell}$ assumed in Step3 – Step6 into $rk'^{L}_{6,\ell}$ respectively, the four 4-bit MFDTs (MFDT(10,ℓ)) of $c^{L}_{5,\ell}$ can derive from MFDT(9,ℓ).

Step11. The values of $\bigoplus c^{L}_{5,\ell}$ can be computed from MFDT(10,ℓ). Then, attackers can judge whether the key is correct or not by examining if Eq.(11) holds.

Complexity Estimation. If the assumed value of the 48-bit key is true, Eq. (11) hold with probability 1. Since Eq. (11) are four 4-bit equations, it is satisfied with $(2^{-4})^4 = 2^{-16}$ even if the assumed key is false. From one set of Eq. (11), the number of candidates for the 48-bit key is reduced from 2^{48} to 2^{32} on average.

In a similar manner, we need $4 (> \lceil \frac{48}{16} \rceil)$ sets of 16-th order differential with different $\mathbf{X}_1$ with $4 \cdot 2^{16} = 2^{18}$ chosen plaintexts in order to identify the true key.

Next, we evaluate the computational complexity for the key recovery attack to 8-round modified LCB. Because the procedure which required the most computational complexity is to identify the 48-bit key by solving Eq. (11), other computational complexities are negligible smaller than this, and are omitted. Therefore, the computational complexity $\mathbf{T}$ is as follows.

$$\mathbf{T} = T_1 + T_2 \approx T_2 \approx 2^{64} \text{ (S-box)},$$
$$T_1 = 2^{18},$$
$$T_2 = 2^8(2^{32} + 2^8(2^{28} + 2^8(2^{24} + 2^8(2^{20} + 2^{16} \cdot 2^{16})))),$$

where T_1 is the computational complexity of 4 sets of 16-th order differential, T_2 is the computational complexity required to determine the key is $T_2 \approx 2^{64}$ times of S-box operation. Because the 8-round modified LCB consists of $64 (= 8 \times 8)$ S-boxes, this computational complexity is equivalent to $2^{64}/64 = 2^{58}$ times of encryption operation.

7 Conclusion

We have studied a higher order differential of LCB. By focusing on the structure of LCB, we found the full-round characteristics of LCB using 1-st order differential. If we use it, it is possible to apply the distinguishing attack to full-round LCB with 2 blocks of chosen plaintext. Then, we also showed an equivalent LCB and described the all key recovery for full-round LCB with only 1 block of known plaintext. Furthermore, we tried to improve the round function of LCB. By the computer experiments, we discovered that there was 5-round characteristic of modified LCB using 16-th order differentials. Then, by using this characteristic and the partial sum technique, it is possible to apply the higher order differential attack to 8-round modified LCB with 2^{18} blocks of chosen plaintext and 2^{58} times of encryption operation. Thus, we think that modified LCB is secure against higher order differential attack shown in this paper.

Our future work is to improve the key scheduling function and to set the number rounds with enough security margin.

References

1. Roy, S., Roy, S., Biswas, A., Baishnab, K.L.: LCB: light cipher block an ultrafast lightweight block cipher for resource constrained IOT security applications. KSII Trans. Internet Inf. Syst. **15**(11), 4122–4144 (2021)
2. Chan, Y.Y., Khor, C.-Y., Teh, J.S., Teng, W.J., Jamil, N.: Differential cryptanalysis of lightweight block ciphers SLIM and LCB. In: Chen, J., He, D., Lu, R. (eds.) EISA 2022. CCIS, vol. 1641, pp. 55–67. Springer, Cham (2022). https://doi.org/10.1007/978-3-031-23098-1_4
3. Lai, X.: Higher order derivatives and differential cryptanalysis. In: Communications and Cryptography, pp. 227–233. Kluwer Academic Publishers (1994)

4. Borghoff, J., et al.: PRINCE – a low-latency block cipher for pervasive computing applications. In: Wang, X., Sako, K. (eds.) ASIACRYPT 2012. LNCS, vol.
   7658, pp. 208–225. Springer, Heidelberg (2012). https://doi.org/10.1007/978-3-642-
   34961-4_14
5. Ferguson, N., et al.: Improved cryptanalysis of Rijndael. In: Goos, G., Hartmanis,
   J., van Leeuwen, J., Schneier, B. (eds.) FSE 2000. LNCS, vol. 1978, pp. 213–230.
   Springer, Heidelberg (2001). https://doi.org/10.1007/3-540-44706-7_15

Bloomier Filters on 3-Hypergraphs

Hyungrok Jo[1]([✉]) and Junji Shikata[1,2]

[1] Institute of Advanced Sciences, Yokohama National University, Yokohama, Japan
{jo-hyungrok-xz,shikata-junji-rb}@ynu.ac.jp
[2] Graduate School of Environment and Information Sciences,
Yokohama National University, Yokohama, Japan

Abstract. A Bloom filter, originally proposed by Bloom in 1970, is a probabilistic data structure used to determine membership in a set with enduring false positive errors. Due to the trade-off between space efficiency and the probability of false positive errors, Bloom filters have found numerous applications in network systems and various fields of information sciences. Chazelle et al. [6] extended this concept to a more versatile data structure known as the Bloomier filter, capable of encoding arbitrary functions. With Bloomier filters, it becomes possible to associate values with specific elements of the domain, enabling more generalized use. In this paper, we propose a variant of Charles and Chellapilla's scheme [5] that utilizes minimal perfect hashings. Specifically, instead of using bipartite random graphs like existing Bloomier filters, we present a space-efficient Bloomier filter with faster creation time based on an analysis of 3-hypergraphs, in comparison to previous results.

Keywords: Bloom filter · Bloomier filter · hypergraph

1 Introduction

A *Bloom filter* is a probabilistic data structure that probabilistically determines whether a specific element is present or absent in a given set. It was initially proposed by B. H. Bloom [1] in 1970 and has since become an essential concept used in network routers, web browsers, databases, and more, to efficiently perform data detection within a limited space. In brief, when querying whether an element belongs to a data structure created using a Bloom filter, it provides an answer of either "probably positive" or "definitely negative". "Probably positive" means that the target element can receive a positive response even if it does not actually belong to the data structure. On the other hand, a response of "definitely negative" guarantees that the target element does not belong to the data structure. This trade-off between reducing memory usage and decreasing search accuracy aims to achieve space-efficiency. As the number of elements in the set increases, the probability of "probably positive" errors also increases.

In 2004, Chazelle et al. [6] designed a *Bloomier filter*, which is an associative array with a Bloom filter that associates added elements with corresponding values. Similar to the Bloom filter, this data structure is space-efficient but has a possibility of false positive errors. In the Bloomier filter, a false positive occurs when a value is returned for a key that is not mapped. However, it will never return an incorrect value for a mapped key. Their main idea came from the creation of lossless expander graphs. In 2008, Charles and Chellapilla [5] improved a construction of Bloomier filter from the creation of minimal perfect hash function [7].

In this paper, we give a space-efficient Bloomier filter from the creation of 3-hypergraphs. We propose how to create the table for the Bloomier filter by leveraging the concept of 3-hypergraphs, which play a role in achieving faster creation. Furthermore, this paper highlights the work of Charles and Chellapilla in 2008, who enhanced the construction of the Bloomier filter by drawing insights from minimal perfect hashing. Our contributions further strengthen the effectiveness and practicality of Charles and Chellapilla's Bloomier filter. The result contributes to the growing body of knowledge in probabilistic data structures and expand the range of practical applications for the Bloomier filter. We briefly provide our contributions comparing the existing results in Table 1. Our proposed construction is most efficient in storage space, while [6] is best in creation time.

Table 1. Comparisons with the earlier k-bit Bloomier filters. Here, $c > 1$, $c_2 = 2.1$, $c_3 = 1.23$, $r \geqslant 2$, ϵ, ϵ': the probability of an error ($\epsilon' > \epsilon$), and n: the size of D, where D is the (large) data set.

Bloomier filter	Creation time	Storing space	Query time	Evaluation time
Chazelle et al. [6]	$O(n \log n)$	$cnr(\log r\epsilon^{-1} + k)$	$O(1)$	$O(1)$
Charles & Chellapilla [5]	$O(c_2 n)$	$c_2 n(\log \epsilon^{-1} + k)$	$O(1)$	$O(1)$
Our proposal	$O(c_3 n)$	$c_3 n(\log \epsilon'^{-1} + k)$	$O(1)$	$O(1)$

The paper is organized as follows: In Sect. 2, we give an introductory explanation of the Bloom filter and some definitions and problems of hypergraph for constructing minimal perfect hash functions. In Sect. 3, we give some brief expositions of the existing Bloomier filters. In Sect. 4, we propose a 1-bit Bloomier filters on 3-hypergraphs. Finally, we conclude some remarks and give open problems in Sect. 6.

2   Preliminaries

2.1   Bloom Filters

Bloom filters are a highly efficient data structure for answering membership queries in a set, offering a remarkably compact representation. Given a set $S \subseteq D$ where D is a large set and $|S| = n$, the Bloom filter requires space $O(n)$ and has the following properties. It can answer membership queries in $O(1)$

time. However, it has one-sided error: Given $x \in S$, the Bloom filter will always declare that x belongs to S, but given $x \in D\backslash S$ the Bloom filter will, with high probability, declare that $x \notin S$. Their space requirements are significantly lower than the theoretical lower bounds for error-free data structures. While they introduce a small probability of false positives (indicating an item is in the set when it is not), they guarantee no false negatives (correctly identifying items in the set). Bloom filters find extensive practical applications in scenarios where storage is limited, and occasional false positives can be tolerated.

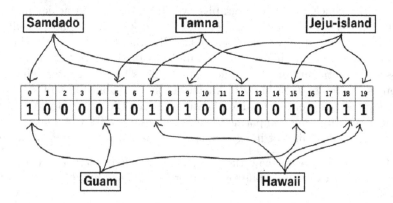

Fig. 1. Example of a Bloom filter for synonym discrimination of Jeju Island

Let's consider a toy example of a Bloom filter shown in Fig. 1. We have constructed a 20-bit Bloom filter with memory to discern a synonym for Jeju Island in South Korea. Assuming all bits in the 20-bit memory are initially set to 0, we added three words related to Jeju Island, namely Jeju-island, Tamna, and Samdado, to the data structure S. The process of adding each word to the data structure S is as follows: From a family of (collision-resistant and efficient) hash functions that uniformly assign 0s and 1s to the 20-bit memory of S, we select three distinct hash functions. Each hash function assigns a 1 to the corresponding memory slot for Jeju-island at positions 9, 15, and 19. Similarly, Tamna is assigned 1 at positions 5, 7, and 18, and Samdado is assigned 1 at positions 0, 5, and 12. Now, when we search for Jeju-island, Tamna, or Samdado in this memory table, they will always receive positive responses based on the three designated hash functions. If we search for the word Guam, which does not belong to S, each hash function will check the corresponding bits at positions 0, 4, and 15, and since at position 4 is 0, it will provide a negative response. However, for the word Hawaii, which also does not belong to S, but has bits assigned to positions 7, 18, and 19, it will erroneously receive a positive response. As such, while a Bloom filter exhibits the mentioned inaccuracies in positive responses, negative responses guarantee a definite absence.

2.2 Hypergraph

For a usage of (minimal perfect) hash functions, we give some preliminaries of hypergraphs, which is a basic structure of perfect hash function. Please see [8] and [11] for details. We define a r-*hypergraph* as follows:

Let $G(V, E)$ be a r-hypergraph with a vertex set V and an edge set $E \subseteq \binom{V}{r}$, the set of r-subsets of V. The k-core of a hypergraph is its maximal induced subgraph having degree at least k. Now we consider some problems for constructing a minimal perfect hash function from m keys into an r-hypergraph with m edges and n vertices. We omit the specific explanation of a minimal perfect hash function. However, it is necessary to consider a problem that the edges of the r-hypergraph must be independent.

Problem 1. For a given r-hypergraph $G = (V, E)$, $|E| = m, |V| = n$, where each $e \in E$ is an r-subset of V, find a function $g : V \to [0, \dots, m-1]$ such that the function $h : E \to [0, \dots, m-1]$ defined as

$$h(e = \{v_1, v_2, \dots, v_r\} \in E) = (g(v_1) + g(v_2) + \cdots + g(v_r)) \pmod{m}$$

is a bijection.

Actually, this problem above does not give the existence of a solution for arbitrary graphs. If the graph G is an acyclic graph, a simple procedure can be used to find values for each vertex. In order to a high probability of constructing a r-hypergraph with independent edges, it is common to use very sparse graphs. So we choose $n = cm$, where c is some constant. If $c = c_r$, it means the constant depending on the cardinality r. As we can see in [11], if $n = cm$ holds with $c > 2$, then the probability p such that G has independent edges, is close to

$$p = e^{1/c} \sqrt{\frac{c-2}{c}} \tag{1}$$

for $n \to \infty$. When $c \leqslant 2.09$, be (1), we can calculate the expected number of times to re-generate the graph until getting an acyclic graph (i.e. a graph is acyclic is equivalent to a graph has independent edges.), which is less than 3 times.

On the other hand, in a case of r-hypergraphs for $r > 2$, we know that there exists a constant c_r depending on r such that if $m \leqslant c_r n$ the probability that a random r-hypergraph has independent edges tends to 1. Specifically, the values are known as $c_2 = 2.1, c_3 = 1.23, c_4 = 1.29$, and $c_5 = 1.41$ in [11]. Since c_r affects the size of vertex set when constructing a table in Bloomier filters, we can say that c_3 seems to be good to choose. In a sense of space-efficiency, there is a trade-off between the cardinality r of each edge of hypergraphs and the accuracy (false positive) of Bloomier filters. If r is increasing, then the probability of false positive $\frac{r}{m}$ for some integer m. However, when r is small enough ($r = 2$ or 3), it is negligible by choosing large enough m. Moreover, the size of the table depends on the size of the vertex set (i.e. $c_r n$, where n is the size of the large data set D). Since the constants c_4 and c_5 are bigger than c_3, there are no benefits on both sides of above.

3   The Existing Bloomier Filters

3.1   Chazelle et al. [6]

Given a set $S \subseteq D$ where D is a large set with $|S| = n$ and a function $f : S \to \{0, 1\}^k$, a Bloomier filter is a data structure that supports queries to the function value. Given $x \in S$, it always outputs the correct value $f(x)$ and if $x \in D \backslash S$ with high probability it outputs '$\bot$', a symbol not in the range of f.

While the traditional Bloom filter enables membership queries on a set, Chazelle et al. [6] extend this concept to a more versatile data structure known as the Bloomier filter, capable of encoding arbitrary functions. With Bloomier filters, it becomes possible to associate values with specific elements of the domain, allowing for a more generalized use. This approach excels in scenarios where the function is defined over a small subset of the domain, a common occurrence in many applications. Bloomier filters find utility in constructing *meta-databases*, specifically directories that encompass a consolidated set of small-scale databases. By utilizing Bloomier filters, information about the database containing each entry is efficiently maintained. This enables users to swiftly navigate to the pertinent databases while bypassing those that hold no connection to the specified entry.

We describe the original idea of the Bloomier filter as the pair of the Bloom filters A and B. First, consider an associative array with possible values of 1 and 2 only. We create two Bloom filters, A and B. Register keys with a value of 1 in A and words with a value of 2 in B. When seeking the corresponding value for a key, both filters are referenced. If the key does not exist in either filter, it means there is no corresponding value for that key. If a key is present in A but not in B, it can be said with high probability that the corresponding value is not 2 but 1. Conversely, if a key is present in B but not in A, it can be said with high probability that the corresponding value is not 1 but 2. A problem arises when false positives occur in the Bloom filter, and both filters indicate the presence of a key. Since it is an associative array, the same key is not added to both Bloom filters. However, it is not possible to determine which filter is providing false information. To address this, create two additional small filters, A_1 and B_1. Register keys in A_1 that result in false positives in B for a value of 1, and register keys in B_1 that result in false positives in A for a value of 1. Then, verify the keys that are said to be present in both A and B using A_1 and B_1. However, there is still a possibility of false positives at this stage. To address this, apply the same solution recursively. Since the pairs of filters are mapped to one side of the higher-level pair and result in false positives on the other side, only register the keys that need to be added. As the process continues, the number of keys to be registered dramatically decreases, reaching a point where it can fit into a deterministic data structure. The number of times the filter hierarchy needs to be traversed is very small, resulting in overall search time in linear time. Furthermore, most of the required space is taken up by the initial filter pairs and is unrelated to n. So far, the data structure and search algorithm have been provided. The method for storing new key-value pairs is as follows. In this case, the program must never set both values for the same key. If the value is 1, add the key to A and check if it also has the key in B (returning a false positive). If B returns a false positive, add the key to the next level, A_1, and continue the process. Once the final level is reached, simply insert the key. Alternatively, if the value is 2, perform the same operation by swapping A and B.

3.2 Charles and Chellapilla [5]

The main part of the Bloomier filter by Charles and Chellapilla [5] is constructing the table using minimal perfect hash function [7]. Especially, the case when $r = 2$, ($c_2 \approx 2.1$ in [11]), it has to do at least 3 trials to generate an acyclic graph.

Algorithm 1. Generate table g on random acyclic graphs

Input: A set $S \subseteq D$ and a function $f : S \to \{0,1\}, c_2 := 2.1$, and an integer $m \geqslant 2$.
Output: Table g and hash functions h_1, h_2, h_3 such that $\forall s \in S : g[h_1(s)] + g[h_2(s)] + h_3(s) \equiv f(s) \pmod{m}$.

1: Let $V = \{0, 1, \ldots, \lceil c_2 n \rceil - 1\}$.
2: **repeat**
3:      Generate $h_1, h_2 : D \to V$ where h_i are chosen independently from $\mathcal{H}$ – a family of hash functions; Let $E = \{(h_1(s), h_2(s)) \mid s \in S\}$.
4: **until** $G(V, E)$ is a simple acyclic graph.
5: Let $h_3 : D \to \mathbb{Z}/m\mathbb{Z}$ be a third independently hash function from $\mathcal{H}$.
6: **for all** T - a connected component of $G(V, E)$ **do**
7:      Choose a vertex $v \in T$ whose degree is non-zero.
8:      $F \leftarrow \{v\}; g[v] \leftarrow 0$.
9:      **while** $F \neq T$ **do**
10:         Let C be the set of vertices in $T \backslash F$ adjacent to vertices in F.
11:         **for all** $w = h_i(s)$ **do**
12:             $g[w] \leftarrow f(s) - g[h_{3-i}(s)] - h_3(s) \pmod{m}$.
13:         **end for**
14:         $F \leftarrow F \cup C$.
15:     **end while**
16: **end for**

A table function $g : V \to \{0, 1\}$ is defined as for every $x \in S$, the equation $f(x) \equiv g(h_1(x)) + g(h_2(x)) \pmod 2$ holds, where $h_1, h_2 : D \to V$. The values $g(v) \in \{0, 1\}$ for $v \in V$ are stored in the table. To evaluate the function f for a given x, we compute the values of $h_1(x)$ and $h_2(x)$, and then sum up the values stored in the table g at these two indices, considering the result modulo 2. Then, it can be extended the method to encode the function $\tilde{f} : D \to \{0, 1, \bot\}$, where $\tilde{f}$ agrees with f on the set S, but assigns the value $\bot$ with high probability on the $D \backslash S$. For achieving this, the same construction of a bipartite random graph $G(V, E)$ is established along with a mapping from S to E using two hash functions h_1 and h_2. Let $m \geqslant 2$ be an integer and $h_3 : D \to \mathbb{Z}/m\mathbb{Z}$ be another independent hash function. We can solve a function $g : V \to \mathbb{Z}/m\mathbb{Z}$ such that the equations

$$f(x) \equiv g(h_1(x)) + g(h_2(x)) + h_3(x) \pmod{m}$$

holds for each $x \in S$.

As the graph G is acyclic, it could be solved these equations efficiently using back-substitution. To evaluate the function f at x we compute one of hash functions among h_1, h_2 and h_3 and then compute $g(h_1(x)) + g(h_2(x)) + h_3(x)$ (mod m). If the computed value is either 0 or 1, output it. Otherwise, we output the symbol $\perp$. It can be checked in Algorithm 2. Here, it can be known

$$\mathrm{Pr}_{x \in D \setminus S}[g(h_1(x)) + g(h_2(x)) + h_3(x) \in \{0, 1\}] = \frac{2}{m}.$$

4   Our Proposals

We only construct a 1-bit Bloomier filter based on Charles and Chellapilla's scheme [5]. The consecutive constructions of general k-bit Bloomier filters and mutable Bloomier filters are omitted and supposed to be constructed in a similar way of [5]. The response set is usually $\{0, 1\}$ for the existing schemes. It allows constructing a bipartite random graph, which has a left set for 0 and a right set for 1. The analysis on these Bloom filters is working on these a bipartite random graph, which is also related to lossless expander graph. Please refer to [2,3,7,10–12] and [13] for details.

In our case, we generalize these approaches to random r-hypergraphs for some integer r. When $r = 2$, it is already discussed in [5] and [6]. If $r > 2$, the response set becomes larger as $\{0, 1, \ldots, r-1\}$. The number of Bloom filters are increasing, but the depth of additional small filters are dramatically decreasing. As argued at the latter of Sect. 2.2, a main target to construct a Bloomier filter is when given a set S of n elements and a function $f : S \to \{0, 1, 2\}$, encode f into a space efficient data structure that allows fast access to the values of f starting with the triple of the Bloom filters. (i.e. the case when $r = 3$). Moreover, it should have a compact encoding of the function $\tilde{f} : D \to \{0, 1, 2, \perp\}$, where $f|_S = f$ and $f(x) = \perp$ with high probability if $x \notin S$. Here, the ultimate goal is to construct an efficient Bloomier filter when D is much larger than S, which is not obvious.

Our construction is also from the creation of minimal perfect hash function [7] as Charles and Chellapilla's scheme but not a bipartite random graph, a random 3-hypergraph $G(V, E)$. We map a set S on the edges of $G(V, E)$ as follows:

Let $h_1, h_2, h_3 : D \to V$ and $h_4 : D \to R$ be hash functions compressing from D to V, respectively. For each $x \in S$, we make an edge $e = (h_1(x), h_2(x), h_3(x))$ and let E be the set of all edges such an e, which gives the fact that $|E| = |S| = n$. Since the argument of an acyclic property of obtained graphs in [5], we remark that it has the condition of $c > 2$, where c is the constant of satisfying $|V| \leqslant c|S|$. It is also mentioned that if $G(V, E)$ is a random graph with $c > 2$, then the graph is acyclic, with probability $e^{1/c}\sqrt{(c-2)/c}$ as mentioned in (1). In our case, it is enough to fix the $c_3 = 1.23$. Then, we can guarantee that our graph is acyclic without the re-generating procedure (i.e. the probability of generating acyclic graph is 1).

Algorithm 2. Generate table g on 3-hypergraph

Input: A set $S \subseteq D$ and a function $f : S \to \{0,1,2\}$, $c_3 := 1.23$ and an integer $m \geqslant 3$.
Output: Table g and hash functions h_1, h_2, h_3, h_4 such that $\forall s \in S : g[h_1(s)] + g[h_2(s)] + g[h_3(s)] + h_4(s) \equiv f(s) \pmod{m}$.
  Let $V = \{0, 1, \ldots, \lceil c_3 n \rceil - 1\}$.
  Generate $h_1, h_2, h_3 : D \to V$ where h_i are chosen independently from $\mathcal{H}$ – a family of hash functions; Let $E = \{(h_1(s), h_2(s), h_3(s)) \mid s \in S\}$.
  Then $G(V, E)$ is an acyclic graph.
  Let $h_4 : D \to \mathbb{Z}/m\mathbb{Z}$ be a third independently hash function from $\mathcal{H}$.
  for all T - a connected component of $G(V, E)$ **do**
    Choose a vertex $v \in T$ whose degree is non-zero.
    $F \leftarrow \{v\}; g[v] \leftarrow 0$.
    while $F \neq T$ **do**
      Let C be the set of vertices in $T \backslash F$ adjacent to vertices in F.
      for all $w = h_{i \pmod 3}(s)$ **do**
        $g[w] \leftarrow f(s) - g[h_{i+1 \pmod 3}(s)] - g[h_{i+2 \pmod 3}(s)] - h_4(s) \pmod{m}$.
      end for
      $F \leftarrow F \cup C$.
    end while
  end for

Mapping to a Table. Let us define a table function $g : V \to \{0, 1, 2\}$ such that for every $x \in S$, the equation $f(x) \equiv g(h_1(x)) + g(h_2(x)) + g(h_3(x)) \pmod 3$ holds. The values $g(v) \in \{0, 1, 2\}$ for $v \in V$ are stored in the table. To evaluate the function f for a given x, we compute the values of $h_1(x)$, $h_2(x)$ and $h_3(x)$, and then sum up the values stored in the table g at these three indices, considering the result modulo 3. We now extend this method to encode the function $\tilde{f} : D \to \{0, 1, 2, \perp\}$, where $\tilde{f}$ agrees with f on the set S, but assigns the value $\perp$ with high probability on the $D \backslash S$.

To achieve this, we employ the same construction of a bipartite random graph $G(V, E)$, along with a mapping from S to E using three hash functions h_1, h_2 and h_3. Let $m \geqslant 3$ be an integer and $h_4 : D \to \mathbb{Z}/m\mathbb{Z}$ be another independent hash function. We solve for a function $g : V \to \mathbb{Z}/m\mathbb{Z}$ such that the equations

$$f(x) \equiv g(h_1(x)) + g(h_2(x)) + g(h_3(x)) + h_4(x) \pmod{m}$$

holds for each $x \in S$.

We always have that G is acyclic, we can solve these equations efficiently using back-substitution. To evaluate the function f at x we compute one of hash functions among h_1, h_2, h_3 and h_4 and then compute $g(h_1(x)) + g(h_2(x)) +$

$g(h_3(x)) + h_4(x) \pmod{m}$. If the computed value is one of $\{0,1,2\}$ we output it. Otherwise, we output the symbol $\perp$. It can be checked in Algorithm 2. Here, we know that

$$\Pr_{x \in D \setminus S}[g(h_1(x)) + g(h_2(x)) + g(h_3(x)) + h_4(x) \in \{0,1,2\}] = \frac{3}{m}.$$

Then, we summarize the properties of 1-bit Bloomier filters as below:

Fix $c_3 = 1.23$ and let $m \geqslant 3$ be an integer, the algorithms described above (Algorithm 2) implement a Bloomier filter for storing the function $\tilde{f} : D \to \{0,1,2,\perp\}$ and the following properties:

1. The expected time for creation of the Bloomier filter is $O(n)$.
2. The space used in $\lceil c_3 n \rceil \lceil \log m \rceil$ bits, where $n = |S|$.
3. Computing the value of the Bloomier filter at $x \in D$ requires $O(1)$ time (4 hash function computations and 3 memory look-ups).
4. Given $x \in S$, it outputs the correct value of $f(x)$.
5. Given $x \notin S$, it outputs $\perp$ with probability $1 - \frac{3}{m}$.

5   Further Discussion

In the works of Chazelle et al. [6] and of Charles and Chellapilla [5], it can be said that they used *lossless expander graph* for constructing a table. Please refer to [4,12] and [13] for details. Especially, there is a famous problem in an area of lossless expander graph, which is called *Densest Subgraph Problem*.

Definition 1 (Densest Subgraph Problem). *Let $G = (V, E)$ be an undirected graph, and let $S = (V_S, E_S)$ be a subgraph of G. Here, the density of S is defined to be* $\text{den}(S) = \frac{E_S}{V_S}$. *The densest sub-graph problem is to find S such that it maximizes* $\text{den}(S)$. *We denote the maximum density by* $\text{Den}(G)$.

In 1984, against the above densest subgraph problem, Goldberg [9] proposed a polynomial time algorithm to find the densest subgraph S whose $\text{den}(S)$ is maximized. The running time of the Goldberg's algorithm is $O(|V||E|\log |V| \log |E|)$. Xie et al. [13] pointed out the connection between the densest subgraph and the lossless expander graphs. By utilizing the Goldberg's algorithm to exclude the non-expanding graphs, it might be possible to create the table of the Bloomier filters more efficiently.

6   Conclusion

Our proposal formalized the case of a 1-bit Bloomier filter. It is necessary to generalize the case of k-bit Bloomier filter, even though it is a quite natural to follow the way of [5]. As mentioned in [5], the efficiency could be earned when we apply the bucketing technique to the suggested algorithm. It is necessary to check if it is applicable. We expect that the properties of the Bloomier filter in a similar way of Charles and Chellapilla, as below: For $\epsilon > 0$ and $\delta \geqslant 4$, $s \geqslant 2$

an integer, let $S \subseteq D$, $|S| = n$ and m, k be positive integers such that $m \geqslant k$. Given $f : S \rightarrow \{0, 1, 2\}^k$, k-bit Bloomier filter is expected to have the following properties

1. The expected time to create the Bloomier Filter is nearly $\tilde{O}(n + m^\delta)$.
2. Computing the value of the Bloomier filter at $x \in D$ requires $O(1)$ hash function evaluations and $O(1)$ memory look-ups.
3. If $x \notin S$, it outputs $\perp$ with probability $1 = O(\epsilon^{-1} 3^{k-m})$.

As a result, we propose a method to construct the Bloomier filter with improved creation time and storage space compared to existing results, by leveraging the concept of 3-hypergraphs with the optimal constant $c_3 = 1.23$.

Acknowledgements. This research was in part conducted under a contract of "Research and development on new generation cryptography for secure wireless communication services" among "Research and Development for Expansion of Radio Wave Resources (JPJ000254)", which was supported by the Ministry of Internal Affairs and Communications, Japan. This work was in part supported by JSPS KAKENHI Grant Number JP22K19773.

References

1. Bloom, B.: Space/time trade-offs in hash coding with allowable errors. Commun. ACM **13**, 422–426 (1970)
2. Botelho, F.C., Pagh, R., Ziviani, N.: Practical perfect hashing in nearly optimal space. Inf. Syst. **38**(1), 108–131 (2013)
3. Belazzougui, D., Venturini, R.: Compressed static functions with applications. In: Proceedings of the Twenty-Fourth Annual ACM-SIAM Symposium on Discrete Algorithms, pp. 229–240. Society for Industrial and Applied Mathematics (2013)
4. Capalbo, M., Reingold, O., Vadhan, S., Wigderson, A.: Randomness conductors and constant-degree lossless expanders. In: Proceedings of the Thirty-Fourth Annual ACM Symposium on Theory of Computing, pp. 659–668 (2002)
5. Charles, D., Chellapilla, K.: Bloomier filters: a second look. In: Halperin, D., Mehlhorn, K. (eds.) ESA 2008. LNCS, vol. 5193, pp. 259–270. Springer, Heidelberg (2008). https://doi.org/10.1007/978-3-540-87744-8_22
6. Chazelle, B., Kilian, J., Rubinfeld, R., Tal, A.: The Bloomier filter: an efficient data structure for static support lookup tables. In: Proceedings of the 15th Annual ACM-SIAM Symposium on Discrete Algorithms (SODA 2004), pp. 30–39 (2004)
7. Czech, Z.J., Havas, G., Majewski, B.S.: An optimal algorithm for generating minimal perfect hash functions. Inf. Process. Lett. **43**(5), 257–264 (1992)
8. Duke, R.: Types of cycles in hypergraphs. In: North-Holland Mathematics Studies, vol. 115, pp. 399–417. North-Holland (1985)
9. Goldberg, A.V.: Finding a maximum density subgraph. University of California Berkeley (1984)
10. Genuzio, M., Ottaviano, G., Vigna, S.: Fast scalable construction of (minimal perfect hash) functions. In: Goldberg, A.V., Kulikov, A.S. (eds.) SEA 2016. LNCS, vol. 9685, pp. 339–352. Springer, Cham (2016). https://doi.org/10.1007/978-3-319-38851-9_23

11. Havas, G., Majewski, B.S., Wormald, N.C., Czech, Z.J.: Graphs, hypergraphs and hashing. In: van Leeuwen, J. (ed.) WG 1993. LNCS, vol. 790, pp. 153–165. Springer, Heidelberg (1994). https://doi.org/10.1007/3-540-57899-4_49

12. Spielman, D.A.: Linear-time encodable and decodable error-correcting codes. IEEE Trans. Inf. Theory **42**(6), 1723–1731 (1996)

13. Xie, T., Zhang, Y., Song, D.: Orion: zero knowledge proof with linear prover time. In: Dodis, Y., Shrimpton, T. (eds.) CRYPTO 2022, Part IV. LNCS, vol. 13510, pp. 299–328. Springer, Cham (2022). https://doi.org/10.1007/978-3-031-15985-5_11

Principal Component Analysis over the Boolean Circuit Within TFHE Scheme

Hyun Jung Doh[1], Joon Soo Yoo[2], Mi Yeon Hong[2], Kang Hoon Lee[2],
Tae Min Ahn[2], and Ji Won Yoon[2(✉)]

[1] Department of Mathematics, Korea University, Seoul, Republic of Korea
smarthammer@naver.com
[2] School of Cybersecurity and Institute of Cybersecurity and Privacy (ICSP), Korea
University, Seoul, Republic of Korea
{sandiegojs,hachikohmy,hoot55,xoals3563,jiwon_yoon}@korea.ac.kr

Abstract. In today's information-driven world, the need to protect personal data while maintaining efficient data processing capabilities is crucial. Homomorphic Encryption (HE) has emerged as a potential solution, allowing secure processing of encrypted information without compromising privacy. However, current HE schemes suffer from slow processing speeds, especially when dealing with high-dimensional data. This paper focuses on leveraging the PCA technique within the Fast Fully Homomorphic Encryption over the Torus (TFHE) scheme to optimize the speed of subsequent algorithms. TFHE offers the advantage of enabling the homomorphic implementation of any circuit but suffers from extensive execution time. We present tailored PCA algorithms for TFHE, utilizing the power method and eigen-shift techniques to extract eigenvalues and eigenvectors. These techniques provide efficient solutions for performing PCA computations within the TFHE framework. By designing a dedicated PCA circuit using TFHE's fundamental homomorphic gates, we achieve efficient evaluation times for PCA. The performance analysis shows execution times of 3.42 h for a 16-bit dataset and 12.22 h for a 32-bit dataset, with potential for further improvement.

Keywords: Homomorphic Encryption · TFHE · Principal Component Analysis

1 Introduction

In the present era, individuals enjoy convenient and unrestricted access to vast amounts of information, facilitated by seamless information exchange and efficient online processing capabilities. However, this convenience gives rise to concerns regarding the vulnerability of important personal information. Consequently, the protection and security of personal data assume paramount importance, with homomorphic encryption emerging as a potential solution.

H. Kim and J. Youn (Eds.): WISA 2023, LNCS 14402, pp. 27–39, 2024.
https://doi.org/10.1007/978-981-99-8024-6_3

Homomorphic Encryption (HE) technology offers a distinctive advantage by enabling the processing of information in an encrypted form. Users of this technology can obtain desired information while preventing the processing institution from accessing personal details. The development and implementation of homomorphic encryption hold the potential to alleviate concerns related to privacy rights infringement, thereby enabling individuals to entrust their information with greater confidence and security.

Nevertheless, the existing homomorphic encryption technology suffers from the drawback of slow processing speed, posing challenges when dealing with high-dimensional information. As the dimensionality of the data increases, the current encryption schemes encounter difficulties in effectively addressing this issue. To overcome this limitation, Principal Component Analysis (PCA) [1] is a statistical methodology capable of reducing the dimensionality of a data matrix. By leveraging PCA, it becomes possible to condense the information into a lower-dimensional space, retaining only the crucial components. This enables the efficient processing of large-dimensional data even within the context of homomorphic encryption.

This paper focuses on leveraging the PCA technique within HE to optimize the speed of subsequent algorithms. To achieve this, we employ the Fast Fully Homomorphic Encryption over the Torus (TFHE) [2] encryption scheme, which is renowned for its Boolean evaluation capabilities. TFHE's distinctive advantage lies in its ability to enable the homomorphic implementation of any circuit through its bootstrapping technique. However, a notable drawback of TFHE is its extensive execution time, which adversely affects performance in terms of speed. Therefore, it is crucial to address this issue in the early stages of the TFHE encryption scheme, particularly for subsequent algorithms like statistical analysis, machine learning, and deep learning.

To implement the PCA technique, we design a dedicated PCA circuit utilizing fundamental homomorphic gates—AND, OR, and XOR—provided by the TFHE library. Notably, the total evaluation time for the PCA algorithm is measured to be 3.42 h for a 16-bit dataset and 12.22 h for a 32-bit dataset, both using a matrix size of 10 by 10. Although the execution time for PCA is considerable, it is important to highlight that subsequent algorithms can greatly benefit from its application once the cloud evaluates the PCA algorithm. Furthermore, to address the limitations of our small dataset, we provide the time complexity of the PCA algorithm as an estimation for larger or real datasets.

Moreover, we present PCA algorithms specifically designed for TFHE, taking into account its unique characteristics. In the context of TFHE, conventional techniques such as the Gaussian elimination trick are not employed for finding the inverse matrix in the encrypted domain. Instead, we propose an alternative approach that leverages the power method and eigen-shift techniques to accurately extract eigenvalues and eigenvectors. This method proves to be more appropriate and efficient for performing PCA computations within the TFHE framework.

This paper introduces the PCA technique to the TFHE scheme, addressing the time-consuming nature of multi-dimensional data analysis with Boolean evaluation. We also propose a more suitable method for the PCA algorithm in the encrypted domain. Furthermore, we conduct timing analysis of PCA implemented using the TFHE scheme. By utilizing the dimensionality reduction capabilities of PCA, TFHE enables advanced machine learning techniques while ensuring the security and privacy guarantees. This synergistic combination of PCA and TFHE presents promising opportunities for unlocking secure and privacy-preserving data analysis.

2   Background

2.1   Homomorphic Encryption (HE)

Rivest et al. [3] first introduce the concept of HE in 1978. HE encompasses four distinct types of schemes with varying capabilities. Partially Homomorphic Encryption (PHE) permits either repeated addition [4,5] or multiplication [6–8] operations, while Somewhat Homomorphic Encryption (SHE) [9,10] enables both addition and multiplication operations. However, SHE has a limitation on the number of times these operations can be performed. Leveled Homomorphic Encryptions (LHE) provide the capability to perform computations on encrypted data using circuits with bounded depths on ciphertexts. Fully Homomorphic Encryption (FHE) represents an enhanced variant of LHE that incorporates the bootstrapping technique, enabling unrestricted computations on encrypted data. Notable schemes within the domain of FHE include BFV [11], CKKS [12], and the primary focus of our discussion, TFHE. The term "fully" implies that an unrestricted number of addition and multiplication operations can be performed, encompassing any function.

Characteristics of TFHE. TFHE exhibits a unique feature wherein plaintext data is encoded using bits, and computations are carried out using a Boolean circuit. When homomorphic operations are performed on ciphertext, noise accumulates due to the computational processes. If the noise level becomes excessive, decryption may become problematic. To address this challenge, TFHE incorporates bootstrapping technology, which facilitates noise reduction. As a result, TFHE enables the decoding of information without significant interference from noise, even when operations are repeatedly applied within arbitrary functions.

Handling Real Numbers in TFHE: Encoding and Decoding Process. In TFHE, when a real number is provided as an input value, it undergoes a specific encoding mechanism. The plaintext representation within TFHE employs an `int32` format, with a fixed bit length of 32. Consequently, only the integer component of the input value is recognized during the encryption process, while the fractional portion, denoted by the decimal point, is excluded.

To address this limitation and enable the expression of both the operations and results as real numbers, we propose a practical and efficient privacy-preserving PCA method. During the encryption process, the input value is multiplied by $2^{length/2}$ where length refers to the bit length, effectively scaling the value. Subsequently, after decryption, the output is divided by $2^{\text{length}/2}$ to restore the original real number representation. This procedure ensures that the homomorphic operations are performed on appropriately scaled values, allowing for the accurate handling of real numbers throughout the encryption and decryption processes.

2.2 Principal Component Analysis (PCA)

A Statistical Approach for Dimensionality Reduction. PCA stands as one of the widely adopted techniques for dimensionality reduction in machine learning. It is a statistical method that explores the primary components within data distributions. When high-dimensional data is provided as input, PCA transforms it into lower-dimensional data as output. The critical objective lies in reducing the dimensionality while preserving the inherent structure of the original data to the greatest extent possible.

To obtain the principal components of the original input matrix, the eigenvalue, and its corresponding eigenvectors are initially computed. The eigenvectors are then arranged in descending order based on the magnitude of their corresponding eigenvalues. Subsequently, to achieve a dimension reduction to d, a reduced basis matrix is derived by selecting d eigenvectors in the prescribed order. This reduced basis matrix serves as the foundation for obtaining a matrix with reduced dimensions, effectively concluding the PCA procedure.

3   Related Work

PCA Within CKKS Scheme. A work by Panda et al. [13] adopted a CKKS scheme that supports the approximate computation on complex numbers by power method. This approach allows vector normalization to be performed using an iterative algorithm of the inverse square root function. However, since the CKKS scheme supports approximate arithmetic over encrypted data, the more homomorphic operation, the accuracy is constrained. Furthermore, the power method in their work is done by iterative computing, rather than directly computing the covariance matrix transformation. This makes the complexity of the power method dependent on the size of the dataset rather than the size of the covariance matrix, thus, the performance is constrained.

4   Our Model

Our proposed model involves a non-interactive two-party computation scenario, where the client transmits encrypted data to the server for evaluation using the Boolean-based TFHE scheme. During the evaluation phase, all data undergo encryption to ensure confidentiality through the security guarantees provided by the hardness of Learning with Errors (LWE) [14] assumption. The protocol operates as follows (Fig. 1):

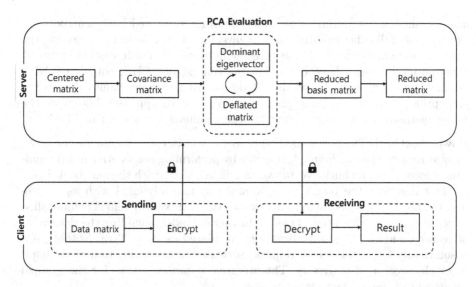

Fig. 1. An overview of our model. The model assumes two-party computation over the TFHE scheme. The server evaluates the PCA algorithm over the encrypted data matrix.

Client. The client encodes the data with a chosen precision (16 or 32-bit) and proceeds to encrypt the data bit by bit, resulting in an LWE ciphertext. The encrypted data is then sent to the server.

Server. The server performs the PCA algorithm on the provided LWE ciphertext using the following steps:

1. Calculation of the mean of the data and centering the data matrix.
2. Computation of the covariance of the centered data.
3. Evaluation of eigenvalues and eigenvectors using the power method and eigenshift techniques.
4. Extraction of the dominant eigenvector and deflation of the data matrix.
5. Construction of the reduced basis matrix and the reduced data matrix.
6. Finally, the server sends the resulting processed data back to the client.

Client. The client decrypts and decodes the received result for further analysis or utilization.

5 PCA over the TFHE Scheme

5.1 Dominant Eigenvector

The primary objective of our research is to derive a reduced matrix possessing diminished dimensions from the original high-dimensional data matrix. To accomplish this, the initial step entails acquiring a reduced basis matrix, comprising a carefully chosen subset of d eigenvectors. In conventional scenarios, the computation and solution of equations facilitate the determination of eigenvectors and eigenvalues. However, within the context of TFHE, equation solving is unattainable without knowledge of the actual numerical values due to the encryption of numbers. Consequently, an alternative approach known as the power method was employed to extract the dominant eigenvector in TFHE.

Power Method. The power method represents an iterative technique employed to approximate the dominant eigenvector by performing consecutive matrix multiplications. First, an initial vector $\mathbf{x}_0$, is utilized, along with the matrix A. Upon the first iteration, the vector $\mathbf{x}_1$ is obtained by multiplying A with $\mathbf{x}_0$. Subsequently, the vector $\mathbf{x}_2$ is computed as $\mathbf{x}_2 = A\mathbf{x}_1 = A^2\mathbf{x}_0$, wherein A is multiplied by $\mathbf{x}_1$ once more. This process can be further extended, enabling the derivation of vector value $\mathbf{x}_k$ at the k-th iteration, calculated as $\mathbf{x}_k = A^k\mathbf{x}_0$. Notably, if k is sufficiently large, the vector value $\mathbf{x}_k$ serves as an approximation of the dominant eigenvector of matrix A. This iterative approach allows for the gradual refinement of the eigenvector estimation.

Algorithm 1. Dominant Eigenvector Algorithm

1: **procedure** DOMEIGENVECTOR(A, I) ▷ N-by-N Matrix A, iteration I
2:   **for** $i = 0, \cdots, N - 1$ **do**
3:    $Z_i \leftarrow \sum_{j=0}^{N-1} A_{ij}$
4:   **end for**
5:   $v \leftarrow \frac{1}{\|Z\|_\infty} Z$
6:   **for** $i = 0, \cdots, I - 2$ **do**
7:    $Z \leftarrow A \cdot v$
8:    $v \leftarrow \frac{1}{\|Z\|_\infty} Z$
9:   **end for**
10:   **return** v ▷ v : Dominant eigenvector
11: **end procedure**

Algorithm 1 is an iterative method for acquiring a dominant eigenvector. This procedure involves conducting I iterations of computations on matrix A to determine the dominant eigenvector. In line 3 of the algorithm, all components of the initial eigenvector, referred to as $\mathbf{x}_0$, are uniformly initialized to a value of 1. Subsequently, the vector $\mathbf{x}_1$ is obtained by performing matrix multiplication between matrix A and vector $\mathbf{x}_0$. Given that each component in $\mathbf{x}_0$ is uniformly set to 1, the i-th component in $\mathbf{x}_1$ is calculated as the sum of all components within the i-th row of matrix A. It is worth noting that, within the context of homomorphic operations, addition operations are known to exhibit greater efficiency than multiplication operations, thereby influencing our chosen implementation strategy.

Given the constrained numerical range of values that can be represented within encrypted numbers, it becomes necessary to devise a strategy aimed at mitigating the numerical magnitude of the matrix resulting from the multiplication of matrix A and vector v (lines 5 and 8). To achieve this, all components of vector Z are divided by the maximum value observed among its constituent elements. This optimization approach serves the purpose of diminishing the overall size of the resultant matrix, thereby facilitating subsequent computational procedures.

5.2   Eigen Shift Procedure

The reduced basis matrix is composed of d eigenvectors, specifically those that correspond to eigenvalues arranged in descending order starting from the largest value. Within the TFHE framework, prioritizing time efficiency, it is advantageous to sequentially select d dominant eigenvectors rather than computing all eigenvectors and subsequently selecting from the computed set. To fulfill this objective, the eigen shift procedure was employed as a viable approach.

Deflated Matrix. After acquiring the dominant eigenvector from matrix A, the second dominant eigenvector of matrix A can be obtained from the deflated matrix S. Specifically, the dominant eigenvector within the deflated matrix corresponds to the second dominant eigenvector in matrix A. By iteratively obtaining the deflated matrix and its dominant eigenvector in this manner, a sequential set of d dominant eigenvectors can be derived, ultimately resulting in a reduced basis matrix.

To obtain the deflated matrix, the eigenvector and its corresponding eigenvalue are utilized. Given a vector $\mathbf{x}$ that satisfies the condition $\mathbf{x}^T \mathbf{v}_{\text{eigen}} = 1$, the deflated matrix S is obtained by subtracting $\lambda_{\text{eigen}} \cdot \mathbf{v}_{\text{eigen}} \mathbf{x}^T$ from matrix A. To ensure operational stability, the normalized eigenvector L is employed in place of the eigenvector as this guarantees $L^T L = 1$.

Eigenvalue. Let v' represent the dominant eigenvector obtained through $I -$ 1 iterations in matrix S, and let v denote the dominant eigenvector obtained through I iterations. In conventional approaches, the eigenvalue corresponding to the dominant eigenvector is determined using the Rayleigh quotient method. However, in our method, the eigenvalue was computed by dividing the first component of $v'' = Sv' = \lambda v'$ by the first component of v', aiming to enhance computational efficiency. This is justified by the fact that the eigenvalue derived from any component of the eigenvector is identical, making it more efficient to obtain it from a single component.

5.3   Details of PCA Algorithm

Algorithm 2 illustrates the comprehensive procedure of PCA within the TFHE scheme that we provide. We present a detailed line-by-line explanation of the algorithm, offering insights into its execution as the following:

Algorithm 2. PCA algorithm

1: **procedure** PCA(A, I, d) ▷ N-by-M Matrix A, iteration I, dimension d

2:    $C \leftarrow \frac{1}{N} \sum_{i=0}^{N-1} A_i^T$

3:    $Z \leftarrow A - 1_N \cdot C^T$

4:    $S \leftarrow \frac{1}{N} Z^T \cdot Z$ ▷ S : covariance matrix of centered data Z

5:    **for** $h = 0, \cdots, d - 2$ **do**

6:        $v' \leftarrow \text{DOMEIGENVECTOR}(S, I - 1)$

7:        $v'' \leftarrow S \cdot v'$

8:        $v \leftarrow \frac{1}{max(|v''|)} v''$ ▷ eigenvector v

9:        $Q \leftarrow \sum v_i^2$

10:       $L \leftarrow \frac{1}{\sqrt{Q}} \times v$ ▷ normalized matrix L

11:       $temp \leftarrow \frac{v_0''}{v_0'}(L \cdot L^T)$

12:       $S \leftarrow S - temp$ ▷ deflated matrix S

13:       $B_h \leftarrow v$ ▷ h-th column of $B = v$

14:   **end for**

15:   $v \leftarrow \text{DOMEIGENVECTOR}(S, I)$ ▷ eigenvector v

16:   $B_{d-1} \leftarrow v$ ▷ reduced basis B

17:   **return** $U = AB$ ▷ U : Reduced Matrix

18: **end procedure**

- (Lines 2 to 4) The matrix Z represents a centered version of the input data matrix A, while the matrix S corresponds to the covariance matrix of Z.
- (Lines 6 to 7) The eigenvector denoted as v' represents the dominant eigenvector obtained after performing $I - 1$ iterations on matrix S, while v'' signifies the dominant eigenvector obtained by performing one additional iteration using the product Sv'.
- (Line 11) Subsequently, the eigenvalue is determined by dividing the first component of the eigenvector v'' by the corresponding first component of the eigenvector v'.
- (Line 8) The vector v is obtained by normalizing v'', dividing it by the maximum value among its vector components. It represents the dominant eigenvector attained after I iterations in matrix S, which is the desired dominant eigenvector.
- (Line 13) This computed eigenvector v is then copied into the h-th column of the reduced basis matrix B.
- (Lines 9 to 12) The deflated matrix S can be obtained by utilizing the normalized eigenvector matrix L derived from the dominant eigenvector v, in conjunction with the associated eigenvalue. This deflated matrix facilitates the computation of the subsequent dominant eigenvector.
- (Lines 15 to 16) Finally, the d-th dominant eigenvector is obtained and placed into the d-th column of matrix B, representing the reduced basis.

– (Line 17) The reduced matrix U can be attained by performing matrix multiplication between matrix A and the reduced basis matrix B.

6   Experiment

Environment. Our research was conducted on a system with Intel i7-7700 CPU working on 3.6 GHz with 8 cores, 48GB RAM, and running Ubuntu 20.04 LTS. Additionally, we employed version 1.1 of the TFHE library for the implementation of the PCA algorithm.

Dataset and Parameter. Our dataset comprises 10 randomly generated data instances, each consisting of 10 features. The small dataset size is a result of the time-consuming nature of Boolean-based construction.

In our experiments, we set the number of power method iterations to 3 and extracted 2 dominant eigenvectors. To evaluate time performance, we conducted measurements using both 16-bit and 32-bit input data encodings.

7   Result

Total Execution Time. The total execution time for PCA is 3.424 h for 16-bit precision and 12.221 h for 32-bit precision. Note that the total execution time excludes encryption and decryption time as it is performed from the client side.

Encryption and Decryption Time. The encryption phase (including encoding) involves the conversion of real-valued inputs into ciphertext representation using a bit format prior to performing PCA. This step was completed rapidly. In the case of the 16-bit precision, it required 0.0716038 s; for the 32-bit precision, the encryption process concluded in 0.11249 s.

The decryption (including decoding) involves converting the ciphertext from its bit format back into real values, producing the resulting decrypted PCA output. For 16-bit precision, it took 8.0997e−05 s. In the case of 32-bit precision, the time required was approximately 1.58725e−04 s.

Table 1. Execution Time of PCA within TFHE scheme. The execution time is measured in hours.

	C	S	v	L	B_h	B_{d-1}	U	Total
16-bit	0.048	1.696	0.410	0.096	0.512	0.410	0.253	3.424
Ratio (%)	1.388	49.540	11.972	2.797	14.953	11.952	7.398	100
32-bit	0.156	5.949	1.474	0.361	1.883	1.476	0.922	12.221
Ratio (%)	1.273	48.683	12.058	2.955	15.404	12.076	7.546	100

Evaluation Time. The total processing time for the category C in Table 1 amounted to 0.048 h in the case of 16-bit encryption, constituting approximately 1.388% of the overall execution time. Similarly, for the 32-bit encryption scheme, the total processing time for this step was 0.156 h, accounting for 1.273% of the total execution time.

S in Table 1 refers to the interval spanning from the computation of matrix C to the derivation of matrix S, constituting lines 3 and 4 in Algorithm 2. This phase involves subtracting the matrix C, the average of each row in matrix A, from A, yielding matrix Z. Subsequently, the transposition of the centered matrix Z is performed, followed by the operation $\frac{1}{N}Z^T Z$, resulting in the covariance matrix S of Z. This step takes most of the time since it requires matrix multiplication taking $O(NM^2)$ whereas other steps are linear transformation with time complexity of $O(NM)$ and inner product with $O(M)$. The total processing time for this step amounted to 1.696 h for 16-bit encryption, representing approximately 49.540% of the overall execution time. For 32-bit encryption, the total processing time for this step was 5.949 h, accounting for 48.683% of the total execution time.

v in Table 1 corresponds to lines 6 to 8 in Algorithm 2 and represents the dominant eigenvector obtained through the I–th iteration of matrix S. The total processing time for this step was 0.410 h for 16-bit encryption, accounting for approximately 11.972% of the overall execution time. Similarly, for 32-bit encryption, the total processing time for this step was 1.474 h, representing 12.058% of the total execution time.

The category indicated as L in Table 1 corresponds to lines 9 and 10 in Algorithm 2. Total processing time for this step amounted to 0.096 h for 16-bit encryption, accounting for approximately 2.797% of the overall execution time. For 32-bit encryption, the total processing time for this step was 0.361 h, representing approximately 2.955% of the total execution time.

B_h in Table 1 corresponds to lines 11 to 13 in Algorithm 2. The total processing time for this step amounted to 0.512 h for 16-bit encryption, constituting approximately 14.953% of the overall execution time. Similarly, for 32-bit encryption, the total processing time for this step was 1.883 h, accounting for 15.404% of the total execution time.

B_{d-1} in Table 1 represent lines 15 and 16 in Algorithm 2. The total processing time for this step was 0.410 h for 16-bit encryption, representing approximately 11.952% of the overall execution time. For 32-bit encryption, the total processing time for this step was 1.476 h, accounting for 12.076% of the total execution time.

U in Table 1 corresponds to line 17 in Algorithm 2. The total processing time for this step amounted to 0.253 h for 16-bit encryption, accounting for approximately 7.398% of the overall execution time. For 32-bit encryption, the total processing time for this step was 0.922 h, representing approximately 7.546% of the total execution time.

8   Discussion and Future Work

8.1   Discussion

Comparative Analysis: Loss of Information in the Encryption-Based Information Processing of PCA Calculations. A comparative evaluation was conducted to assess the impact of encrypting input values on the information processing performed during PCA calculations. Specifically, the same data matrix was examined under two conditions: PCA calculation performed in plain text versus PCA calculation executed with encrypted input values.

The findings reveal that during the process of information processing in encrypted form, a certain degree of information loss occurs. This loss is attributed to the precision of the input encoding and the encryption-based operations employed during PCA calculations. As a result, the transformed data exhibits variations compared to the original, unencrypted data matrix. This phenomenon necessitates careful consideration of the potential trade-off between privacy preservation through encryption and the preservation of information integrity in the context of PCA calculations.

8.2   Future Work

Improved Computational Efficiency by Modifying Eigenvector Normalization in PCA Algorithm. Within the PCA algorithm, lines 8 and 11 involve the normalization of eigenvectors. It is important to note that while both normalizations occur, they serve different purposes and adopt different formats.

Line 8 in Algorithm 2 pertains to the derivation of all eigenvectors to be output. The eigenvector is obtained after I iterations using matrix S. In this case, to achieve unity, all components of the eigenvector are divided by the largest component before deriving the result. As a result, the absolute value of the largest number in the eigenvector becomes 1, while the absolute values of the remaining components are less than 1. Consequently, the sum of the squares of these components is greater than 1.

On the other hand, line 11 in Algorithm 2 involves the normalization of eigenvectors to obtain the deflated matrix. In this step, the goal is to find a matrix L such that the multiplication of L^T and L equals 1. To achieve this, the eigenvector is divided by the sum of the squares of all its components. As a result, in this particular case, the absolute value of the largest component is less than 1, while the sum of the squares of all components equals 1.

It is worth mentioning that if the process in line 8 in Algorithm 2 is eliminated and only the normalization in lines 9 to 11 is applied to the eigenvectors, it would lead to a reduction in computational effort and significantly faster execution of the PCA algorithm. Since multiplication operations in TFHE tend to be time-consuming, omitting the step of multiplying all $(d - 1)$ eigenvectors by real numbers can yield substantial time savings. Although the proportionality uniformity in the derived eigenvectors may be reduced, the resulting values are still valid, allowing for the successful acquisition of the reduced matrix even with the improved execution time.

9   Conclusion

This paper introduces the application of PCA within the TFHE scheme to optimize the execution time of subsequent algorithms. By leveraging the dimensionality reduction capabilities of PCA and designing a dedicated circuit using TFHE's homomorphic gates, we address the challenge of slow processing speeds in high-dimensional data analysis. Additionally, we propose tailored PCA algorithms that utilize the power method and eigen-shift techniques for efficient computations within the TFHE framework. Future work can explore further optimizations and applications of PCA within TFHE to enhance its performance and expand its capabilities.

Acknowledgements. This work was supported by an Institute of Information & Communications Technology Planning Evaluation (IITP) grant funded by the Korea government (MSIT) (No. 2021-0-00558-003, Development of National Statistical Analysis System using Homomorphic Encryption Technology).

References

1. Abdi, H., Williams, L.: Principal component analysis. Wiley Interdisc. Rev. Comput. Stat. **2**, 433–459 (2010)
2. Chillotti, I., Gama, N., Georgieva, M., Izabachène, M.: TFHE: fast fully homomorphic encryption over the torus. J. Cryptol. **33**, 34–91 (2020). https://doi.org/10.1007/s00145-019-09319-x
3. Rivest, R., Shamir, A., Adleman, L.: A method for obtaining digital signatures and public-key cryptosystems. Commun. ACM **21**, 120–126 (1978)
4. Goldwasser, S., Micali, S.: Probabilistic encryption & how to play mental poker keeping secret all partial information. In: Providing Sound Foundations for Cryptography: On the Work of Shafi Goldwasser and Silvio Micali, pp. 173–201 (2019)
5. Damgård, I., Geisler, M., Krøigaard, M.: Efficient and secure comparison for online auctions. In: Pieprzyk, J., Ghodosi, H., Dawson, E. (eds.) ACISP 2007. LNCS, vol. 4586, pp. 416–430. Springer, Heidelberg (2007). https://doi.org/10.1007/978-3-540-73458-1_30
6. ElGamal, T.: A public key cryptosystem and a signature scheme based on discrete logarithms. IEEE Trans. Inf. Theory **31**, 469–472 (1985)
7. Rivest, R., Adleman, L., Dertouzos, M., et al.: On data banks and privacy homomorphisms. Found. Secure Comput. **4**, 169–180 (1978)
8. Paillier, P.: Public-key cryptosystems based on composite degree residuosity classes. In: Stern, J. (ed.) EUROCRYPT 1999. LNCS, vol. 1592, pp. 223–238. Springer, Heidelberg (1999). https://doi.org/10.1007/3-540-48910-X_16
9. Brakerski, Z., Gentry, C., Vaikuntanathan, V.: (Leveled) fully homomorphic encryption without bootstrapping. ACM Trans. Comput. Theory (TOCT) **6**, 1–36 (2014)

10. Boneh, D., Goh, E.-J., Nissim, K.: Evaluating 2-DNF formulas on ciphertexts. In: Kilian, J. (ed.) TCC 2005. LNCS, vol. 3378, pp. 325–341. Springer, Heidelberg (2005). https://doi.org/10.1007/978-3-540-30576-7_18

11. Fan, J., Vercauteren, F.: Somewhat practical fully homomorphic encryption. Cryptology ePrint Archive (2012)

12. Cheon, J.H., Kim, A., Kim, M., Song, Y.: Homomorphic encryption for arithmetic of approximate numbers. In: Takagi, T., Peyrin, T. (eds.) ASIACRYPT 2017. LNCS, vol. 10624, pp. 409–437. Springer, Cham (2017). https://doi.org/10.1007/978-3-319-70694-8_15

13. Panda, S.: Principal component analysis using CKKS homomorphic encryption scheme. Cryptology ePrint Archive (2021)

14. Regev, O.: On lattices, learning with errors, random linear codes, and cryptography. J. ACM (JACM) 56(6), 1–40 (2009)

A Security Analysis on MQ-Sign

Yasuhiko Ikematsu[1], Hyungrok Jo[2(✉)], and Takanori Yasuda[3]

[1] Institute of Mathematics for Industry, Kyushu University, 744, Motooka, Nishi-ku, Fukuoka 819-0395, Japan
ikematsu@imi.kyushu-u.ac.jp
[2] Institute of Advanced Sciences, Yokohama National University, 79-7, Tokiwadai, Hodogaya-ku, Yokohama 240-8501, Japan
jo-hyungrok-xz@ynu.ac.jp
[3] Institute for the Advancement of Higher Education, Okayama University of Science, 1-1, Ridaicho, Kita-ku, Okayama 700-0005, Japan
tyasuda@ous.ac.jp

Abstract. MQ-Sign is a variant of the UOV signature scheme proposed by Shim et al. It has been suggested as a candidate for the standardization of post-quantum cryptography in Republic of Korea (known as KpqC). Recently Aulbach et al. proposed a practical key recovery attack against MQ-Sign-RS and MQ-Sign-SS with a simple secret key S. In this paper, we propose another attack that is valid for the case of a general secret key S.

Keywords: Post-quantum cryptography · Multivariate public key cryptography · KpqC

1 Introduction

Post-Quantum Cryptography (PQC) [2] is a new generation cryptographic system that distinguishes itself from conventional cryptographic systems that rely on the hardness of integer factorization problems, and is globally popularized due to its resistance to attacks by Shor's quantum algorithm [10]. Currently, the National Institute of Standards and Technology (NIST) [7] is working towards the standardization of practical post-quantum cryptography systems that provide both adequate security and practicality. The ultimate objective is to promote these cutting-edge cryptographic systems in the near future. NIST announced the results [8] of its third round of selection in July 2022, with CRYSTALS-Kyber being chosen for the KEM category, and CRYSTALS-Dilithium, Falcon, and SPHINCS+ being selected for the signature category.

In February 2022, the Korean Post-Quantum Cryptography Competition (KpqC, for short)[1] was launched in South Korea for the standardization of post-quantum cryptography. In November 2022, the Round 1 of KpqC was announced, and 7 candidates (3 Lattice-based, 3 Code-based, and 1 Graph-based) were

---

[1] The Korean Post-Quantum Cryptography Competition, www.kpqc.or.kr.

H. Kim and J. Youn (Eds.): WISA 2023, LNCS 14402, pp. 40–51, 2024.
https://doi.org/10.1007/978-981-99-8024-6_4

selected in the Public Key Encryption/Key-Establishment Algorithms category, while 9 candidates (5 Lattice-based, 1 Code-based, 1 Multivariate-based, 1 Isogeny-based, and 1 MPCitH-based) were selected in the Digital Signature Algorithms category.

In the pursuit of post-quantum digital signature schemes, multivariate cryptography has emerged as a promising candidate. MPKC (Multivariate Public Key Cryptography) is based on the hardness of the Multivariate Quadratic polynomial problem (MQ problem, for short), which asks to solve a system of multivariate quadratic equations over a finite field. MPKC is attractive due to its fast signature verification and small signature sizes. In particular, UOV [6] and Rainbow [5] have been actively researched as leading schemes in the area of MPKC in recent years. However, it is essential to note that Rainbow scheme [5], which was a finalist of NIST PQC standardization, has been broken by the attack proposed by Beullens [3]. Therefore, careful selection and analysis of multivariate signature schemes are necessary to ensure their security in practice.

The MQ-Sign [9] is a UOV-based signature scheme proposed by Shim et al., which was submitted to the KpqC competition for the standardization of post-quantum cryptography in the Republic of Korea. MQ-Sign acquired to reduce the size of secret key by making the central map of UOV sparse and to improve signing performance by using the block inversion method. There are 4 types of MQ-Sign, which are denoted by "MQ-Sign-{R/S}{R/S}" with the suffixes "R" and "S". The first slot {R/S} stands for the selection of the Vinegar × Vinegar quadratic parts using Random polynomials or Sparse polynomials. The second slot {R/S} stands for the selection of the Oil × Vinegar quadratic parts using Random polynomials or Sparse polynomials. We note that MQ-Sign-RR is basically same as the structure of an original UOV scheme. Recently, Aulbach et al. [1] proposed a practical key recovery attack against MQ-Sign-{R/S}S, combining the sparsity of the central map with a secret key S having a simple form. They have checked in [1] that their attack recovered the secret key in a few second for the proposed parameter of security level 5.

In this paper, we propose another attack against MQ-Sign-{R/S}S which is valid for the case of a general secret key S. The attack by Aulbach et al. [1] recovers the secret key by solving a linear system, which is obtained by exploiting the sparseness of the central map $\mathcal{F}$ and assuming that the form of the secret key S is simple. In contrast, our attack can handle a general secret key S. We first construct a system of quadratic equations involving the components of S, its inverse matrix $\mathcal{T} := S^{-1}$, and the central map $\mathcal{F}$. To solve this system, we classify the equations into various subsystems and guess some variables by brute force, obtaining a system of linear equations. Finally, we recover the secret key S by solving the linear system in polynomial time. We also provide the experimental results of our attack, which broke the proposed parameters of security level 1, 3, and 5 in [9] by a usual laptop within about 30 min.

This paper is organized as follows. In Sect. 2, we provide the explanation of the UOV signature scheme and its variant, MQ-Sign(-RS). In Sect. 3, we give a detailed description of a series of attack methods against MQ-Sign-RS. In

Sect. 4, we demonstrate the results of implementation performed to validate the effectiveness of our attack. In Sect. 5, we conclude our results.

2　MQ-Sign

In this section, we explain the constructions of the UOV (Unbalanced Oil and Vinegar) signature scheme and its improved variant, MQ-Sign.

2.1　UOV

Let $\mathbb{F}_q$ be a finite field. Here, we briefly recall the construction of the UOV signature scheme [6]. Let v and o be two positive integers such that $v > o > 0$ and set $n := v + o$. We use two variable sets $\mathbf{x}_v = (x_1, \ldots, x_v)$, and $\mathbf{x}_o = (x_{v+1}, \ldots, x_n)$, and put $\mathbf{x} = (\mathbf{x}_v, \mathbf{x}_o)$. We call the first variables $\mathbf{x}_v$ the *vinegar variables* and the second variables $\mathbf{x}_o$ the *oil variables*.

Key Generation: Randomly choose o quadratic polynomials in the variables $\mathbf{x}$ in the following form:

$$f_1(\mathbf{x}) = f_1(\mathbf{x}_v, \mathbf{x}_o) = \sum_{i,j=1}^{v} a_{i,j}^{(1)} x_i x_j + \sum_{i=1}^{v} \sum_{j=v+1}^{n} a_{i,j}^{(1)} x_i x_j,$$

$$\vdots \qquad\qquad (1)$$

$$f_o(\mathbf{x}) = f_o(\mathbf{x}_v, \mathbf{x}_o) = \sum_{i,j=1}^{v} a_{i,j}^{(o)} x_i x_j + \sum_{i=1}^{v} \sum_{j=v+1}^{n} a_{i,j}^{(o)} x_i x_j.$$

Here, each coefficient $a_{i,j}^{(k)}$ is randomly chosen from the finite field $\mathbb{F}_q$. Then, the set $\mathcal{F} = (f_1, \cdots, f_o)$ is called a *central map* of the UOV scheme. Once we randomly choose an invertible linear map $\mathcal{S} : \mathbb{F}_q^n \to \mathbb{F}_q^n$, the public key is given by the composite $\mathcal{P} := \mathcal{F} \circ \mathcal{S} = \{p_1, \cdots, p_o\}$, which is a set of o quadratic polynomials. Moreover, the secret key is $\{\mathcal{F}, \mathcal{S}\}$.

Signature Generation: Given a message $\mathbf{m} = (m_1, \ldots, m_o) \in \mathbb{F}_q^o$ to be signed, a signature $\mathbf{s}$ is generated as follows. First, randomly choose an element $\mathbf{c} = (c_1, \ldots, c_v) \in \mathbb{F}_q^v$. Second, we can easily obtain a solution $\mathbf{d} \in \mathbb{F}_q^o$ to the equations

$$f_1(\mathbf{c}, \mathbf{x}_o) = m_1, \cdots, f_o(\mathbf{c}, \mathbf{x}_o) = m_o,$$

since they are o linear equations in oil variables $\mathbf{x}_o$ from the form of (1). If there is no solution, we choose another element $\mathbf{c}$. Finally, we compute $\mathbf{s} = \mathcal{S}^{-1}(\mathbf{c}, \mathbf{d}) \in \mathbb{F}_q^n$, which is a solution to $\mathcal{P}(\mathbf{x}) = \mathbf{m}$. This $\mathbf{s} \in \mathbb{F}_q^n$ is a signature of the message $\mathbf{m}$.

Verification: It is performed by checking whether $\mathcal{P}(\mathbf{s}) = \mathbf{m}$.

2.2 MQ-Sign-RS

MQ-Sign used here refers specifically to MQ-Sign-RS. MQ-Sign is constructed by making the central map in (2) sparse as follows.

$$f_1(\mathbf{x}) = \sum_{i,j=1}^{v} \alpha_{i,j}^{(1)} x_i x_j + \sum_{i=1}^{v} \beta_i^{(1)} x_i x_{(i+1-2 \pmod o))+v+1},$$

$$\vdots$$

$$f_k(\mathbf{x}) = \sum_{i,j=1}^{v} \alpha_{i,j}^{(k)} x_i x_j + \sum_{i=1}^{v} \beta_i^{(k)} x_i x_{(i+k-2 \pmod o))+v+1}, \qquad (2)$$

$$\vdots$$

$$f_o(\mathbf{x}) = \sum_{i,j=1}^{v} \alpha_{i,j}^{(o)} x_i x_j + \sum_{i=1}^{v} \beta_i^{(o)} x_i x_{(i+o-2 \pmod o))+v+1}.$$

Here each $\beta_i^{(k)}$ is randomly chosen from $\mathbb{F}_q^{\times}$. The linear and constant terms are omitted as they are not relevant in our attack. The signature generation and verification are identical to those of the original UOV scheme.

3 Our Proposed Attack

In this section, we describe our attack against MQ-Sign-RS. In Sect. 3.1, we explain the representation of quadratic polynomials. In Sect. 3.2, we describe the representation of some quadratic polynomials in the central map of MQ-Sign-RS. In Sects. 3.3, 3.4 and 3.5, we state the idea of our attack and describe the algorithm to break MQ-Sign-RS.

3.1 Preliminary

We recall a relation between quadratic polynomials and square matrices. For a homogeneous quadratic polynomial

$$g(\mathbf{x}) = \sum_{1 \leqslant i \leqslant j \leqslant n} g_{ij} x_i x_j \in \mathbb{F}_q[\mathbf{x}],$$

we define the upper triangular matrix G^{up} by

$$G^{\mathrm{up}} := \begin{pmatrix} g_{11} & g_{12} & \cdots & g_{1n} \\ 0 & g_{22} & \cdots & g_{2n} \\ \vdots & \vdots & \ddots & \vdots \\ 0 & 0 & \cdots & g_{nn} \end{pmatrix} \in \mathbb{F}_q^{n \times n}.$$

Then, we obtain the following equality

$$g(\mathbf{x}) = \mathbf{x} \cdot G^{\mathrm{up}} \cdot {}^t\mathbf{x},$$

where ${}^t\mathbf{x}$ denotes the transpose of $\mathbf{x}$. It is clear that the map $g \mapsto G^{\mathrm{up}}$ is a bijective map between the set of homogeneous quadratic polynomials in $\mathbb{F}_q[\mathbf{x}]$ and the set of upper triangular (square) matrices of size n. Let $\mathcal{S}$ be a linear map on $\mathbb{F}_q^n$ and let S be its corresponding matrix of size n. Then, we have

$$g \circ \mathcal{S}(\mathbf{x}) = \mathbf{x} \cdot S \cdot G^{\mathrm{up}} \cdot {}^tS \cdot {}^t\mathbf{x}.$$

However, since $S \cdot G^{\mathrm{up}} \cdot {}^tS$ is not an upper triangular matrix in general, the corresponding upper triangular matrix of $g \circ \mathcal{S}(\mathbf{x})$ is not equal to $S \cdot G^{\mathrm{up}} \cdot {}^tS$.

To avoid this inequality, it is necessary to consider symmetric matrices. For the above quadratic polynomial $g(\mathbf{x})$, we define the following symmetric matrix:

$$G := G^{\mathrm{up}} + {}^tG^{\mathrm{up}}.$$

Then, the corresponding symmetric matrix of $g \circ \mathcal{S}(\mathbf{x})$ is equal to

$$S \cdot G \cdot {}^tS.$$

Thus, if $(F_1, \ldots, F_o)$ and $(P_1, \ldots, P_o)$ are the corresponding symmetric matrices of the central map $\mathcal{F} = (f_1, \ldots, f_o)$ and the public key $\mathcal{P} = (p_1, \ldots, p_o)$, then we have

$$(P_1, \ldots, P_o) = \left(SF_1{}^tS, \ldots, SF_o{}^tS \right),$$

where S are the corresponding matrices of size n to the secret key $\mathcal{S}$. As a result, it is considered that the symmetric matrices of the public key $\mathcal{P}$ inherit some properties of the symmetric matrices of the central map $\mathcal{F}$.

Remark 1. Aulbach et al. [1] proposed a practical attack against MQ-Sign-{R/S}S in the case where S can be written as the secret key $S = \begin{pmatrix} 1_v & 0 \\ * & 1_o \end{pmatrix}$.

3.2   Representation Matrices of the Central Map of MQ-Sign-RS

From the construction of the central map (2) of MQ-Sign-RS, the representation matrices $F_1, \ldots, F_o$ have the special form as follows:

$$F_1 = \begin{pmatrix} \begin{array}{c|c} * & \begin{matrix} \beta_1^{(1)} & & & & \vdots & & & \\ & \beta_2^{(1)} & & & \vdots & & & \\ & & \ddots & & \vdots & & & \\ & & & \beta_{v-o}^{(1)} & \vdots & & & \\ & & & & \vdots & \beta_{v-o+1}^{(1)} & & \\ & & & & \vdots & & \ddots & \\ & & & & \vdots & & & \beta_o^{(1)} \\ \hdashline \beta_{o+1}^{(1)} & & & & \vdots & & & \\ & \ddots & & & \vdots & & & \\ & & & \beta_v^{(1)} & & & & \end{matrix} \\ \hline * & \mathbf{0} \end{array} \end{pmatrix}$$

$$F_2 = \begin{pmatrix} \begin{array}{c|c} * & \begin{matrix} 0 & \beta_1^{(2)} & & & & & & \\ & & \ddots & & & & & \\ & \vdots & & \beta_{v-o}^{(2)} & & & & \\ & \vdots & & & \beta_{v-o+1}^{(2)} & & & \\ & \vdots & & & & \ddots & & \\ & \vdots & & & & & \beta_{o-1}^{(2)} & \\ \beta_o^{(2)} & \vdots & & & & & & 0 \\ \hdashline & \beta_{o+1}^{(2)} & & & & & & \\ & & \ddots & & & & & \\ & & & \beta_v^{(2)} & & & & \end{matrix} \\ \hline * & \mathbf{0} \end{array} \end{pmatrix}$$

$$F_3 = \begin{pmatrix} & 0 & 0 & \beta_1^{(3)} & & & & \\ & & \vdots & & \ddots & & & \\ & & \vdots & & & \beta_{v-o}^{(3)} & & \\ & & \vdots & & & & \beta_{v-o+1}^{(3)} & \\ * & & \vdots & & & & & \ddots & \\ & \beta_{o-1}^{(3)} & \vdots & & & & & & \beta_{o-2}^{(3)} \\ & \beta_o^{(3)} & \vdots & & & & & & 0 \\ & & \beta_{o+1}^{(3)} & & & & & & 0 \\ & & & \ddots & & & & \\ & & & & \beta_v^{(3)} & & & \\ \hline & * & & & 0 & & & \end{pmatrix}$$

$$F_4 = \begin{pmatrix} & 0 & 0 & 0 & \beta_1^{(4)} & & & & \\ & & & \vdots & & \ddots & & & \\ & & & \vdots & & & \beta_{v-o}^{(4)} & & \\ & & & \vdots & & & & \beta_{v-o+1}^{(4)} & \\ * & & & \vdots & & & & & \ddots & \\ & \beta_{o-2}^{(4)} & & \vdots & & & & & & \beta_{o-3}^{(4)} \\ & & \beta_{o-1}^{(4)} & \vdots & & & & & & 0 \\ & & & \beta_o^{(4)} & \vdots & & & & & 0 \\ & & & & \beta_{o+1}^{(4)} & & & & & 0 \\ & & & & & \ddots & & & \\ & & & & & & \beta_v^{(4)} & & \\ \hline & * & & & & 0 & & & \end{pmatrix}$$

We omit F_5 and later. We denote the right-hand side of F_i as F_i' ($i = 1, \ldots, o$).

3.3   The Idea of Our Attack

Now we describe the idea of our proposed attack. First, our purpose is to find o linear independent vectors $\mathbf{t}_1, \ldots, \mathbf{t}_o \in \mathbb{F}_q^n$ such that

$$^t\mathbf{t}_i \cdot P_k \cdot \mathbf{t}_j = 0, \quad p_k(\mathbf{t}_i) = 0 \quad (1 \leqslant i, j, k \leqslant o). \tag{3}$$

It is well-known that if such vectors are recovered from the public key $\{p_1, \ldots, p_o\}$, then any signature can be forged easily.

Next, we utilize the special structure of $F_1, F_2, \ldots, F_o$ as described above. We set $T := {}^tS^{-1}$, denote by $\mathbf{t}_1, \ldots, \mathbf{t}_o$ the $v+1, \ldots, o$-th column vectors in T, and put $T' := (\mathbf{t}_1 \cdots \mathbf{t}_o)$. Since S is the secret key, we see that these vectors $\mathbf{t}_1, \ldots, \mathbf{t}_o$ satisfy the above condition (3). Moreover, since $P_i = S \cdot F_i \cdot {}^tS$, we have $P_i \cdot T = S \cdot F_i$. From this, we obtain the following relations:

$$P_1 \cdot T' = S \cdot F_1', \quad P_2 \cdot T' = S \cdot F_2', \quad P_3 \cdot T' = S \cdot F_3', \tag{4}$$
$$\cdots, \qquad P_o \cdot T' = S \cdot F_o'.$$

Furthermore, by setting $S = (\mathbf{s}_1 \cdots \mathbf{s}_n) \in \mathbb{F}_q^{n \times n}$, we have the following relations using the description in Subsect. 3.2.

$$P_1 \cdot \mathbf{t}_o = \beta_o^{(1)} \cdot \mathbf{s}_o, \quad P_2 \cdot \mathbf{t}_1 = \beta_o^{(2)} \cdot \mathbf{s}_o, \quad P_3 \cdot \mathbf{t}_2 = \beta_o^{(3)} \cdot \mathbf{s}_o, \tag{5}$$
$$\cdots, \qquad P_o \cdot \mathbf{t}_{o-1} = \beta_o^{(o)} \cdot \mathbf{s}_o.$$

Similarly, by (4), we have

$$\beta_o^{(3)} \cdot P_2 \cdot \mathbf{t}_1 = \beta_o^{(2)} \cdot P_3 \cdot \mathbf{t}_2,$$
$$\beta_{o-1}^{(4)} \cdot P_3 \cdot \mathbf{t}_1 = \beta_{o-1}^{(3)} \cdot P_4 \cdot \mathbf{t}_2,$$
$$\beta_{o-2}^{(5)} \cdot P_4 \cdot \mathbf{t}_1 = \beta_{o-2}^{(4)} \cdot P_5 \cdot \mathbf{t}_2, \tag{6}$$
$$\vdots$$
$$\beta_3^{(o)} \cdot P_{o-1} \cdot \mathbf{t}_1 = \beta_2^{(o-1)} \cdot P_o \cdot \mathbf{t}_2.$$

Remark 2. By (5), we see that the matrix $(P_1 \cdot \mathbf{t}_o \ P_2 \cdot \mathbf{t}_1 \cdots P_o \cdot \mathbf{t}_{o-1})$ with size $n \times o$ is of rank one, since each column vector is generated by $\mathbf{s}_o$.

We would like to find $\mathbf{t}_1, \ldots, \mathbf{t}_o$ by solving the Eqs. (5) and (6). Here, note that if we set $\mathbf{t}_i' := \beta_o^{(i+1),-1} \cdot \mathbf{t}_i$, then $\mathbf{t}_1', \ldots, \mathbf{t}_o'$ also satisfy (3). Thus, it is enough to find $\mathbf{t}_1', \ldots, \mathbf{t}_o'$ to break MQ-Sign-RS. Then, the above relations are rewritten as follows:

$$P_1 \cdot \mathbf{t}_o' = P_2 \cdot \mathbf{t}_1' = P_3 \cdot \mathbf{t}_2' = \cdots = P_o \cdot \mathbf{t}_{o-1}'. \tag{7}$$

Also,

$$P_2 \cdot \mathbf{t}_1' = P_3 \cdot \mathbf{t}_2',$$
$$P_3 \cdot \mathbf{t}_1' = \gamma^{(1)} \cdot P_4 \cdot \mathbf{t}_2',$$
$$P_4 \cdot \mathbf{t}_1' = \gamma^{(2)} \cdot P_5 \cdot \mathbf{t}_2', \tag{8}$$
$$\vdots$$
$$P_{o-1} \cdot \mathbf{t}_1' = \gamma^{(o-3)} \cdot P_o \cdot \mathbf{t}_2',$$

where $\gamma^{(i)} := \beta_{o-i}^{(i+2)} \cdot \beta_{o-i}^{(i+3),-1} \cdot \beta_o^{(3)} \cdot \beta_o^{(2),-1}$ $(i = 1, \ldots, o-3)$, which are unknown for an attacker.

We solve the above linear equations by guessing some $\gamma^{(i)}$ with brute force. By doing so, we can obtain the vectors $t_1', \ldots, t_o'$ that are forgeable with any signature. In the following subsections, we describe the algorithm to solve the above Eqs. (7) and (8).

3.4 How to Recover t_1' and t_2'

First step is to recover to t_1' and t_2'.

From (8), since $\begin{pmatrix} t_1' \\ t_2' \end{pmatrix}$ is a non-zero element of the right kernel of the following matrix

$$\begin{pmatrix} P_2 & -P_3 \\ P_3 & -\gamma^{(1)} \cdot P_4 \end{pmatrix} \in \mathbb{F}_q^{2n \times 2n},$$

the determinant of this matrix is zero. Since $\gamma^{(1)}$ is unknown, an attacker must collect candidates of $\gamma^{(1)}$. Therefore, we collect $\gamma_1 \in \mathbb{F}_q^\times$ such that the determinant of the matrix $\begin{pmatrix} P_2 & -P_3 \\ P_3 & -\gamma_1 \cdot P_4 \end{pmatrix}$ is zero, which gives us the set Γ_1 defined as

$$\Gamma_1 := \left\{ \gamma_1 \in \mathbb{F}_q^\times \,\middle|\, \det \begin{pmatrix} P_2 & -P_3 \\ P_3 & -\gamma_1 \cdot P_4 \end{pmatrix} = 0 \right\}.$$

Next, for such a $\gamma_1 \in \Gamma_1$, we find $\gamma_2 \in \mathbb{F}_q^\times$ such that the rank of the following matrix is less than $2n$:

$$\begin{pmatrix} P_2 & -P_3 \\ P_3 & -\gamma_1 \cdot P_4 \\ P_4 & -\gamma_2 \cdot P_5 \end{pmatrix} \in \mathbb{F}_q^{2n \times 3n}.$$

Similarly, we define

$$\Gamma_2 := \left\{ (\gamma_1, \gamma_2) \in \mathbb{F}_q^\times \times \mathbb{F}_q^\times \,\middle|\, \begin{array}{l} \det \begin{pmatrix} P_2 & -P_3 \\ P_3 & -\gamma_1 \cdot P_4 \end{pmatrix} = 0, \\[12pt] \mathrm{Rank} \begin{pmatrix} P_2 & -P_3 \\ P_3 & -\gamma_1 \cdot P_4 \\ P_4 & -\gamma_2 \cdot P_5 \end{pmatrix} < 2n \end{array} \right\}.$$

We construct Γ_i for $i \geqslant 3$ in a similar way. When the number of Γ_i is small for some i, we compute the right kernel of

$$\begin{pmatrix} P_2 & -P_3 \\ P_3 & -\gamma_1 \cdot P_4 \\ \vdots & \vdots \\ P_{i+2} & -\gamma_i \cdot P_{i+3} \end{pmatrix}$$

for all $(\gamma_1, \ldots, \gamma_i) \in \Gamma_i$ in order to recover (t_1', t_2'). It is worth noting that there exist some candidates of (t_1', t_2') in this step.

3.5   How to Recover the Other Vectors $t_3', \ldots, t_o'$

In this subsection, we utilize the possible values of t_1', t_2' obtained in Subsect. 3.4 to deduce the remaining vectors $t_3', \ldots, t_o'$. By (7) and (3), we have the following linear equations regarding t_3':

$$P_2 \cdot t_1' - P_4 \cdot t_3' = 0, \quad {}^t t_1' \cdot P_k \cdot t_3' = 0, \quad {}^t t_2' \cdot P_k \cdot t_3' = 0 \quad (k = 1, \ldots, o).$$

By solving this linear equations, we obtain t_3'.

Similarly, we have the following linear equations regarding t_ℓ' for $\ell = 4, \ldots, o$:

$$P_2 \cdot t_1' - P_{(\ell+1 \pmod o)} \cdot t_\ell' = 0, \quad {}^t t_j' \cdot P_k \cdot t_\ell' = 0 \quad (j = 1, \ldots, \ell-1, \ k = 1, \ldots, o)$$

Once we obtain $t_1', \ldots, t_o'$, we check if those satisfy the condition (3). If not, we re-select another pair of t_1' and t_2'.

4   Implementation Results and Complexity Analysis

4.1   Experiments

In this subsection, we report the implementation results of our attack described in Sect. 3. All experiments in this subsection were conducted on a system with Apple M1 (8 cores), 16 GB memory, macOS Ventura 13.3 ver. and using Magma V2.27-8 [4].

We conducted experiments to measure the timings of our attack for three parameters proposed in the original document [9]. For each parameter, we executed 5 experiments. Note that in our experiments we computed only $\Gamma_1, \Gamma_2, \Gamma_3$ and found the candidates of the pair (t_1', t_2'). All experiments were successful. In Table 1, we present the timings of our attack for each parameter.

4.2   Complexity

From Table 1, we assume that $\#\Gamma_1 \approx \#\Gamma_2 \approx \cdots \approx \#\Gamma_{o-3} \leqslant q$. To compute Γ_1, we need to perform $q \times (2n)^3$ operations. Similarly, to compute Γ_2, we need $\#\Gamma_1 \times q \times (2n)^3$ operations, and so on for $\Gamma_3, \ldots, \Gamma_{o-3}$. The total complexity to find t_1', t_2' is therefore $O(oq^2 n^3)$. To find $t_3', \ldots, t_o'$, we need to solve linear systems in n variables $o-3$ times, which results in a complexity of $O(on^3)$. Thus, the overall complexity of our attack is

$$O(oq^2 n^3).$$

The complexity of our attack for level 1 is $46 \times 2^{16} \times 118^3 = 2^{28.4}$. For level 3, the complexity is $72 \times 2^{16} \times 184^3 = 2^{29.7}$, and for level 5, the complexity is $96 \times 2^{16} \times 244^3 = 2^{30.5}$.

Table 1. Timings of proposed attack algorithm and the cardinality of Γ_i ($i = 1, 2,$ and 3) for the cases of security level 1, 3, and 5.

(q, v, o)	$\#\Gamma_1$	$\#\Gamma_2$	$\#\Gamma_3$	Cputime (s)
$(2^8, 72, 46)$	19	18	16	96
	21	18	16	99
	19	18	16	96
	19	18	16	95
	18	18	16	94
$(2^8, 112, 72)$	33	30	28	527
	30	30	28	514
	29	30	28	505
	31	30	28	517
	28	30	28	502
$(2^8, 148, 96)$	41	42	40	1613
	45	42	40	1644
	40	42	40	1602
	39	41	40	1077
	37	42	40	981

5   Conclusion

MQ-Sign is a UOV-based signature scheme proposed by Shim et al. and submitted to the KpqC competition. Recently, Aulbach et al. proposed a practical key recovery attack against MQ-Sign-{R/S}S for the case where the secret key $\mathcal{S}$ has a simple form. Their attack was proposed by utilizing two properties: (i) Oil × Vinegar quadratic parts in the central map are sparse, and (ii) the secret key $\mathcal{S}$ has the form of $\begin{pmatrix} 1_v & 0 \\ * & 1_o \end{pmatrix}$. In this paper, we proposed an attack against MQ-Sign-{R/S}S without property (ii). Due to our experiments, all the proposed parameters of MQ-Sign-RS can be broken in 30 min. Since our attack exploits only property (i), it can be applied to MQ-Sign-SS without modification. On the other hand, since MQ-Sign-{S/R}R do not have property (i), our methodology is not adaptable. As a result, it is considered that MQ-Sign-SR and MQ-Sign-RR are secure among the four types of MQ-Sign.

Acknowledgements. This research was in part conducted under a contract of "Research and development on new generation cryptography for secure wireless communication services" among "Research and Development for Expansion of Radio Wave Resources (JPJ000254)", which was supported by the Ministry of Internal Affairs and Communications, Japan. This work was also supported by JSPS KAKENHI Grant Number JP19K20266, JP22K17889 and JP20K03741, Japan.

References

1. Aulbach, T., Samardjiska, S., Trimoska, M.: Practical key-recovery attack on MQ-Sign. Cryptology ePrint Archive (2023). https://ia.cr/2023/432
2. Bernstein, D.-J., Buchmann, J., Dahmen, E. (eds.): Post-Quantum Cryptography. Springer, Heidelberg (2009). https://doi.org/10.1007/978-3-540-88702-7
3. Beullens, W.: Breaking rainbow takes a weekend on a laptop. In: Dodis, Y., Shrimpton, T. (eds.) CRYPTO 2022. LNCS, vol. 13508, pp. 464–479. Springer, Cham (2022). https://doi.org/10.1007/978-3-031-15979-4_16
4. Bosma, W., Cannon, J., Playoust, C.: The Magma algebra system. I. The user language. J. Symbolic Comput. **24**(3–4), 235–265 (1997)
5. Ding, J., Schmidt, D.: Rainbow, a new multivariable polynomial signature scheme. In: Ioannidis, J., Keromytis, A., Yung, M. (eds.) ACNS 2005. LNCS, vol. 3531, pp. 164–175. Springer, Heidelberg (2005). https://doi.org/10.1007/11496137_12
6. Kipnis, A., Patarin, J., Goubin, L.: Unbalanced oil and vinegar signature schemes. In: Stern, J. (ed.) EUROCRYPT 1999. LNCS, vol. 1592, pp. 206–222. Springer, Heidelberg (1999). https://doi.org/10.1007/3-540-48910-X_15
7. National Institute of Standards and Technology, Post-Quantum Cryptography Standardization. https://csrc.nist.gov/projects/post-quantum-cryptography
8. National Institute of Standards and Technology, Post-quantum cryptography, Round 3 Submission. https://csrc.nist.gov/Projects/post-quantum-cryptography/post-quantum-cryptography-standardization/round-3-submissions
9. Shim, K.-A., Kim, J., An, Y.: MQ-Sign: a new post-quantum signature scheme based on multivariate quadratic equations: shorter and faster (2022). https://www.kpqc.or.kr/images/pdf/MQ-Sign.pdf
10. Shor, P.-W.: Algorithms for quantum computation: discrete logarithms and factoring. In: Proceedings 35th Annual Symposium on Foundations of Computer Science, pp. 124–134. IEEE (1994)

Network and Application Security

Research on Security Threats Using VPN in Zero Trust Environments

Eunyoung Kim[1(✉)] and Kiwook Sohn[2]

[1] National Security Research Institute, Daejeon 34044, South Korea
eykim@nsr.re.kr
[2] Department of Computer Science and Engineering, Seoul National University
of Science and Technology, Seoul 01811, South Korea
kiwook@seoultech.ac.kr

Abstract. The United States issued an executive order requiring all federal agencies to adopt the Zero Trust security framework, and instructed each federal government department to devise a plan for its implementation. This development has generated a great deal of interest in the Zero Trust security framework in many countries. In Korea, the Ministry of Science and ICT and the Korea Internet & Security Agency (KISA) are actively promoting the establishment of guidelines for the implementation of Zero Trust in public institutions. Discussions on policies and models for the introduction of Zero Trust began with the launch of the Zero Trust security forum on October 26, 2022. Accordingly, this paper examines and conducts experiments on security threats that may arise within a Zero Trust environment in the Zero Trust Network Access (ZTNA) system. Despite the adoption of Zero Trust in many network environments, existing firewall or VPN devices are still in use. We discuss potential security threats that Zero Trust environments may encounter due to vulnerabilities in these existing network devices and propose countermeasures to mitigate such threats.

Keywords: Zero Trust Network Access · Security Threats ·
Vulnerability · VPN · Firmware

1 Introduction

The Biden administration in the United States issued an executive order aimed at enhancing the country's cyber security [1]. The order specifically called on federal agencies and cloud service providers to implement Zero Trust security policies and comply with the corresponding principles. The COVID-19 pandemic has prompted countries worldwide to quickly adopt Zero Trust models that are tailored to their specific environments [4]. The Zero Trust Security model was initially introduced by John Kindervag of Forrester Research in 2010 [3], and it has been developed and implemented by industry leaders such as Google's Beyond Corp and Microsoft's AZURE. The CSA (Cloud Security Alliance) is also promoting the use of Software Defined Perimeter (SDP) as the best technology for implementing the Zero Trust framework. In this paper, we will explore potential scenarios for security threats that may arise in the Zero Trust framework and examine their configuration and attack possibilities. Additionally, we will outline various security measures that can be employed to mitigate these threats.

2   Zero Trust 5 Pillars

2.1   Zero Trust Concept

Traditional security frameworks used network segmentation to physically isolate networks and provide security. However, the concept of Zero Trust which means "Zero-Trust trust no one, trust nothing" in a network-based security framework, gained widespread attention after the US federal government announced its transition to Zero Trust for cybersecurity and digital infrastructure protection in January 2022 [5–7]. The COVID-19 pandemic has also led to a surge in remote work environments, making Zero Trust-based remote work environments more critical and companies are taking swift steps to enhance their work environment accordingly. In practice, Zero Trust as defined in NIST SP800-207, evaluates the security level of the five pillars of assets (users, devices, network, application workload, and data) and establishes new security policies based on them. Zero Trust also provides a maturity model for each pillar and companies implement systems based on the Zero Trust maturity model that is appropriate to their current situation. Then the 5 Pillars of Zero Trust are described.

Identity: This refers to verifying the identity and access control for all users who attempt to access the company's IT assets.
Device: This includes all endpoint devices that attempt to access the company's network.
Network/Environment This refers to processing all data shared via the network separately from users (Identity) and devices (Device) based on encrypted communication.
Application Workload: This includes computing management that can be programmed, such as physical and virtual servers.
Data: This refers to continuously monitoring data access based on user authority, especially for critical data.

We can see that the fundamental principles require all communication to be secure, regardless of the network location where users connect. Furthermore, strict authentication procedures should be applied for internal network access to all resources, including all endpoint devices that users attempt to access. All organizations must also maintain the integrity and security status of their assets by monitoring the internal resource status to keep them safe and secure. The five Pillars of Zero Trust provide a solid foundation for companies and organizations to improve their security posture. However, as Zero Trust is a relatively new concept, there is no one-size-fits-all approach and organizations may choose to further subdivide the Pillars to better suit their needs. For example, some organizations may include "data protection" or "application security" as additional Pillars. Despite these variations, the fundamental principles of Zero Trust remain the same and companies should focus on ensuring that all communication is secure. The internal resources are monitored and kept in a secure state and strict authentication procedures are applied to

2.2   Approaches to Applying Zero Trust to the US DoD

The US Department of Defense (DoD) has recognized the need to adopt Zero Trust quickly in response to constant external environmental changes [2]. This includes establishing a new system configuration and budget execution that can be composed of 3139 with the Zero Trust architecture, adopting and integrating Zero Trust functionality, technology, solutions, and processes. The personnel, education, and expertise development process are also important aspects to address Zero Trust requirements [9]. The four strategic objectives for implementing Zero Trust in the DoD are: adoption of a Zero Trust culture, protection and defense of DoD information systems, technology acceleration, and implementation of Zero Trust. The article also suggests referencing other resources such as NSA's Issues Guidance on Zero Trust Security Model, CISA's Zero Trust Maturity Model, and OMB's Federal Zero Trust Strategy in addition to the NIST 800-207 and DoD Zero Trust Strategy. Overall, it is clear that the DoD is taking Zero Trust seriously and is making efforts to implement it as quickly and effectively as possible. This will be crucial for protecting sensitive information and systems from cyber threats in an ever-changing environment. It is encouraging to see countries like New Zealand, Singapore, and the UK taking steps to adopt Zero Trust security measures to protect their critical information infrastructures from cyber-attacks. The COVID-19 pandemic has accelerated the trend towards remote work, which has increased the risk of cyber-attacks, making it essential to implement ZTA. In Singapore, the government's focus on quick incident response through the GCSOC (Government Cyber Security Operations Centre) is commendable. The government's adoption of Zero Trust security for critical systems and the implementation of GTBA (Government Trust-Based Architecture) will undoubtedly strengthen application and system security [8]. The UK's National Cyber Security Centre has released Zero Trust design principles, which emphasize the importance of identity and authentication for users and devices and monitoring of device and service status. However, it is concerning to see that the adoption of Zero Trust security measures outside the UK is lagging behind. The adoption of Zero Trust security measures by various governments and organizations is a positive development. It is critical to continue to educate and train personnel to understand the importance of Zero Trust security measures and incorporate them into their security strategies [14].

It's interesting to see how different countries are approaching the adoption and implementation of Zero Trust security. New Zealand and Singapore are taking proactive steps to deploy Zero Trust in response to the changing cybersecurity landscape, others, like Japan, seem to be lagging behind. It's important to note that the adoption and implementation of Zero Trust security is a complex process that requires significant investment of resources, including time, money, and expertise. Therefore, it's understandable that some countries may be hesitant to embrace it fully. However, given the increasing sophistication of cyber-attacks and the high cost of data breaches, it's becoming increasingly clear that Zero Trust security is a critical component of any comprehensive cybersecurity strategy.

2.3   Analysis of Published Zero Trust Security Frameworks

In this section, we will describe the Zero Trust model proposed by Google, Microsoft, and Netflix, which is operated through the Zero Trust framework system. Figure 1 provides a comparison of the Zero Trust models of Google, Microsoft and Netflix. Google's Zero Trust model focuses on protecting data by implementing strict access control measures and continuously monitoring user activity. Google's model also emphasizes the use of strong authentication methods such as multi-factor authentication to ensure that only authorized users can access sensitive data. Microsoft's Zero Trust model, on the other hand, emphasizes the importance of verifying device health and implementing identity and access management controls [10]. Microsoft's model also incorporates the use of conditional access policies to restrict access based on user context, such as location and device. Both Google and Microsoft's Zero Trust models are designed to provide enhanced security and protect against data breaches. However, each model has its unique approach and focus. Figure 1 provides a visual representation of the differences between the three models. It shows that while Google's model emphasizes user authentication and access control, Microsoft's model places more emphasis on device health and identity management.

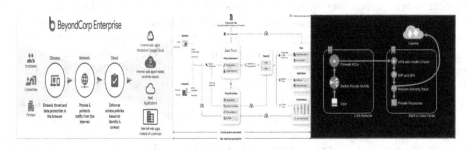

Fig. 1. Google Beyond Corp vs. MS Azure vs. Netflix LISA Zero Trust Model Comparison

First, We will explain Google's Zero Trust model. Google's Zero Trust model is an approach to enhancing security that assumes untrusted access for all users, devices, and network traffic. Since this model does not trust the internal network, each user and device must be individually authenticated and granted permission based on their ID authentication for network requests and data access. These security rules are based on predefined security policies and access control is enforced accordingly, with users and devices requiring authentication every time they connect.

Second, Microsoft's Zero Trust model in Azure includes Identity and Access Management (IAM) technology based on Azure Active Directory (AAD) [11]. The Zero Trust model in Azure verifies access to all users, devices, and applications to enhance data protection for users and businesses. The Azure Zero Trust model is structured around three main principles. First authentication requests for all devices, users, and applications. Second only necessary permissions are granted to each user and device based on the principle of least privilege. Thrid all access is verified based on the real-time status of users and devices.

Finally, let's describe Netflix's Zero Trust model [12]. The LISA (Least-privilege, Identity, Security, and Automation) Zero Trust model in Netflix is centered around Identity and Access Management (IAM), which plays a significant role in authenticating and verifying users and devices. The LISA model was proposed taking into account various security aspects and was designed based on four basic principles: Least-privilege, Identity, Security, and Automation. Table 1 shows the four basic principles of LISA Model.

Table 1. LISA model's four basic principles

Principle	Description
Least-privilege	The model minimizes access permissions for users and devices to prevent unnecessary access permission grants
Identity	The LISA model is centered around Identity and Access Management (IAM) systems that authenticate and verify users and devices, verifying users' IDs and passwords and performing device security verification. IAM systems also provide additional security verification using various authentication factors
Security	This model uses Transport Layer Security (TLS) to encrypt data communication to enhance security and applies additional security technologies to enhance application and device security
Automation	The LISA model enhances security through automated processes, and uses Continuous Integration/Continuous Deployment (CI/CD) pipelines to automate application deployment and updates, protecting internal resources from security threats

In addition, the LISA model is first and foremost used on a cloud-based infrastructure by Netflix. Through the LISA model, Netflix is able to protect its data, ensure the security of customer information, and enhance security in cloud-based services by verifying users and devices. One of the key differences between the LISA model and other Zero Trust models is that it has the advantage of being able to leverage existing firewall or VPN equipment to implement the Zero Trust framework.

3   Security Threats to ZTNA

In this chapter, we will discuss potential security threats that may arise when implementing a Zero Trust framework, and describe the experimental results based on these assumptions. One of the main advantages of the Zero Trust framework is its ability to protect against various types of cyber threats, including phishing attacks, malware infections, and data breaches. However, despite the implementation of a Zero Trust framework, security threats may still occur. To confirm this, we conducted simulations using a vulnerability-based attack scenario, and describe the actual results based on these assumptions.

3.1   Zero Trust Security Threat Scenarios

Most of the proposed models for Zero Trust have primarily focused on access control for end devices and access data by strengthening user authentication when accessing the Zero Trust framework. This access control method is in a situation where there is no prior knowledge of whether the user is a legitimate or illegitimate user, and which device the user will use to access. Therefore, network equipment (such as VPN and firewall, which are traditional security concepts) located at the forefront of the Zero Trust framework must allow all network access requests made to that domain or IP address. Based on all the user information that has been accessed, access control for the user's access status and the requested data is carried out based on the internal policies of the Zero Trust model.

After access request through user authentication, Zero Trust's network is approached through the concept of "Divide and Rule" to prepare for unexpected hacking attacks, identifying important assets. The network is divided into "micro-segments," and this is used to easily exclude and isolate the network in case of a security incident. In order to apply the concept of security domains, Google's Beyond Corp applies policies based on device information, current status, and related user information, rather than applying service and data access policies based on employee's actual location or connected network. This approach eliminates traditional VPN concepts and creates a secure work environment on any network. On the other hand, Netflix's LISA (Location Independent Security Access) places strong authentication and device security as a top priority and differs from Google's Zero Trust concept, which excludes VPNs and firewalls. However, this structure has attracted a lot of attention as a way for many companies to implement Zero Trust without incurring significant costs. In the case of the aforementioned LISA, it is also an advantage to have the time of existing or VPN equipment, but all security threats that existed prior to the introduction of exceptional trust are looking at the last point that must be observed. That is, firewall and VPN network equipment can obtain undisclosed or publicly disclosed vulnerabilities through firmware analysis [13,15,18–21], and it has been confirmed that remote information collection of such equipment can be performed through login with administrator privileges. Figure 2 shows a security threat scenario in a Zero Trust environment utilizing VPN.

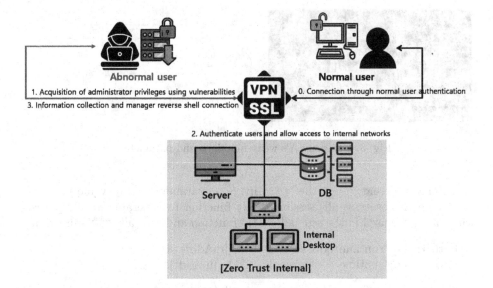

Fig. 2. Security Threat Scenario in Zero Trust Environment Using VPN

In this paper, we aim to verify the possibility of various malicious information gathering and intrusion through public or private vulnerabilities of existing network devices such as firewalls and VPNs when implementing Zero Trust using existing network equipment, similar to the LISA model [14,17].

3.2   Security Vulnerabilities for Zero Trust-Based VPN Equipment

We conducted vulnerability research on the A company VPN equipment, which is widely used in many public institutions and organizations. As a result, we identified an undisclosed remote code execution vulnerability that allows remote system commands to be executed without logging in to the A company VPN equipment. Although the string '/' cannot be used among the requestable strings, we circumvented this constraint and conducted an exploit to allow free use of system commands. As a result, we judged that this vulnerability could be universally used regardless of library versions or compilation environments if the same code were created [16].

The A company VPN equipment has a vulnerability that allows system commands to be inserted and executed in the session_***.csp path in the web service. However, the file in this path does not exist in the actual equipment's file system. Therefore, the functionality processed when requesting the session_***.csp is implemented in the mod_***.so file, as shown in Fig. 3. When the user enters '2' as the type parameter, the process_all_session_***() function is called during the processing of the page.

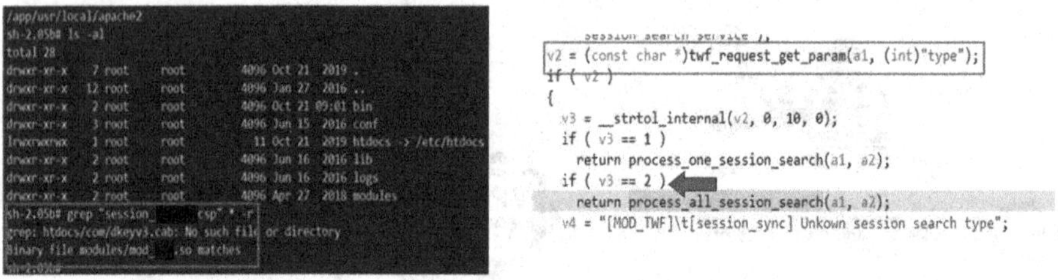

Fig. 3. Company A's weak functions and parameters

After that, the ip parameter value is utilized in the process_all_session_***() function to generate two file paths, which are later used in the scp_all_***() function and scp_all_***() function.

Path 1: /etc/runtime/qdb/session_***_[ipAddr].db
Path 2: /etc/runtime/cookie/cookie_***_[ipAddr].tar.gz

However, the first path (/etc/runtime/qdb/session_***_[ipAddr].db) is used in the qdbm_***() function call when it returns "TRUE".

The qdbm_open() function creates a file with the specified path entered by the user and then reopens the created file for use. However, if the input path contains the '/' character, an error occurs during file creation, and the scp_all_***() and scp_all_***() functions, which have a system command execution vulnerability, are not called. The scp_all_***() function requests the cluster daemon (the daemon on the corresponding device) to execute the command created using the ip parameter. The snprintf() function generates the command using the ip parameter. Therefore, if the ip parameter is entered in the format ';command;', a separate system command can be inserted. Similarly, the scp_all_***() function requests the cluster daemon to execute the command created using the input parameters. The snprintf() function generates a command using the ip parameter. Therefore, if the ip parameter is entered in the format ';command;', a separate system command can be inserted.

To summarize, if a system command is entered in the format "type=2&ip=;cmd;" in the session_***.csp path, scp_all_***() function is executed 2 times and scp_all_***() function is executed 4 times. However, the path delimiter character ('/') must not be present. The exploit process for this vulnerability involves implementing the send_***() function. This function sends the IP address, port number, and system command to the target device, allowing the system command to be executed on the target device. However, the '/' character cannot be used.

The vulnerability allows system commands to be executed but the path separator character ('/') cannot be used. To bypass this limitation, the bind_***() function was developed as shown in Fig. 4. The bind_***() function was developed to bypass the constraint that the path separator character ('/') cannot be used in system commands. The function performs the following steps:

1. Outputs the hexadecimal value of the path separator character (0x2f) using the echo command to create a script file (filename: a).
2. Sends the 'chmod 777 a' command to grant execute permission (no path separator).
3. Sends the 'sh a' command to execute the script file.

```
def bind_send_cmd( ipAddr, port, cmd ):

#Replace the '/' character in the input command with the hexadecimal value ₩x2f
cmd = cmd.replace('/', '₩₩x2f')

# Create a script file by outputting the '/' character from the command entered with the echo command
payload = 'echo -e "' + cmd + '₩₩nrm -rf ₩₩x2fetc₩₩x2fruntime ₩₩x2fqdb₩₩x2f session_sync*₩₩nrm -rf a" >
a'

# 1) Create a script file with the echo command
result = send_cmd( ipAddr, port, payload )
print result

# 2) Grant execution permission to the created script file
cmd = 'chmod 777 a'
result = send_cmd( ipAddr, port, cmd )
print result

# 3) Execute the created script file
cmd = 'sh a'
result = send_cmd( ipAddr, port, cmd )
print result
```

Fig. 4. Implementation of the bind_***() function

When the generated script is executed, the incorrectly created file and the script file a are removed by the user-inputted command. Finally, when the IP address, port number, and system command are sent to the bind_*** function, the system command is executed on the target device.

The discovered vulnerability allows an attacker to obtain a reverse shell by executing a command that connects to it. As shown in Fig. 5, the vulnerability requires three requests to be made to execute a system command. Upon the first request, a shell script file is created, and on the second request, a temporary file is created in the /etc/runtime/qdb/ path. Finally, on the third request, the shell script is executed, and the temporary file is removed, along with the script file. In addition, since the vulnerability is currently unpatched in the corresponding firmware version, detailed firmware version information is not disclosed.

Fig. 5. Step-by-step screen for vulnerability execution

3.3   Security Vulnerability Countermeasure Techniques

We have verified and experimented with the possibility of remote access based on undisclosed vulnerabilities using VPN devices that can operate in a Zero Trust environment. Then, we describe how to respond to attacks using device-based vulnerabilities.

Patch Management: We must quickly apply security patches provided by each network system manufacturer to maintain the latest security status. Additionally, we should monitor vulnerabilities in our operating systems and apply patches quickly when vulnerabilities are discovered.

Access Control: Access control policies should be applied to differentiate access rights between regular users and users with administrator privileges, and to grant appropriate access rights as needed. In a Zero Trust environment, there is often no administrator account with full access rights to the system, as there is no root account with such privileges. Therefore, access to system resources should be limited to a minimum and appropriate permissions should only be granted when necessary.

Monitoring and Log Analysis: Real-time monitoring and log analysis of the system should be carried out to detect any abnormal access attempts or behavior and to take immediate response measures.

Security Awareness Training: Security awareness training should be provided to all users to enhance their awareness of security threats and their ability to respond to them.

Integrity Verification: In a Zero Trust environment, the integrity of the system should be verified using technologies such as security certificates. Verification must be performed to ensure that the system has not been changed or tampered with.

Backup and Recovery Plan: Backup and recovery plans should be established to prepare for system failures or data loss, and these plans should be reviewed and updated regularly.

Establishing and implementing these security measures is an important factor in enhancing the security of the system in a Zero Trust environment. However, it is difficult to establish security measures targeting undisclosed vulnerabilities in reality. Therefore, if we discover such vulnerabilities in the system, we should apply the above security measures as a baseline, and enhance real-time monitoring of abnormal user behavior for the possibility of remote access and manipulation of system resources using undisclosed vulnerabilities. In other words, access to the system with administrator privileges should not be supported remotely as much as possible. Although ordinary users may not have a significant impact on the system as a whole even if they are subjected to hacking attacks from external sources in a Zero Trust environment, vulnerability attacks on users with administrator privileges can cause many problems throughout the system. Therefore, in a Zero Trust environment, access control policies should be defined for ordinary users based on the resources of the access area and the data they want to access, and access control for the access area must be carried out before granting administrator privileges.

4   Conclusion

In this paper, we conducted experiments and configurations to study the security threats that may arise through vulnerability research on existing network equipment that can be applied under a Zero Trust environment. Through firmware analysis of the equipment, we secured a vulnerability that could penetrate the system with admin privileges and confirmed remote system infiltration and access through reverse shells. Therefore, when introducing the new Zero Trust framework proposed in this paper, rather than simply strengthening user authentication with a more robust policy based on the security threats presented in the paper, real-time monitoring of abnormal user behavior and security measures should be reviewed for all network equipment.

References

1. Rose, S.: NIST Special Publication 800-207, Zero Trust Architecture (2020)
2. Department of Defense (DoD): Zero Trust Reference Architecture (2022)
3. Kindervag, J.: Build security into your network's DNA: the zero trust network architecture, pp. 1–26. Forrester Research Inc. (2010)
4. Sudakshina, M., Khan, D.A., Jain, S.: Cloud-based zero trust access control policy: an approach to support work-from-home driven by COVID-19 pandemic. New Gener. Comput. **39**, 599–622 (2021). https://doi.org/10.1007/s00354-021-00130-6
5. Kerman, A., Borchert, O., Rose, S., Tan, A.: Implementing a zero trust architecture. Technical report, The MITRE Corporation (2020)
6. Anil, G.: A zero trust security framework for granular insight on blind spot and comprehensive device protection in the enterprise of Internet of Things (E-IOT). BMS Institute of Technology (2021)
7. Uttecht, K.D.: Zero Trust (ZT) concepts for federal government architectures. Massachusetts Institute of Technology, Lexington, United States (2020)
8. CSA Singapore: The Singapore Cybersecurity Strategy 2021 (2021). https://www.csa.gov.sg/Tips-Resource/publications/2021/singapore-cybersecurity-strategy-2021
9. CISA USA: Zero Trust Maturity Mode, Pre-decisional Draft (2021). https://www.cisa.gov/sites/default/files/publications/CISA%20Zero%20Trust%20Maturity%20Model_Draft.pdf
10. Ward, R., Beyer, B.: BeyondCorp: a new approach to enterprise security (2014)
11. Hwang, M.J.: Microsoft zero trust network strategy and implementation plan. Microsoft Cyber Security Solutions Group (2020)
12. Zimmer, B.: Location independent security approach (LISA). USENIX Security (2018)
13. Wright, C., Cowan, C., Morris, J., Smalley, S., Kroah-Hartman, G.: Linux security module framework. In: Ottawa Linux Symposium, vol. 8032, pp. 6–16 (2002)
14. Kim, S.Y., Jeong, K.H., Hwang, Y.N., Nyang, D.H.: Abnormal behavior detection for zero trust security model using deep learning. In: Korea Information Processing Society Collection of Academic Papers, vol. 28, no. 1, pp. 132–135 (2021)
15. Sun, P., et al.: Hybrid firmware analysis for known mobile and IoT security vulnerabilities. In: 2020 50th Annual IEEE/IFIP International Conference on Dependable Systems and Networks (DSN). IEEE (2020)
16. Rastogi, A., Nygard, K.E.: Software engineering principles and security vulnerabilities. In: CATA, pp. 180–190 (2019)
17. Corteggiani, N., Camurati, G., Francillon, A.: Inception: system-wide security testing of real-world embedded systems software. In: Proceedings of the USENIX Security Symposium (2018)
18. Chen, D.D., Egele, M., Woo, M., Brumley, D.: Towards automated dynamic analysis for Linux-based embedded firmware. In: Proceedings of the Network and Distributed System Security Symposium (NDSS) (2016)
19. Costin, A., Zarras, A., Francillon, A.: Automated dynamic firmware analysis at scale: a case study on embedded web interfaces. In: Proceedings of the ACM on Asia Conference on Computer and Communications Security (ASIACCS) (2016)
20. Davidson, D., Moench, B., Ristenpart, T., Jha, S.: FIE on firmware: finding vulnerabilities in embedded systems using symbolic execution. In: Proceedings of the USENIX Security Symposium (2013)
21. Abeni, L., Kiraly, C.: Investigating the network performance of a real-time Linux Kernel. In: Proceedings of the 15th Real Time Linux Workshop (2013)

A Blockchain-Based Mobile Crowdsensing and Its Incentive Mechanism

Yan Zhang[1], Yuhao Bai[1], Soojin Lee[1], Ming Li[2],
and Seung-Hyun Seo[3]([✉])

[1] The Department of Electronic and Electrical Engineering, Hanyang University,
Seoul 04763, Korea
{z2021189899,byh2018,tssn195}@hanyang.ac.kr
[2] The Department of computer and information Engineering,
Henan Normal University, Xinxiang 453007, Henan, China
liming@htu.edu.cn
[3] School of Electrical Engineering, Hanyang University (ERICA),
Ansan 15588, Korea
seosh77@hanyang.ac.kr

Abstract. Mobile crowdsensing (MCS) has become a crucial paradigm
for the efficient implementation of large-scale sensing tasks in smart
cities. However, untrustworthy mobile users often contribute lower-
quality data and attempt to manipulate reward distributions unfairly.
These problems will indirectly make mobile users more passively participate in the sensing task. To address these challenges, we propose a
novel MCS system model that combines the public blockchain and the
consortium blockchain. To provide an effective data quality evaluation,
we introduce an advanced Sybil-resistant account grouping method and
employ an enhanced grouping truth discovery algorithm to evaluate data
quality accurately. Additionally, we suggest an adjustable fair reward distribution mechanism based on the Shapley value to promote equitable
reward distribution. The proposed model provides a more dependable
and effective means of achieving high-quality services for society.

Keywords: MCS · Blockchain · Quality evaluation · Shapley value ·
Incentive mechanism

1 Introduction

The advancement of Internet of Things (IoT) communication technology and the
widespread use of mobile smart devices have led to innovative approaches in data

This work was supported by the MSIT (Ministry of Science and ICT), Korea, under
the ITRC (Information Technology Research Center) support program (IITP-2023-
2018-0-01417) supervised by the IITP (Institute for Information & Communications
Technology Planning & Evaluation)
This work was supported by Science and Technology Research Project of Henan
Province (Grant No. 212102210413).

collection. In the context of large-scale sensing tasks in smart cities, traditional sensor-based data collection methods pose challenges in terms of cost and system maintenance [1]. Mobile crowdsensing (MCS) emerges as a solution to address these challenges by leveraging collaborative sensing using mobile smart devices. In most existing MCS networks, a centralized platform serves as a trusted third party, with mobile users playing crucial roles as data requesters and collectors [2]. Data collectors collect data using mobile smart devices to provide high-level servers under low infrastructure conditions [3]. However, the reliance on centralized platforms in MCS networks introduces vulnerabilities such as denial of service attacks and data leakage [4]. Furthermore, issues of mutual distrust can arise between the platform, task publishers, and data collectors in centralized MCS networks. Collusion between the platform and task publishers can result in unauthorized modifications to task and reward information. Likewise, collusion among data collectors can lead to data duplication and free-riding, where rewards are obtained through the submission of similar data. Consequently, security, trust, and user privacy in centralized MCS networks warrant significant attention from researchers.

Blockchain technology, with its decentralized, tamper-proof, and pseudonymous characteristics, holds promise for the development of secure and reliable MCS networks. The current MCS system based on a public blockchain faces challenges of performance and privacy, which can be mitigated by integrating a consortium blockchain to efficiently handle computationally intensive tasks while ensuring transaction efficiency and relative privacy. To meet the societal demand for high-quality services, the MCS platform must attract a sufficient number of mobile users to participate in sensing tasks. Therefore, a quality-driven incentive mechanism, leveraging accurate data quality assessment to ensure fair reward, is crucial to motivate more mobile users to engage in sensing tasks.

This paper presents a hybrid blockchain based MCS system model, aiming to enhance the security and reliability of the mobile users' MCS platform. We propose a quality-driven incentive mechanism that combines an effective quality evaluation method with a fair reward distribution mechanism. This approach ensures that the incentive mechanism is aligned with the assessment of data quality, promoting fairness and encouraging active participation of mobile users.

2   Literature Review

Zou et al. [5] proposed a decentralized hybrid blockchain framework and a location privacy-preserving optimization mechanism (LPPOM) to achieve a trade-off between user privacy and system efficiency. Zhu et al. [6] utilized delegated proof of stake(DPOS) and practical Byzantine fault tolerance(PBFT) consensus protocols in the decentralized crowdsourcing platform, which can significantly improve the transaction verification efficiency and reduce the transaction latency and energy consumption of the crowdsourcing system. Tong et al. [7] designed a hybrid blockchain framework and a reputation-based practical Byzantine fault tolerance (R-PBFT) consensus protocol to improve transaction throughput and fault tolerance of the crowdsourcing platform. Most of the above research work discusses the application of combined public and private chains to solve privacy protection and system performance in crowdsourcing. [5–7] utilized hybrid blockchain to prevent data from being exposed in the public blockchain to provide user privacy. However, malicious workers may attempt to perform the same task multiple times and deceitfully receive multiple rewards. Therefore, we apply a grouping truth discovery algorithm for data quality evaluation, which helps reduce rewards for similar data submissions.

In the blockchain-based MCS system proposed by Huang et al. [8], temporal stability and spatial correlation of data are used for outlier data detection. In addition, truth discovery methods and machine learning methods such as clustering are also often used in data aggregation and outlier detection [9]. Among them, truth discovery algorithms are potential data integration solutions that can more accurately identify real information from noisy data. Wang et al. [10] accurately estimate the truth using a group truth discovery algorithm. But the accuracy of the group truth discovery algorithm is greatly affected by the interference of malicious data. Quality detection and evaluation through the data quality calculation method used in the above literature is the basis of many quality-driven incentive mechanisms.

Most existing Quality-driven incentive mechanisms are all aimed at the benefit of the platform and social welfare, ignoring the interests of mobile users as the main influencing factor of high-quality data collection and multi-user participation in the MCS platform [11–13]. Especially for a decentralized MCS platform, we should focus on the interests of mobile users and solve the problem of reward distribution for mobile workers. Table 1 compares the main related works of blockchain-based mobile crowdsensing model.

Table 1. Comparison of related works for mobile crowdsensing based on blockchain

ref.	Main problem perspective	Blockchain	Consensus mechanism	Data quality evaluation	Privacy protection
[5]	System security, performance and privacy	Hybrid	POW	.	O
[6]	blockchain performance, privacy	Hybrid	DPOS, PBFT	.	O
[7]	limited transaction throughtput, task privacy, low fault-tolerance of pbft	Hybrid	R-PBFT	.	O
[8]	centralized platform security, data anomaly	Public	POW	temporal stability, spatial correlation	X
[9]	centralized platform security, verifier's computational overhead, data quality assessment	Public	Credit-based verifier selection	clustering, fuzzy mathematics	X
[10]	centralized platform security, blockchain performance, inaccurately estimated truth	Public	.	truth discovery	X
Ours	system security, performance and data privacy, data quality evaluation, unfair reward distribution	Hybrid	POW, PBFT	truth discovery	O

3   System Model

In this section, we proposed a hybrid blockchain-based mobile crowdsensing model including a data quality evaluation and a fair reward distribution. The proposed model is composed of public blockchain and consortium blockchain in consideration of effective public data collection and privacy of collected data. The MCS system based on public blockchain offers a means to effectively engage a large user base and establish a secure environment for information exchange. There is a consortium blockchain for each type of task and interest, and related policy makers, institutions, and companies participate as blockchain nodes. Leveraging the transaction efficiency, relative privacy, and security advantages offered by the consortium chain, computationally intensive tasks within the sensing process can be efficiently accomplished. Figure 1 depicts the blockchain-based MCS (BCMCS) model, while a detailed description of the entities involved is provided below.

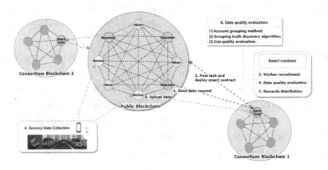

Fig. 1. The blockchain-based MCS (BCMCS) model.

(1) Mobile users: Mobile users participate as both data requesters and mobile workers. Data requesters formulate task requirements and establish data quality evaluation rules, subsequently transmitting data request information to the agent nodes of the relevant consortium chain. Mobile workers employ mobile devices to conduct data sensing and upload data at designated locations, earning corresponding rewards upon task completion.

(2) Public chain miners: These transaction verifiers record and permanently store transactions within the chain. Their primary responsibility is to maintain the secure interaction and data consistency of the public chain through the consensus protocol.

(3) Consortium chain members: In accordance with smart city application scenarios, multiple consortium chains can be created, jointly participated in, and managed by various associated institutions. Consortium chain members consist of relevant stakeholders, with nodes possessing higher reputation values included in the transaction verification set. The most reputable nodes

are designated as agent nodes. The consortium chain assumes responsibilities such as releasing sensing tasks, recruiting mobile workers, evaluating data quality, and distributing rewards. Agent nodes deploy task-related smart contracts within the consortium chain and collaborate with data requesters to publish sensing task information and final task reward assignment results to the public chain. They are responsible to act as a gate way node to transfer information between public network and consortium network.

4 Proposed Approach

We present a Blockchain-based Mobile Crowdsensing (BCMCS) model comprising a blockchain platform and a group of mobile users, denoted as $U = \{1, 2, \ldots, n\}$. In this model, data requesters initiate data request messages that are transmitted to the agent node. After successful verification of the data request information by the transaction verification set of the consortium chain within a specified time threshold, the agent node of the consortium chain publishes the set of sensing tasks $T = \{T_1, T_2, \ldots, T_m\}$ to the public chain. Mobile workers participate in sensing tasks by submitting a deposit to the worker recruitment contract within the consortium chain. Upon completion of several sensing tasks by worker i, the corresponding sensing data is packaged into a set $D_i = \{(d_j^i, t_j^i)|\tau_j \in T_i\}$ and submitted to the relevant contract for data quality evaluation. Once all sensing data from the workers is collected, the smart contract initiates automatic execution and proceeds to calculate the account grouping results for each user. Subsequently, for each task $\tau_j \in T_i$, the platform obtains an aggregated result d_j using the grouping truth discovery algorithm. This aggregated result represents the estimated truth for the given task, and the user's weight and collected data quality are evaluated based on it. Upon completion of the data quality evaluation, the reward distribution contract is triggered, and the distribution of rewards takes place using the task's budget deposit and the results of the quality evaluation. The following sections provide detailed descriptions of the truth-discovery-based data quality assessment and reward distribution mechanisms.

4.1 Account Grouping Method

Within the mobile crowdsensing (MCS) network, a prevalent issue arises wherein users create multiple identities. This behavior is exploited by malicious users who leverage multiple identities to engage in sensing tasks, either by uploading similar data to obtain excessive rewards or by submitting multiple false data to manipulate the final data aggregation outcomes. To combat such Sybil attacks, inspired by Wang's work [10,15], we utilize a Jensen-Shannon divergence-based (D-JS) approach to detect accounts exhibiting similar task trajectories, aiming to identify accounts with high similarity and group them together, assigning a lower weight to their uploaded data to mitigate the influence of malicious data on the accuracy of ground truth discovery.

The calculation equation of the degree of difference based on Jensen-Shannon (JS) divergence is as follows:

$$JS(i||j) = (\sum_{d^i \in D_i, d^j \in D_j} d^i \times log\frac{2d^i}{d^i + d^j} + \sum_{d^i \in D_i, d^j \in D_j} d^j \times log\frac{2d^j}{d^i + d^j}) \times \frac{1}{2(\sum_{d^i \in D_i} d^i + \sum_{d^j \in D_j} d^j)} \quad (1)$$

Among them, d^i and d^j are data in data sets D_i and D_j uploaded by two accounts i and j, respectively. JS divergence is improved based on $Kullback - Leibler(KL)$ divergence, and its symmetry is more suitable for calculating the difference degree of task sets.

4.2   Grouping Truth Discovery Algorithm

To extract truth information from noisy data provided by untrustworthy users, We use the account grouping method based on JS divergence to group accounts, and $G = \{g_1, g_2, ..., g_k, ...\}$ is the grouping result. We then proposed an improved group truth discovery algorithm (I-GTDA) that can estimate the truth accurately even in the presence of a Sybil attack. The Table 2. explains the symbolic meanings of the group discovery algorithm.

Table 2. Symbolic explanation in grouped truth discovery algorithms.

Symbol	Explanation
n, m	Number of users, number of tasks
$D_i = \{(d_j^i, t_j^i) \vert \tau_j \in T_j\}$	Dataset collected by account i
$D = \{D_i \vert i \in U\}$	Dataset collected by mobile users
τ_j	jth task
d_j^i	The data collected by account i for task τ_j
G, g_k	The result of account grouping, the kth group
d_j^k, w_j^i	The data mean of group g_k corresponds to task τ_j, and the weight of account i in group g_k
$\hat{d}_j^k, \hat{w}_k$	The data aggregation result of group g_k corresponds to task τ_j, the weight of group g_k
d_j^*, w_i	The true value of the data corresponds to task τ_j, the weight of account i
e_j^*	the last round's estimated truth for task τ_j
t_j^i	A timestamp of a mobile worker i's sensing data for task τ_j
σ, p	a small constant real number, an arbitrary positive real number

The data of each task τ_j is aggregated by the group. The smart contract calculates the weight of each account in each group g_k using Eq. (2).

$$w_j^i = \frac{(|d_j^i - \bar{d}_j^k| + \sigma)^{-p}}{\sum_{i \in g_k}(|d_j^i - \bar{d}_j^k| + \sigma)^{-p}} \quad (2)$$

The $\hat{d}_j^k$ is the mean value of data uploaded by accounts in group g_k for task τ_j. d_j^i is the data collected by account i for task τ_j. The data aggregation calculation equation of the kth group g_k corresponding to the task τ_j is as follows:

$$\hat{d}_j^k = \frac{\sum_{i \in g_k} w_j^i d_j^i}{\sum_{i \in g_k} w_j^i} \quad (3)$$

The group weight of the kth group g_k corresponding to the task τ_j is calculated as follows:

$$\hat{w}_k = 1 - \frac{|g_k|}{|U_j|} \tag{4}$$

The $|g_k|$ indicates the number of accounts in the group g_k, and the $|U_j|$ indicates the number of accounts participating in the task τ_j.

Compared with the random initialization of the truth ground of each task in the traditional truth discovery algorithm, Eq. (5) is used to initialize the truth ground of each task in the group truth discovery algorithm.

$$d_j^* = \frac{\sum_{g_k \in G} \hat{w}_k \hat{d}_j^k}{\sum_{g_k \in G} \hat{w}_k} \tag{5}$$

Then we will evaluate the weight of each account participating in task τ_j using Eq. (6). Using the idea of the inverse distance weighting method, the weight of the account decreases as the gap between the uploaded data and the truth ground increases.

$$w_i = \frac{(|d_j^i - e_j^*| + \sigma)^{-p}}{\sum_{i \in U_j} (|d_j^i - e_j^*| + \sigma)^{-p}} \tag{6}$$

The e_j^* denotes the last round's estimated truth for task τ_j. The calculation of the ground truth value of the task τ_j is jointly determined by the data uploaded by the account and the account weight of the previous round. The truth evaluation is calculated as follows:

$$e_j^* = \frac{\sum_{i \in U_j} w_i d_j^i}{\sum_{i \in U_j} w_i} \tag{7}$$

We assume $\{d_j^* | \tau_j \in T\}$ is the ground truth of task τ_j discovered by the truth discovery algorithm. To evaluate the quality level of the collected data, we use distance functions $d(\bullet)$ to calculate the similarity between the collected data d_j^i and the truth ground d_j^*. The smaller $d(d_j^i, d_j^*)$, the higher the quality of the data collected d_j^i. The range of Q_j^i is [0,1]. The data quality is calculated as follows:

$$Q_j^i = 1 - \frac{d(d_j^i, d_j^*)}{\sum_{i \in U} d(d_j^i, d_j^*) + \sigma} \tag{8}$$

4.3   Reward Distribution Mechanism

The mobile workers participating in the task acts as a player in the cooperative game model. $N = \{1, 2, \cdots, n\}$ is the set of all participants, and S is a cooperative alliance composed of $|S|$ participants. For each cooperative alliance $S \subseteq N$, $v(S)$ represents the utility function of the income obtained from the cooperation of alliance S, and all cooperative utility values $v(S)$ are greater than the single user's utility value $v(i)$, where $i \in S$. The following is the utility function of the cooperative alliance based on data quality and a fixed total reward budget.

$$v(S) = \frac{B_j \times (|N|^h + 10) \sum_{i \in S} Q_j^i}{|S|^h + 10} \tag{9}$$

where B_j is the total reward for task τ_j, and Q_j^i is the quality of data collected by participant i. h is used to adjust the fairness of reward distribution, and $h \geq 0$.

The larger h is, the users with higher data quality will get more rewards, and users with lower quality will get fewer rewards.

We apply Shapley value [16], which is distribution scheme that distributes the total surplus generated by the coalition of all players. The distribution result is decided by how much each individual contributes to the alliance. The reward distribution calculation $\theta_i(v)$ of each mobile worker i participating in the cooperative game is as follows:

$$\theta_i(v) = \sum_{S \in N \setminus \{i\}} [v(S \cup \{i\}) - v(S)] \frac{|S|!(|N| - |S| - 1)!}{|N|!} \tag{10}$$

where $|S|$ and $|N|$ are the number of elements in set S and set N respectively, participant $i \in N$.

5   Experiments and Security Analysis

5.1   Security Analysis

The application of the blockchain eliminates the security threats brought by the centralized platform and realizes data consistency, tamper-proof, and distributed data storage in the network. During the operation of the entire system, the verification nodes of the public chain and the consortium chain are not crossed. Private information and public information are stored separately, ensuring the privacy and security of users and data. Also, a malicious user might creates multiple IDs and submits multiple responses to the same task in an attempt to receive more rewards. The proposed model uses a grouping truth discovery algorithm to score the data. Therefore, if one user submits multiple identical responses, the data quality will be measured as low and get reduced rewards. Therefore, our model is resistant to Sybil attack.

5.2   Experiment Setup and Performance Metrics

In the experiment of evaluating the account grouping algorithm, we recruited 12 mobile users in our system, among them are 10 legal users and 2 Sybil attackers. Each legal user has only one account to join the sensing tasks, and each Sybil attacker has 5 accounts to perform tasks. The percentage of malicious workers is equal to the percentage of legal accounts. However, the higher the activeness of the malicious account, the greater the damage to the sensing task. The activeness of each account i is defined as follows:

$$\alpha_i = \frac{|T_i|}{m} \tag{11}$$

where $|T_i|$ is the number of tasks performed by account i and m is the total number of tasks. In our experiment, each account has to perform at least two task, and thus $\alpha_i \in [0.2, 1]$.

To effectively compare the accuracy of the I-GTDA algorithm and the GTD algorithm [10], we set two reference variables γ and μ, the difference between malicious data and normal data, and the participation ratio of Sybil accounts.

$$\gamma = |\bar{d}_j^k - \bar{d}_j^{\bar{m}}| \tag{12}$$

where $\bar{d}_j^k$ is the average value of data perceived by the normal account for task τ_j, and $\bar{d}_j^{\bar{m}}$ is the average value of data collected by the detected Sybil account for task τ_j.

$$\mu = \frac{|U_n|}{|U|} \tag{13}$$

where $|U_n|$ is the number of malicious users participating in the task, and $|U|$ is the number of all users participating in the task.

To demonstrate the usefulness and fairness of the reward distribution proposed in this paper, we use the same data quality or user reputation value and total reward B_j to compare the weight-based proportional distribution (W-Proportional), the scheme proposed by Yang et al. (Y-Shapley) [17] and the I-Shapley scheme proposed in this paper. In our scheme, it is assumed that the data quality set corresponding to the participating user set $N = \{a_1, a_2, a_3, a_4, a_5\}$ is $\{Q_1 = 0.1, Q_2 = 0.15, Q_3 = 0.3, Q_4 = 0.25, Q_5 = 0.2\}$. The parameter h is set to 0, 1, 1.5 respectively.

The following metrics are used to analyze the performance of the D-JS and I-GTDA algorithms.

Adjusted rand index (ARI): This is a widely used criterion to evaluate the performance of clustering algorithms. The range of the ARI value is $[-1, 1]$. And the larger the ARI value, the better the clustering effect.

Mean absolute error (MAE) [10]: This is used to measure the error between the estimated ground truth obtained by the truth discovery algorithm and the ground data. The smaller the MAE value, the higher the accuracy of the truth discovery algorithm.

5.3 Result Analysis

Account Grouping Method Evaluation. We use ARI to evaluate the performance of the D-JS method proposed in this paper and compare it with the AG-TS and AG-TR methods proposed in [15]. Figure 2 shows the ARI values of the three account grouping methods for different levels of activeness among legal accounts and Sybil accounts. We fix the activeness of legal users at $\alpha = 0.2, 0.5$, or 0.8. The activeness of Sybil attackers varies, with α set to 0.2, 0.5, and 1, respectively. From Fig. 2, we observe that when the activity level of Sybil attackers ranges from 0.2 to 0.5, the ARI values of all three methods increase as the activity level of the Sybil attackers increases. However, when the activity level of Sybil attackers is 1, all Sybil attackers are grouped together, resulting in a decrease in the ARI value. This is because the three methods are based on task sets. Nevertheless, this result still allows for the distinction between Sybil attackers and legal users. In Fig. 2(c), it can be seen that when the activity level of normal users is 0.8, there is a high similarity in task sets among legal users, leading to a performance degradation of the AG-TS method that relies solely on task sets. In contrast, the D-JS method based on JS divergence considers the task set sequence, time series and collected data set simultaneously, which makes the difference degree calculation between accounts more accurate. Therefore, even when the Sybil attackers have lower activity levels, the D-JS method can still demonstrate better performance.

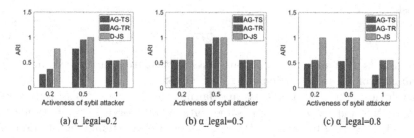

(a) α_legal=0.2   (b) α_legal=0.5   (c) α_legal=0.8

Fig. 2. ARI comparison of different account grouping methods.

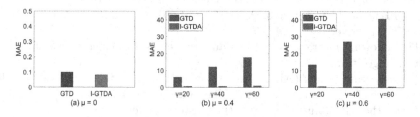

(a) μ = 0   (b) μ = 0.4   (c) μ = 0.6

Fig. 3. MAE comparison of different truth discovery algorithms.

Grouping Truth Discovery Algorithm Evaluation. MAE was used to measure the accuracy of the I-GTDA and the GTD algorithm. As shown in (a) of Fig. 3, when there is no interference from malicious data, the accuracy of the two methods is quite high, and then the I-GTDA algorithm outperforms the GTD algorithm. The (b) and (c) in Fig. 3 show the algorithm evaluation results under different malicious user participation ratios. When the proportion of malicious user participation increases or malicious data interference increases, the accuracy of the GTD algorithm will decrease significantly, but the I-GTDA algorithm has always maintained a high accuracy. Therefore, the I-GTDA algorithm is more suitable for realistic scenarios where Sybil attackers exist.

Reward Distribution Mechanism Evaluation. Figure 4 compares the results of three different reward distribution schemes as the value of h is adjusted. In Fig. 4(a), when $h = 0$, the reward distribution results of the I-Shapley scheme and the W-Proportional scheme are nearly identical. Similarly, in Fig. 4(b), when h is adjusted to 1, the I-Shapley distribution results closely match the Y-Shapley results. However, in Fig. 4(c), when h is set to 1.5, the I-Shapley reward distribution favors users who provide high-quality data, allocating lower rewards to users who provide low-quality data. When adjusting the h value, it is worth noting that the reward for each user should be no less than 0. For example, it can be seen from Fig. 5 that when the value of h is greater than or equal to 2, there are users whose reward is less than 0, so the value of h at this time is inappropriate. As a result, by adjusting the value of h appropriately, the I-Shapley scheme effectively incentivizes users to submit high-quality data, making it well-suited for mobile crowdsensing scenarios.

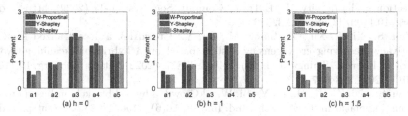

Fig. 4. Comparison of different reward distribution schemes.

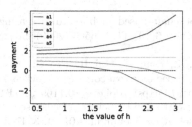

Fig. 5. The effect of the change of h value on the user's reward.

6 Conclusion

In this paper, we propose a BCMCS system model. The application of the public chain realizes a completely decentralized reward distribution model. The consortium chain ensures the privacy and security of participating users. Furthermore, to encourage mobile users to join the MCS platform, a quality-driven incentive mechanism is proposed in this paper. By achieving fair reward distribution based on accurate quality assessment, more mobile users are motivated to join the perception task. In future work, this paper will conduct further research on the consensus mechanism of blockchain, the design of benefit distribution, and the realization of the system.

References

1. Liu, Y., Kong, L., Chen, G.: Data-oriented mobile crowdsensing: a comprehensive survey. IEEE Commu. Surv. Tutorials **21**(3), 2849–2885 (2019). https://doi.org/10.1109/COMST.2019.2910855

2. Zhao, C., Yang, S., Yan, P., Yang, Q., Yang, X., McCann, J.: Data quality guarantee for credible caching device selection in mobile crowdsensing systems. IEEE Wireless Commun. **25**(3), 58–64 (2018). https://doi.org/10.1109/MWC.2018.1700299
3. Vahdat-Nejad, H., Asani, E., Mahmoodian, Z., Mohseni, M.H.: Context-aware computing for mobile crowd sensing: a survey. Futur. Gener. Comput. Syst. **99**, 321–332 (2019)
4. Cheng, X., He, B., Li, G., Cheng, B.: A survey of crowdsensing and privacy protection in digital city. IEEE Trans. Comput. Soc. Syst. 1–17 (2022). https://doi.org/10.1109/TCSS.2022.3204635
5. Zou, S., Xi, J., Xu, G., Zhang, M., Lu, Y.: CrowdHB: a decentralized location privacy-preserving crowdsensing system based on a hybrid blockchain network. IEEE Internet Things J. **9**(16), 14803–14817 (2022). https://doi.org/10.1109/JIOT.2021.3084937
6. Zhu, S., Cai, Z., Hu, H., Li, Y., Li, W.: zkCrowd: a hybrid blockchain-based crowdsourcing platform. IEEE Trans. Ind. Inform. **16**(6), 4196–4205 (2020). https://doi.org/10.1109/TII.2019.2941735
7. Tong, W., Dong, X., Shen, Y., Zhang, Y., Jiang, X., Tian, W.: CHChain: secure and parallel crowdsourcing driven by hybrid blockchain. Futur. Gener. Comput. Syst. **131**, 279–291 (2022)
8. Huang, J., et al.: Blockchain-based mobile crowd sensing in industrial systems. IEEE Trans. Ind. Inform. **16**(10), 6553–6563 (2020). https://doi.org/10.1109/TII.2019.2963728
9. An, J., Liang, D., Gui, X., Yang, H., Gui, R., He, X.: Crowdsensing quality control and grading evaluation based on a two-consensus blockchain. IEEE Internet Things J. **6**(3), 4711–4718 (2019). https://doi.org/10.1109/JIOT.2018.2883835
10. Wang, E., et al.: Trustworthy and efficient crowdsensed data trading on sharding blockchain. IEEE J. Sel. Areas Commun. **40**(12), 3547–3561 (2022). https://doi.org/10.1109/JSAC.2022.3213331
11. Wen, Y., et al.: Quality-driven auction-based incentive mechanism for mobile crowd sensing. IEEE Trans. Veh. Technol. **64**(9), 4203–4214 (2015). https://doi.org/10.1109/TVT.2014.2363842
12. Tan, W., Liu, J., Liang, Z., Ding, K.: Based on bid and data quality incentive mechanisms for mobile crowd sensing systems. In: 2022 IEEE 25th International Conference on Computer Supported Cooperative Work in Design (CSCWD), pp. 89–94 (2022). https://doi.org/10.1109/CSCWD54268.2022.9776098
13. Li, M., Lin, J., Yang, D., Xue, G., Tang, J.: QUAC: quality-aware contract based incentive mechanisms for crowdsensing. In: 2017 IEEE 14th International Conference on Mobile Ad Hoc and Sensor Systems (MASS), pp. 72–80 (2017). https://doi.org/10.1109/MASS.2017.45
14. Bai, Y., Hu, Q., Seo, S.H., Kang, K., Lee, J.J.: Public participation consortium blockchain for smart city governance. IEEE Internet Things J. **9**(3), 2094–2108 (2022). https://doi.org/10.1109/JIOT.2021.3091151
15. Lin, J., Yang, D., Wu, K., Tang, J., Xue, G.: A sybil-resistant truth discovery framework for mobile crowdsensing. In: 2019 IEEE 39th International Conference on Distributed Computing Systems (ICDCS), pp. 871–880 (2019). https://doi.org/10.1109/ICDCS.2019.00091
16. Shapley, L.S., et al.: A Value For N-person Games, vol. 2, pp. 307–317 (1953)
17. Yang, S., Wu, F., Tang, S., Gao, X., Yang, B., Chen, G.: On designing data quality-aware truth estimation and surplus sharing method for mobile crowdsensing. IEEE J. Sel. Areas Commun. **35**(4), 832–847 (2017). https://doi.org/10.1109/JSAC.2017.2676898

A New Frontier in Digital Security: Verification for NFT Image Using Deep Learning-Based ConvNeXt Model in Quantum Blockchain

Aji Teguh Prihatno[1] , Naufal Suryanto[1] , Harashta Tatimma Larasati[1] ,
Yustus Eko Oktian[2,3] , Thi-Thu-Huong Le[2,3] , and Howon Kim[1(✉)]

[1] School of Computer Science and Engineering, Pusan National University,
Busan 609735, Republic of Korea
howonkim@pusan.ac.kr
[2] Blockchain Platform Research Center, Pusan National University,
Busan 609735, Republic of Korea
[3] IoT Research Center, Pusan National University, Busan 609735, Republic of Korea

Abstract. Non-Fungible Tokens (NFTs) have transformed the digital
asset landscape with unique ownership verification. However, securing
NFT images remains a crucial challenge. This paper proposes a verification framework for NFT images in a quantum blockchain environment.
We explore the fundamentals, characteristics, and security challenges
of NFT images. We examine the significance of quantum computing
for digital security, highlighting vulnerabilities in classical encryption.
We discuss existing image verification techniques and their limitations,
leading to our proposed methodology that combines quantum-inspired
approaches with a Deep Learning-based model. Additionally, we investigate the potential of ConvNeXt as a part of Deep Learning methods to
enhance NFT image verification security and trust. Our comprehensive
technique combines the Deep Learning-based method with a quantum
blockchain to ensure the integrity, scalability, and validity of NFT images.
Experimental evaluation demonstrates the feasibility and effectiveness
of our approach. We discuss implications, including comparisons, limitations, and future research areas. This research advances digital security,
providing insights into NFT image verification in the quantum computing era and laying the foundation for secure NFT ecosystems, promoting
adoption across various domains.

This research was supported by the MSIT (Ministry of Science and ICT), Korea, under
the ITRC (Information Technology Research Center) support program (IITP-2023-
2020-0-01797) supervised by the IITP (Institute for Information & Communications
Technology Planning & Evaluation) and also supported by the MSIT (Ministry of
Science and ICT), Korea, under the Convergence security core talent training business
(Pusan National University) support program (IITP-2023-2022-0-01201) supervised
by the IITP (Institute for Information & Communications Technology Planning &
Evaluation).

Keywords: NFT · quantum blockchain · deep learning · digital security · ConvNeXt

1 Introduction

The rise of Non-Fungible Tokens (NFTs) has revolutionized the digital asset landscape, offering a novel approach to verifying the ownership and authenticity of digital content. NFTs have gained significant popularity in various domains, including art, collectibles, and virtual assets. However, the security of NFT images remains a critical concern [1], as they are susceptible to tampering, counterfeiting, and unauthorized duplication. Ensuring the integrity and trustworthiness of NFT images is paramount for maintaining the value and credibility of these digital assets. Digital security measures have traditionally relied on classical encryption algorithms to protect sensitive data. However, the advent of quantum computing poses significant challenges to classical cryptographic schemes, as quantum computers have the potential to break many of the currently deployed encryption methods [2]. This vulnerability requires innovative approaches to secure NFT images in the quantum era.

This paper proposes a verification framework for NFT images in a quantum blockchain environment to address NFT image authenticity and integrity security concerns. We use quantum computing and blockchain technology to develop a robust and tamper-resistant verification methodology [3]. Our approach uses quantum-inspired verification techniques to enhance the security and trustworthiness of NFT images while leveraging blockchain's decentralized and immutable nature to ensure transparency and audibility. To establish the foundation for our research, we first delve into the fundamentals of NFT images, exploring their unique characteristics and the security challenges they face. We analyze the vulnerabilities of classical encryption algorithms in the context of quantum computing and discuss the need for quantum-resistant cryptographic schemes [4]. Additionally, we survey existing image verification techniques and highlight their limitations in providing comprehensive security for NFT images. Building upon this background, we introduce our proposed methodology that combines Deep Learning-based ConvNext model approaches with the power of quantum blockchain technology [5].

We present a comprehensive technique that ensures the integrity and validity of NFT images, even in the presence of quantum computing threats. Through experimental evaluation and analysis, we demonstrate the feasibility and effectiveness of our approach to providing robust security for NFT images. This research's findings contribute to the digital security field by addressing the emerging challenges of NFT image verification in the quantum computing era. By establishing secure and trustworthy NFT ecosystems, our work promotes the widespread adoption of NFTs across various domains, fostering confidence and value in the digital asset landscape. The remaining structure of the paper is as follows.

Section 2 provides an overview of the related work in NFT image verification and quantum blockchain. In Sect. 3, we describe the dataset used for conducting our experiments and evaluating the effectiveness of our proposed methodology. Section 4 presents our methodology for verifying NFT images that utilize various ConvNeXt models and a concept quantum blockchain. Section 5 describes the proposed design architecture of NFT image verification in a quantum blockchain environment. Section 6 presents the results obtained from applying our methodology to the NFT image dataset and compares it with the ConvNeXt-based model. Section 6 comprises a comprehensive discussion and analysis of the results, highlighting its advantages, limitations, and areas for further improvement. In the final section, Sect. 7, we summarize the key findings of our research and provide concluding remarks.

2 Related Work

The use of NFT verification to identify potential con artists has been supported in a number of papers and methodologies. Galis et al. [6] has proposed a rapid and creative method for approximating pattern matching for plagiarism detection utilizing an NDFA-based method that greatly improves performance compared to other similarity measures already in use. In order to trace partial matches faster, the suggested approach makes use of local thresholds at the node level and a sliding window notion. The method is especially useful for platforms and ecosystems that are NFT-ready and driven by blockchain. However, the method has a high potential computational cost since it computes every feasible suffix for each node.

In the context of blockchain-based non-fungible tokens (NFTs), Pungila et al. [7] employed a novel method to do approximate pattern-matching for plagiarism detection. The authors combine an NDFA (Non-Deterministic Finite Automaton) method with a sliding window idea and local thresholds at the node level to trace partial matches more quickly. They tested their method and found that it acts adequately similarly to other similarity measures currently used in text mining for plagiarism detection. However, they are precautionary because their proposed approach might only be appropriate for some plagiarism detection tasks. It is still being determined how well the authors' approach will perform in different circumstances after testing it in a number of real-world scenarios and with various similarity tests used in plagiarism detection. Furthermore, the accuracy of the authors' method needs to be thoroughly analyzed.

3 Datasets

An openly available dataset from Kaggle was used in this study [10]. The dataset contains 9761 records from the Crypto Coven NFT project, each represented by a unique folder containing three images: an original size image labeled as os, a preview version labeled as preview, and a smaller thumbnail version labeled as a thumbnail. These images are in .png format and were collected via the OpenSea API. The images don't fit into any particular genre and instead exhibit a variety of NFT arts. All images were resized to a uniform 224 by 224 pixels for processing purposes. Subsequently, the images were divided into training, validation, and test subsets in the proportion of 60%, 20%, and 20%, respectively. Considering the complexities and variability in real-world scenarios, augmentation techniques were applied to increase the robustness and generalizability of the model. These techniques included random modifications to the input images' rotation, brightness, shear, horizontal flip, and scale, thus effectively enlarging the sample size of the training data and allowing the model to learn from a broader range of instances. This data expansion and variation help the ConvNeXt model to adapt and generalize across diverse image techniques.

4   Methodology

4.1   NFT Concept

Users can participate in our system by becoming content creators or consumers. The content creators make the original NFT assets, upload the assets on IPFS, and store the corresponding metadata on-chain. Before our system successfully accepts this new NFT mint, our Image Plagiarism Checker (IPC) will validate the uploaded digital assets using the deep learning-based ConvNeXt method. Only assets with below 0.3 similarity score can be accepted. On the other side of the system, consumers browse the NFT on our platform through the available Application Programming Interface (API), obtain the relevant on-chain metadata, make payments, and download the image from the IPFS. Because of the proposed IPC, consumers can make a safe payment knowing that the NFT they bought will likely not be a copycat. In the following paragraphs, we describe each component from our proposals in more detail.

4.2   NFT Image Verification Using ConvNeXt

ConvNeXts, built from common ConvNets (convolutional neural networks) modules, outperform Transformers in terms of accuracy, scalability, and resilience across all significant benchmarks. ConvNeXt is incredibly easy to use and maintains the effectiveness of regular ConvNets while being completely convolutional for training and testing [11]. Utilizing grouped convolution with the same number of groups as channels, ConvNeXt employs depthwise convolution. Depthwise convolution is comparable to self-weighted attention's sum operation because both exclusively combine the information in the spatial dimension and act on a per-channel basis [12]. Compared to the Swin Transformers model, every transformer block produces an inverted bottleneck. Concatenating four blocks results in an output that quadruples the size of the hidden dimensions. ConvNeXts imitates this concept by creating an inverted bottleneck with a 4-to-1 expansion ratio. It was discovered that it improves the model's performance [13].

The ConvNeXt block [11], depicted in Fig. 1, is a fundamental component within the ConvNeXt architecture, comprising four branches; each encompasses a 1×1 convolutional layer generating 96 output channels. Subsequently, a 7×7

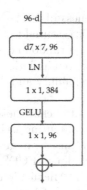

Fig. 1. ConvNeXt block architecture.

convolutional layer with 96 output channels and a stride of 2 is applied to perform downsampling. The output feature maps of the four branches are then concatenated along the channel dimension, resulting in a feature map with a fourfold increase in the number of channels compared to the input. This concatenated feature map is subsequently fed through a sequence of two 1×1 convolutional layers. The initial 1×1 convolutional layer has 384 output channels, while the subsequent 1×1 convolutional layer has 96 output channels. Finally, the output of the last 1×1 convolutional layer is combined with the input feature map using a residual connection. Furthermore, from the ConvNeXt block architecture, incorporating downsampling layers and residual connections play a vital role in preserving information from the input feature map and facilitating the training of deep ConvNeXt networks. By utilizing the gating mechanism within the ConvNeXt block, the network can selectively integrate information from different branches, thereby enhancing the network's representative capacity.

The ConvNeXt block illustrated in Fig. 1 constitutes a straightforward and efficient building block that can be stacked to construct a deep ConvNeXt network. The specific configuration of the convolutional layers and the gating mechanism can be adjusted to optimize the network's performance for various computer vision tasks. The ConvNeXt block consists of a series of convolutional layers followed by a gating mechanism. The input feature map is divided into multiple branches, transforming a distinct convolutional layer set. These transformed feature maps are subsequently merged using a gating function, which learns to integrate information from the different branches selectively.

4.3   Quantum Blockchain

Quantum blockchain offers Non-Fungible Tokens (NFTs) the benefit of providing distinctive and genuine tokens by integrating the greatest aspects of blockchain technology. NFTs are digital assets such as artwork, collectibles, or virtual real estate that serve as ownership or authenticity proof tokens. By utilizing the capabilities of quantum computing and communication, quantum blockchain improves the security and uniqueness of NFTs. Quantum blockchain also provides computing efficiency, which is essential for Metaverse apps to operate correctly. Additionally, it uses quantum randomness, which generates random bits via qubit series, to guard against manipulation by users and programs. This significantly improves the NFTs' reliability and dependability in the blockchain-based Metaverse system.

The NFT platform is built on a blockchain network that is quantum-resistant. The coming threat of quantum computing, which would make conventional cryptography obsolete, motivated this strategic choice. We suggest replacing the present digital signature technique, ECDSA (widely used in blockchain networks), with the LMS (Leighton-Micali Signature) algorithm [14], a hash-based signature scheme. The adoption of LMS over alternatives such as XMSS (eXtended Merkle Signature Scheme) stems from careful technical deliberation rather than a random choice. Regarding key generation, signing, and verifying performance, LMS typically surpasses XMSS. This is due to several variables, including using a Merkle tree with a constant height, simplifying the implementation, and lowering the stack use. Furthermore, LMS uses a one-time signature (OTS) method that is less complex than XMSS and requires fewer hash function evaluations. In addition, LMS uses a more effective technique to compute the public key, which compresses computation time and uses less memory [15]. The LMS algorithm resists to assaults that take advantage of discrete logarithm problems and large-number factorization, which present serious vulnerabilities in quantum computing. Therefore, we can confidently state that our system is immune to these types of attacks, ensuring its durability and integrity even when quantum computing becomes widely used in the future.

On top of this blockchain, a smart contract similar to Ethereum Virtual Machine (EVM) exist to provide fair and deterministic logics for creators and consumers. This EVM smart contract handles day-to-day NFT tasks such as minting and transfers following the ERC-721 or ERC-1155 standard.

5   Proposed Approach

The proposed approach initiates at the creator's side and includes numerous crucial processes, including image creation, image verification, minting, and ultimately storage in the Quantum Blockchain Network. The creator starts by creating an original work of digital art that will be issued as a Non-Fungible Token NFT. Upon finalizing the image, the designer employs a Deep Learning-based ConvNeXt model known as the Image Plagiarism Checker (IPC) to ensure the image's authenticity and originality. IPC works by examining the image's features and comparing them with a simulation database of images. If there are significant similarities with any image in the database, the image may be flagged as potential plagiarism. IPC's output classes can range from 'original' to 'plagiarized' depending on the detected degree of similarity. After verification, the image flows through the minting process, which turns the digital artwork into an NFT and encodes essential information, including the artist's identity, ownership information, and the specific characteristics of the artwork. The InterPlanetary File System (IPFS), a decentralized file storage system, obtains the NFT after minting, assuring the data's accessibility and permanence. The NFT is then safely kept on the Quantum Blockchain Network, a blockchain architecture that can resist quantum attacks and offers the highest level of security.

On the other hand, the buyer's side with an API that makes it possible to interface with the Quantum Blockchain Network in order to search for and get NFT images offered for sale on the NFT marketplace. Each NFT image that is for sale is specifically identifiable and traceable on the Quantum Blockchain Network, and the prospective buyer can choose from a variety of them. After deciding on a suitable NFT image, the buyer can complete the transaction on the NFT marketplace, such as OpenSea, CryptoPunks, or Nifty Gateway; then, the buyer should complete the purchase under the terms of the underlying smart contract. Once this transaction has been completed, the blockchain ledger will be updated to reflect the transfer of ownership from the creator to the buyer. A buyer can reliably purchase authentic NFTs through this secure and transparent approach.

Figure 2 shows our proposed method Quantum Blockchain network's NFT image verification architecture. It is based on the particular that no instrument is built into the Blockchain to verify that the person minting an NFT is legitimately entitled to the asset they are minting.

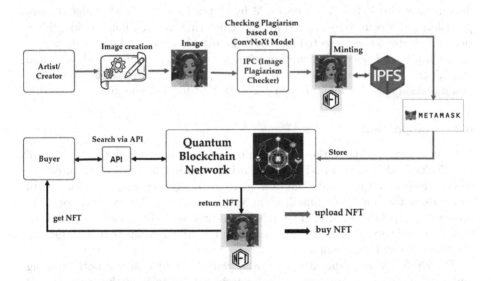

Fig. 2. Proposed architecture for NFT image verification.

6 Experiment Results and Comparison

This study uses the latest CNN-based development, which is part of the deep learning method, namely the ConvNeXt model [8], from which we compare various ConvNeXt variant methods with the same object as a form of the progress of the author's previous research [9]. In this paper, NFT image verification is still a developing issue discussed in a case study with Quantum Blockchain technology.

6.1 Experimental Setup

The hyperparameters must be set to optimal and equivalent values to guarantee the best results for NFT Images verification. This study established the same hyperparameters for all ConvNeXt model varieties. The Adam optimizer, also comprehended as leaky averaging, is a prominent deep-learning training method that uses exponentially weighted moving averages to regulate the momentum and second moment of the gradient. This optimizer is more efficient than the traditional stochastic gradient descent (SGD) method, which omits the impact of outliers in that it records the relative prediction error of the loss function through a weighted average. ReLU activation was determined over other activation functions like tanh and sigmoid because it is less computationally expensive and improves upon the vanishing gradient problem. The default learning rate value of 0.001 was utilized in most Keras optimizers, and a 128-dimension embedded dimension was selected. With only 128 bytes per face, this model offered more precision and was initially utilized for face clustering, verification, and identification. Batch size 64 was selected because it is suitable for the volume of data used in the study, and selecting a mini-batch size with a power of 2 is advised, and 100 epochs have been chosen for the training. Furthermore, triplet semi-hard loss was chosen as this loss function performs best for verifying image similarity.

6.2 Comparison

In this work, we evaluated the Triplet Semi-Hard Loss model with the variation of ConvNeXt models to verify NFT images using the same dataset for one threshold score, which is 0.3 to obtain the best score for analyzing image plagiarism. In comparison to ConvNeXt Small, ConvNeXt Base, and ConvNeXt Large, the proposed Deep Learning-based ConvNeXt XLarge with Triplet Semi-Hard Loss maintains the lowest loss and maximum accuracy, which means that NFT picture verification may be guaranteed.

ConvNeXt XLarge surpasses the other variations in terms of both training and validation loss, according to the experimental results of the training and validation losses across several models. ConvNeXt XLarge has the best learning and generalization skills among the studied models, with the lowest training loss of 0.1129 and validation loss of 0.1801. The second-best performance is provided by ConvNeXt Large, which has a training loss of 0.2565 and a validation loss of 0.3132. ConvNeXt Base follows with a training loss of 0.2895 and a validation loss of 0.3543. ConvNeXt Small records the largest losses, with training losses of

0.3267 and validation losses of 0.4857. The pattern found suggests that model size considerably affects learning ability, with larger models doing better. This might be explained by the greater model complexity and capability of representation that come with larger models. The model's capacity to generalize to new data would be significantly impacted by overfitting, thus it is imperative to prevent this from happening as the model size grows. Figure 3 shows the comparison of training and validation loss from all ConvNeXt models.

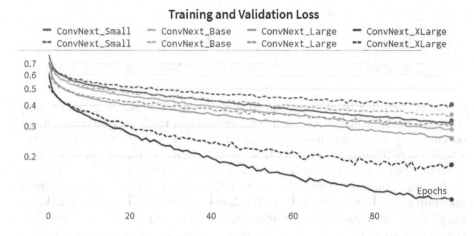

Fig. 3. Comparison of training and validation loss across all ConvNeXt models.

We discover that the ConvNeXt XLarge model beats all other models after examining the experimental results of the training and validation losses at an image similarity score threshold of 0.3. ConvNeXt XLarge outperforms other versions in learning and generalization, with a training score of 0.9185 and a validation score of 0.788, showing a greater degree of performance when confirming NFT images. The ConvNeXt Large model, which reports a training score of 0.7546 and a validation score of 0.6883, displays the second-best performance, followed by the ConvNeXt Base model, which gives a training score of 0.7134 and a validation score of 0.6307. With a validation score of 0.6109 and a training score of 0.6945, the ConvNeXt Small model has the lowest ratings. These findings demonstrate that larger models are more efficient at learning complicated patterns in the data, improving the accuracy of their image verification. This is due to their higher complexity and representational capacity. To avoid overfitting and preserve model effectiveness, it's crucial to find a balance. Figure 4 describes the comparison of training and validation loss from all ConvNeXt models respect to the threshold score 0.3.

When comparing the experimental findings for the Precision-Recall Area Under Curve (AUC) of picture similarity across many models, we can see that each model-ConvNeXt XLarge, Large, Base, and Small-performed remarkably well, producing scores that were very close to perfect. The ConvNeXt XLarge

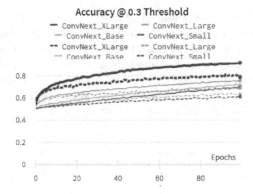

Fig. 4. Comparison of training results among all ConvNeXt models for threshold 0.3.

model, on the other hand, boasts an AUC of 1, which is a flawless score, showing that this model achieves the ideal balance between recall and precision, hence offering the most efficient image verification. The scores of the three models, ConvNeXt Large (0.9992), ConvNeXt Base (0.9997), and ConvNeXt Small (0.9999), are interestingly also quite near to 1, indicating that these models perform well in the task of picture verification. The ConvNeXt model architecture's ability to maintain excellent precision and recall balance for this specific task, regardless of model size, is demonstrated by their nearly equal performance. Figure 5 describes the comparison of training and validation loss from all ConvNeXt models respect to Precision-Recall AUC metric.

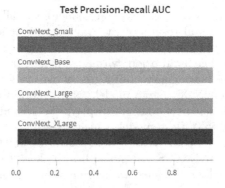

Fig. 5. Comparison test results among all ConvNeXt models for Precision-Recall AUC.

7   Conclusion

In conclusion, this study has pushed the boundaries of digital security, particularly in the realm of non-fungible tokens (NFTs), by proposing and validating an effective verification process for NFT images utilizing a Deep Learning-based ConvNeXt model integrated with Quantum Blockchain. The research has convincingly shown that the ConvNeXt XLarge model outperforms its smaller counterparts in learning and generalizing the image verification task. This affirms the idea that larger models, with their greater complexity and representation power, can better learn intricate patterns in the data and consequently enhance image verification accuracy.

The utilization of Quantum Blockchain technology offers an added layer of security, ensuring the system's resilience even against the anticipated threats of quantum computing. This synergy of Deep Learning and Quantum Blockchain can pave the way for future developments in the secure handling and verification of digital assets like NFTs. It also highlights the potential of these technologies to address complex digital security concerns in an increasingly interconnected and digital world.

Future work could extend to exploring the efficiency and effectiveness of this model in larger, more diverse datasets, as well as the potential integration of other post-quantum cryptographic algorithms. This would further ensure the robustness and adaptability of the model in a dynamic digital landscape, thus continuing the exploration of new frontiers in digital security.

References

1. Hrenyak, A.: Implications of non-fungible tokens for the online artist (2022)
2. Shor, P.W.: Algorithms for quantum computation: discrete logarithms and factoring. In: Proceedings 35th Annual Symposium on Foundations of Computer Science, pp. 124–134. Santa Fe, NM, USA (1994). https://doi.org/10.1109/SFCS.1994.365700
3. Vardhan Singh Rawat, H., Bisht, D., Kumar, S., Dangi, S.: Rise of blockchain-based non-fungible tokens (NFTs): overview, trends, and future prospects. In: Skala, V., Singh, T.P., Choudhury, T., Tomar, R., Abul Bashar, M. (eds.) Machine Intelligence and Data Science Applications. LNDECT, vol. 132, pp. 1–10. Springer, Singapore (2022). https://doi.org/10.1007/978-981-19-2347-0_1
4. Mattsson, J.P., Smeets, B., Thormarker, E.: Quantum-Resistant Cryptography. arXiv preprint arXiv:2112.00399 (2021)
5. Guo, X., Zhang, G., Zhang, Y.A.: Comprehensive review of blockchain technology-enabled smart manufacturing: a framework, challenges and future research directions. Sensors **23**(1), 155 (2023). https://doi.org/10.3390/s23010155
6. Galiş, D., Pungilă, C., Negru, V.: A fast NDFA-based approach to approximate pattern-matching for plagiarism detection in blockchain-driven NFTs. In: Wrembel, R., Gamper, J., Kotsis, G., Tjoa, A.M., Khalil, I. (eds.) DaWaK 2022. LNCS, vol. 13428, pp. 53–58. Springer, Cham (2022). https://doi.org/10.1007/978-3-031-12670-3_5
7. Pungila, C., Galis, D., Negru, V.: A new high-performance approach to approximate pattern-matching for plagiarism detection in blockchain-based non-fungible tokens (NFTs). ArXiv Preprint ArXiv:2205.14492 (2022)
8. Chollet, F.: Keras Applications. https://keras.io/api/applications/. Accessed 12 June 2023

9. Prihatno, A., Suryanto, N., Oh, S., Le, T., Kim, H., et al.: NFT image plagiarism check using EfficientNet-based deep neural network with triplet semi-hard loss. Appl. Sci. **13**, 3072 (2023)
10. Wang, H.: Crypto Coven. https://www.kaggle.com/datasets/harrywang/crypto-coven. Accessed 10 June 2023
11. Liu, Z., Mao, H., Wu, C., Feichtenhofer, C., Darrell, T., Xie, S.: A convnet for the 2020s. In: Proceedings of the IEEE/CVF Conference on Computer Vision and Pattern Recognition, pp. 11976–11986 (2022)
12. Singh, A.: ConvNext: The Return Of Convolution Networks. https://medium.com/augmented-startups/convnext-the-return-of-convolution-networks-e70cbe8dabcc. Accessed 13 June 2023
13. Kinyan, S.: An overview of ConvNeXt. https://www.section.io/engineering-education/an-overview-of-convnext/. Accessed 13 June 2022
14. Bernstein, D., Lange, T.: Post-quantum cryptography-dealing with the fallout of physics success. Cryptology EPrint Archive (2017)
15. Campos, F., Kohlstadt, T., Reith, S., Stöttinger, M.: LMS vs XMSS: comparison of stateful hash-based signature schemes on ARM Cortex-M4. In: International Conference on Cryptology in Africa, pp. 258–277 (2020)

AE-LSTM Based Anomaly Detection System for Communication Over DNP 3.0

Ilhwan Ji⬤, Seungho Jeon⬤, and Jung Taek Seo⁽⊠⁾⬤

Gachon University, Seongnam-daero, 1342 Seongnam-si, Republic of Korea
{ilhwan1013,shjeon90,seojt}@gachon.ac.kr

Abstract. Energy Management System (EMS) communicates with power plants and substations to maintain the reliability and efficiency of power supplies. EMS collects and monitors data from these sources and controls power flow through commands to ensure uninterrupted power supply, frequency and voltage maintenance, and power recovery in the event of a power outage. EMS works in a Distributed Network Protocol (DNP) 3.0-based network environment that is considered secure due to its unique security features and communication methods. However, cyberattacks exploiting the vulnerability of the DNP 3.0 protocol can manipulate the power generation output, resulting in serious consequences such as facility malfunction and power outages. To address this issue, this paper identifies security threats in power system networks, including DNP 3.0, and proposes an AI-based anomaly detection system based on DNP 3.0 network traffic. Existing network traffic target rule-based detection methods and signature-based detection methods have defects. We propose an AI-based anomaly detection system to compensate for defects in existing anomaly detection methods and perform efficient anomaly detection. To evaluate the performance of the AI-based anomaly detection system proposed in this paper, we used a dataset containing normal network traffic and nine types of attack network traffic obtained from the DNP 3.0 communication testbed, and experiments showed 99% accuracy, 98% TPR, and 1.6% FPR, resulting in 99% F-1 score. By implementing these security measures, power system network environments, including EMS, can be better protected against cyber threats.

Keywords: ICS · SCADA · EMS · AI-based Anomaly Detection System

1 Introduction

The Energy Management System (EMS) communicates with power plants and substations acquires and monitors data from substations and plants for the stability, continuity, real-time, and economic efficiency of power supply, and transmits trans-mission and substation system and power output control commands. These functions control the power flow to perform uninterruptible power supply, frequency maintenance in a specific range, voltage maintenance within a particular range, and recovery during a power outage [1]. The power control network that includes EMS is based on Distributed Network Protocol 3.0 (DNP 3.0).

© The Author(s), under exclusive license to Springer Nature Singapore Pte Ltd. 2024
H. Kim and J. Youn (Eds.): WISA 2023, LNCS 14402, pp. 91–104, 2024.
https://doi.org/10.1007/978-981-99-8024-6_8

The power control network using the DNP 3.0 communication method was considered safe thanks to the inherent security of DNP 3.0 and the communication method that performs communication only by resuming communication of the master device [2]. Cyberattacks against EMS using vulnerabilities in these DNP 3.0 protocols can cause financial and physical damage, such as facility malfunction and power outages, through arbitrary adjustment of the power generation output of the plant. Traditional network traffic target rule-based detection methods and signature-based detection methods are flawed. For rule-based detection methods, rule update cycles to respond to rapidly changing attacks cannot keep up with the rate of change in the attack. For signature-based detection methods, unknown attacks cannot be detected [3, 4]. An anomaly detection method using AI is required to compensate for the weaknesses of these existing anomaly detection methods and effective detection based on the DNP 3.0 packet.

In this paper, we analyze vulnerabilities in the DNP3.0-based power system network environment, including EMS, and propose an AI-based anomaly detection system to respond to cyberattacks using these vulnerabilities. The anomaly detection system presented in this paper consists of DNP 3.0 parser, feature preprocessor, and autoencoder-based long short-term memory classifier. DNP 3.0 parser produces more than 100 features around all properties and time-related data of DNP 3.0, such as source and destination IP addresses and ports that can be extracted from DNP 3.0 raw traffic collected from substations and power plants. In addition, it plays a role in converting the derived flow data into the same format and format for learning classifiers and abnormal detection. Feature preprocessor performed normalization and label-encoding on feature for efficient AE-LSTM (Autoencoder - Long Short Term Memory) classifier learning and abnormal detection using data collected by DNP 3.0 Parser. AE-LSTM classifier classifies normal data and abnormal data based on the input data. In order to evaluate the detection performance of an anomaly detection system with the above configuration, a high performance of 99% accuracy, 98% TPR, 1.6% FPR, and 99% F-1 Score was derived in this experiment using "DNP3 intrusion detection dataset," a dataset containing normal network traffic and nine types of attack network traffic obtained from the DNP 3.0 communication testbed. The contribution of this paper is three-fold:

- We present DNP 3.0 based power system security vulnerabilities and risk analysis, including EMS.
- We propose abnormal detection system based on AE-LSTM for the EMS communication section based on DNP 3.0
- For the AE-LSTM-based anomaly detection system presented in this paper, high performance of 99% accuracy, 98% TPR, 1.6% FPR, and 99% F-1 Score was derived using "DNP3 intrusion detection data set", a dataset containing normal network traffic and nine attack network traffic obtained from the DNP 3.0 communication testbed.

The remainder of this paper is organized as follows. Section 2 introduces research related to AI-based anomaly detection in DNP 3.0-based Industrial Control System/Supervisory Control and Data Acquisition (ICS/SCADA). Section 3 analyzes the power system network, including EMS, and analyzes the risks that may occur in the power system network, including EMS. Section 4 presents an AI-based anomaly detection system for detection and response to threats. In Sect. 5, the conclusions and future research directions are presented.

2   Related Works

Radoglou-Grammatikis et al. [5] proposed a network flow-based intrusion and anomaly detection and prevention technique called DIDEROT that uses supervised and unsupervised machine learning. Network flows are classified by decision tree models trained on various attacks based on the Rodofile dataset [6] and normal behavior collected from real substation traffic. The anomaly detection model detects anomalies by enabling autoencoders when data flows are classified as malicious flows. The response module causes the SDN controller to delete a specific flow if a malicious activity or abnormality is found. The evaluation results of the abnormal detection model showed that the autoencoder and decision tree achieved high accuracy and F1-score with 99.7% and 99.1% for decision trees and 95.1% and 95.3% for autoencoder, respectively.

V. Kelli et al. [7] designed the internal vulnerabilities of DNP3.0 and implemented the attacks found through nine DNP 3.0 attack scenarios. This paper generated a DNP 3.0 environment normal and cyberattack dataset by implementing nine DNP 3.0 attack scenarios. They presented a machine learning-based multi-model cyberattack classification IDS trained to recognize DNP3 attacks. As a result of the experiment, high accuracy and f1-score were achieved with 97% accuracy and 88% f1-score in the DNN-based anomaly detection model.

I. Siniosoglou et al. [8] proposed an Intrusion Detection System (IDS) specifically designed for smart grid environments using Modbus/TCP (Transmission Control Protocol) and DNP 3.0 protocols. The proposed IDS, called anoMaly Detection aNd claSificAction (MENSA), was designed to adopt a new autoencoder-Generative Adversarial Network (GAN) architecture to detect anomalies and classify cyberattacks on Modbus/TCP and DNP 3.0. As a result of the experiment, MENSA achieved high accuracy and F1-score with 99% accuracy and 98% F1 score for Rodofile dataset, a DNP 3.0 data set.

3   Power System Network

3.1   Analysis of Power System Network Communication Method

The communication structure of the power SCADA system, including EMS, is shown in Fig. 1. Table. 1 presents the components of the power SCADA system. The power system network comprises a remote terminal unit (RTU), SCC SCADA, RCC SCADA, and EMS. RTU transmits status information of the power plant and substation to the upper system and receives commands from the upper system. SCC SCADA monitors and controls the 154 kV radial power system. It also performs remote operations of unmanned substations. RCC SCADA controls the 154 kV LOOP power system and provides a service, monitoring information for the main system operation and power generation status of substations and power plants, balancing power demand and supply. If necessary, RCC SCADA adjusts the power generation output of the power plant. Also, the power system network consists of EMS, which reduces the power loss rate by maintaining the rated frequency of the substation [1, 10]. DNP 3.0 transmits status information from substations and plant RTUs to EMS and SCADA and receives control commands.

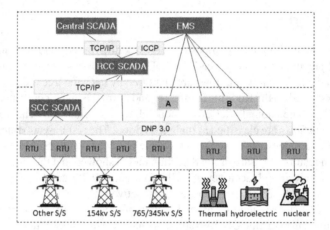

Fig. 1. Power system network configuration diagram including EMS [9]

Table 1. Describe the main functions of the power system components.

Component	Unit Function	Key Function
EMS	Data Acquisition	Obtaining system data for real-time power plants and substations remotely
	Monitoring and Control	Displaying the system status, checking the alarm, and performing remote control
	Automatic power Generation Control	Maintaining the rated frequency, automatically controlling the power generation output, and minimizing the power generation fuel cost
	Economic Dispatch	Allocating generator power economically and reflecting the cost of fuel in the middle
	Contingency Analysis	Analyzing the system status of the assumed failure and extracting the violation cases
	State Estimation	- Estimating the current system state based on acquisition/model data - Creating solutions for all system analyses and DTSs
RCC SCADA	Distant monitoring	Remotely monitoring the LOOP power system

(continued)

Table 1. (*continued*)

Component	Unit Function	Key Function
	Distant control	Remotely controlling the LOOP power system
	Distant measurement	Displaying key system operation information
SCC SCADA	Distant monitoring	Displaying the operation status of substation facilities
	Distant control	Remotely operating unmanned substation facilities
	Distant measurement	Displaying remote metering information for substation facilities

Line A of Fig. 1 is where EMS acquires information based on DNP 3.0 for the substation RTU. EMS collects operational data such as load power, frequency and voltage of substations, reserved power, and operational status of transmission and substation facilities. Based on the collected information, EMS monitors operational status, such as power loss rate at substations and failure of substation facilities.

Line B of Fig. 1 is a data communicating location based on DNP 3.0 for other power plants, including the current power plant infrastructure and renewable energy power plant. EMS acquires and monitors the operational status data of the power plant. Based on monitoring information, the generator terminal voltage is controlled by telephone to maintain the safety of the power system, efficient use of reactive power, and customer-proper voltage.

DNP 3.0 is a widely used protocol in ICS to automate the control and supervision of production processes in the electrical, oil, and water industries. In particular, DNP 3.0 is used as the SCADA protocol in power plant environments, including smart grids, to communicate between field devices and master stations [11]. The power control network using the DNP 3.0 communication method was considered safe owing to the inherent security of DNP 3.0 and the method that performs communication only by resuming communication of the master device [2]. In critical infrastructure, including power systems, attacks on the DNP 3.0 protocol can have serious consequences, including financial damage and physical and human casualties.

3.2 Risk Analysis of DNP 3.0-Based Communication Systems

Table 2 presents the security risks that may occur in the environment with the serial DNP 3.0 and lists the vulnerabilities for DNP 3.0 released by ICS-CERT and Digital Bond. Possible security risks were classified into infringing on confidentiality, availability, and integrity, and the causes of each risk were presented [12, 13].

Suppose an attacker uses the vulnerability in Table 2 to conduct a cyber-attack on EMS. In that case, it can result in service suspension of EMS by an unauthorized request packet of DNP 3.0 and stop the performance of RTU functions of substations or power

Table 2. Security risks that may arise in DNP 3.0 communication environments.

Risk Type	Description
Points List Scan	During the information gathering phase, gather information about the attackable DNP 3.0 data points - plaintext communication
Function Code Scan	Gathering information about the attackable DNP function code during the information-gathering phase - plaintext communication
Disable Unsolicited Responses	An attacker could disable unsolicited response functionality on the field control by setting the application layer function code to Disable Unsolicited Responses to disrupt alarms and other key events - lack of authentication mechanisms and improper behavior detection
Unauthorized Miscellaneous	Unauthorized DNP 3.0 client sends undefined requests - an absence of an authentication mechanism
Stop Application	An attacker can stop an application on the field controller by sending a packet with the function code of the application layer set to 0x12 (Stop Application) to the field controller - lack of authentication mechanisms and improper behavior detection
Unsolicited Response Storm	An attacker performs a denial-of-service attack by sending many response packets with the function code of the application layer set to 0x82 (Unsolicited Responses) to the control system server - lack of authentication mechanisms and improper behavior detection
Cold Restart	An attacker sends a request packet with the application layer function code set to 0X0D (Cold Restart) to the field controller, causing the field controller to become out of service - lack of authentication mechanisms and improper behavior detection
Time Change Attempt	Change the time information of a field device - an absence of an authentication mechanism
Warm Restart	An attacker can delete configuration initialization and events, such as removing audit evidence from the field control, by sending a packet with the application layer function code set to 0X0E (Warm Restart) to the field control - an absence of an authentication mechanism

(continued)

Table 2. (*continued*)

Risk Type	Description
Failed Checksum Error	Checksum checks are disabled to prevent integrity from being guaranteed - lack of authentication mechanism and plaintext communication

plants through stop application packet transmission to on-site RTU devices and EMS. When such an attack occurs, the EMS cannot perform efficient power transmission, reception, and production control. Additionally, arbitrary control, including arbitrary power generation control, can cause failures and destroy power generation facilities when performing data forgery attacks bet\ween the attacker's EMS and the plant using insufficient mutual authentication. In order to respond to cyber-attacks based on these DNP 3.0 vulnerabilities, it is necessary to identify and respond to cyber-attacks in advance through the DNP 3.0 packet target anomaly detection system.

4 Proposed AI-Based Anomaly Detection System

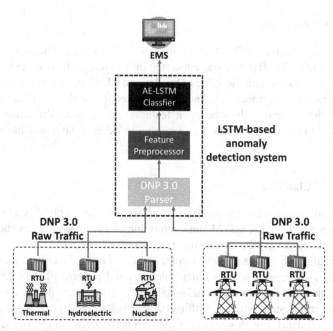

Fig. 2. DNP 3.0-based network environment EMS network traffic-based anomaly detection system application configuration diagram

Figure 2 shows the proposed anomaly detection system overview in DNP 3.0-based network environment EMS. The anomaly detection system is in front of the EMS. It performs anomaly detection for all DNP 3.0 network packets generated at substations and power plants and accessed by the EMS. The component of the anomaly detection system is the DNP 3.0 parser, which converts DNP 3.0 raw traffic into a file in a certain format for learning the anomaly detection based-on AE-LSTM classifier. In addition, there are "feature preprocessor" that selects specific feature and preprocesses to increase the efficiency and accuracy of AE-LSTM-based classifier and AE-LSTM classifier that classifies normal and abnormal traffic based on input data. The anomaly detection model is designed based on AE-LSTM to reflect the time series characteristics of network packets that are continuously generated every certain cycle, and real-time anomaly detection is performed based on this.

4.1 DNP 3.0 Parser

DNP 3.0 parser is responsible for converting DNP 3.0 raw traffic collected from substations and plants into a consistent format for classifier learning. The DNP 3.0 parser collects DNP 3.0 packets and generates traffic data for data contained within a specific period. DNP 3.0 parser generates traffic consisting of more than 100 features, including the packet feature and the packet data's statistical values, such as the source IP address, destination IP address and port address in the raw traffic.

4.2 Feature Preprocessor

The input value of the AE-LSTM classifier must be numeric data. Therefore, the shape extracted from the DNP 3.0 parser was converted into an integer type value by applying label encoding to the non-numeric value of the data. In addition, data normalization was carried out to prevent deterioration in learning the detection model originating from the differences in the range of values between features. As the normalizer, the min-max scaler is applied to change each data to a minimum value of 0 and a maximum value of 1, was applied.

4.3 AE-LSTM Classifier

LSTM is a variant of the recurrent neural network specialized for processing sequential data such as time series data. LSTM can capture long-term dependencies and patterns of data by selectively forgetting or remembering information. LSTM is a suitable model for processing time series data because a combination of input data, memory cells, and gates can identify long-term temporal dependencies and patterns of data. In addition, using AI in an anomaly detection system, abnormal behavior can be determined in depth by learning control system network traffic characteristics (sequences, average values, temporary-related data). For this reason, we developed an AE-LSTM-based anomaly detection system. For the anomaly detection model learning the characteristics of the input data, the encoder is a stacked bidirectional LSTM, and the decoder is designed as a one-way LSTM model. An encoder takes consecutive packet data as input, and the decoder is trained to output identical data. The encoder is m-1(x_(t-m) ~ x_(t-1)) consecutive packet data are received as input, and the decoder is trained to output the same data. For the purpose of learning to detect actual abnormal behavior, the input of the encoder is used equally. After that, when a difference between the value predicted by the encoder and the actual observed value of x_t occurs above the threshold, it is detected as abnormal behavior.

5   Evaluation

5.1   Dataset Description

Table 3. Feature list used to learn and validate anomaly detection models

Feature List
'flow ID', 'source IP', 'destination IP', 'source port', 'destination port', 'duration', 'TotalFwdPkts', 'TotalBwdPkts', 'TotLenfwdDL', 'TotLenfwdTR', 'TotLenfwdAPP', 'TotLenbwdDL', 'TotLenbwdTR', 'TotLenbwdAPP', 'DLfwdPktLenMAX', 'DLfwdPktLenMIN', 'DLfwdPktLenMEAN', 'DLfwdPktLenSTD', 'TRfwdPktLenMAX', 'TRfwdPktLenMIN', 'TRfwdPktLenMEAN', 'TRfwdPktLenSTD', 'APPfwdPktLenMAX', 'APPfwdPktLenMIN', 'APPfwdPktLenMEAN', 'APPfwdPktLenSTD', 'DLbwdPktLenMAX', 'DLbwdPktLenMIN', 'DLbwdPktLenMEAN', 'DLbwdPktLenSTD', 'TRbwdPktLenMAX', 'TRbwdPktLenMIN', 'TRbwdPktLenMEAN', 'TRbwdPktLenSTD', 'APPbwdPktLenMAX', 'APPbwdPktLenMIN', 'APPbwdPktLenMEAN', 'APPbwdPktLenSTD', 'DLflowBytes/sec', 'TRflowBytes/sec', 'APPflowBytes/sec', 'FlowPkts/sec', 'FlowIAT_MEAN', 'FlowIAT_STD', 'FlowIAT_MAX', 'FlowIAT_MIN', 'TotalFwdIAT', 'fwdIAT_MEAN', 'fwdIAT_STD', 'fwdIAT_MAX', 'fwdIAT_MIN', 'TotalBwdIAT', 'bwdIAT_MEAN', 'bwdIAT_STD', 'bwdIAT_MAX', 'bwdIAT_MIN', 'DLfwdHdrLen', 'TRfwdHdrLen', 'APPfwdHdrLen', 'DLbwdHdrLen', 'TRbwdHdrLen', 'APPbwdHdrLen', 'fwdPkts/sec', 'bwdPkts/sec', 'DLpktLenMEAN', 'DLpktLenMIN', 'DLpktLenMAX', 'DLpktLenSTD', 'DLpktLenVAR', 'TRpktLenMEAN', 'TRpktLenMIN', 'TRpktLenMAX', 'TRpktLenSTD', 'TRpktLenVAR', 'APPpktLenMEAN', 'APPpktLenMIN', 'APPpktLenMAX', 'APPpktLenSTD', 'APPpktLenVAR', 'ActiveMEAN', 'ActiveSTD', 'ActiveMAX', 'ActiveMIN', 'IdleMEAN', 'IdleSTD', 'IdleMAX', 'IdleMIN', 'frameSrc', 'frameDst', 'TotPktsInFlow', 'mostCommonREQ_FUNC_CODE', 'mostCommonRESP_FUNC_CODE', 'deviceTroubleFragments', 'pktsFromMASTER', 'pktsFromSLAVE'

The dataset used in this paper is the DNP 3.0 intrusion detection dataset [14], which is related to nine DNP 3.0 protocol network attacks (Common Network Control) in the DNP 3.0 environment due to a lack of security risk types and authentication mechanisms, plain text communication, and inappropriate behavior detection. The types of attacks included in the dataset are shown in Table 4. The dataset contains DNP 3.0 flow statistics (CSV format). In this work, we used data generated by converting packets collected every 45 s among the data provided by the data set into DNP 3.0 flow statistics.

Table 4. Attack Types Included in "DNP3 Intrusion Detection Dataset"

Risk Type	Description
Disable Unsolicited Message Attack	This attack targets a DNP3 outstation/slave, establishing a connection with it while acting as a master station. The false master then transmits a packet with the DNP3 Function Code 21, which requests to disable all the unsolicited messages on the target
Cold Restart Attack	The malicious entity acts as a master station and sends a DNP3 packet that includes the "Cold Restart" function code. When the target receives this message, it initiates a complete restart and sends back a reply with the time window before the restart process
Warm Restart Attack	This attack is similar to the "Cold Restart Message" but aims to trigger a partial restart, re-initiating a DNP3 service on the target outstation
Enumerate Attack	This reconnaissance attack aims to discover which DNP3 services and functional codes are used by the target system
Info Attack	This attack constitutes another reconnaissance attempt, aggregating various DNP3 diagnostic information related the DNP3 usage
Initialization Attack	This cyberattack is related to Function Code 15 (Initialize Data). It is an unauthorized access attack, which demands from the slave to reinitialize possible configurations to their initial values, thus changing potential values defined by legitimate masters
MITM-DoS Attack	In this cyberattack, the cyberattack is placed between a DNP3 master and a DNP3 slave device, dropping all the messages coming from the DNP3 master or the DNP3 slave
Replay Attack	This cyberattack replays DNP3 packets coming from a legitimate DNP3 master or DNP3 slave
Stop Application Attack	This attack is related to Function Code 18 (Stop Application) and demands the slave stop its function so that the slave cannot receive messages from the master

Table 3 shows a list of features used in the experiment. The dataset contains 102 functions, including 'Flow ID,' 'Source IP,' 'Target IP,' and 'Source Port.' In this work, correlation analysis was performed using Pearson correlation coefficients for all features to improve the efficiency and detection rate of the anomaly detection model. Ninety-five features were used for model learning and verification, excluding features with low correlation rates and features representing time series. The number of data used in the training and testing of anomaly detection systems used 10,000 normal data on the model train, 2,650 normal data for verification, and 300 abnormal data with the same distribution by attack type. Some intervals were selected within the normal data interval to insert abnormal data for verification and testing.

5.2 Experimental Setup

The AE-LSTM anomaly detection model designed in this experiment has an Auto-Encoder structure, including an LSTM layer. Input data first passes through the Convolutional 1D Layer with 512 nodes, passes through the Dense Layer with 128 nodes, and generates compressed data through the Bidirectional LSTM Layer with 64 nodes for data reduction. Subsequently, compressed data goes through the LSTM layer with 64 nodes, followed by the Dense Layer with 128 nodes contrary to the input order, and the Convolutional 1D Layer with 512 nodes. Afterward, the difference between the model-produced output and observed data is calculated using the mean squared error (MSE). If the difference value is more than a threshold value (when the precision and recall of the anomaly detection model are the same), it is detected as an anomaly.

5.3 Performance Index

Accuracy, True Positive Rate (TPR), False Positive Rate (FPR), and F-1 Score were used as metrics for measuring the performance of the anomaly detection model in this experiment. Accuracy is an indicator of whether the detection system correctly classifies normal data from collected data into normal data and abnormal data into abnormal data by defining the ratio of correctly classified data to the total data. TPR is the ratio of the number judged above divided by the total number of abnormal data. It is an evaluation index that evaluates how well the data to be detected has been found. FPR is an evaluation index that evaluates the proportion of normal events or behaviors that are misclassified as abnormal in a system. It is an evaluation index used to measure the overall accuracy of the F-1 Score model.

5.4 Experiment Result

Figure 3 shows the anomaly detection results over the DNP 3.0 network packet, the blue points in Fig. 3 mean normal data, and the orange point means anomalies. A straight red line indicates a threshold for detecting abnormal behavior. The threshold value was set to the value when the precision and recall of the anomaly detection model were the same. High precision means low false detection of normal data, and high reproducibility means low false detection of abnormal data [15]. Since these two performance indicators are generally in a trade-off relationship, we derived thresholds by considering the two indicators evenly without bias [16]. Figure 3-(A) is the result of anomaly detection without applying the moving average to the data, and Fig. 3-(B) is the result of anomaly detection by applying the moving average to the data. By applying the moving average to the data, it can be confirmed that abnormal data is highlighted, as shown in Fig. 3-(B), by smoothing the difference between the data predicted by the model and the observed data.

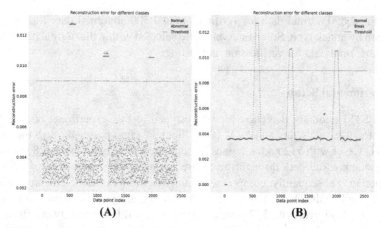

Fig. 3. (A) Anomaly detection results when moving average is not applied. (B) Anomaly detection results when moving average is applied.

Table 5. DNP 3.0 Target Classification Performance Comparison with Traditional Methods.

reference	dataset	method	ACC	TPR	FPR	F-1
Radoglou-Grammatikis et al. [5]	[6]	**Autoencoder**	0.951	1	0.098	0.953
V. Kelli et al. [7]	[13]	**DNN**	0.990	0.954	-	0.883
I. Siniosoglou et al. [8]	[6]	**GAN**	**0.994**	0.983	**0.003**	0.983
Our model	[13]	**AE-LSTM**	0.990	0.984	0.016	**0.990**

Table 5 shows the performance comparison between the AE-LSTM-based anomaly detection model presented in this paper and the abnormal behavior classification study targeting DNP 3.0 in the existing ICS/SCADA environment.

As a result of the experiment, the AE-LSTM-based anomaly detection model presented in this paper derived high performance of 99% accuracy, 98% TPR, 1.6% FPR, and 99% F-1 Score, and most of the performance is like or higher than that suggested in previous studies.

6   Conclusions and Future Research

This paper identified the security concerns of the communication over the DNP 3.0-based power system network, including EMS, by analyzing the current DNP 3.0-based communication environment with substations and power plants. To solve this, it was proposed to apply an AI-based anomaly detection system for EMS communication locations. The experimental results show that most cyber-attacks using DNP 3.0 protocol vulnerabilities can be detected when applying the anomaly detection system presented in this paper to EMS communication.

We shall study the application plan and considerations for the AI-based anomaly detection system for actual power systems in the near future.

Acknowledgements. This work was supported by Institute of Information & communications Technology Planning & Evaluation (IITP) grant funded by the Korea government (MSIT) (RS-2023–00241376, Development of security monitoring technology based network behavior against encrypted cyber threats in maritime environment).

References

1. Jae-guk, Y.: Energy management system (EMS) operation status and improvement plan. NARS Pending Rep. **157**, 1–141 (2016)
2. Ji Woong, J., Huy Kang, K.: A study on vulnerabilities of serial based DNP in power control fields. J. Korea Inst. Inf. Secur. Cryptol. **23**(6), 1143–1156 (2013)
3. New Mirai Variant Attacks Apache Struts Vulnerability, https://searchsecurity.techtarget.com/news/252448779/New-Mirai-variant-attacks-Apache-Struts-vulnerability. Accessed 09 June 2023
4. Kolias, C., Kambourakis, G., Stavrou, A., Voas, J.: DDoS in the IoT: Mirai and other botnets. Computer **50**(7), 80–84 (2016)
5. Radoglou Grammatikis, P., Sarigiannidis, P., Efstathopoulos, G., Karipidis P., Sarigiannidis, A.: DIDEROT: an intrusion detection and prevention system for dnp3-based SCADA systems. In: Proceedings of the 15th International Conference on Availability Reliability and Security, pp. 1–8, Association for Computing Machinery, Virtual Event Ireland (2020)
6. Rodofile, N., Radke, N., Foo E.: Framework for SCADA cyber-attack dataset creation. In: Proceedings of the Australasian Computer Science Week Multiconference, Association for Computing Machinery, USA, pp. 1–10 (2017)
7. Kelli, V.: Attacking and defending DNP3 ICS/SCADA systems. In: 2022 18th International Conference on Distributed Computing in Sensor Systems (DCOSS), pp. 183–190. IEEE, USA (2022)
8. Siniosoglou, I., Radoglou-Grammatikis, P., Efstathopoulos, G., Fouliras, P., Sarigiannidis, P.: A unified deep learning anomaly detection and classification approach for smart grid environments. IEEE Trans. Netw. Serv. Manage. **18**(2), 1137–1151 (2021)
9. Jungwook, K., Eui Young, S., Seung Hyun, K., Joong-Kyum, K., Yongbeum, Y.: 2021/22 KSP policy consultation report Czech republic smart systems resilience 4.0 for the Czech republic, Korea development institute, Korea (2022)
10. Pil Sung, W., Balho H, K.: Establishment of cyber security countermeasures amenable to the structure of power monitoring & control systems. Trans. Korean Inst. Electr. Eng. **67**(12), 1577–1586 (2018)
11. East, S., Butts, J., Papa, M., Shenoi, S.: A taxonomy of attacks on the dnp3 protocol. In: Palmer, C., Shenoi, S. (eds.) ICCIP 2009. IAICT, vol. 311, pp. 67–81. Springer, Heidelberg (2009). https://doi.org/10.1007/978-3-642-04798-5_5
12. DNP, DNP3 Application Note AN2013–004b Validation of Incoming DNP3 Data (2014)
13. Sungmoon, K., Hyung-uk, Y., Yi Sang, H., Shon, T.S.: DNP3 protocol security and attack detection method. J. Adv. Navig. Technol. **18**(4), 353–358 (2014)
14. Radoglou-Grammatikis, P., Kelli, V., Lagkas, T., Argyriou, V., Sarigiannidis, P.: DNP3 Intrusion Detection Dataset, IEEE Dataport (2022)

15. Razib, M., Javeed, D., Khan, M., Alkanhel, R., Muthanna, M.: Cyber Threats detection in smart environments using SDN-enabled DNN-LSTM hybrid framework. IEEE Access **10**, 53015–53026 (2022)
16. Sun, X., Houfeng, W.: Adjusting the precision-recall trade-off with align-and-predict decoding for grammatical error correction. In: Proceedings of the 60th Annual Meeting of the Association for Computational Linguistics, pp. 686–693. Computational Linguistics Dublin (2022)

Privacy and Management

Systematic Evaluation of Robustness Against Model Inversion Attacks on Split Learning

Hyunsik Na[1], Yoonju Oh[1], Wonho Lee[2], and Daeseon Choi[3]

[1] Department of Software, Graduate School of Soongsil University,
Seoul 07027, South Korea
{rnrud7932,ohyoonju}@soongsil.ac.kr
[2] Department of Software, Under-Graduate School of Soongsil University,
Seoul 07027, South Korea
james020907@naver.com
[3] Department of Software, Soongsil University, Seoul 07027, South Korea
sunchoi@ssu.ac.kr

Abstract. Split learning is a new training paradigm that divides a neural network into two parts and performs operations on the client and server, respectively. However, it does not directly transmit the client's original data to the server, and the intermediate features transmitted by the client allow an attacker to guess the original data via model inversion attacks. In this study, we conducted a quantitative evaluation to compare the performances of three existing defense technologies to prevent such threats to data privacy. For systematic experiments, we used two datasets and three target classification models and measured how well previous defenses maintained model accuracy and resisted model inversion attacks. Our results showed that Laplacian noise-based defense has little practical effect, NoPeekNN has a large performance variation, and differential privacy is somewhat helpful in defense; however, the larger the client-side model, the lower the task performance. Finally, further research is needed to overcome the limitations of previous defenses.

Keywords: Deep Neural Networks · Split Learning · Model Inversion Attack · Data Privacy Protection

1 Introduction

Society is demanding larger-scale AI owing to the development of 6G networks and AI industry, as well as the diversification of data and devices. Consequently, the cost of maintaining data storage and GPUs on a central server owned by a service provider is increasing exponentially. In addition, the requirement for network capacity to transmit vast amounts of data from users (or clients) continues to increase. Moreover, threats to data security may arise while transferring clients' data to the server, and infringements of data privacy may occur if the server uses or spies on the client's data improperly [2].

© The Author(s), under exclusive license to Springer Nature Singapore Pte Ltd. 2024
H. Kim and J. Youn (Eds.): WISA 2023, LNCS 14402, pp. 107–118, 2024.
https://doi.org/10.1007/978-981-99-8024-6_9

Split learning is one of the solution to the above problems. It divides DNNs into two parts to form a split neural network, which uses the first few layers as the client-side model and remaining layers as the server-side model. The client-side model calculates the data embedded in the local device to provide the server-side model with intermediate features. Subsequently, the server-side model calculates and outputs the results of the final task. Because the client and server share only intermediate features, they do not expose the client's original data. Moreover, the service provider's burden can be eased because the client's local device supports part of the model learning. However, some studies [6,9] still emphasize that data privacy can be compromised even in split learning environments. A server or client with a malicious intent can attempt a model inversion attack via intermediate features sent by the client (victim), which can reconstruct the original data form, thereby damaging the client.

In this study, we conducted quantitative experiments to evaluate the performance of previous defense technologies in preventing model inversion attacks in split learning environments. Most defense technologies experience a certain level of decline in task performance to protect data privacy and require additional time and computational costs. In addition, we question whether data privacy can be sufficiently protected because it still has a similar appearance to the original data despite the decrease in the quality of the reconstructed image that results from previous defenses. Therefore, we analyzed their actual effects through a model inversion attack according to hyperparameters of various defenses in the same environment under the ability of attackers to be stronger than the original papers of previous defense techniques. In addition, we observed whether the defenses could effectively protect data privacy at a level of model performance degradation acceptable to the service provider and users.

Contributions. Some studies have attempted to resist model inversion attacks by injecting noises [1,13] or minimizing distance correlation [14] in split learning scheme. However, it is not possible to directly compare the results of each defense approach across datasets and architectures from different studies. Our study addresses this limitation by performing experiments under equivalent experimental settings. We systematically compared the effects of previous defense approaches based on various datasets and model architectures. Moreover, we discuss the limitations of previous defense approaches, which are currently insufficient to respond to attacks.

2   Background

2.1   Split Learning

A split neural network f has a total of L layers, and the upper part of model $f_{1:l}$ is set to the client-side model f_{client} and lower part of model $f_{l:L}$ is set to the server-side model f_{server} based on any split point illustrated in Fig. 1(a). When we train f_{client} and f_{server}, the client sends intermediate features I_l to the server.

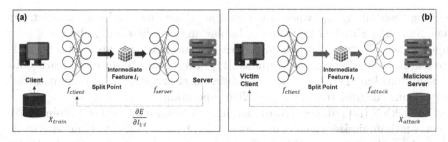

Fig. 1. (a): Split learning architecture with two parties. (b): Model inversion attack architecture.

The server then calculates the loss E between the model output and labels and provides gradients $\partial E / \partial I_l$ to the client for back-propagation. In addition, the client has an arbitrary training dataset X_{train} that is not accessible to the server. However, the server has sufficient knowledge of the domain, dimension, and size of the data because it is fully aware of the use of f. Finally, the client queries the test dataset X_{test} to learn f to perform the desired task.

2.2 Model Inversion Attacks

In a split learning scenario, an attacker who can attempt model inversion attacks may be a malicious server or client if the concept of a federated learning scenario is added. The attacker can build an inverse network f_{attack} to reconstruct a computed I_l using the victim client's training or test data as the original data $x \in X$. f_{attack} has a different structure than f_{client}, receives a vector of the same size as I_l as an input, and then outputs a vector of the same size and dimension as x. The attacker has an attack dataset X_{attack} that is different from X_{train} and X_{test} but similar to their distributions. The attacker can iteratively query X_{attack} at f_{client} and input the intermediate features received from f_{client} into f_{attack} to obtain a reconstructed image x_{recon}. The parameters of f_{attack} are updated by minimizing the error between X_{attack} and x_{recon}, and the attacker typically uses the L_2 distance function as an objective function. Namely, f_{attack} can be optimized by the following formula:

$$f_{attack} = minimize_{f_{attack}} \frac{1}{m} \sum_{i=1}^{m} ||f_{attack}(f_{client}(x_{attack_i})) - x_{attack_i}||_2^2 \quad (1)$$

An illustration of model inversion attacks is shown in Fig. 1(b).

2.3 Defenses Against Model Inversion Attacks

Approaches to improving resistance against model inversion attacks in split learning environments can be largely divided into two types: injecting noise and minimizing distance correlation. Among noise-based defenses, the Laplacian noise-based defense [13] injects noises into the intermediate features before sending them to f_{server}, where the noises are drawn from a Laplacian distribution. Similarly, Shredder [8] trained a Laplacian noise distribution by using noise injection as a learning process to reduce the information content of intermediate features. In addition, some studies [11] have been introduced to learn noise distributions based on the concept of differential privacy, which minimizes task performance degradation during gradient operations.

NoPeekNN [14] reduces reconstruction performance by further training a loss term, which minimizes the distance correlation between the input and intermediate features. Furthermore, B-SL [10] adds binarized activation within the model, which minimizes the distance correlation between the input and intermediate features as the goal of NoPeekNN. Otherwise, it reduces the computational costs with memory by applying a sign function to all model weights and adding batch normalization.

As mentioned above, various studies have aimed to defend against model inversion attacks in split learning environments; however, some studies have limitations in preventing vulnerabilities in the training phase. In this study, we focused on defense technologies that can counter attacks from a malicious server during the training and test stages and performed systematic evaluations on three defense technologies: Laplacian noise [13], NoPeekNN [14], and differential privacy [11].

3   Implementations of Previous Defense Approaches on Training Phase

3.1   Laplacian Noise

The authors of [13] injected random noise belonging to a Laplacian distribution before sending intermediate features to the server to counter model inversion attacks in a split learning environment. They experimented with a Laplacian distribution average μ of zero and noise scales σ of 0.1, 0.5, and 1.0. We applied a larger noise scale, such as $\sigma \in [1.0 : 6.0]$, to inject more noise than in the original study.

3.2   NoPeekNN

The authors of [14] added a distance correlation loss term to the training stage to induce maximum information on the original data to be left on the intermediate features when a client provides the vectors. They optimized it simultaneously with the commonly used cross-entropy loss term as follows:

$$loss_{nopeek} = \alpha \times (DCOR(x, I)) + CCE(y_{true}, y_{pred}) \tag{2}$$

where α represents scalar weights, and the intensity of the attacks may be adjusted accordingly. We analyzed the effectiveness of the attacks based on $\alpha \in [0.1 : 10000.0]$. Meanwhile, $DCOR$ is a distance correlation loss term between x and I, and CCE is a cross-entropy loss of the predicted class and ground-truth class, i.e., the original classification task loss term.

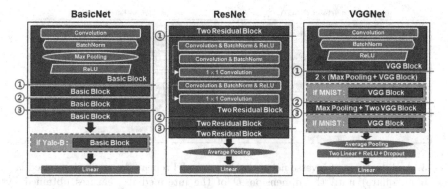

Fig. 2. Architectures of target classification models. The red lines represent split points.

3.3 Differential Privacy

Differential privacy was first introduced in [1]. They proposed differentially private stochastic gradient descent (DPSGD), which updates a model by clipping the gradient of each parameter calculated through a neural network and then injects some noises drawn from a Gaussian distribution into each clipped gradient. The gradient clipping and noise injection processes are as follows:

$$\overline{g}(x) \leftarrow g(x)/max(1, \frac{||g(x)||_2}{C})$$
$$\widetilde{g} \leftarrow \overline{g}(x) + \mathcal{N}(0, \sigma^2 C^2 \mathbf{I})$$

(3)

where $g(\cdot)$, C, and σ denote the gradient calculation, gradient norm bound, and noise scale, respectively. We fixed C at 1.0 and set σ as 1.3 or 3.0.

4 Experimental Settings

4.1 Datasets

We experimented on a handwritten digit classification task and face recognition task using the MNIST [3] and Yale-B [4] datasets. MNIST, which consists of ten classes of gray-scale images of size 28×28, contains 60,000 training data and 10,000 test data. Among them, 40,000 were set as training data, 10,000 were used as the attacker training dataset, and 5,000 were used as the attacker test dataset.

The Yale-B dataset is a gray-scale facial database of 38 subjects. Among them, we selected ten subjects and removed images that were so dark that it was difficult to identify their faces. Additionally, we resized each image to 64×64 size to increase the classification performance and doubled it with horizontal flipping. Subsequently, eight images for each subject were taken as a test dataset and the remainder as a training dataset, with 582 and 80 images, respectively. Additionally, some of the remaining data were used as the attacker training and test datasets with 490 and 100 images, respectively.

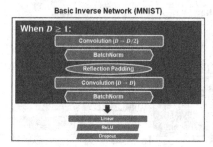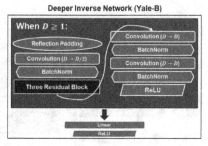

Fig. 3. Architectures of inverse networks. Each model repeated convolution-based layers (blue square) until the dimension D of the intermediate features obtained by attacker's data reached to 1 (Color figure online).

4.2   Target Classification Models

To experiment on the two datasets, we built three types of convolutional neural networks. Because the sizes of each dataset were 28×28 and 64×64, the depth of each model was stacked deeper in the Yale-B dataset. First, we built a "Basic-Net" consisting of four convolutional layers, a batch normalization layer, a max pooling layer, a leaky ReLU activation layer, and a linear layer in the bottom. Second, we formed a "ResNet"-based model with the addition of a residual block [5] and added one average pooling layer before the linear layer instead of the max pooling layers. Third, we modified a VGG-based architecture [12] to build a "VGGNet" that is deeper than Basicnet, with two additional linear layers. The architectures of the models are shown in Fig. 2, and their split points are separated into three parts. In Sect. 5, we denote each model along with its split points as '[model name] [split point]'.

When training the target models, we used an Adam optimizer [7] and set an initial learning rate of 0.005, which was reduced by 0.8 times for every 10 steps. In addition, the MNIST and Yale-B datasets were trained for 30 and 50 epochs, respectively, and the batch size was set to 64. The cross-entropy loss was minimized to optimize the model, and the model parameters with the smallest losses were used for the final trained model. In addition, VGGNet for classifying the Yale-B dataset was excluded from the experiments because it did not properly learn.

4.3   Inverse Models

The inverse models f_{attack} used by an attacker have different input values for each situation because the images in each dataset and intermediate features provided by the client-side model f_{client} are unequal in size. Therefore, convolutional layers were added until the dimension of the input intermediate features reached 1, as shown in Fig. 3, so that the final outputs were vectors of the same size as the original input images. The inverse models were trained for 100 epochs, and an Adam optimizer with a batch size of 64 was used. It had a learning rate of 0.001, with a reduction by 0.8 times for every 10 steps.

4.4 Evaluation Matrix

In general, defense techniques must satisfy two objectives: (1) maintainability of task performance and (2) resistance to attacks. In this study, the following evaluation indices were used to evaluate the extent to which each defense technique satisfied the two objectives.

Classification Accuracy. If defenses were applied in the model training and inference time, task performance was mostly reduced. We measured the classification accuracy to assess the ability to maintain task performance by calculating the cross-entropy, which can be formulated as

$$L_{acc} = \frac{1}{n} \sum_{i=1}^{n} CCE(f_{server}(f_{client}(x_i)), y_{true}) \tag{4}$$

where the lower L_{acc} is, the better the task is maintained.

L_2 Distance. To evaluate the ability of an attacker to reconstruct an input image, we first measured the Euclidean distance between the original and reconstructed images:

$$L_{l2} = \frac{1}{n} \sum_{i=1}^{n} (x_i - x_{recon})^2 \tag{5}$$

where the higher L_{l2} is, the better the defensive performance.

Structural Similarity. Structural Similarity (SSIM) [15] is a statistical value used to measure perceptual quality in terms of human color perception. It is expressed as

$$SSIM(A, B) = l(A, B) \times c(A, B) \times s(A, B) \tag{6}$$

where A and B are images in the spatial domain, and l, c, and s are the luminance, contrast, and structure comparisons, respectively. These can be calculated using the average μ and standard deviation σ of the two images as follows:

$$l(A, B) = \frac{2\mu_A\mu_B + c_1}{\mu_A^2 + \mu_B^2 + c_2}, \quad c(A, B) = \frac{2\sigma_{AB} + c_2}{\sigma_A^2 + \sigma_B^2 + c_2}, \quad s(A, B) = \frac{\sigma_{AB} + c_3}{\sigma_A\sigma_B + c_3} \tag{7}$$

where c_1, c_2, and c_3 are constraints. The lower $L_{SSIM} = \frac{1}{n}\sum_{i=1}^{n} SSIM(x_i, x_{recon})$ is, the better the defensive performance.

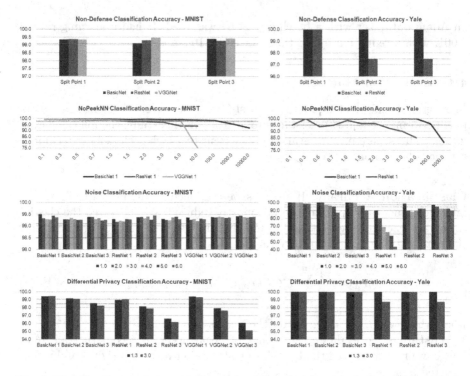

Fig. 4. Classification performance of models with each defense technique. The primary axis is classification accuracy (Color figure online).

Visualization. Finally, qualitative evaluations were performed using visualization. The lower the quality of x_{recon} and the more difficult it is to infer the original image through it, the better the defense approach. Note that when we attacked the Yale-B classification models, the number of data points for training the inverse model held by the attacker was only 490. Therefore, when attempting an attack, there is a possibility that it will be reconstructed as a person with a similar appearance (a person existing in the attacker's dataset), rather than a person with a complete original image. With reference to this point, we assumed that some data privacy would be exposed even when a person with a similar appearance was reconstructed.

5   Experimental Results

5.1   Classification Performance Evaluation

Figure 4 shows the performance results of the original task without defense and the degree to which the three defense technologies affect the classification. First, BasicNet, ResNet, and VGGNet achieved classification accuracies of more than 99.10% and 97.50% for the MNIST and Yale-B datasets, respectively, at three split points. We set this as the recommended Maginot Line (green line) for performance degradation. In addition, we assumed that the minimum Maginot Line (red line) with no problems performing the classification task was 98.5% and 95.0%, respectively.

First, it can be confirmed that the Laplacian noise-based defense maintains the classification accuracy above the green line, even if the noise scale is raised to 6.0 in the MNIST classification. In other words, there was little damage to the task performance. In contrast, the Yale-B classification showed a relatively sensitive performance degradation. The larger the noise scale, the greater the accuracy reduction. In particular, ResNet responds significantly to noise. Next, we tested the performance of NoPeekNN on the first split point of the three models. In general, accuracy decreased as the weight α of the distance correlation loss increased. When classifying MNIST, BasicNet 1, ResNet 1, and VGGNet 1 fell below the red line when $\alpha = 10.0, 1.5$, and 2.0 or higher, respectively. However, a relatively high α could be allowed for the Yale-B classification. When BasicNet 1 and ResNet 1 had $\alpha = 10,000$ and 3.0 or higher, respectively, the accuracy fell below the red line.

Finally, the greater the noise scale σ, the lower the accuracy when we adopt differential privacy. In the MNIST classification, the application of $\sigma = 3.0$ to the BasicNet 3 model fell short of the minimum Maginot Line of the task, and ResNet and VGGNet maintained their performance only when the split point was 1. When applying differential privacy in split learning, the parameters updated by gradients with added noise were limited to the client-side model. In other words, when the split point was located at the bottom of the model, the parameters affected by noise increased significantly. Therefore, we can conclude that the desired result has been obtained. In addition, we observed that the application of differential privacy did not significantly affect task performance in the case of Yale-B classification.

5.2   Data Privacy Evaluation

We evaluated the performance of model inversion attacks for each model based on the inverse model f_{attack} in Sect. 4.3. In MNIST and Yale-B classifications, we set 10,000 and 490 attacker training data sizes and tested the attack performance using 10,000 and 80 test data, respectively. Most importantly, for BasicNet 1, ResNet 1, and VGGNet 1 (Only MNIST) without defense technology, attacks on MNIST classification generated reconstructed images with L_2 distances of 0.0241, 0.0271, and 0.0251, respectively, and 0.0272 and 0.0319 for the Yale-B classification. In addition, the SSIM was 0.7999, 0.7627, and 0.7969 for MNIST classification and 0.3681 and 0.2660 for Yale-B classification. These values are shown in Fig. 5 as the green line (L_2) and red line (SSIM), respectively.

In Fig. 5, the injection of Laplacian noise into all models up to the noise scale σ 6.0 did not improve L_2 or SSIM. That is, it can be confirmed that the defense performance did not improve for MNIST classification. However, the Yale-B classification can hinder reconstruction to some extent. In addition, we observed that a person different from the original image was reconstructed in Fig. 6. NoPeekNN

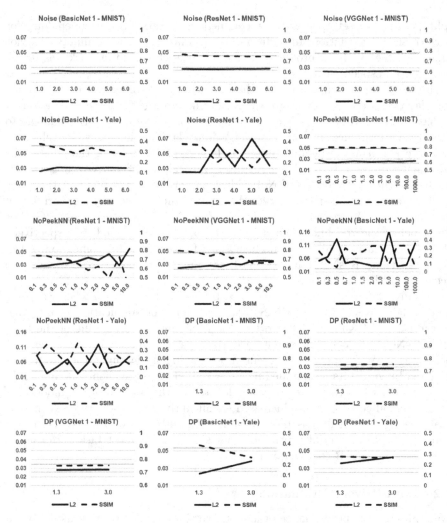

Fig. 5. Quality of the reconstructed images for each defense technique. The horizontal axis represents noise scale or weight for NoPeekNN loss. The primary axis represents L_2 distance, and the auxiliary axis shows the SSIM value.

was able to improve the resistance against attacks in general, except with the MNIST classification model using BasicNet 1. When NoPeekNN was applied to the Yale-B classification model, the defense performance according to the weight α was not enhanced linearly. Because this technology is applied to training loss and gradually improves robustness according to iterative training, there may be variations between training. In other words, it is necessary to pay attention to the training settings, such as the hyperparameter settings. Nevertheless, this induced difficulty in identifying the subject in the original image, as shown in Fig. 6 according to some α. Finally, differential privacy did not affect MNIST

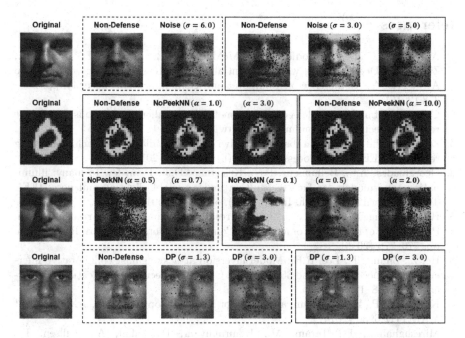

Fig. 6. Visualization of reconstructed images according to each defense. The square of solid lines represents BasicNet 1, the square of dotted lines represents ResNet 1, and the square of double lines represents VGGNet 1.

classification. However, in the Yale-B classification model, the larger the noise scale, the more positive the defense. Looking at the corresponding reconstructed images in Fig. 6, when the noise scale $\sigma = 3.0$ was applied to each of the two models, the image was reconstructed as a person different from the original.

6 Conclusion

In this study, we systematically evaluated three approaches to defend against model inversion attacks in the split learning scheme. As a result, the Laplacian noise-based method had limitations in responding to attacks, and NoPeekNN had a very large variation in training and requires careful tuning of the defenders. In addition, differential privacy is limited because it is difficult to maintain the model performance depending on the split point. An interesting future work is to explore an advanced defense mechanism to resolve the limitations of previous works mentioned in this study.

Acknowledgements. This work was supported by Institute of Information & communications Technology Planning & Evaluation (IITP) grant funded by the Korea government(MSIT) (No. 2021-0-00511, Robust AI and Distributed Attack Detection for Edge AI Security).

References

1. Abadi, M., Chu, A., Goodfellow, I., McMahan, H.B., Mironov, I., Talwar, K., Zhang, L.: Deep learning with differential privacy. In: Proceedings of the 2016 ACM SIGSAC Conference on Computer and Communications Security, pp. 308–318 (2016)
2. Chang, L., et al.: 6g-enabled edge AI for metaverse: challenges, methods, and future research directions. J. Commun. Inf. Netw. **7**(2), 107–121 (2022)
3. Deng, L.: The MNIST database of handwritten digit images for machine learning research. IEEE Signal Process. Mag. **29**(6), 141–142 (2012)
4. Georghiades, A.S., Belhumeur, P.N., Kriegman, D.J.: From few to many: illumination cone models for face recognition under variable lighting and pose. IEEE Trans. Pattern Anal. Mach. Intell. **23**(6), 643–660 (2001)
5. He, K., Zhang, X., Ren, S., Sun, J.: Deep residual learning for image recognition. In: Proceedings of the IEEE Conference on Computer Vision and Pattern Recognition, pp. 770–778 (2016)
6. He, Z., Zhang, T., Lee, R.B.: Model inversion attacks against collaborative inference. In: Proceedings of the 35th Annual Computer Security Applications Conference, pp. 148–162 (2019)
7. Kingma, D.P., Ba, J.: Adam: a method for stochastic optimization. arXiv preprint arXiv:1412.6980 (2014)
8. Mireshghallah, F., Taram, M., Ramrakhyani, P., Jalali, A., Tullsen, D., Esmaeilzadeh, H.: Shredder: learning noise distributions to protect inference privacy. In: Proceedings of the Twenty-Fifth International Conference on Architectural Support for Programming Languages and Operating Systems, pp. 3–18 (2020)
9. Pasquini, D., Ateniese, G., Bernaschi, M.: Unleashing the tiger: inference attacks on split learning. In: Proceedings of the 2021 ACM SIGSAC Conference on Computer and Communications Security, pp. 2113–2129 (2021)
10. Pham, N.D., Abuadbba, A., Gao, Y., Phan, T.K., Chilamkurti, N.: Binarizing split learning for data privacy enhancement and computation reduction. IEEE Trans. Inf. Forensics Secur. **18**, 3088–3100 (2023)
11. Ryu, J., et al.: Can differential privacy practically protect collaborative deep learning inference for IoT? Wireless Netw. 1–21 (2022)
12. Simonyan, K., Zisserman, A.: Very deep convolutional networks for large-scale image recognition. arXiv preprint arXiv:1409.1556 (2014)
13. Titcombe, T., Hall, A.J., Papadopoulos, P., Romanini, D.: Practical defences against model inversion attacks for split neural networks. arXiv preprint arXiv:2104.05743 (2021)
14. Vepakomma, P., Singh, A., Gupta, O., Raskar, R.: NoPeek: information leakage reduction to share activations in distributed deep learning. In: 2020 International Conference on Data Mining Workshops (ICDMW), pp. 933–942. IEEE (2020)
15. Wang, Z., Bovik, A.C., Sheikh, H.R., Simoncelli, E.P.: Image quality assessment: from error visibility to structural similarity. IEEE Trans. Image Process. **13**(4), 600–612 (2004)

Vulnerability Assessment Framework Based on In-The-Wild Exploitability for Prioritizing Patch Application in Control System

Seong-Su Yoon, Do-Yeon Kim, Ga-Gyeong Kim, and Ieck-Chae Euom[✉]

System Security Research Center, Chonnam National University, Gwangju, Republic of Korea
skymoonight@jnu.ac.kr, iceuom@chonnam.ac.kr

Abstract. With the increasing understanding of attackers towards the characteristics of control systems and the growing connectivity with information technology, security incidents targeting control systems are on the rise. The number of vulnerabilities related to these incidents are increasing every year, making it impossible to apply timely patches for all vulnerabilities. The current common vulnerability assessment framework, which is considered the basis for vulnerability patching, has limitations in that it does not consider the weaponization after vulnerability discovery and does not adequately reflect the exploitability in real-world "in-the-wild" environments. Therefore, in this study, we propose an approach to evaluate the in-the-wild exploitability and risk of vulnerabilities occurring in control systems based on publicly available data. To achieve this, we define criteria for classifying attacker skill levels and improve the existing CVSS metrics by introducing new factors for evaluating exploitability and risk. By applying this evaluation approach, we can identify vulnerabilities in control systems that are likely to be exploited in real-world scenarios, enabling prioritized patching and proactive defense against advanced persistent threat (APT) attacks.

Keywords: Vulnerability Assessment · Exploitability · Exploit Code Maturity · Ease of Exploit · CVSS · ICS-CERT

1 Introduction

Industrial Control Systems (ICS) are systems that monitor and control the operational process of critical national infrastructure and industrial processes, widely used in power generation, electricity, gas, refining, and petrochemical fields. Therefore, timely patching based on vulnerability risk assessments is crucial to prevent national losses due to cyberattacks.

However, the current Common Vulnerability Scoring System (CVSS) base score, which serves as the standard for vulnerability patching, does not consider temporal factors. As a result, while the post-attack severity is evaluated as an impact index, the risk of current exploitation is not assessed [1]. The temporal score is only performed limitedly by the manufacturers of individual digital assets, and the evaluated score tends to decrease rather than reflect the urgency by reducing the existing evaluated base score [2].

Security professionals in IT, OT, and ICS rely on basic vulnerability scores for patch management. However, these scores overlook the temporal aspect, specifically the weaponization of vulnerabilities. As a result, the present-time exploitation potential remains unassessed, despite evaluating the impact after an attack.

ICS plays a critical role in monitoring and controlling operational processes in national infrastructure facilities and industrial settings. However, maintaining facility availability poses challenges, making it difficult to promptly address newly disclosed vulnerabilities or vulnerabilities exploited during operations.

This paper aims to evaluate vulnerability risk within the operational life cycle of control systems by considering the evolving capabilities and exploitability of attackers. Furthermore, it proposes a new metric for assessing exploitability based on existing vulnerability and exploit information sources and suggests a method for combining this with existing risk assessment metrics.

2 Scoring System of Vulnerability

2.1 Common Vulnerability Scoring System, CVSS

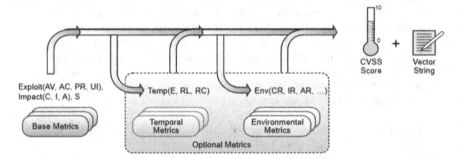

Fig. 1. CVSS scoring method

CVSS provides an open framework for conveying the impact and characteristics of vulnerabilities [3]. It defines three evaluation groups: the base metric, which represents the static attribute information of vulnerabilities; the temporal metric, which captures the characteristics of vulnerabilities that change over time; and the environmental metric, which reflects the characteristics of vulnerabilities considering the user environment.

The scoring methodology of CVSS follows the structure shown in Fig. 1, where a risk rating from 0 to 10 is calculated based on exploitability, impact, and scope for the base score. Depending on the objective, it is possible to calculate a vulnerability severity score by including the temporal score and environmental score calculation formulas.

However, CVSS evaluates the severity solely based on the attribute information of vulnerabilities and does not consider the weaponization that occurs after their discovery. This limitation prevents a comprehensive assessment of exploitability and risk, leading to an incomplete evaluation.

2.2 Exploit Prediction Scoring System, EPSS

CVEs with shifting EPSS scores

EPSS scores can shift around because of new information (e.g CPE data is available now, an exploit is published, etc)

CVE-2022-46631 70.1% +64.8%	CVE-2021-31170 60.4% +46.4%	CVE-2020-17127 2.9% -35.4%	CVE-2020-17156 2.9% -35.4%	CVE-2018-8432 33.3% -15.2%	CVE-2009-2497 48.1% +11.5%
CVE-2022-46634 70.1% +64.8%	CVE-2021-31188 49.2% +37.0%	CVE-2020-17129 2.9% -35.4%	CVE-2020-17159 2.9% -35.4%	CVE-2004-0480 80.1% -13.7%	CVE-2006-3226 16.8% +11.0%
CVE-2020-17124 4.4% -59.1%	CVE-2020-17122 2.9% -35.4%	CVE-2020-17148 2.9% -35.4%	CVE-2023-29084 18.4% -21.7%	CVE-2020-17144 25.3% -11.9%	CVE-2022-35713 1.2% -10.4%
CVE-2020-17125 4.4% -59.1%	CVE-2020-17123 2.9% -35.4%	CVE-2020-17150 2.9% -35.4%	CVE-2006-3227 44.8% +21.2%	CVE-2009-0091 48.1% +11.5%	CVE-2012-0002 79.7% +10.2%

Fig. 2. EPSS Scores

EPSS (Exploit Prediction Scoring System) is an evaluation framework used to predict exploitability, aiming to assess the likelihood of a vulnerability being exploited in advance [4]. It utilizes artificial intelligence technologies to analyze the characteristics of vulnerabilities, publicly available exploit code, previous attack cases, exploit patterns, and more, quantifying the exploitability for each vulnerability as shown in Fig. 2 and assigning prioritization based on the exploitability. EPSS provides predicted exploit probabilities for the currently known 204,563 vulnerabilities.

The existing CVSS primarily focuses on evaluating the static elements of discovered vulnerabilities and does not consider post-discovery weaponization information. Additionally, it fails to adequately reflect detailed exploitability and risk by scoring vulnerabilities with generalized metrics, thus lacking the ability to sufficiently represent real-world exploitability in In-the-wild environments.

EPSS overcomes these limitations of CVSS by considering dynamic exploitability and predicting exploit probabilities through a combination of real-world data and technical analysis. It takes into account the evolving nature of vulnerabilities and provides a more comprehensive assessment of exploitability.

3 Related Works

Several studies have assessed vulnerability severity by utilizing publicly available vulnerability and exploit information.

Jung et al. [5] defined evaluation criteria for the "exploit code maturity" attribute of CVSS's temporal metric using reference URLs and tag information from publicly available vulnerabilities. They automated the evaluation and prioritized patches based on scores, aiming to leverage contextual information on exploit ease. However, the evaluated scores only reduce severity and lack the ability to track vulnerability weaponization levels.

Singh et al. [6] calculated CVSS's temporal metric scores using exploit code maturity and patch level information derived from vulnerability data. They used these scores, along with base metric information, to calculate exploit frequency and estimate quantitative security risk. However, the criteria for judging exploit code maturity lack standardization and heavily rely on empirical judgment.

Bulut et al. [1] introduced three attributes - Weaponized Exploit (WX), Utility, and Opportune - to assess vulnerability exploitability. They evaluated these attributes using reference links in Exploit DB, Metasploit, GitHub, and expert judgment. These attributes were included as additional weighting factors in severity score calculation, altering the severity values. However, relying on expert judgment hinders consistent evaluations and lacks clear criteria for quantifying risk scores. Moreover, existing studies neglect vulnerabilities in operational technology (OT) and industrial control system (ICS) environments, failing to capture real-world exploitability. Table 1 classifies these studies based on research characteristics, highlighting their limitations.

Table 1. Characteristics of studies related to vulnerability exploitability evaluation

Paper	Evaluation Attribute		Domain		
	Weaponization Level	Exploitability	IT	OT	ICS
Jung. B et al. [5]	O	X	O	X	X
Singh. U.K et al. [6]	O	X	O	X	X
Bulut et al. [1]	O	X	O	X	X

4 In-The-Wild Risk Assessment Method for Vulnerabilities

In this study, considering the operational environment of control systems and the limitations of CVSS and existing related research, this study proposes an evaluation approach to assess the risk of vulnerabilities based on the attacker's skill level and the likelihood of exploitation within a specified time frame. Figure 3 illustrates the overall process of in-the-wild risk score (WRS) assessment study conducted in this research.

4.1 Evaluate Attacker Skill Level and Likelihood of Exploiting In-The-Wild Vulnerabilities

This study defines classification criteria for assessing the skill level of attackers in control systems based on exploit code maturity. The relevant evaluation metrics are defined as 'Not Defined', 'Unproven', 'Proof of Concept', 'Functional', and 'High', which correspond to the time elements in the existing CVSS. To overcome the lack of consistency in defining classification criteria across organizations, which results in different assessments, objective criteria based on publicly available data from vulnerability and exploit sources were established.

Collecting Vulnerability/Exploit Data. The data utilized in this study can be classified into two categories: vulnerability-related and exploit-related data. Firstly, the vulnerability data consists of Common Vulnerabilities and Exposures (CVE) [7] and Common Platform Enumeration (CPE) [8] provided by the National Vulnerability Database (NVD), as well as Common Weakness Enumeration (CWE) [9] and Common Attack

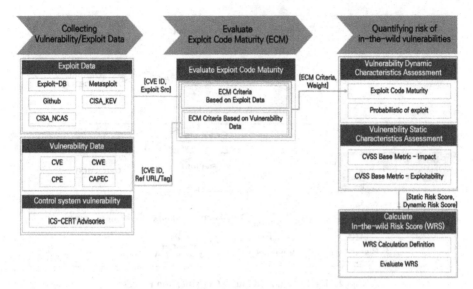

Fig. 3. In-the-wild risk score (WRS) assessment process

Pattern Enumeration and Classification (CAPEC) [10] provided by MITRE. As standardized sources of information for vulnerabilities occurring in operational technology and industrial control system environments, ICS-CERT advisories [11] provided by the Cybersecurity and Infrastructure Security Agency (CISA) offer insights into vulnerability types occurring in these environments and enable the establishment of assessment approaches considering them.

Secondly, for exploit code maturity classification and severity assessment considering operational technology and industrial control system environments, the exploit data includes Exploit-DB [12] and Github [13], which provide information corresponding to Proof of Concept (PoC) level used in previous studies. For Functional-level information, CISA provides Known Exploited Vulnerability (KEV) information [14], which offers details about vulnerabilities that have been actually exploited, and the National Cyber Awareness System (NCAS) [15] provides information on security issues, vulnerabilities, and exploits occurring in national-level infrastructure and Advanced Persistent Threat (APT) groups. Lastly, for High-level information, Rapid7's Metasploit [16] provides automated attack module information for vulnerabilities.

Each piece of collected vulnerability information has associations based on specific attribute information, whereas exploit information is linked to vulnerability information based on the source vulnerability identifier CVE.

Evaluation of the Exploit Code Maturity (ECM). The maturity of exploit codes, which is also an evaluation attribute of the existing CVSS temporal score, has been classified based on each organization's own criteria without standardized classification criteria. In this study, we defined classification criteria from two perspectives: the collected vulnerability information source and the exploit information source (Fig. 4).

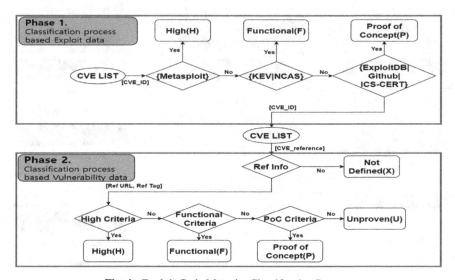

Fig. 4. Exploit Code Maturity Classification Process

Classification Criteria Based on Exploit Sources. The classification criteria of exploit code maturity based on exploit information were defined according to the level of vulnerability weaponization information provided, similar to earlier studies. CVE information included in Metasploit, which provides an automated module for penetration testing, is classified as 'High' among indicators of exploit code maturity, while CVE information included in CISA's KEV and NCAS, which provides vulnerability information that has been exploited in real-world environments, is classified as 'Functional'. Additionally, CVE information included in Exploit-DB and Github, which provides PoC information for verifying the feasibility of an attack, is classified as 'Proof of Concept' among indicators of attack code maturity. Furthermore, based on the characteristics of industrial control system operation, which considers the vulnerability itself as a risk factor, ICS-CERT information was included in the 'Proof of Concept' classification criteria. Table 2 shows the defined criteria for classifying exploit information based on the exploit information source.

Table 2. Classification Criteria Based on Exploit Sources

Exploit Code Maturity	Classification Criteria
High	{Metasploit}
Functional	{KEV I NCAS}
Proof of Concept	{ExploitDB I Github I ICS-CERT}

Classification Criteria Based on Vulnerability Sources. The classification criteria based on vulnerability information were defined to classify the attack code maturity of CVEs that do not have any associated exploit information or newly discovered CVEs. In order to achieve this, an associated analysis of CVE-Exploit information sources was performed on the URL and tag information that make up the CVE reference information. The relevant reference information was based on the 'cve_references' field information, which provides URLs containing recommendations, patch information, exploitation information, and analysis reports related to vulnerabilities, as well as tag information for each reference content.

The reference URLs used for the analysis included 13,307 out of a total of 204,563 CVEs, and the corresponding tag information consisted of 18 tags. The CVE-Exploit association analysis for defining the classification criteria was carried out through statistical analysis of reference URLs and tag frequency for all CVEs and CVEs with existing exploit information. The existing exploit information for CVEs included 26,329 at the PoC level, 2,658 at the Functional level, and 4,236 at the High level.

The statistical analysis of URL information is based on URL information included in CVEs that are mapped to exploit information. The URL information extracted at each level measures the discovery frequency in the corresponding attack code maturity CVE group. Next, the tag information statistical analysis is performed with both independent tags and tag combinations. Exploit information-associated CVEs are extracted for each attack code maturity level, along with their tags and tag combinations. Then, tag and tag combination discovery frequencies are measured for each level of CVEs. Based on the URL analysis results, URLs providing weaponization information with a probability of 25% or more for each level were selected as classification criteria after eliminating duplicates. The tag analysis results selected the top discovery frequency independent tags and tag combinations for each level as classification criteria. Additionally, to classify common top tags and tag combinations such as 'Vendor Advisory' and 'Third Party Advisory', additional URL classification criteria were selected based on connection information with the CVE Numbering Authority (CNA). Furthermore, considering operational technology and industrial control system environments, URL information connected to 'US Government Resource,' a unique top tag in PoC level CVEs, was added as a classification criterion for CNA-LR (CVE Numbering Authority of Last Resort) [17], which assigns CVE IDs for vulnerabilities in fields beyond the scope of traditional CNA roles, such as industrial control systems and medical equipment. Table 3 shows the final vulnerability information-based classification criteria.

Table 3. Classification criteria based on vulnerability information

Exploit Code Maturity	Classification Criteria
High	{CNA(Vendor/Products, Vulnerability Researcher) Link & (['Exploit', 'Third Party Advisory', 'VDB Entry'] Tag)}
Functional	{CNA(Vendor/Products, Vulnerability Researcher) Link & ['Third Party Advisory', 'VDB Entry']}| {'packetstormsecurity' Link}

(continued)

Table 3. (*continued*)

Exploit Code Maturity	Classification Criteria
Proof of Concept	{CNA-LR & (['Exploit'] l 'US Government Resource' Tag)}l{'securityfocus' l 'xforce.ibmcloud' l 'exploit-db' l 'securitytracker' l 'secunia.com' l 'osvdb.org' Link}
Unproven	Not satisfy any rules above
Undefined	Unable to obtain information

4.2 Quantifying Risk of In-The-Wild Vulnerabilities

We evaluated the vulnerability risk by assigning a weight (1–5) across five categories representing the attacker's skill level in terms of exploit code maturity. We aimed to increase the severity score considering both the probabilistic of exploit (PoE) and the attacker's skill level. In this calculation, we utilized the EPSS, which takes into account the risk and urgency of vulnerability exploitation within 30 days, in order to leverage probabilistic numeric information.

The ease of exploitation (EoE) quantifies the actual exploitability and feasibility by considering the attacker's skill level and vulnerability exploitation trends. By integrating the attacker's skill level and the probabilistic in-the-wild exploitability, this approach surpasses the limitations of the existing CVSS, allowing score to exceed the conventional limit of 10 points. This comprehensive approach provides insights into the actual risk and urgency of the vulnerabilities, taking into account both the availability of exploits over time and static and dynamic characteristics of the vulnerabilities.

This paper devised in-the-wild risk score (WRS) calculation formula. The calculation formula calculates a score between 0 and 15 by applying the exploitability derived in this paper to the existing CVSS base score formula. In the calculation formula, Imp indicates the impact score of the base score, Exp denotes the exploitability score of the base score, and the calculation formulas for EoE and WRS are as follows:

$$EOE = PoE(cve\_id) * ECM(cve\_id) \tag{1}$$

$$WRS_{(S=U)} = Imp(cve\_id) + Exp(cve\_id) + EoE \tag{2}$$

$$WRS_{(S=C)} = 1.08 * [Imp(cve\_id) + Exp(cve\_id) + EoE] \tag{3}$$

4.3 Case Study

Using CVSS(v3.1) scores, we evaluated EoE for 4,180 CVEs available in CISA ICS-CERT Advisories. Identifying CVEs with CVSS at 7.0 or higher for each percentile range of EoE values calculated between 1 and 5, 58 CVEs had an EoE score at 1.25 or higher, accounting for about 2% of the total vulnerabilities. This suggests that when considering the exploitation probability based on the attacker's skill level, the number of actual exploited vulnerabilities is significantly low. Figure 5 illustrates the distribution of high-risk vulnerabilities subject to exploitation according to EoE ranges. Consequently, instead of establishing patch strategies for numerous vulnerabilities, it enables an efficient patch strategy for a small number of high-risk vulnerabilities (Table 4).

Table 4. Number of CVEs by Ease of Exploitation (EoE)

Ease of Exploitation (EoE)	# of CVE
EoE < 1.25	2,722
1.25 ≤ EoE < 2.5	21
2.5 ≤ EoE < 3.75	14
3.75 ≤ EoE	23

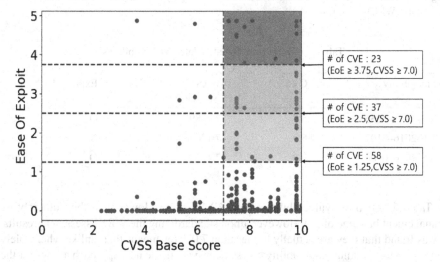

Fig. 5. Common vulnerability scoring system (CVSS) base score-ease of exploitation

We have conducted a WRS assessment that yields scores ranging from 0 to 15 for all CVEs, and in order to observe changes in score distribution compared to the existing CVSS, we have standardized the calculated WRS scores to a range of 0 to 10. Compared to the CVSS, which was predominantly focused on high scores, the risk stratification according to the dynamic characteristics of vulnerabilities, such as exploitability levels, has led to changes in score distribution, as illustrated in Fig. 6.

Additionally, by conducting a comparative analysis of the CVSS and standardized WRS scores based on the 7.0 assessment criterion for critical infrastructure vulnerabilities, We discovered that the number of previously managed vulnerabilities has decreased by approximately 98%, from 2,780 to 49.

Furthermore, we discovered that some vulnerabilities with originally low CVSS scores have higher WRS scores than those with high initial CVSS scores, as demonstrated

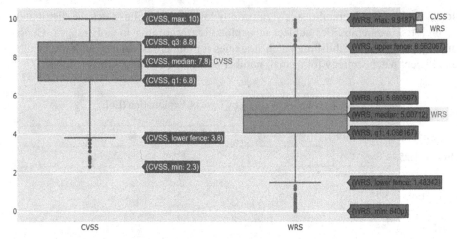

Fig. 6. Distribution of the common vulnerability scoring system (CVSS) score and in-the-wild risk score (WRS)

Table 5. Discovered Threat-Related Vulnerabilities

Vulnerability	CVSS	WRS (standardized)	Exploited
CVE-2015–7855	6.5	7.5689	O
CVE-2016–2107	5.9	7.1763	X
CVE-2016–0800	5.9	7.1292	O

in Table 5. All three vulnerabilities have CVSS scores lower than the vulnerability management baseline of 7.0. However, upon standardizing the WRS assessment results, it was found that they are actually higher than 7.0. This means that, unlike when solely relying on the existing vulnerability assessment system, the new approach allows for the identification of novel threats and potential threats.

In fact, among these three vulnerabilities, CVE-2016–0800, which has a CVSS score of 5.9, is still considered to be dangerous for aging servers and equipment using vulnerable protocols such as SSLv2 in control system environments. Furthermore, it has been exploited in campaigns by The Budworm espionage group specifically targeting government and multinational electronic product control systems.

As depicted in Fig. 7, we compared the effectiveness of CVSS and the proposed evaluation method WRS for 4180 vulnerabilities disclosed by ICS-CERT. Based on CISA's APT analysis report and threat information, 23 vulnerabilities used in exploit campaigns were identified out of 4180 vulnerabilities. When using CVSS scores 7.0 or higher as a criterion, only 14 out of 2780 CVEs were identified, yielding a coverage of about 60% and an identification efficiency of only about 0.5%. Conversely, when applying WRS normalization with a score of 10 (equivalent to CVSS 7.0), 49 CVEs were identified, with 16 being relevant. Coverage increased by about 9% compared to CVSS, and identification efficiency improved by about 32%.

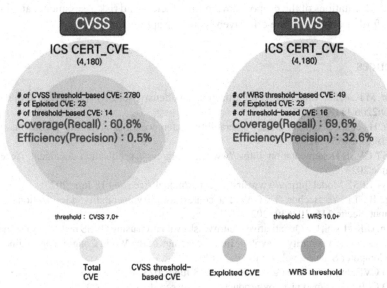

Fig. 7. Comparison of CVSS and WRS application results in terms of vulnerability exploitation identification

5 Conclusion

This paper highlights limitations in providing comprehensive severity information for control system vulnerabilities due to real-world constraints and shortcomings in existing CVSS and vulnerability assessment research. To address these limitations, we collected additional data on industrial control system vulnerabilities and APT attack information. We proposed a new metric called "ease of exploitation," which considers only the attacker's skill level among the static properties and dynamic characteristics of control system vulnerabilities that change over time. Furthermore, we have calculated a new indicator, WRS (in-the-wild risk score), which represents the risk of being exploited in an in-the-wild environment by combining this new metric with the existing vulnerability risk assessment formula. We applied this assessment to disclosed control system vulnerabilities and compared them to traditional CVSS-based prioritization strategies to determine that they can be effective in prioritizing defense against exploits and mitigating risk.

This study aims not only to identify vulnerabilities with a high likelihood of exploitation but also to consider the unique attributes of the vulnerabilities. By doing so, it enables defenders to comprehensively assess how easily the vulnerabilities can be exploited and what impacts they may have on the organization, thereby facilitating the establishment of effective defense systems.

For future work, we plan to identify the residual threats of vulnerabilities with proactive defense measures by considering patch information for vulnerabilities that are not currently taken into account. Additionally, we aim to conduct statistical analysis to address the limitations of the proposed weighting factors and risk assessment calculation formula, further enhancing the effectiveness of our approach.

References

1. Bulut, M.F., et al.: Vulnerability prioritization: an offensive security approach. arXiv preprint arXiv:2206.11182 (2022)
2. Yang, H., et al.: Better not to use vulnerability's reference for exploitability prediction. Appl. Sci. **10**(7), 2555 (2020)
3. FIRST CVSS Documentation. https://www.first.org/cvss/specification-document. Accessed 18 June 2023
4. FIRST EPSS Model. https://www.first.org/epss/model.Accessed 18 June 2023
5. Jung, B., Li, Y., Bechor, T.: CAVP: a context-aware vulnerability prioritization model. Comput. Secur. **116**, 102639 (2022)
6. Singh, U.K., Joshi, C.: Quantitative security risk evaluation using CVSS metrics by estimation of frequency and maturity of exploit. In: Proceedings of the World Congress on Engineering and Computer Science, vol. 1, pp. 19–21 (2016)
7. NVD CVE. https://nvd.nist.gov/. Accessed 18 June 2023
8. NVD CPE. https://nvd.nist.gov/products/cpe. Accessed 18 June 2023
9. MITRE CWE. https://cwe.mitre.org/. Accessed 18 June 2023
10. NVD CAPEC. https://capec.mitre.org/. Accessed 18 June 2023
11. CISA ICS-CERT Advisories. https://www.cisa.gov/uscert/ics/advisories?items_per_page=All. Accessed 18 June 2023
12. Exploit-DB. https://exploit-db.com. Accessed 18 June 2023
13. Github. https://github.com/nomi-sec/PoC-in-GitHub/. Accessed 18 June 2023
14. CISA. https://www.cisa.gov/known-exploited-vulnerabilities-catalog/. Accessed 18 June 2023
15. CISA. https://www.cisa.gov/uscert/ncas/alerts/. Accessed 18 June 2023
16. Rapid7. https://rapid7.com/. Accessed 18 June 2023
17. MITRE. https://www.cve.org/Program Organization/CNA s. Accessed 18 June 2023

Patchman: Firmware Update Delivery Service Over the Blockchain for IoT Environment

Yustus Eko Oktian[1,2], Uk Jo[3], Simon Oh[3], Hanho Jeong[3], Jaehyun Kim[3],
Thi-Thu-Huong Le[1,2], and Howon Kim[3(✉)]

[1] Blockchain Platform Research Center, Pusan National University,
Busan 609735, Republic of Korea
yustus@islab.re.kr
[2] IoT Research Center, Pusan National University,
Busan 609735, Republic of Korea
[3] School of Computer Science and Engineering, Pusan National University,
Busan 609735, Republic of Korea
{jouk,simon,hanho,jaehyun}@islab.re.kr, howonkim@pusan.ac.kr

Abstract. This paper proposes `Patchman`, a firmware binary delivery service for the Internet of Things ecosystem leveraging blockchain. When a new firmware patch is available, vendors make a bid in the smart contract for anyone to join as firmware distributors. For each successful delivery to targeted devices, distributors are rewarded with tokens. Meanwhile, devices gain a reputation score every time they successfully install an update. To ensure fairness, we develop secure exchange protocols using *proof-of-delivery* and *proof-of-installation*. Those proofs are verifiable in the blockchain. Therefore, the firmware update delivery can be executed safely without centralized third-party control.

Keywords: Firmware Update · Blockchain · IoT

1 Introduction

Providing firmware updates for Internet of Things (IoT) devices is crucial to prevent previous security attacks (e.g., Mirai [1]) from happening again in the future. With the sheer number of IoT devices (i.e., expected to reach 29 billion in 2030 [9]), performing a full-scale firmware update operation becomes even more challenging. Traditional centralized architecture is vulnerable to failure and scalability problems. Hence, exploring a distributed solution is always beneficial for the IoT community going forward.

Some studies suggest using peer-to-peer (P2P) networks such as Gnutella, BitTorrent, or IPFS as a medium to transmit the binary decentrally. However, such an approach cannot be executed perfectly out of the box. First, compared to popular files such as pirated music/movies, firmware binaries will most likely fail to attract much interest in the P2P community. Few distributors will seed the files, resulting in a lower upload/download speed. Second, because anyone can redistribute the binary, malicious adversaries may reverse-engineered it and

H. Kim and J. Youn (Eds.): WISA 2023, LNCS 14402, pp. 131–142, 2024.
https://doi.org/10.1007/978-981-99-8024-6_11

share the tampered version with the community. Therefore, it is crucial to (i) provide incentives so that many people are willing to host the binary files and (ii) provide an integrity guarantee to the shared binary files.

Solving those mentioned issues fairly without the involvement of centralized third-party control complicates the challenges. In particular, distributors may deliver the firmware binary to devices first. But, since distributors and devices do not trust each other, we cannot guarantee that the devices will pay after receiving the binary. Similarly, devices may pay the delivery fee in advance. However, such action cannot guarantee that distributors will send the binary after receiving payment. This *fair exchange* problem is usually solved through an authorized third party as a trusted escrow service. However, we cannot rely on a single entity to perform this process in a decentralized environment.

In this paper, we tackle those challenges by proposing `Patchman`, a decentralized firmware binary (or patch) delivery service for the IoT ecosystem leveraging blockchain. Specifically, we develop secure exchange protocols using key commitment and on-chain encryption to solve the fair exchange problem. Distributors first encrypt the binary and commit the decryption key in the blockchain. After receiving encrypted binary from distributors, devices create a *proof-of-delivery* and submit it to the blockchain. Successful submission of the proof will reveal the decryption key for devices and reward the distributors, providing a win-win solution for both of them. Aside from solving fair exchange, we also develop a *proof-of-installation* as a way for vendors to safely track which devices have successfully installed given firmware binary, despite not being personally in charge of the delivery process.

2 Problem Definition

2.1 Trust Model

We set the following trust models in `Patchman`. First, IoT devices trust their vendors, and they will install any binary that comes from vendors. Second, vendors and devices are assumed not to collude with one another. Third, brokers do not trust vendors/devices, and vice versa. Fourth, all parties trust the blockchain network such that smart contract operations are always hard-to-tamper and deterministic.

2.2 Security Goals

We design `Patchman` to satisfy the following security goals.

1. **Fair Exchange** – Distributors should only get paid if they successfully deliver the binary to devices. The exchange between firmware binary and money reward must be performed fairly without any intervention of a centralized third party.
2. **Patch Integrity** – Malicious distributors may redistribute fake binaries instead of the original ones. Thus, we should be able to check if the binary is altered during the transmission. We should also be able to determine the source origin of the binary.

3. **Patch Availability** – Devices should be able to download binaries from multiple sources so that the system has a low probability of downtime while providing cheaper costs than a centralized cloud.
4. **Patch Confidentiality** – Despite allowing anyone to redistribute the binary, only the vendors and devices should know about the firmware binary. Distributors (and other intermediaries) should not be able to use the binary.
5. **Patch Correctness** – Vendors should understand whether devices have received the binary and whether they have successfully installed the firmware binary.

3   Patchman Delivery Service

The firmware update is performed batch-to-batch, where we split the process of updating devices only to a few devices at a time. This scheme allows system developers to employ a customized prioritization strategy. For example, assuming that developers know the operating location of each IoT device, they can target specific devices (e.g., those in healthcare) to be prioritized by including their public keys in the first batch. Alternatively, developers can also prioritize devices by their role (e.g., devices that serve the role of service providers should get the update first). The token rewards and update duration can be configured to stimulate urgency in the distributors (e.g., by giving high rewards on a relatively small time window) so that they will quickly distribute the binary to devices.

3.1   Components

The followings are the main components of our proposals.

Vendors. IoT vendors are denoted as v. Vendors create IoT devices and are responsible for maintaining their firmware. Every vendor has the following: (i) a private/public keys pair (SK_v, PK_v) and (ii) a list of self-produced IoT devices public keys $\{PK_1, PK_2, ..., PK_d..., PK_D\}$. Multiple competing IoT vendors join the blockchain network and participate in maintaining and generating blocks.

Devices. IoT devices are denoted as d. Devices private/public keys pair (SK_d, PK_d) and vendors public key PK_v is embedded in devices during manufacturing. Devices do not necessarily become blockchain nodes, so getting information from the blockchain can be achieved through trusted intermediaries (e.g., nearby trusted IoT gateways).

Brokers. Brokers are denoted as b. Anyone can participate to become brokers, which are untrusted agents to redistribute firmware binaries from vendors. They have a private/public key pair (SK_b, PK_b) and become blockchain nodes but do not generate blocks.

Blockchain. The blockchain is designed to support smart contract SC such as in Ethereum Virtual Machine (EVM), and use a high-performance consensus algorithm such as Practical Byzantine Fault Tolerance (PBFT). The blockchain is a hybrid between permissioned and permissionless. Anyone can connect and see the information in the blockchain network. However, only vendors are allowed to create blocks.

3.2 Protocol

The overall protocol can be divided into six big stages: (i) firmware creation, (ii) firmware download, (iii) firmware redistribution, (iv) complaint (optional), (v) firmware installation, and (vi) reward distribution.

Firmware Creation. Vendors first prepare the binary file and relevant metadata. After that, they will host the binary temporarily in their server and upload the metadata in the blockchain through Binary Smart Contract BSC (c.f., Algorithm 1). Detailed steps are as follows.

1. Vendors first do:
   - Create a binary firmware update file U and intentionally hide a secret message m inside the binary. This secret is revealed only when devices successfully install the firmware in this batch.
   - Form a hash $m^{id} = \text{H}(m)$. The $\text{H}(\cdot)$ is a secure cryptographic hash function, for example, using SHA-256 or KECCAK-256 algorithm.
   - Make a random key $l = \text{Gen}(1^\lambda)$. The $\text{Gen}(\cdot)$ is a secure pseudorandom generator function, and λ is a security parameter.
   - Specify a list of eligible devices $\hat{D} = \{PK_1, PK_2, ..., PK_d, ..., PK_D\}$ to be updated in this batch. All devices can be identified by their public key PK_d, with D indicating the total number of devices.
   - Encrypt l with devices public key, which is $\forall d \in \hat{D}, k_d = \text{PKE}_{PK_d}(l)$. The $\text{PKE}(\cdot)$ is a secure asymmetric encryption algorithm using ECC encryption.
   - Form a list of encrypted keys $\hat{K} = \{k_1, k_2, ..., k_d, ..., k_D\}$. Note that the order of d is the same in $\hat{D}$ and $\hat{K}$.
   - Make a Merkle Root hash $\tau = \text{MerkleRoot}(\hat{D}, \hat{K})$. The $\text{MerkleRoot}(\cdot)$ is a function to generate a Merkle Root.
   - Encrypt the binary file $\hat{U} = \text{E}_l(U)$. The $\text{E}(\cdot)$ is a secure symmetric encryption such as the AES algorithm.
   - Form a hash $\hat{U}^{id} = \text{H}(\hat{U})$.
2. Vendors deploy new BSC to the blockchain network and put the following metadata:
   - $\tau, D, \hat{U}^{id}, m^{id}$ from the previous steps.
   - The public key of vendors PK_v.
   - The time limit required for registration Δ^{regis}, binary update Δ^{update}, and complaint $\Delta^{complain}$.
   - The firmware version U^{ver} and device model U^{type}.

Algorithm 1. Binary Smart Contract (BSC)

1: Initialize merkleRoot = τ, totalDevice = D
2: Initialize binaryHash = $\hat{U}^{id}$, secretHash = m^{id}
3: Initialize regisDeadline = now + Δ^{regis}
4: Initialize updateDeadline = regisDeadline + Δ^{update}
5: Initialize complainDeadline = updateDeadline + $\Delta^{complain}$
6: Initialize firmwareVersion = U^{ver}, deviceType = U^{type}
7: Initialize deliveryReward = $R^{delivery}$, installReward = $R^{install}$
8: Initialize requiredDeposit = β, owner = PK_v
9: Initialize numberOfDelivered = 0, numberOfInstalled = 0
10: Initialize brokers = $\emptyset$, devices = $\emptyset$ ▷ List of brokers, devices
11: Initialize finalized = False

12: **procedure** DEPOSIT($PK_b, \hat{U}^{url}, \beta'$)
13:     revert if now > regisDeadline
14:     revert if β' < requiredDeposit
15:     brokers[PK_b].deposit = β'
16:     brokers[PK_b].url = $\hat{U}^{url}$
17:     emit **Deposited**($PK_b, \hat{U}^{url}$)

18: **procedure** SUBMITPOD($PK_b, PK_d, r, s, k_d, \tau^{path}, \text{Sign}_{SK_d}(\alpha_{BSC}, s, PK_b)$)
19:     revert if now > updateDeadline
20:     revert if $PK_b \notin$ brokers
21:     revert if devices[PK_d].delivered = True
22:     revert if H(r) $\neq s$
23:     revert if **VerifyPath**($PK_d \parallel k_d, \tau^{path}$, merkleRoot) = False
24:     revert if **Ver**$_{PK_d}$(**Sign**$_{SK_d}(\alpha_{BSC}, s, PK_b)$, address(this) $\parallel s \parallel PK_b$) = False
25:     devices[PK_d].delivered = True
• 26:   devices[PK_d].broker = PK_b
27:     emit **Delivered**(PK_b, PK_d, r)

28: **procedure** SUBMITPOI($PK_b, PK_d, \hat{m}^{id}, \text{Sign}_{SK_d}(\alpha_{BSC}, \hat{m}^{id}, PK_b)$)
29:     revert if now > updateDeadline
30:     revert if $PK_b \neq$ devices[PK_d].broker
31:     revert if devices[PK_d].delivered = False or devices[PK_d].installed = True
32:     revert if **Ver**$_{PK_d}$(**Sign**$_{SK_d}(\alpha_{BSC}, \hat{m}^{id}, PK_b)$, address(this) $\parallel \hat{m}^{id} \parallel PK_b$) = False
33:     devices[PK_d].installed = True
34:     devices[PK_d].secret = $\hat{m}^{id}$
35:     emit **Installed**(PK_b, PK_d)

36: **procedure** COMPLAIN($PK_d, PK_b, \bar{U}, r, s, \text{Sign}_{SK_b}(\bar{U}^{id}, \hat{U}^{id}, s, PK_d)$)
37:     revert if now > complainDeadline
38:     revert if $PK_b \neq$ devices[PK_d].broker
39:     revert if devices[PK_d].delivered = False or devices[PK_d].installed = True
40:     revert if H(r) $\neq s$
41:     revert if **Ver**$_{PK_b}$(**Sign**$_{SK_b}(\bar{U}^{id}, \hat{U}^{id}, s, PK_d)$, H($\bar{U}$) $\parallel$ binaryHash $\parallel s \parallel PK_d$) = False
42:     revert if H(DECRYPT($\bar{U}, r$)) = binaryHash
43:     brokers[PK_b].malicious = True
44:     transfers brokers[PK_b].deposit to PK_v ▷ Deposit is confiscated
45:     emit **Complained**(PK_d, PK_b)

Algorithm 1. Binary Smart Contract (BSC) continued

1: **procedure** CLAIMREWARD(PK_b, PK_d)
2:     revert if now < complainDeadline
3:     revert if $PK_b \neq$ devices[PK_d].broker
4:     revert if brokers[PK_b].malicious = True
5:     revert if devices[PK_d].delivered = False or devices[PK_d].claimed = True
6:     deliveryBill = deliveryReward ÷ (totalDevice - numberOfDelivered)
7:     deliveryReward = deliveryReward - deliveryBill
8:     numberOfDelivered++
9:     devices[PK_d].claimed = True
10:    transfer deliveryBill to PK_b
11:    emit **Claimed**($PK_b, PK_d,$ deliveryBill)

12: **procedure** FINALIZE(PK_v, m)
13:    revert if now < complainDeadline
14:    revert if $PK_v \neq$ owner
15:    revert if finalized = True
16:    revert if H(m) ≠ secretHash
17:    **for all** $PK_d \in$ devices **do**
18:        **if** devices[PK_d].secret = H($m \parallel PK_d$) **then**
19:            installBill = installReward ÷ (totalDevice - numberOfInstalled)
20:            installReward = installReward - installBill
21:            numberOfInstalled++
22:            transfer installBill to devices[PK_d].broker
23:            increase PK_d reputation score ++
24:            increase PK_v reputation score ++
25:    finalized = True
26:    emit **Finalized**($PK_v,$ address(this))

27: **function** ENCRYPT($\hat{U}, r$)
28:    **return** $\mathrm{E}_r(\hat{U})$

29: **function** DECRYPT($\bar{U}, r$)
30:    **return** $\mathrm{D}_r(\bar{U})$

- The total reward R for all brokers, and split the reward for delivery $R^{delivery}$ and installation $R^{install}$, where $R = R^{delivery} + R^{install}$.
- The deposit amount requirement for brokers β.

3. Vendors wait until BSC is deployed. After that, vendors save the BSC address α_{BSC}, which will be used as pointers to collect metadata. Finally, vendors temporarily host the $\hat{U}$ in their server until Δ^{regis} ends.

Firmware Download. Brokers make a deposit to smart contracts and download the firmware from vendors. After successful binary and metadata validation, brokers host the binary for devices. Detailed operations within are described as follows.

4. Before Δ^{regis} ends, interested brokers do:

- Make a deposit β' to BSC (i.e., calling DEPOSIT($\cdot$) method). The broker public key PK_b and the public URL for redistribution $\hat{U}^{url}$ will be stored in BSC.
- Download the firmware binary from vendors' servers. The vendors may host several binaries simultaneously, and brokers use α_{BSC} to indicate which binary they are interested in.

5. Vendors send $(\hat{U}, \hat{D}, \hat{K})$ to brokers.
6. Brokers verify payload:
   - Form $\hat{U}^{id'} = \text{H}(\hat{U})$.
   - Verify that $\hat{U}^{id'} = \hat{U}^{id}$.
   - Reconstruct $\tau' = \text{MerkleRoot}(\hat{D}, \hat{K})$.
   - Make sure that $\tau' = \tau$.

   If everything is valid, brokers open the $\hat{U}^{url}$ to the public so that devices can begin requesting firmware downloads.

Firmware Redistribution. Brokers begin redistributing the firmware to devices by re-encrypting the original firmware with random encryption keys. Devices need to sign the *proof-of-delivery* (PoD) to obtain the decryption key from brokers. Brokers submit the signed PoD to the blockchain to claim delivery rewards later. The following steps are performed within Δ^{update}.

7. Devices determine whether they need the update. If so, they download the binary from brokers by sending (α_{BSC}, PK_d) to $\hat{U}^{url}$. Similar to vendors' cases, brokers may host multiple different batches of firmware binaries at the same time. Therefore, α_{BSC} is used as an identifier.
8. Brokers do:
   - Check if devices are included in this batch $PK_d \in \hat{D} = 1$.
   - Form a Merkle Path $\tau^{path} = \text{MerklePath}(PK_d \parallel k_d, \tau)$. The MerklePath($\cdot$) is a function to create a path from the leaf to the root.
   - Make a random challenge $c = \text{Gen}(1^\lambda)$.
   - Send (c, τ^{path}, k_d) to devices.
9. Devices do:
   - Make sure that brokers indeed have the firmware binary and metadata that they need by performing VerifyPath($PK_d \parallel k_d, \tau^{path}, \tau$) = 1. The VerifyPath($\cdot$) checks whether we can make Merkle Root τ from given leaf $PK_d \parallel k_d$ and Merkle Path τ^{path}.
   - Sign the challenges $\text{Sign}_{SK_d}(c)$ and send to brokers. The Sign($\cdot$) is an asymmetric digital signature generation function using, e.g., the ECDSA algorithm.
10. Brokers do:
   - Verify $\text{Ver}_{PK_d}(\text{Sign}_{SK_d}(c), c) = 1$. The Ver($\cdot$) is an asymmetric digital signature verification function using, e.g., the ECDSA algorithm.
   - Create a random encryption key $r = \text{Gen}(1^\lambda)$.
   - Form $s = \text{H}(r)$.
   - Re-encrypt the binary $\bar{U} = \text{E}_r(\hat{U})$, using ENCRYPT($\cdot$) method.
   - Form $\bar{U}^{id} = \text{H}(\bar{U})$.

– Send $(\bar{U}, s, \mathtt{Sign}_{SK_b}(\bar{U}^{id}, \hat{U}^{id}, s, PK_d))$ to devices.
11. Devices do:
   – Create $\bar{U}^{id} = \mathtt{H}(\bar{U})$.
   – Verify $\mathtt{Ver}(\mathtt{Sign}_{SK_b}(\bar{U}^{id}, \hat{U}^{id}, s, PK_d), \bar{U}^{id} \parallel \hat{U}^{id} \parallel s \parallel PK_d) = 1$. Devices later can use this $\mathtt{Sign}_{SK_b}(\bar{U}^{id}, \hat{U}^{id}, s, PK_d)$ to complain in case brokers lie about the committed decryption key s to devices.
   – Send PoD payload $\mathtt{Sign}_{SK_d}(\alpha_{BSC}, s, PK_b)$ to brokers.
12. Brokers upload $(PK_b, PK_d, r, s, k_d, \tau^{path}, \mathtt{Sign}_{SK_d}(\alpha_{BSC}, s, PK_b))$ to smart contract using SUBMITPOD($\cdot$) method.

Firmware Installation. Devices perform triple decryptions: (i) decrypt the binary from brokers, (ii) decrypt the secret key, and (iii) decrypt the binary from vendors. After installing the binary, devices learn about the secret message, which is then submitted to the blockchain as *proof-of-installation* (PoI). Details of these operations can be described as follows.

13. Devices learn the decryption key r from SUBMITPOD($\cdot$) transaction that is submitted in the previous step. Devices then do the following:
   – Call the DECRYPT($\cdot$) method and obtain $\hat{U} = \mathtt{D}_r(\bar{U})$. The $\mathtt{D}(\cdot)$ is a symmetric decryption function, counterpart of $\mathtt{E}(\cdot)$.
   – Form $\hat{U}^{id'} = \mathtt{H}(\hat{U})$.
   – Verify that $\hat{U}^{id'} = \hat{U}^{id}$.
   – Decrypt $l = \mathtt{PKD}_{PK_d}(k_d)$. The $\mathtt{PKD}(\cdot)$ is a asymmetric decryption function, counterpart of $\mathtt{PKE}(\cdot)$.
   – Decrypt $U = \mathtt{D}_l(\hat{U})$.
   – Install U and obtain m.
   – Form PoI payload $\hat{m}^{id} = \mathtt{H}(m \parallel PK_d)$.
   – Send $(PK_d, \hat{m}^{id}, \mathtt{Sign}_{SK_d}(\alpha_{BSC}, \hat{m}^{id}, PK_b))$ to brokers.
14. Brokers upload $(PK_b, PK_d, \hat{m}^{id}, \mathtt{Sign}_{SK_d}(\alpha_{BSC}, \hat{m}^{id}, PK_b))$ to BSC by calling SUBMITPOI($\cdot$) method.

Complaint. Brokers can cheat devices by giving fake decryption keys. Brokers initially encrypted $\hat{U}$ with r, $\bar{U} = \mathtt{E}_r(\hat{U})$. However, they intentionally generate a fake decryption key r' (i.e., $r' \neq r$), form $s' = \mathtt{H}(r')$, and send s' to devices. At this moment, devices cannot verify if this s' (and r' behind it) can actually decrypt $\bar{U}$. Devices use an optimistic approach and assume that brokers are honest. Therefore, devices sign and make PoD. After receiving PoD, brokers submit PoD and (r', s') using the SUBMITPOD($\cdot$) method. This transaction is considered valid, and BSC can process it. However, when r' is revealed and devices try to decrypt $\bar{U}$, they found out that $\hat{U}' \neq \hat{U}, \hat{U}' = \mathtt{D}_{r'}(\bar{U})$. To solve this issue, we allow devices to make a complaint request to BSC by submitting $PK_b, \bar{U}, r, s, \mathtt{Sign}_{SK_b}(\bar{U}^{id}, \hat{U}^{id}, s, PK_d)$ using COMPLAIN($\cdot$) method within $\Delta^{complain}$ window. If brokers are found to be malicious, BSC will confiscate brokers' deposits.

Reward Distribution. Rewards are distributed only to honest participants. In this case, brokers obtain tokens for submissions of the PoD and PoI. Meanwhile, devices and vendors increase their reputation scores for successfully performing a firmware update. The details are as follows.

15. Brokers wait until the $\Delta^{complain}$ expires, then do:
    - Make a claim transaction (PK_b, PK_d) using CLAIMREWARD$(\cdot)$ method.
    - Obtain a slice of $R^{delivery}$ for successfully processed the PoD.
16. Vendors wait until the $\Delta^{complain}$ expires, then do:
    - Terminate the process by uploading (PK_v, m) with FINALIZE$(\cdot)$ method.
    - Brokers obtain a slice of $R^{install}$ for successfully processed the PoI.
    - Devices and vendors' reputations are increased.

Once the BSC is closed, this batch is completed, and the BSC state can not be altered anymore. If one or a few devices are not successfully installed on this batch, they can be included in the next batch.

4   Security Analysis

In this section, we evaluate our proposal and prove it can provide security goals as described in Sect. 2. This discussion assumes that the underlying cryptography algorithm and the blockchain network are secure. We also assume that devices do not leak secrets, such as decrypted firmware binary, encryption keys, and PoI secret messages, to the public.

Fair Exchange. The economic (and sociological) model plays an important role in forcing honest behavior from participants. First, devices may not want to provide PoD payloads for brokers after receiving the binary. However, only by releasing PoD payloads will devices get the encryption key to decrypt the received binary. Second, brokers can decide to break the exchange protocol by not submitting the PoD or PoI payloads to the smart contract. However, they will lose incentives $(R^{delivery}, R^{install})$ by doing so. Furthermore, devices can try to make new exchange protocols with other brokers if they find previous brokers unresponsive. Third, brokers can try to cheat devices by committing (and later revealing) a fake encryption key during PoD exchanges. However, when devices detect such action, they can make a complaint, and brokers will lose their deposit (c.f., complaint stage from Sect. 3 for details).

Patch Integrity. Integrity is enforced by utilizing hash and digital signatures. The binary firmware is accompanied by cryptographic hash $\hat{U}^{id} = H(U)$, which can be used to prove if there is any tampering during binary transmission. Furthermore, vendors must provide digital signatures when providing transactions $\text{Sign}_{SK_v}(\text{Tx})$ to deploy BSC. Devices need to check that creator of BSC is PK_d and $\hat{U}^{id}$ is stored in BSC to determine the true source of the transmitted binary.

Table 1. Feature comparison of our proposal with previous works

Research	Fair Exchange	Integ.	Avail.	Confi.	Corre.
Leiba et al. [6,7]	ZKP	✓	✓	–	–
Baza et al. [2]	ZKP & ABE	✓	✓	–	–
Puggioni et al. [8]	ZKP	✓	✓	–	–
Lee J.H. [5]	Key-Commit	✓	✓	✓	–
Zhao et al. [11]	DAPS & OABS	✓	✓	–	–
Tapas et al. [10]	BitTorrent Choking	✓	✓	–	–
Fukuda et al. [4]	Access Control	✓	✓	–	–
Patchman	On-Chain Encrypt	✓	✓	✓	✓

Legend: (✓) means included, (–) means not included.

Patch Availability. Availability is solved by incentivizing multiple brokers. Thus, it depends heavily on the number of brokers interested in rehosting the binary. With attractive incentive models, many brokers will likely participate in our system to rehost the device binary.

Patch Confidentiality. Confidentiality is achieved through end-to-end encryption. The binary in the given batch is encrypted with shared key l, which is $\hat{U} = \mathrm{E}_l(U)$. That key is then encrypted with device public key $k_d = \mathrm{PKE}_{PK_d}(l)$. Thus, only legitimate devices with SK_d can decrypt and obtain original firmware U. Furthermore, vendors will use different key l', which $l' \neq l$, in the next batch to provide confidentiality between batches.

Patch Correctness. Correctness is realized through PoI. When devices install the binary, a secret message m will be revealed to the devices. Because the submission of PoI to BSC only reveals $\hat{m}^{id} = \mathrm{H}(m \parallel PK_d)$, it prevents devices from seeing and stealing each other m. Devices also cannot resubmit $\hat{m}^{id}$ from other devices and claim it as their own since such $\hat{m}^{id}$ is only valid for a specific device. With these traits, vendors can be confident that only devices whose PoI are successfully processed on-chain have installed the firmware binary.

Note that since we focus on firmware delivery, the actual scheme to realize m revelation is beyond the scope of this paper. An idea to achieve this is, for example, allowing devices to hash small parts of the registry configuration, indicating that the firmware state has been updated. In this case, the resulting hash will be used as m.

5   Related Work

To our knowledge, Leiba et al. [7] propose the first study about fair exchange for IoT firmware update by leveraging Zero-Knowledge Contingent Payment (ZKCP) protocol [3] and smart contract. In their initial [7] and extended work

[6], they use Zero-Knowledge Proof (ZKP) to build *proof-of-delivery* (PoD) between distributors and devices. Those works inspire many other researchers to build similar concepts, which results in many variations, each with its own fair exchange methods and security goals guarantee. A comparison summary can be seen in Table 1.

Baza et al. [2] use the same ZKP as in [7] for PoD but replace the token reward with a reputation system and add attribute-based encryption (ABE) for access control. Puggioni et al. [8] also use ZKP but introduce a new hub entity to outsource heavy cryptographic operations from devices. Lee J.H. [5] proposes an on-chain key-commit scheme as PoD, where distributors first commit the hash of the encryption key in the smart contract, then later submit PoD, including the correct key, to get the reward. Zhao et al. [11] propose to use double authentication preventing signature (DAPS) and outsource attribute-based signature (OABS) for their PoD. Tapas et al. [10] divides the firmware into multiple parts, and distributors will transfer one part at a time to devices. Each part delivery is a fair exchange, and devices must pay to get the next part. If devices do not pay, distributors will choke their traffic from the BitTorrent network so that they cannot get any parts from other distributors. Fukuda et al. [4] enforce an access control mechanism to build a fair exchange. Distributors must send the firmware to devices to get rewards, and devices must sign PoD to update their firmware state in the smart contract. Failing to do so will result in losing access to the network.

Patchman is also inspired by the works of Leiba et al. [7]. However, unlike previous studies, we use an on-chain encryption scheme to enforce fair exchange in our system. On-chain encryption is relatively more efficient than using ZKP [2]. Our approach also does not require any trusted setup or specific environment like if using access control [4], attribute-based cryptography [11], or BitTorrent choking [10]. More importantly, previous research does not consider patch confidentiality, so distributors can see the binary. Also, they only guarantee delivery without knowing whether the devices have successfully installed the binary. Only our works fully support all security goals, as seen in Table 1.

6 Conclusion

We have described Patchman, a decentralized firmware update delivery service for IoT leveraging blockchain. Entities can register as brokers and help redistribute binary from vendors to devices in exchange for *proof-of-delivery* incentives. Devices can install the binary and submit the *proof-of-installation* to gain a reputation increase. Those proofs are verifiable in the blockchain to guarantee security and fairness for all participants. Since we share our early design in this paper, detailing the deposit, reward, and reputation system will be carried out in the future. Furthermore, implementation and feasibility analysis will also be our immediate future work.

Acknowledgements. This research was supported by the MSIT(Ministry of Science and ICT), Korea, under the Convergence security core talent training business(Pusan National University) support program(IITP-2023-2022-0-01201) supervised by the IITP(Institute for Information & Communications Technology Planning & Evaluation) and also supported by the MSIT(Ministry of Science and ICT), Korea, under the ITRC(Information Technology Research Center) support program(IITP-2023-2020-0-01797) supervised by the IITP(Institute for Information & Communications Technology Planning & Evaluation).

References

1. Antonakakis, M., et al.: Understanding the Mirai Botnet. In: 26th USENIX Security Symposium (USENIX Security 2017), pp. 1093–1110 (2017)
2. Baza, M., Nabil, M., Lasla, N., Fidan, K., Mahmoud, M., Abdallah, M.: Blockchain-based firmware update scheme tailored for autonomous vehicles. In: 2019 IEEE Wireless Communications and Networking Conference (WCNC), pp. 1–7. IEEE (2019)
3. Bitcoin Wiki: Zero knowledge contingent payment (2020). https://en.bitcoin.it/wiki/Zero_Knowledge_Contingent_Payment
4. Fukuda, T., Omote, K.: Efficient blockchain-based IoT firmware update considering distribution incentives. In: 2021 IEEE Conference on Dependable and Secure Computing (DSC), pp. 1–8. IEEE (2021)
5. Lee, J.: Patch transporter: incentivized, decentralized software patch system for WSN and IoT environments. Sensors 18(2), 574 (2018)
6. Leiba, O., Bitton, R., Yitzchak, Y., Nadler, A., Kashi, D., Shabtai, A.: IoTPatchPool: Incentivized delivery network of IoT software updates based on proofs-of-distribution. Pervasive Mob. Comput. 58, 101019 (2019)
7. Leiba, O., Yitzchak, Y., Bitton, R., Nadler, A., Shabtai, A.: Incentivized delivery network of IoT software updates based on trustless proof-of-distribution. In: 2018 IEEE European Symposium on Security and Privacy Workshops (EuroS&PW), pp. 29–39. IEEE (2018)
8. Puggioni, E., Shaghaghi, A., Doss, R., Kanhere, S.S.: Towards decentralized IoT updates delivery leveraging blockchain and zero-knowledge proofs. In: 2020 IEEE 19th International Symposium on Network Computing and Applications (NCA), pp. 1–10. IEEE (2020)
9. Statista: Number of internet of things (IoT) connected devices worldwide from 2019 to 2021, with forecasts from 2022 to 2030 (2023). https://www.statista.com/statistics/1183457/iot-connected-devices-worldwide/
10. Tapas, N., Yitzchak, Y., Longo, F., Puliafito, A., Shabtai, A.: P4uiot: pay-per-piece patch update delivery for IoT using gradual release. Sensors 20(7), 2156 (2020)
11. Zhao, Y., Liu, Y., Tian, A., Yu, Y., Du, X.: Blockchain based privacy-preserving software updates with proof-of-delivery for internet of things. J. Parallel Distrib. Comput. 132, 141–149 (2019)

Security Risk Indicator for Open Source Software to Measure Software Development Status

Hiroki Kuzuno[1]([⊠])(ID), Tomohiko Yano[2], Kazuki Omo[3], Jeroen van der Ham[4], and Toshihiro Yamauchi[5](ID)

[1] Graduate School of Engineering, Kobe University, Kobe, Japan
kuzuno@port.kobe-u.ac.jp
[2] Intelligent Systems Laboratory, SECOM CO., LTD, Tokyo, Japan
[3] SIOS Technology, Inc., Tokyo, Japan
[4] Faculty for Electrical Engineering, Mathematics and Computer Science,
University of Twente, Enschede, The Netherlands
[5] Faculty of Environmental, Life, Natural Science and Technology,
Okayama University, Okayama, Japan

Abstract. Recently, open source software (OSS) has become more mainstream. Therefore, the security of OSS is an important topic in information systems that use OSS. When vulnerabilities are discovered in OSS, it is difficult to fix or address for each information system developer or administrator. Existing security studies propose classifying vulnerabilities, estimating vulnerability risks, and analyzing exploitable vulnerabilities. However, it is still difficult to understand the threat of exploited vulnerabilities, and the development status of OSS used in information system operations. Determining whether vulnerabilities and the OSS development status are security risks is challenging. In this study, we propose a security risk indicator for OSS to address these problems. The proposed method calculates security risk indicators by combining vulnerability information with the development status of OSS. The proposed security risk indicator of OSS is a criterion for security measures during the operation of information systems. In the evaluation, we verified whether the proposed security risk indicator can be used to identify the threats of multiple OSS and the calculation cost of the security risk indicators.

1   Introduction

The use of open source software (OSS) has become mainstream in information systems. OSS development is often conducted by volunteer developer communities, and it is difficult for information system operators and developers to understand OSS development status. It leads to security risks of OSS that are a low activity of OSS development, and not fixing OSS vulnerabilities, then, OSS is a new target of cyber attack that exploits security risks to compromise information systems using OSS [1].

The development status of each OSS may not be known when many OSS are used in an information system. In addition, it is difficult to determine whether vulnerabilities should be addressed as security measures for OSS as this depends on the operational environment of the information system and the trend of attacks that exploit the vulnerabilities.

Several analysis methods for the impact of vulnerabilities have been proposed in studies on existing software vulnerabilities [2], an assessment of the vulnerabilities risk [3,4], and the exploitability of the use of vulnerabilities [5]. Another analysis method is proposed for each reported vulnerability to determine the likelihood of its use in an attack [6,7].

In the operation of information systems, the implementation of security measures against OSS is desirable when the operator judges that immediate updates or scheduled maintenance are necessary. Therefore, existing methods have the following issues.

Problem: Understanding the security risks of OSS

Existing methods identify software security threats based on vulnerabilities reported for OSS and decide whether to update the software as a security measure. However, to get an indication of the security risk of OSS developed by third parties, information on the development status of OSS is important; This is based on whether vulnerabilities are being fixed or not, and whether the development of OSS is continuing.

In this study, we propose a security risk indicator calculated by linking the development status and vulnerability information of an OSS. It is a security measure used to judge whether to take security risks for the OSS used in information systems. The OSS security risk indicator enables a continuous and comprehensive understanding of vulnerabilities and the development status, which can be used as a criterion for updating or scheduled maintenance in information systems.

The objective of the OSS security risk indicator is quickly and continuously identify the presence or absence of OSS security risks to support updating OSS and reviewing its use. We collected vulnerability information from the National Vulnerability Database (NVD) [8], and OSS information from the list of packages managed by Linux distributions with a GitHub repository to calculate the proposed security risk indicator. To calculate the security indicator, the software identification name included in the vulnerability information was used to link the OSS information. The system then uses the Common Vulnerability Scoring System (CVSS) to give an indication towards vulnerability risk [9]. Next, the criticality score, which quantifies the development status of OSS [10], is used to calculate a security risk indicator for OSS.

We are aware that a CVSS score does not express risk itself, however we feel that it does provide some first indication that may be helpful for assessing OSS. The research contributions in this paper are as follows:

1. We propose a security risk indicator for OSS that links vulnerabilities and OSS information to utilize the indicator in security measures for OSS. We calculated the security risk indicator of the OSS in Linux distributions and made it possible to provide a security risk indicator for various OSS.
2. To evaluate the proposed OSS security risk indicator, we verified whether it is possible to identify the OSS security risk and the impacts of known

Table 1. Vulnerabilities Information

Item	Description
CVE	A list of common identifiers for publicly known cybersecurity vulnerabilities
CPE	A structured naming scheme for systems, software, and packages
CVSS	A characteristics and severity of software vulnerabilities
KEV	A list of active exploitation vulnerabilities

Table 2. OpenSSF Criticality Score [10]

Parameter (S_i)	Description
created_since	Time since the project was created (in months)
updated_since	Time since the project was last updated (in months)
contributor_count	Count of project contributors (with commits)
org_count	Count of distinct organizations that contributors belong to
commit_frequency	Average number of commits per week in the last year
recent_releases_count	Number of releases in the last year
closed_issues_count	Number of issues closed in the last 90 days
updated_issues_count	Number of issues updated in the last 90 days
comment_frequency	Average number of comments per issue in the last 90 days
dependents_count	Number of project mentions in the commit messages

vulnerabilities. We also evaluated the computational cost of calculating the security risk indicators for several packages in a particular Linux distribution.

2 Background

2.1 Vulnerability Information

Vulnerabilities are mis-implementation flaws that affect software behavior and can be used for attacks. Table 1 lists the vulnerability information used in this study. Common Vulnerabilities and Exposures (CVE) is the vulnerability identifier [11], and a unique number is assigned to each vulnerability. Common Platform Enumeration (CPE) is a list of common platforms that indicates the hardware or software versions of vulnerabilities that have been reported [12].

The CVSS was used to quantify vulnerabilities and includes CVSSv2 and CVSSv3. CVSS were calculated by considering several factors depending on those necessary for vulnerability exploitation and the threat level [9]. In addition, the known exploited vulnerabilities catalog (KEV) is used in actual attacks to exploit vulnerabilities. It is a database of high security risk vulnerabilities that have been exploited in the wild [13].

2.2 OSS Information

OSS Criticality Score: Many organizations use OSS, operating systems, libraries, databases, and infrastructure software, such as language processing systems. The development status of each OSS is complicated. The following formula to quantify the development status of OSS as a criticality score.

$$C_{project} = \frac{1}{\sum_i \alpha_i} \sum_i \alpha_i \frac{\log(1 + S_i)}{\log(1 + \max(S_i, T_i))} \tag{1}$$

where, $C_{project}$ is an OSS project, and a weight α_1 and a threshold T_i are defined for each S_i parameter in Table 2. The criticality score takes the range $0 \leq C_{project} \leq 1$, where 0 means not critical (least-critical) and 1 means critical (most-critical). The criticality score can be used to quantify the development status of an OSS because it changes according to the activity of development.

OSS Package Management: Linux distribution facilitates the introduction of OSS by considering the dependencies among OSS distribution package management. Debian GNU/Linux manages and distributes OSS in the `deb` package format [14]. The `deb` package contains `changelog` includes the package version, update date and information, and the `control` comprises architecture and OSS repository information.

3   Assumed Situation

The model in this study assumes that a high security risk indicator is calculated from vulnerability information and the development status as OSS information.

Assumed Environment: In the assumed model, the environment in which security risk indicators can be calculated is as follows:

- OS: OSS managed as a package (e.g., Debian GNU/Linux)
- OSS: Packages are managed by the OS, and developer information can be referenced (e.g., GitHub repository)
- Vulnerability Information: Vulnerability information with CVE numbers for the OSS have been released. CVSSv3 numbers can be calculated.
- OSS information: The repository is registered on GitHub, OSS Criticality Score can be calculated.

Assumed Scenario: As a possible scenario, consider that the security risk indicators of OSS are variable. The development status of OSS may not be constant. The activity of development is referred in Table 1. In addition to past vulnerabilities, new vulnerabilities are expected to be discovered and CVE registrations and CVSS will be added. Therefore, the development status is delayed that conducts increasing of security risk, because a developer has less motivation, then does not update OSS.

For example, the frequency of updates to development repositories decreases for packaged libraries used by many OSS on computers. In addition, a certain number of past vulnerabilities have been reported, and newly discovered vulnerabilities have not been addressed or corrected. The proposed security risk indicator for OSS assumes that the security risk indicator increases if the OSS in the assumed model follows the assumed scenario.

4   Approach

4.1   Requirement

The proposed measurement enables the calculation of the security risk indicator of OSS based on vulnerability and OSS information by specifying monitoring targets for OSS deployed in computers. We aimed to satisfy the following requirements:

Requirement: We assume attacks that exploit vulnerabilities in OSS installed on computers (i.e., privilege escalation attacks and denial of service attacks) and attacks that exploit the development status of OSS. The vulnerability and OSS information of the monitored OSS were obtained periodically, and security risk indicators were calculated.

4.2   Design

An overview of the OSS security risk indicators is shown in Fig. 1 that illustrates the flow of calculating the security risk indicator for OSS. A list of vulnerability information and OSS information on the computer to be monitored is maintained to fulfill these requirements. Vulnerability and OSS information were quantified and combined to calculate OSS security risk indicators.

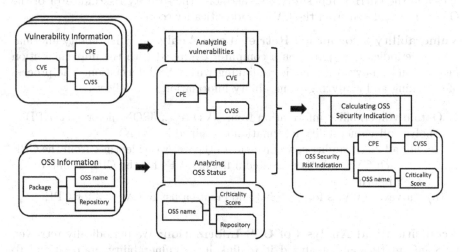

Fig. 1. Design overview of OSS security risk indicator calculation

Vulnerability Information: In the proposed security risk indicator for OSS, the vulnerability information used to identify the vulnerabilities of OSS running on computers. Vulnerability information uniquely identifies vulnerabilities (e.g., CVE), information that identifies vulnerable software (e.g., CPE), and information that quantifies vulnerabilities (e.g., CVSS).

OSS Information: In the calculation of the proposed OSS security risk indicator, the OSS information used to monitor the development status of OSS running on computers. OSS information quantifies the development status of the OSS (e.g., criticality score).

Security Risk Indicator: To regularly assess the risk of OSS, the vulnerability information and security risk indicators of OSS proposed using OSS information are calculated as follows.

- Linking vulnerability information to OSS information: Software identifiers included in vulnerability information are linked to OSS information.
- Calculation of security risk indicator: The security risk indicator is calculated by combining the harmonic mean of all score values (e.g., CVSS) of vulnerabilities associated with the OSS information and the score values obtained from the OSS information (e.g., criticality score).

4.3   Implementation

To monitor the OSS running on computers, the environment assumed for implementation is the Debian GNU/Linux OS and x86_64 CPU architecture.

In the implementation method, vulnerability information was obtained and analyzed from the NVD. OSS information was obtained and analyzed from packages and the GitHub repository. Furthermore, the security risk indicator of the OSS was calculated from the CVSS and criticality score.

Vulnerability Information Retrieval and Analysis: Vulnerability information is periodically acquired on a computer equipped with the implementation method and analyzed to enable its linking with OSS information. The process of obtaining and analyzing vulnerability information is as follows:

1. Obtain vulnerability information from NVD (e.g., JSON file or Web API)
2. Analyze all vulnerability information contained in the NVD
    (a) For all vulnerabilities, we investigate the software identifier from the CPE for each CVE. We then created a list of CVEs for the CPE to link to the OSS information
    (b) Survey all CVEs for CVSSv3 and create a list of CVSSv3 for CPEs

Acquisition and Analysis of OSS Information: We periodically retrieved OSS information and analyzed it to link it to vulnerability information. To retrieve OSS information from Debian, we used the management function of the deb package and the description information of the files included in the deb package. The OSS information acquisition and analysis processes are as follows:

1. The deb package management functionality is used to obtain information on the list of OSS packages on a computer

2. Use the **deb** package management functionality to obtain the source code of the **deb** package for each OSS
   (a) Search the **control** file for all **deb** packages and get GitHub repository information
   (b) If GitHub repository information exists, calculate and record a criticality score for each OSS **deb** package
   (c) Generate software identifiers that can be tied to CPEs for each OSS **deb** package

Linking Vulnerability Information to OSS Information: Vulnerability and OSS information are linked for each OSS, and a security risk indicator for the OSS is calculated from the CVSS and criticality score for OSS.

1. The **deb** package management functionality was used to obtain information from a list of OSS packages on the computer
2. Do the following for all **deb** packages in the following order
   (a) Obtain CVE and CVSS lists from CPE using software identifiers that can be linked to CPE for **deb** packages
   (b) Obtain the list of criticality scores calculated for the **deb** package
   (c) Calculate OSS security risk indicators from the CVS list and the criticality score list for the **deb** package

Security Risk Indicators for OSS: To calculate the security risk of OSS, we use a normalized CVSS list in the range of $0 \le cvss_i \le 0.5$. CVSS list for OSS $\{cvss_1, cvss_2, \ldots, cvss_n\}$, and criticality score cs_{date} normalized within $0 \le cs_i \le 0.5$. As OSS, calculate the security risk indicator S_{oss} of the **deb** package as follows.

$$S_{oss} = \frac{\sum_{i=1}^{n} w1_i}{\sum_{i=1}^{n} \frac{w1_i}{cvss_i}} + cs_{date} \tag{2}$$

where, $\{w1_1, w1_2, \ldots, w1_n\}$ are the weights for each CVSS, and cs_{date} is the criticality score of the values of the measurement date and time. Let S_{oss} have the range $0 \le S_{oss} \le 1$, where 0 means no risk and 1 means risky.

The OSS security risk indicator can be used to quantify and capture a composite of the CVSS, which quantifies the vulnerability of the OSS, and the criticality score, which indicates the level of development activity. Moreover, the OSS security risk indicator can be used as a constant to understand the variation in the risk associated with OSS.

5 Evaluation

5.1 Purpose and Environment

The evaluation items and their contents were as follows:

1. Assessment of security risk indicators for OSS
   The proposed OSS security risk indicator was calculated for 142 OSS in 11 programming languages. To evaluate whether it is possible to comprehensively understand whether OSS is at security risk or not.
2. Exploited vulnerability handling of security risk indicator for OSS
   We evaluated whether the OSS security risk indicators were affected by the vulnerabilities registered in KEV.
3. Time to calculate security risk indicators for OSS
   We measured the time required to calculate the proposed OSS security risk indicator for OSS packages managed in a Linux environment.

Environment: Computer with an Intel(R) Core(TM) i7-12700H CPU (2.30 GHz, 14 cores) and 16 GB of memory was used as the computing environment for evaluating security risk indicators for the OSS, and Debian GNU/Linux 12.0 (Linux kernel 5.4.0, x86_64). The calculating security risk indicator of OSS was implemented in 610 lines in Python. The CVSSv3 included in the NVD is the numerical value based on Base Score Metrics [8], and the threshold for the criticality score calculation is the default parameter used [10].

5.2 Assessment of Security Risk Indicators

To evaluate the security risk indicator of OSS, we measured the security risk indicator of OSS for 142 OSS of 11 programming languages (C, C++, C#, Java-based, JavaScript-based, PHP, Go, Python, Ruby, Rust, and Shell). These results are shown in Figs. 2, 3, and 4. The CVE and CVSS for the past year were used at the date of each criticality score measurement.

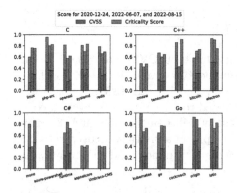

Fig. 2. OSS Security Risk Indicators 1 (5 selected from each language)

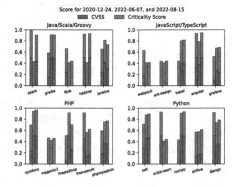

Fig. 3. OSS Security Risk Indicators 2 (5 selected from each language)

Figures 2, 3, and 4 show that Rails has the highest security risk indicator as of August 15, 2022, and that their CVSS and criticality score have increased due

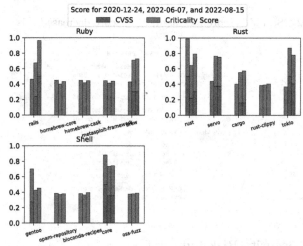

Table 3. Number of evaluated 142 OSS for KEV

Item	# of software	# of vulnerabilities
KEV information	404	914
KEV of evaluated OSS	12	27

Fig. 4. OSS Security Risk Indicators 2 (5 selected from each language)

to vulnerability reports. The OSS with the lowest security risk indicator as of August 15, 2022, was Oss-fuz, with no vulnerabilities reported in the past year and no increase in the criticality score. Similar increases or decreases in security risk indicators can be observed for other OSS.

Using a certain security risk indicator, it is possible to comprehensively survey multiple OSS and compare the number of vulnerability reports and the development status of OSS over a period of time. Therefore, it is possible to determine the change in dangers related to OSS from the OSS security risk indicator.

5.3 Exploited Vulnerability Handling of Security Risk Indicators

In this evaluation, we investigated whether the registration of vulnerabilities in KEV affected the security risk indicators of the 142 OSS evaluated. Table 3 shows how many of the 142 OSS evaluated were included in the KEV.

The evaluation results are listed in Table 4. It shows the detailed and affected results of vulnerabilities of the evaluated 142 OSS are included in KEV.

For the 19 vulnerabilities of nine software packages, the security risk indicator changed after the vulnerabilities were registered in the KEV. In particular, six software packages (Linux, Jenkins, phpMyAdmin, Salt, Airflow, and Rails) have an increased security risk indicator that can be captured because the vulnerability registration and measurement of the security risk indicator were similar. By contrast, three software packages (OpenSSL, Redis, and Core) decreased the security risk indicator. This is because vulnerability registration and the fixing are closed dates, and active development is captured. Moreover, the seven vulnerabilities of Linux and Spark, on the security risk indicator could not be captured because of the time lag between vulnerability registration.

Table 4. KEV of evaluated 142 OSS ($\nearrow$ is score increased, $\searrow$ is score decreased,—is out of range)

Software	CVE	Published	Fixed	Fluctuation
Linux	CVE-2019-13272	2021-12-10	2022-06-10	$\nearrow$
Linux	CVE-2016-5195	2022-03-03	2022-03-24	$\nearrow$
Linux	CVE-2021-22600	2022-04-11	2022-05-02	$\nearrow$
Linux	CVE-2022-0847	2022-04-25	2022-05-16	$\nearrow$
Linux	CVE-2014-3153	2022-05-25	2022-06-15	$\nearrow$
Linux	CVE-2013-6282	2022-09-15	2022-10-06	—
Linux	CVE-2013-2596	2022-09-15	2022-10-06	—
Linux	CVE-2013-2094	2022-09-15	2022-10-06	—
Linux	CVE-2021-3493	2022-10-20	2022-11-10	—
Linux	CVE-2023-0266	2023-03-30	2023-04-20	—
OpenSSL	CVE-2014-0160	2022-05-04	2022-05-25	$\searrow$
Redis	CVE-2022-0543	2022-03-28	2022-04-18	$\searrow$
Spark	CVE-2022-33891	2023-03-07	2023-03-28	—

Software	CVE	Published	Fixed	Fluctuation
Jenkins	CVE-2018-1000861	2022-02-10	2022-08-10	$\nearrow$
Jenkins	CVE-2019-1003030	2022-03-25	2022-04-15	$\nearrow$
Jenkins	CVE-2019-1003029	2022-04-25	2022-05-16	$\nearrow$
Grafana	CVE-2021-39226	2022-08-25	2022-09-15	—
Core	CVE-2019-6340	2022-03-25	2022-04-15	$\searrow$
Core	CVE-2018-7602	2022-04-13	2022-05-04	$\searrow$
phpMyAdmin	CVE-2009-1151	2022-03-25	2022-04-15	$\nearrow$
Salt	CVE-2020-11652	2021-11-03	2022-05-03	$\nearrow$
Salt	CVE-2020-11651	2021-11-03	2022-05-03	$\nearrow$
Salt	CVE-2020-16846	2021-11-03	2022-05-03	$\nearrow$
Airflow	CVE-2020-11978	2022-01-18	2022-07-18	$\nearrow$
Rails	CVE-2016-0752	2022-03-25	2022-04-15	$\nearrow$
Rails	CVE-2014-0130	2022-03-25	2022-04-15	$\nearrow$

5.4   Calculation Time of Security Risk Indicator

The time required to calculate the proposed OSS security risk indicator was evaluated by calculating the OSS security risk indicators for 142 Debian packages. Ten measurements were taken for each OSS, and the average values were calculated and summed. The NVDs were assumed to have been analyzed, and the download times for the `deb` package were not included.

The calculation of the security risk indicator of OSS required a total of 24 min and 40 s, with an average time of 10.27 s and a median of 6.0 s per `deb` package. The OSS that took the longest calculation time was Cataclysm-DDS, which took 2 min and 28 s, and the OSS that required the least time to calculate was Linux, which required 4 s.

6   Discussion

6.1   Considerations

Evaluation Consideration: To evaluate the proposed OSS security risk indicator, we verified whether it was possible to identify OSS fluctuation from exploited vulnerabilities. We also evaluated the computational cost of the security risk indicators for several packages included in a particular Linux distribution.

The calculation results of the security risk indicators for the proposed OSS showed that the security risk indicators varied for all OSS situations, indicating that it is possible to identify changes in the disclosed vulnerabilities or OSS development status. Moreover, we identified that KEV has an impact on the security risk indicator for OSS. The proposed OSS security risk indicator monitors several OSS on a running computer. It is possible to continuously monitor the security risks of OSS that are actually used in the information systems.

From the performance evaluation results, the calculation of the OSS security risk indicator required an average of 10.27 s per package count. Periodically calculating the OSS security risk indicator on a computer may affect the computer's performance.

However, the main cost is the time required to acquire the package infor-mation. We believe that if the OSS security risk indicator is calculated on an ongoing, periodic basis, the direct overhead on the OS and application operations can be reduced using less computationally demanding calculation time.

Approach Consideration: In the calculation of the proposed security risk indicator for OSS, the CVSS, which quantifies the risk of vulnerability as vulnerability information, and the criticality score obtained from the development repository as OSS information are used as specific information for OSS. The proposed security risk indicator for OSS does not identify vulnerabilities. However, if the existence of vulnerabilities that could be used for attacks is identified and as development stagnates, the security risk increases, and the possibility of future attacks is considered to be high.

To continue the operation of information systems using OSS, software for attack mitigation measures must be developed based on the results of the security risk indicators. In addition, to use the security risk indicator of OSS as a criterion for security measures, it is necessary to estimate the risk of OSS running on a computer. Moreover, we will attempt to develop a framework to further grasp the vulnerabilities and possibility of attacks for each development status and to provide information at all times.

6.2 Limitations

OSS Security Risk Indicator: The proposed OSS security risk indicator is obtained from the package information of each OSS as a starting point. The criticality score cannot be calculated if the package information does not include developer information. In the case of OSS introduced from sources other than package management, it is difficult to supplement the usage status, and investigation and analysis of the executable files of the entire OSS are necessary.

Target OSS: The OSS security risk indicators alone may not reliably capture the development, modification, and availability status of an OSS. In the future, it will be important to analyze the source code modification history, bug trackers, provided patches as the fix status, communication tools such as mailing lists, and materials in the OSS distribution environment. We plan to consider this information that can be used to calculate security risk indicators by considering, the necessity of each piece of OSS to cover the latest OSS threat cases [1].

7 Related Work

Vulnerability Analysis: An analysis method of vulnerabilities classifies the trends of vulnerabilities used in attacks [15]. The timing of actual attacks has also been investigated [5], and the exploitable risk of vulnerability and the impact of using the attack have also been discussed [2, 3].

Vulnerability Exploit Estimation: Disclosed vulnerabilities have been quickly used in an attack [16]. VEST tries to analyze the attack likelihood and disclosure timing of vulnerabilities to mitigate the impact of vulnerabilities [17]. EPSS also analyzes the likelihood of an actual attack on a vulnerability [6,7].

Vulnerability Classification: Deep learning and machine learning methods have been proposed to analyze the type and summary of vulnerabilities and automatically classify vulnerabilities [18,19]. In addition, an estimation method concerning the danger of vulnerabilities and the priority of countermeasures using CVSS was proposed [4,20].

Vulnerability Management: The timing of vulnerability disclosure, its effects, and patch provisions have been analyzed [21–23].

8   Conclusion

In this study, we proposed a security risk indicator for OSS that is increasingly being used in information systems, to handle the security risk of OSS. The proposed method calculated a security risk indicator for an OSS by combining the CVSS and quantification of the OSS development status.

The OSS security risk indicator could be referred to as one of the decision criteria and first indication for security measures because it can continuously grasp the security risk of OSS based on its vulnerability information and OSS development status. In the evaluation, we used the security risk indicator for OSS to verify whether it was possible to determine the security risks for multiple OSS and the impacts of known vulnerabilities in KEV. We also applied the security risk indicator to Linux distributions and verified the cost of calculating the OSS.

Acknowledgment. This work was partially supported by the Japan Society for the Promotion of Science (JSPS) KAKENHI Grant Number JP19H04109, JP22H03592, JP23K16882, and ROIS NII Open Collaborative Research 2022 (22S0302)/2023 (23S0301).

References

1. Ladisa, P., Plate, H., Martines, M., Barais, O.: SoK: taxonomy of attacks on open-source software supply chains. In: Proceedings of 2023 IEEE Symposium on Security and Privacy, pp. 1509–1526. IEEE (2023). https://doi.ieeecomputersociety.org/10.1109/SP46215.2023.00010
2. Allodi, L.: Economic factors of vulnerability trade and exploitation. In: Proceedings of the 24th ACM SIGSAC Conference on Computer and Communications Security, pp. 1483–1499. ACM (2017). https://doi.org/10.1145/3133956.3133960
3. Allodi, L., Massacci, F.: Security events and vulnerability data for cybersecurity risk estimation. Risk Anal. **37**(8), 1606–1627 (2017). https://doi.org/10.1111/risa.12864

4. Nikonov, A., Vulfin, A., Vasilyev, V., Kirillova, A., Mikhailov, V.: System for esti-mation CVSS severity metrics of vulnerability based on text mining technology. In: Proceedings of the 2021 Information Technology and Nanotechnology, pp. 1–5. IEEE (2021) https://doi.org/10.1109/ITNT52450.2021.9649232

5. Householder, D, A., Chrabaszcz, J., Warren, D., Spring, M, J.: Historical analysis of exploit availability timelines. In: Proceedings of the 13th USENIX Workshop on Cyber Security Experimentation and Test, USENIX (2020)

6. Jacobs, J., Romanosky, S., Adjerid, I., Baker, W.: Improving vulnerability remedi-ation through better exploit prediction. J. Cybersecurity **6**(1) (2020). https://doi.org/10.1093/cybsec/tyaa015

7. Jacobs, J., Romanosky, S., Edwards, B., Adjerid, I., Roytman, M.: Exploit pre-diction scoring system. Digital Threats Res. Pract. **2**(3), 1–17 (2021). https://doi.org/10.1145/3436242

8. NIST, National Vulnerability Database. https://nvd.nist.gov/. Accessed 18 Aug 2022

9. FIRST, Common Vulnerability Scoring System SIG. https://www.first.org/cvss/. Accessed 18 Aug 2022

10. OpenSSF, Open Source Project Criticality Score (Beta). https://github.com/ossf/criticality_score. Accessed 18 Aug 2022

11. MITRE, Common Vulnerabilities and Exposures. https://www.cve.org/. Accessed 18 Aug 2022

12. NIST, Official Common Platform Enumeration Dictionary. https://nvd.nist.gov/products/cpe. Accessed 18 Aug 2022

13. CISA, Known Exploited Vulnerabilities Catalog. https://www.cisa.gov/known-exploited-vulnerabilities-catalog. Accessed 8 Apr 2023

14. Debian Project, Debian GNU/Linux (online). https://www.debian.org/. Accessed 18 Aug 2022

15. Williams, M.A., Dey, S., Barranco, C., Naim, M.S., Hossain, S.M., Akbar, M.: Analyzing evolving trends of vulnerabilities in national vulnerability database. In Proceedings of 2018 IEEE International Conference on Big Data, pp. 3011–3020. IEEE (2018). https://doi.org/10.1109/BigData.2018.8622299

16. Martin, H., Jana, K., Elias, B., Pavel, C.: Survey of attack projection, prediction, and forecasting in cyber security. IEEE Commun. Surv. Tutor. **21**(1), 640–660. IEEE (2018). https://doi.org/10.1109/COMST.2018.2871866

17. Chen, H., Liu, J., Liu, R., Park, N., Subrahmanian, S.V.: VEST: a system for vul-nerability exploit scoring & timing. In: Proceedings of the Twenty-Eighth Interna-tional Joint Conference on Artificial Intelligence, pp. 6503–6505 (2019). https://doi.org/10.24963/ijcai.2019/937

18. Minh, L.H.T., et al.: DeepCVA: automated commit-level vulnerability assess-ment with deep multi-task learning. In: Proceedings of 36th IEEE/ACM Interna-tional Conference on Automated Software Engineering, pp. 717–729. IEEE (2021). https://doi.org/10.1109/ASE51524.2021.9678622

19. Siewruk, G., Mazurczyk, W.: Context-aware software vulnerability classification using machine learning. IEEE Access **9**, 88852–88867 (2021). https://doi.org/10.1109/ACCESS.2021.3075385

20. Walkowski, M., Krakowiak M., Jaroszewski, M., Oko, J., Sujecki, S.: Automatic CVSS-based vulnerability prioritization and response with context information. In Proceedings of International Conference on Software, Telecommunications and Computer Networks, pp. 1–6 (2021). https://doi.org/10.23919/SoftCOM52868.2021.9559094.559094

21. Mitra, S., Ransbotham, S.: The effects of vulnerability disclosure policy on the diffusion of security attacks. Inf. Syst. Res. **26**(3), 565–584 (2015). https://doi.org/10.1287/isre.2015.0587

22. Boechat, F., et al.: Is vulnerability report confidence redundant? pitfalls using temporal risk scores. IEEE Secur. Priv. **19**(4), 44–53 (2021). https://doi.org/10.1109/MSEC.2021.3070978

23. Walkowski, M., Oko, J., Sujecki, S.: Vulnerability management models using a common vulnerability scoring system. Appl. Sci. **11**, 8735 (2021). https://doi.org/10.3390/app11188735

Attacks and Defenses

Defending AirType Against Inference Attacks Using 3D In-Air Keyboard Layouts: Design and Evaluation

Hattan Althebeiti, Ran Gedawy, Ahod Alghuried, Daehun Nyang, and David Mohaisen(✉)

University of Central Florida, Orlando, USA
mohaisen@ucf.edu

Abstract. Augmented reality (AR) interaction methods are leaning towards more natural techniques, such as voice commands, hand gestures, and in-air tapping for input. From a security perspective, however, recent works have demonstrated that these methods, such as in-air tapping, are vulnerable to inference attacks where an adversary is capable of reconstructing input in the virtual environment using low-level hand-tracking data with high accuracy. This paper addresses the defense of in-air tapping mechanisms against inference attacks by developing and evaluating a 3D curved keyboard for input. Our design exploits the symmetry between the virtual and physical worlds enabling the inference attack in the first place and increasing the uncertainty of the adversary by manipulating the geometric aspects of this keyboard plane in 3D. We evaluate our design through numerous experiments and show it to be robust against inference attacks, where the adversary's accuracy in obtaining the correct input text is reduced to 0% (from 87%) and at most to just 18% within the top-500 candidate reconstructions.

Keywords: AR/VR · Inference · Privacy · Defense

1 Introduction

The emerging usage of new interaction methods in AR/VR environments is shown to result in serious privacy and security risks. For example, Shi *et al.* [21] developed an eavesdropping attack that analyzed the captured facial movements from the AR/VR Head Mounted Display's (HMD) motion sensors and inferred sensitive speech and speaker information from this low-level sensor data. Meteriz-Yildiran *et al.* [19] showed that low-level hand tracking data captured by a motion sensor could be feasibly used to infer the users typed data, including sensitive data such as username and passwords, effectively keylogging the victims' inputs with up to 87% accuracy. The key insight in the developed attack by Meteriz-Yildiran *et al.* is that the projection of the keyboard in the AR environment has a fixed structure in a 2D plane that can be estimated using those

© The Author(s), under exclusive license to Springer Nature Singapore Pte Ltd. 2024
H. Kim and J. Youn (Eds.): WISA 2023, LNCS 14402, pp. 159–174, 2024.
https://doi.org/10.1007/978-981-99-8024-6_13

low-level tracking data with high accuracy and feasibly due to the relatively limited set of possibilities for keyboard layouts in 2D. Meteriz-Yildiran *et al.* also demonstrated a defense to the attack that "jitters" the keyboard, thus allowing the limited adversary observations from which the adversary could learn the position of the keyboard. However, this defense is shown to have limited usability [19].

This work aims to address the latter risk and associated attack on AR IO by investigating the development of new and advanced text entry methods. Specifically, we examine a tilted 3D QWERTY keyboard and its capability in alleviating the input inference attacks utilized by Meteriz-Yildiran *et al.* [19]. The key insight exploited in alleviating the impact of the inference attack on AR IO through a "curved" keyboard is by breaking the symmetry and predictability of the keyboard structure that allowed the attack to succeed in the first place. Namely, the curved keyboard is represented by N 2D planes in AR environment, significantly increasing the search space for the likely keyboard position in space, and reducing the likelihood of key inference attacks significantly. Our experiments demonstrate that an adversary will not be able to infer the typed text with the 3D keyboard as effectively. Namely, the pinpoint accuracy of the new keyboard using the same inference technique due to Meteriz-Yildiran *et al.* ranged from 0% to 18%. Moreover, the maximum pinpoint accuracy was just 33% assuming a very powerful adversary who computed all the possible keyboard reconstructions, in contrast to a more realistic adversary that is constrained to estimating the keyboard from the top-k reconstructions (e.g., top-5, top-100, or even top-500).

Contributions. The key contributions of this paper are as follows. (1) We present, implement, and demonstrate a new text entry method, a 3D QWERTY keyboard, in the AR space that is customized to alleviate the input inference attack on 2D AR keyboards. (2) We customize the inference attack on in-air tapping keyboards for AR/VR devices proposed by [19] for the 3D keyboard inference. (3) We evaluate our text entry method using extensive experiments and show that it significantly alleviates the input inference attacks while being highly usable.

Organization. The paper is organized as follows. Section 2 discusses the related work. Section 3 defines the system and threat models. Section 4 is the proposed design and technical details. Section 5 discusses the evaluation and results. Section 6 is the discussion. Section 7 concludes this paper.

2   Related Work

The most popular method of text entry in virtual environments is by using hardware, such as a hand-held controller. However, this method is characterized by high error rate and latency. Gupta *et al.* [11], Chen *et al.* [9], and Markussen *et al.* [18] developed word-gesture text entry methods, each of which uses a planar keyboard similar to SHARK2 developed by Kristensson and Zhai [15]. The main idea of SHARK2 is combining regular tapping on a stylus keyboard with gesturing on the stylus keyboard for familiar words. Yanagihara *et al.* [27] proposed a cubic keyboard, which is a 3D word-gesture text entry method for virtual environments where users enter a word by drawing a stroke with the hand-held controller. Meteriz-Yildiran *et al.* [29] developed AirType, a 2D in-air tapping keyboard, on which the main attack discussed in this paper is launched. Yanagihara *et al.* [28] also proposed another cubic keyboard for virtual environments but with a curved layout, controlled by the hand-held controller.

Keylogging inference attacks date back over 50 years when Bell Laboratory researchers discovered that the emanating electromagnetic spikes from a teletype terminal could be used to decode secure communications [7]. Later on, keylogging inference attacks became more advanced and powerful. Generally, the related work in this space is categorized into temporal and spatial: attacks utilizing temporal information, such as the timing of key press and release events [25,30], and attacks utilizing spatial information to reveal the location of and distance between keys on the keyboard [3,17,26]. This work focuses on inference attacks that utilize spatial information in the AR/VR domain. In this space, Meteriz-Yildiran *et al.* [19] showed that low-level hand tracking data captured by a motion sensor can be used to infer the user's typed data. Sun *et al.* [22] proposed a video-assisted keystroke inference framework that uses video recordings of tablet backside motion to infer the user's typed inputs. Jin *et al.* [12] inferred users' typed input through the vibrations of the desk where the keyboard is placed.

Blocking keylogging inference attacks is inherently difficult due to the difficulty of analytically describing some physical systems, thus most efforts have been focused on attack mitigation (alleviation) under specific assumptions. To this end, the mitigation mechanisms for keylogging inference attacks focused on three approaches (1) **Impedance.** Defense mechanisms that impede the adversary from accessing the compromising signal [6,10]. (2) **Obfuscation.** Mechanisms that obfuscate the side channel, so that even when the signals are still accessible to the adversary, limited useful information is obtained from the acquired signals [4,16]. (3) **Concealment.** Mechanisms that conceal essential information from the adversary, so that the obtained signals alone will not be enough for the adversary to successfully launch a keylogging attack [1,5].

Our proposed work falls into the third category, concealment, as the geometric aspects of our proposed text entry method are concealed from the adversary.

3   System and Threat Model

System Model. Our model includes an in-air tapping keyboard, HMD with an AR application, and a user. Upon launching the AR application, the user attaches the keyboard to an arbitrary location in the virtual environment. The AR HMD then tracks the user's hand movements and detects the key taps on the keyboard by checking if a fingertip collides with a key in space. The keyboard layout can be freely resized by the user.

Hand Tracking. Hand tracking is crucial for the AR user and the adversary. For the user, hand tracking allows typing on the in-air keyboard. For the adversary, hand tracking facilitates the inference attack. Most AR HMDs [23] have built-in hand-tracking capabilities, which allows the users to efficiently type on the AR keyboards. On the other hand, an adversary may obtain the hand-tracking data by one of a few possible methods, e.g., hand-tracking sensors. Hand tracking sensors, such as the leap motion controller [24], provide various spatial information about hands and fingers, including the tip positions of all fingers and their pointing directions, the position of the palm center, and the palm normal. This information is called low-level hand-tracking data.

Threat Model.. Our threat model includes a user typing on an AR keyboard, and an adversary trying to infer what the user types by exploiting the user's hand-tracking data. To gain access to the victim's hand traces, an adversary might utilize a number of possible methods, which we cover in the following scenarios. **Scenario 1: Using an AR HMD.** The adversary may use an AR HMD similar to the one used by the user for typing, where the adversary is expected to sit close to the AR user, put on the AR HMD, and the AR HMD will record the victim's hand data as done by the AR HMD of the user. While efficient, this scenario exposes the adversary as he has to be close enough to the user to capture accurate hand traces. **Scenario 2: Remote collection by malware.** The adversary may embed malicious software (malware) in the user's AR HMD. The malware can be then used to record the victim's hand-tracking data and send it to the adversary through an API invocation. This scenario is more stealthy and requires no extra hardware by the adversary, although more expensive as the adversary has to inject malware into the user's HMD beforehand. **Scenario 3: Collection using tracking devices** In this scenario, the adversary uses a hand tracker device, such as the leap motion controller [24], positioned near the victim. The device is small and can be easily hidden by the adversary, and a recent version of this device can support wireless setup [20], allowing the adversary to collect hand-tracking data remotely.

4   Design and Methodology

4.1   Design Justification

Why do Inference Attacks on AR Work? By analyzing the work proposed by Meteriz-Yildiran *et al.* [19], we concluded that the inference attacks on AR input mechanisms, and the air-taping keyboards in particular, are highly successful for the following two reasons. 1. **Visibility and exposure.** During an AR typing session, the user's typing space is typically visible to the adversary. An adversary can therefore obtain high-level information about the keyboard plane by only observing the victim's activity in the physical space to interact with the virtual space stealthily. 2. **Symmetry.** Using the QWERTY keyboard in the AR environment makes the projected keyboard and the virtual hand models **symmetrical** to the physical keyboard and the user's actual hands movements.

An adversary exploits this observation to obtain the specific location of keys on the keyboard, reconstruct the keyboard as a whole, and infer the user input. By knowing the keyboard used in the virtual space is a flat 2D QWERTY keyboard, the adversary has knowledge about the positions of the keys relative to one another and that the keys are of fixed size. By obtaining just two keys' positions and the associated transformations from the victim's plane, the adversary can infer the rest of the keys. Therefore, an adversary can map the virtual space associated with the keyboard to the physical space.

Key Insight: Breaking the Symmetry. The visibility and exposure reason high-lighted above as a key factor in enabling the attack by allowing adversaries to collect low-level features for inference is unavoidable for most AR applications. Limiting exposure and visibility for input would thus be a significant design challenge. To address the inference attack, we focus on the symmetry aspect. We believe it is very natural to anticipate that a defense to those attacks should be focusing on breaking such symmetry. While breaking such symmetry may not necessarily eliminate the attacks altogether, we anticipate that it will raise the cost of the attack significantly (i.e., attack alleviation).

There are several possible techniques that could be used for breaking this symmetry, which we review in the following. (1) **Key Shuffling.** One such possibility to break the symmetry is to dynamically shuffle the key positions every time the virtual keyboard is launched through keyboard refreshing. This approach clearly breaks the symmetry by randomizing the keys positions and making it infeasible for the adversary to learn the specific position of a key in the virtual space by exploiting the consistent and repeated patterns of key taps that amplify language characteristics. (2) **Keyboard Jittering.** Another approach to break the symmetry is to manipulate the virtual location of the keyboard through jittering, thus altering the physical location of the key taps.

Shortcomings. While the key shuffling approach is widely used in banking apps, its use is limited to short inputs, e.g., passwords, and is rarely used as a main input mechanism for being impractical with poor usability. In particular, given that the users are familiar with the QWERTY keyboard as a fixed and deterministic layout, randomizing the keys would mean that the users would be inconvenienced, become slower at using the keyboard, and be more likely prone to errors, all of which are essential usability metrics. Certainly, the usability of this approach can be improved by exploring the trade-off of between security and usability through determining the frequency at which the keyboard is randomized. Nevertheless, the fundamentals of the attack and the shortcomings in terms of usability will be manifested in such a trade-off design.

The keyboard approach, while effective at significantly reducing the attack surface, it has significant usability drawbacks. Namely, the frequent jittering of the keyboard causes the users to feel dizzy. Similarly, exploiting the trade-off between security and usability could be a problem but would still maintain the fundamentals of the attack.

4.2   3D AR Keyboard Design

Our Approach. Our approach to breaking the symmetry is to project the physical QWERTY keyboard on a 3D plane in the virtual space. By using this technique, the key sizes are no longer consistent across all keys. Moreover, the transformation angles and positions of the keys will vary widely, which makes it highlight infeasible for an adversary to obtain an accurate mapping between the victim's virtual space and the physical space. On the other hand, and from a usability standpoint, the same exact structure of the basic QWERTY keyboard will be utilized, alleviating the issues in the key shuffling approach. Similarly, this approach employs a fixed keyboard (although in 3D), thus addressing the shortcomings in the jittering approach. We hypothesize that maintaining the structure of the keyboard will have favorable usability features that we will uncover.

General Design. We developed an in-air tapping curved QWERTY keyboard and used it to evaluate the effectiveness of the inference attack on air-tapping keyboards. We implemented the curved keyboard using the *Unity game engine* and utilized the *Magic leap 1* as an HMD. The keyboard surface is bent spherically inwards towards the user. The keyboard uses a 3D word gesture text entry method for a more immersive experience when compared with the 2D word gesture text entry methods. Upon launching an AR application, the system shows the keyboard plane and two hand models as virtual objects. Figure 1 shows the keyboard in the first user's view with the hand models.

Keys Selection and Detection. The keys selection is done through the virtual hand models, which mirror the user's actual hands via the hand tracking feature of the AR HMDs. The AR HMD detects if a key is selected by checking if the fingertip of the index finger collides with the key in space. The keys are set to green by default, and when the user's index fingertip collides with a key, the key turns into blue and plays a "click" sound, providing the user with visual/audio cues. Accordingly, a user enters the letters of an intended word by tapping keys sequentially using their index finger. The typed words are displayed to the user above the keyboard. The AR keyboard is designed so that the keys in the center of the keyboard resemble the keys of the basic QWERTY keyboard in terms of the keys' transformation, while a transformation angle is applied to the keys towards the edges of the keyboard. This design ensures the symmetry between the physical and the virtual keyboards is broken through the transformation angles of the edge keys while still maintaining high usability through the remaining keys design.

4.3   Technical Details

We adapted the same attack by Meteriz-Yildiran *et al.* [19] where the attacker uses a hand tracking device near the victim to collect the low-level hand tracking data to infer the typed text. The pipeline input is the low-level hand-tracking data and the final output is the list of text inferences ordered from best to worst.

Fig. 1. The user's view of the 3D AR keyboard.

Similarly, the keylogging inference attack consists of keystroke detection and identification. The keystroke detection consists of (1) *deep key tap localization* and (2) *key tap localization refinement*. The key identification consists of (1) *candidate Key center generation*, (2) *candidate Keyboard Reconstruction*, and (3) *best-to-worst ordering*.

Keystroke Detection (1): Deep Key Tap Localization. A Convolutional Neural Network (CNN) is used to localize the key taps from the input time domain data stream. We address the change in the input data to sensor proximity through a pre-processing step, followed by applying the CNN and then localization. In the preprocessing, we ensure that different spatial configurations of the sensor do not affect the tracking data time-domain data conversion. Namely, we obtain the following features from the low-level hand tracking data: (1) *Finger tips:* The tip position of each finger for the palm center (f_p), (2) *Direction:* The pointing direction of each finger for the normal vector of the palm (f_d), and (3) *Velocity:* The velocity of each fingertip (f_v). Eventually, the hand features are represented as $X = \{x_t\}_{t=1}^{T}$, where the t-th frame is $x_t = [f_p \ f_d \ f_v]^T$. A data segment $s(t_s, t_e)$ is a slice that includes the frames between the start and end.

Network Architecture. We utilize a multi-head CNN to localize the key taps from the input data stream. The hand tracker sampling rate is 80 frames per second (fps), each key tap is interpreted as 375 ms (or 30 frames). Each head of the CNN takes an input sub-segment with the shape of height 5 fingers, width of 30 frames, and depth of 3 dimensions. The convolution kernel size covers 3 frames with stride 1. In our implementation, we made several modifications to fit our use case, compared to [19]. First, a single CNN model was used instead of two, since users tend to use only one hand while typing on the curved keyboard. Second, some CNN model parameters, including the number of epochs and batch size, were tuned to decrease the validation loss.

Localization. Segments are generated by sliding a fixed-length window on the data stream. The multi-head CNN takes the input segments and outputs a confidence score of each segment, determining the confidence a key tap occurred in that segment. Redundant detection is excluded by applying a non-max suppression to ensure that the most confident predictions are kept and that the kept predictions are all disjoint. We denote the segments and their predicted confidence scores as $\mathsf{P} = \{(sm, \tau m)\}_{m=1}^{M}$, where τm is the confidence score. The segments with a confidence score below a certain predefined threshold are excluded. The key tap points of the remaining segments are estimated by fetching the position of the index fingertip at the midpoint of the window. Given the ground truth key tap segments GT, each key tap segment is associated with a ground truth segment that is closest to the key tap segment in time.

For each association, the intersection over-union (IoU) is measured. For two segments, $S_1(t_1, t_2)$ and $S_2(t_3, t_4)$, where t_1 and t_3 are the start time, t_2 and t_4 are finish time, and $t_3 > t_1$, the IoU between S_1 and S_2 is defined as $\min(0, t_2 - t_3)/(t_4 - t_1)$, which takes values in $[0, 1]$. The result of this step is a set of associations of segments with ground truth and their IoU values: $\mathsf{A} = \{(sm, gtl ,IoU)\}$, where sm is the key tap segment, gtl is ground truth segment and IoU is the intersection over the union between the given segment and the ground truth segment. The associations with IoU below a predefined IoU threshold are eliminated, ensuring a key tap segment with a high IoU with a ground truth segment is kept while inaccurate key tap segments are eliminated.

Metrics. We interpret the segments in A as true positives, $P \backslash A$ as false positives, $GT \backslash A$ as false negatives, and the remaining segments as true negatives. We set the classification threshold to 0.5, based on trials for an optimal trade-off.

Keystroke Detection (2): Key Tap Localization Refinement. For a more accurate localization, the previously obtained key tap points are further refined through a series of steps. 1. **Keyboard plane estimation:** A keyboard plane is estimated from the key tap points, where a plane in 3D is defined by a normal vector perpendicular to the plane, a point on the plane, and a scalar. Thus, the fitting plane to the estimated 3D key tap points is obtained using a regression model that minimizes a linear least square error between the points and the plane. 2. **Reducing the false positives:** The trace of the fingertip of each key tap window is checked and is eliminated if it does not cross the previously estimated plane, as that means it does not represent any key on the keyboard. 3. **Refining the key tap points:** To improve the spatial precision of key tap points, the intersection point where fingertips cross the estimated keyboard plane is used instead of the midpoint of the key tap window. 4. **Dimension reduction:** The estimated 3D key tap points are reduced to 2D by first creating an orthonormal basis containing the normal of the plane. Then, we change the basis for the key tap points and obtain 2D key tap points by eliminating the component in the direction of the normal vector. This step reduces the complexity of obtaining a similarity transformation between the points in the virtual and physical planes. Since all the key tap points lay on the same plane, the dimensionality reduction causes no loss of information.

Key Identification (1): Candidate Key Center Generation. From the refined key tap points, candidates for key centers are deduced. The relationship between the key centers and the key tap points is observed as follows: when each key center is considered as the cluster centroid of that particular key, each key tap point will belong to the cluster of the tapped key. Optimally, the number of clusters should equal the number of unique keys pressed in a session. However, this number is unknown. As such, cluster groups with different numbers are generated using a weighted agglomerative (bottom-up) hierarchical clustering. First, all key tap points are treated as singleton clusters with uniform weights, then cluster group C is iteratively updated by merging the closest clusters considering the weights. We use the Euclidean distance to find the closest clusters, then merge them through weighted vector averaging. Each update to the cluster group C adds a cluster group to the set of cluster groups G with a different cluster count. Since the number of unique keys in a session is upper bounded by the total number of keys, any cluster group with more clusters than the total number of AR keyboard keys is eliminated. The **output** of this step is a set of cluster groups, G, where each cluster group has a different cluster count.

Key Identification (2): Candidate Keyboard Reconstruction. In this step, the keyboard reconstructions are output by overcoming two challenges, which we highlight as follows. 1. **Adversary/victim coordinates mapping**: Since the user's coordinates system differs from the adversary's, the geometric instances are expressed differently. We consider two pairs of the adversary and victim plane points to address this issue and compute their similarity transform T (translation, rotation, uniform scaling). By applying the similarity transform T to all obtained key tap points from the victim's plane, the key tap points are mapped to the corresponding keys on the AR keyboard. 2. **Obtaining corresponding pairs of points:** After obtaining the similarity transform T, the user's key tap points K can be easily transformed into the adversary's keyboard as $K' = T(K)$, associating each key tap position k' in K' with its corresponding key by checking the key area where the key tap position k' falls. However, the adversary lacks two corresponding points from both planes, precluding correct transformation. Also, the adversary does not know which cluster corresponds to which key. To resolve this issue, the likelihood of each cluster C belonging to any unique key j for each cluster group C in the set of cluster groups G was considered. Candidate keyboard reconstructions are obtained by computing the transformation using all possible center and key pairs.

Key Identification (3): Best-to-worst Ordering. In this step, inaccurate reconstructions caused by the incorrect center and key pairings are excluded. Accurate reconstructions are known to meet certain characteristics measured using the following inference measurements. 1. **Scaling factor.** The keyboard size should not be too large or too small, as too small keyboards will have poor usability because they will be hard for the users to tap the right keys while too large keyboards can get out of the range of the HMD frame. 2. **Outliers ratio.** Outliers are key tap points falling outside the estimated keyboard area. Ideally, all key tap points should fall into the area of some key. Although the optimal value for the scaling factor is zero, a small number of outliers are expected and accepted. Based on the previous description, the scaling factor measures the ratio of the outliers to all key tap points. 3. **Number of clusters.** Optimally, the number of clusters should equal the number of unique keys found after the transformation. This is achieved if the clustering process is accurate, dividing the key tap points into clusters of unique keys. Based on the previous description, this measure quantifies the difference between the number of clusters and the found keys.

First, some reconstructions are eliminated by enforcing a scaling factor limit. Then, a linear regression model is utilized to estimate the combined effect of (2) and (3) on the correctness of the reconstructions. The model takes (2) and (3) as inputs, and outputs the associated correctness score. We first train the regression model with the correctness scores measured using the normalized Levenshtein similarity between the estimated and the ground truth strings. Upon training, (2) and (3) of each candidate reconstructions are forwarded to it, and the reconstructions are sorted in decreasing order with respect to their correctness score. The **final output** of the pipeline are the sorted reconstructions i.e., the best to worst ordering of the keyboard reconstructions.

5   Evaluation

We evaluated the end-to-end pipeline of the inference attack on the 3D keyboard design (attack mitigation) and our keyboard's usability to ensure that 3D structure does not affect performance metrics (effectiveness, efficiency, and satisfaction).

5.1   User Study

First, we carried out a comparative usability analysis to evaluate the usability of our developed AR keyboard model. We compared our model against two text entry methods: the baseline keyboard and AiRType [29]. In the baseline keyboard, the user moves the cursor through the ray coming out of the controller to target different keys, then pulls the trigger button to select the keys. In AiRType, the user selects the key by directly tapping the target key with any of their fingers. For this evaluation, we measured the usability based on the standard ISO 9241-11 [2] model of usability.

Usability Study Setup. We collected data from 10 users. The users' ages (in years) ranged between 20 and 36, including 7 males and 3 females. None of the users had any previous experience with AR text entry techniques and none was trained before performing the experiments. The users were asked to wear Magic leap 1 HMD and type the same sequence of words (an e-mail of length 105, 5 random strings of length 8, and 3 passwords of lengths 15, 10, and 5).

The ISO usability model defines three metrics: (1) *effectiveness*, (2) *efficiency*, and (3) *satisfaction*. The effectiveness measures the percentage of incorrect key

Table 1. The average usability test results. The effectiveness is expressed as a percentage, the efficiency in terms of cps, and the satisfaction as a percentage

	Effectiveness	Efficiency	Satisfaction
Baseline	8.02	0.604	74.5
AiRType	5.83	0.624	81.5
Our model	7.38	0.381	68.0

taps, the efficiency measures the task completion time by the user, measured the number of characters typed per second, and the satisfaction represents the System Usability Scale (SUS) score of the design. We measure the satisfaction by a standardized system usability questionnaire score [8].

Usability Study Results. The usability test measurements from our keyboard, AiRType, and the baseline keyboard are shown in Table 1. For the effectiveness metric, our curved keyboard model is observed to be more effective than the baseline keyboard and has a slightly worse effectiveness than the AiRType keyboard.

For the efficiency metric, the curved keyboard was shown to be less efficient in terms of the number of typed characters per second. We assume that this is because the participants in our case were inexperienced and not sufficiently trained before using the system. Users tend to be more cautious and slow when using our design, in contrast to the standard flat keyboard design. For the satisfaction metric, our model achieved average satisfaction. We anticipate that the efficiency and satisfaction will significantly increase if participants gain more experience with using the system and dealing with this novel design of keyboards. We also anticipate that involving a larger number of participants with different backgrounds related to using AR keyboards can help us in general to gain better insights into the efficiency of users using the curved keyboard. The results, however, are promising and can be further viewed alongside the security provided by the keyboard in mitigating the inference attack.

5.2   End-to-End Pipeline

Experimental Setup. For this set of experiments, we used Magic Leap 1 as the AR HMD, and Leap Motion Controller as the hand tracker. The leap motion controller can track hands within a 60-cm distance. Hence the adversary is assumed to implant it close to the victim. With the wireless version of the leap motion controller, the adversary will be able to obtain hand-tracking data effortlessly at distance. Magic Leap 1, on the other hand, detects hands within 80 cm distance.

In this experiment, we used five participants, including one female and four males with ages ranging from 25 to 36.

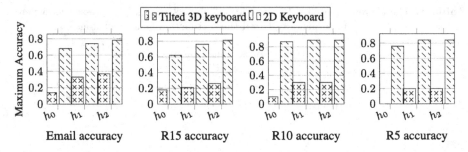

Fig. 2. Comparison of h_0, h_1 and h_2 email, R15, R10, and R5 accuracies between flat and curved VR keyboard

Evaluation Metrics: We evaluated the accuracy of the text inference using the normalized Levenshtein similarity. We compute the pinpoint, h-hop, and top-k accuracy [22]. In the h-hop accuracy, the predicted h-hops from the actual keys are considered a correct prediction. h_0 (or 0-hop accuracy) represents pinpoint accuracy, h_1 represents one key hop from the predicted to the actual key pressed, and h_2 represents two key hops from the actual key pressed.

We use h-hop to show that an adversary will not be able to achieve meaningful predictions even when utilizing the closest key hops. The top-k accuracy represents the maximum accuracy within k inferences in the best-to-worst ordering.

Keystroke Detection. We first collected data from two users while typing 54 random pangrams (108 in total). This data is split into 96 pangrams for training and 12 pangrams for testing. To create the ground truth, we labeled the key tap segments from each data sample as 1 and labeled the disjoint background segments as 0. To train the CNN, we used Adam optimizer [13] with a learning rate of 0.001, L2 regularization with a penalty of 0.001, and the weighted binary cross-entropy as our loss function.

Key Identification. We used the same data from training the CNN of the *keystroke detection* phase to train the linear regression model for the *best-to-worst ordering.*

End-to-End Pipeline. We collected data from 3 other users while typing an e-mail of length 105, randomly selected from the Enron dataset [14]. We call this data the Email dataset. We also collected short data sequences while the users were typing random text, resembling typing passwords, with lengths of 5, 10, and 15. We call this data the R5, R10, and R15 datasets. In this experiment, we aim to gauge the ability of the adversary to obtain meaningful long-text inputs, e.g., writing an e-mail, or short-text scenarios, e.g., login credentials. We feed the E-mail, R5, R10, and R15 datasets and associated low-level artifacts to the pipeline, and the output is a set of reconstructions, ordered from best to worst, for each dataset.

Table 2. The maximum h_0, h_1, and h_2 accuracy for the top 500 reconstructions

	Email			R15			R10			R5		
	h_0	h_1	h_2	h_0	h_1	h_2	h_0	h_1	h_2	h_0	h_1	h_2
User 1	0.14	0.33	0.37	0.18	0.21	0.21	0.05	0.20	0.20	0.00	0.20	0.20
User 2	0.10	0.16	0.16	0.05	0.13	0.26	0.07	0.30	0.30	0.00	0.00	0.00
User 3	0.14	0.30	0.32	0.13	0.13	0.13	0.10	0.30	0.30	0.00	0.20	0.20

Table 3. The maximum h_0, h_1, and h_2 accuracy for the maximum reconstructions.

	Email			R15			R10			R5		
	h_0	h_1	h_2	h_0	h_1	h_2	h_0	h_1	h_2	h_0	h_1	h_2
User 1	0.19	0.26	0.27	0.50	0.69	0.69	0.40	0.40	0.40	0.50	0.60	0.60
User 2	0.27	0.33	0.39	0.38	0.43	0.56	0.36	0.60	0.70	0.31	0.40	0.40
User 3	0.38	0.38	0.38	0.41	0.41	0.41	0.45	0.45	0.45	0.33	0.33	0.33

Experiment Results. Table 2 shows the h_0, h_1, and h_2 accuracies obtained for the Email, R15, R10, and R5 datasets for each user. These values are obtained considering the top-500 reconstructions. We also considered a scenario in which an adversary has sufficient resources and can compute the inferences using the maximum number of reconstructions that can be obtained. This results in a huge number of keyboard reconstructions. For user 1, there are 473,850 keyboard reconstructions for the e-mail data, 31,850, 234,650, and 109,850 keyboard reconstructions for each sequence in R5, R10, and R15, respectively. The difference in the number of keyboard reconstructions is due to the number of key taps, which is upper bounded by the number of centers. Table 3 shows the results of the h_0, h_1, and h_2 accuracies in the previously described scenario.

Overall, the results show that our model is a highly secure text entry method against the inference attack in contrast to the two alternatives. The pinpoint accuracy of inferring the typed text is 0% in most of the cases, and it reaches just 50% in the worst case when an adversary is able to generate all possible keyboard reconstructions, which is highly optimistic and impractical in many real-world scenarios.

The maximum pinpoint accuracy for the top 500 constructions is 15%, 18%, 18%, and 3% for the Email, R15, R10, and R5 data, respectively. Compared to the 2D keyboard model [19], where the authors achieved a maximum pinpoint accuracy of 68%, 62%, 87%, and 76% for Email, R15, R10, and R5 data, respectively, our 3D keyboard is resilient. Overall, this experiment shows that our proposed keyboard model is highly effective in defending against input inference attacks.

Figure 2 compares the accuracy of text inference from our 3D keyboard model and the flat keyboard model [19]. In particular, these results show that, without any exception, the adversary's inference accuracy on our model is consistently much lower than that of the flat keyboard, which confirms that our model is significantly more robust against the keylogging inference.

6   Discussion and Limitations

The defense's success mainly depends on the adversary's knowledge of the geometric aspects of the text entry method. The following steps of the pipeline influence that:

Key Tap Localization Refinement–Keyboard Plane Estimation. We assume the adversary estimates the keyboard plane as a regular 2D plane. This is how almost all keyboards are represented in the AR environments, replicating the physical QWERTY keyboard structure, not as a spherical 3D plane. This results in inaccurate plane estimation.

Candidate Keyboard Reconstructions. For obtaining the relevant keyboard reconstructions, the adversary has to overcome the problem of mapping the coordinates system from the victim's plane to his plane. As proposed by [19], this challenge can be overcome by obtaining two corresponding pairs of points from both planes. A transformation vector that maps the points from the different planes is then computed and later used to map each point from the victim's to the adversary's plane. However, this is not applicable in our model, as the transformation between points is inconsistent across all points. This is because different points have different rotation angles in the titled 3D space, especially keys on the sides of the keyboard. Obtaining the transformation vector using only two pairs of points will not guarantee the accurate transformation of all the points in the victim's plane to the physical AR plane because different points on the 3D plane will have different transformations that need to be accurately calculated.

Due to the inaccurate estimation of the keyboard plane, in the **best-to-worst ordering step**, several reconstructions will be incorrectly excluded. This is because some of the key tap points of these reconstructions are considered outliers, as they do not fall in the estimated plane area. This is because the keyboard plane wasn't estimated correctly in the first place. If considering the correct 3D plane, more keyboard reconstructions would be included in the final output.

Limitations. Our work has the following limitations.

Usability. Although our model proved to be highly robust against input inference attacks, the usability of the model could still be improved. We anticipate that the usability can be significantly enhanced if participants had enough training before using the keyboard. Our model is seen to provide a trade-off between usability and security. By reducing how the keyboard is bent, the keyboard will gradually convert to a flat keyboard, and hence the usability will improve but at the expense of affecting security.

Strong Threat Model. In our future work, we will explore our model's security against a stronger threat model. An adversary could obtain more information about the geometric aspects of our proposed model by observing the victim's typing patterns long enough. We will test the security of our model against an adversary with such a level of knowledge. We anticipate this model's security to be lower, although exploring a quantification and contrast with the 2D keyboard model remains open.

7 Conclusion

This paper presented and evaluated a new keyboard model for text entry in the AR space. The proposed model is robust against keylogging inference attacks, specifically attacks exploiting the user's hand-tracking data based on the observation that the hands follow specific typing patterns. The maximum keylogging pinpoint accuracy against this curved keyboard was found to be 18% for the top 500 keyboard reconstructions, making a keylogging attack against this keyboard is impractical.

References

1. High resolution time level 2. http://web.archive.org/web/2017 1017013909/ (2017). Accessed 17 Oct 2017
2. 9241-11:2018, I.: Ergonomics of human-system interaction. https://www.iso.org/ obp/ui/#iso:std:iso:9241:-11:ed-2:v1:en
3. Ali, K., Liu, A.X., Wang, W., Shahzad, M.: Keystroke recognition using WiFi signals. In: ACM MobiCom (2015)
4. Anderson, R., Kuhn, M.: Low cost countermeasures against compromising electromagnetic computer emanations. US Patent 6,721,423 (2004)
5. Askarov, A., Zhang, D., Myers, A.C.: Predictive black-box mitigation of timing channels. In: ACM CCS (2010)
6. Asonov, D., Agrawal, R.: Keyboard acoustic emanations. In: IEEE S&P, pp. 3–11 (2004)
7. Boak, D.G.: A history of us communications security, NSA 1973 (1973)
8. Brooke, J.: SUS-A Quick and Dirty Usability Scale. CRC Press, Boca Raton (1996)
9. Chen, S., Wang, J., Guerra, S., Mittal, N., Prakkamakul, S.: Exploring word-gesture text entry techniques in virtual reality. In: CHI EA, pp. 1–6 (2019)
10. Chizeck, H.J., Bonaci, T.: Brain-computer interface anonymizer. US Patent App. 14/174,818 (2014)
11. Gupta, A., Ji, C., Yeo, H.S., Quigley, A., Vogel, D.: RotoSwype: word-gesture typing using a ring. In: ACM CHI (2019)
12. Jin, K., et al.: ViViSnoop: someone is snooping your typing without seeing it! In: IEEE CNS (2017)
13. Kingma, D.P., Ba, J.: Adam: a method for stochastic optimization. In: Bengio, Y., LeCun, Y. (eds.) ICLR (2015). http://arxiv.org/abs/1412.6980
14. Klimt, B., Yang, Y.: The Enron corpus: a new dataset for email classification research. In: Boulicaut, J.-F., Esposito, F., Giannotti, F., Pedreschi, D. (eds.) ECML 2004. LNCS (LNAI), vol. 3201, pp. 217–226. Springer, Heidelberg (2004). https://doi.org/10.1007/978-3-540-30115-8_22

15. Kristensson, P.O., Zhai, S.: Shark2:a large vocabulary shorthand writing system for pen-based computers. In: ACM UIST (2004)
16. Kuhn, M.G., Anderson, R.J.: Soft tempest: hidden data transmission using electromagnetic emanations. In: Aucsmith, D. (ed.) IH 1998. LNCS, vol. 1525, pp. 124–142. Springer, Heidelberg (1998). https://doi.org/10.1007/3-540-49380-8_10
17. Liu, X., Zhou, Z., Diao, W., Li, Z., Zhang, K.: When good becomes evil: keystroke inference with smartwatch. In: ACM CCS (2015)
18. Markussen, A., Jakobsen, M.R., Hornbæk, K.: Vulture: a mid-air word-gesture keyboard. In: ACM CHI (2014)
19. Meteriz-Yidiran, U., Yildiran, N.F., Awad, A., Mohaisen, D.: A keylogging inference attack on air-tapping keyboards in virtual environments. In: IEEE VR, pp. 765–774 (2022)
20. Nefes: Data kit untethers USB devices for wireless VR setups. https://bit.ly/3VbqQG8 (2017). Accessed 12 Mar 2020
21. Shi, C., et al.: Face-mic: Inferring live speech and speaker identity via subtle facial dynamics captured by AR/VR motion sensors. In: ACM MobiCom (2021)
22. Sun, J., Jin, X., Chen, Y., Zhang, J., Zhang, R., Zhang, Y.: Visible: video-assisted keystroke inference from tablet backside motion. In: NDSS (2016)
23. Sun, K., Wang, W., Liu, A.X., Dai, H.: Depth aware finger tapping on virtual displays. In: ACM MobiSys (2018)
24. Tracking: Leap motion controller (2021). https://www.ultraleap.com/product/leap-motion-controller/. Accessed 07 May 2021
25. Vila, P., Kopf, B.: Loophole: timing attacks on shared event loops in chrome. In: USENIX Security (2017)
26. Wang, H., Lai, T.T.T., Roy Choudhury, R.: Mole: motion leaks through smartwatch sensors. In: ACM MobiCom (2015)
27. Yanagihara, N., Shizuki, B.: Cubic keyboard for virtual reality. In: ACM SUI (2018)
28. Yanagihara, N., Shizuki, B., Takahashi, S.: Text entry method for immersive virtual environments using curved keyboard. In: ACM VRST (2019)
29. Yildiran, N.F., Meteriz-Yildiran, U., Mohaisen, D.: AiRType: an air-tapping keyboard for augmented reality environments. In: IEEE VR (2022)
30. Zhang, K., Wang, X.: Peeping tom in the neighborhood: keystroke eavesdropping on multi-user systems. In: USENIX Security (2009)

Robust Training for Deepfake Detection Models Against Disruption-Induced Data Poisoning

Jaewoo Park, Hong Eun Ahn, Leo Hyun Park, and Taekyoung Kwon[✉]

Graduate School of Information, Yonsei University, Seoul, South Korea
{jaewoo1218,ahnhe9227,dofi,taekyoung}@yonsei.ac.kr
http://seclab.yonsei.ac.kr/

Abstract. As Generative Adversarial Networks continue to evolve, deepfake images have become notably more realistic, escalating societal, economic, and political threats. Consequently, deepfake detection has emerged as a crucial research area to deal with these rising threats. Additionally, deepfake disruption, a method that introduces proactive perturbations to genuine images to thwart deepfake generation, has arisen as a prospective defense mechanism. While adopting these two strategies simultaneously seems beneficial in countering deepfakes, this paper first highlights a concern related to their co-existence: genuine images gathered from the Internet, already imbued with disrupting perturbations, can lead to data poisoning in the training datasets of deepfake detection models, thereby severely affecting detection accuracy. This problem, despite its practical implications, has not been adequately addressed in previous deepfake detection studies. This paper proposes a novel training framework to address this problem. Our approach purifies disruptive perturbations during model training using a reverse process of the denoising diffusion probabilistic model. This purification process, faster than the leading method called DiffPure, enables successful deepfake image generation for training and significantly curtails accuracy loss in poisoned datasets. Demonstrating superior performance across detection models, our framework anticipates broad applicability. Our implementation is available at https://github.com/seclab-yonsei/Anti-disrupt.

Keywords: Deepfake · Deepfake Detection · Deepfake Disruption · Data Poisoning · Adversarial Purification

1 Introduction

Generative Adversarial Networks (GANs) [5] have demonstrated exceptional performance in the realm of face manipulation. Rapid advancements in GAN-based deepfake technology [2,13,22] have led to the creation of highly sophisticated deepfake images that are nearly indistinguishable to the human eye. When exploited in cybercrimes, deepfake videos can inflict substantial political, social,

H. Kim and J. Youn (Eds.): WISA 2023, LNCS 14402, pp. 175–187, 2024.
https://doi.org/10.1007/978-981-99-8024-6_14

and economic damage, necessitating robust defense strategies. In this context, two countermeasures are currently under investigation: reactive deepfake detection and proactive deepfake disruption. Deepfake detection [17, 26] is a technology that employs deep learning models to discern whether an input image is authentic or fabricated. Techniques for deepfake detection include spatial-based detection [23], which seeks visual artifacts; frequency-based detection [30], which identifies features in the frequency domain; and biological signal-based detection [4], which leverages biological signals. Conversely, deepfake disruption [24] aims to obstruct the generation of deepfakes by introducing disruptive perturbations to the authentic image. This method, inspired by existing adversarial attacks [6, 14, 19], utilizes a gradient of loss as a perturbation that maximizes the distortion of the deepfake generator output.

The two defense techniques, each with distinct roles, naturally coexist within a deepfake environment. However, this prompts a fundamental question: *Are there any complications arising from the simultaneous adoption of both countermeasures?* Due to the divergent objectives of detection and disruption, we have found that disruption can inadvertently contribute to the issue of data poisoning, leading to a substantial decrease in detection model accuracy. Disruption techniques aim to ensure that images uploaded by users onto the Internet are safeguarded from use as deepfake images, while detection techniques necessitate the generation of a training dataset from deepfake images downloaded from the Internet. Therefore, the training dataset for detectors can potentially be contaminated through the inclusion of disrupted images. While these issues may arise in real-world applications, they have not been previously addressed. To tackle this problem, it's crucial to ensure the effective operation of the deepfake generator. Adversarial defense techniques can be implemented to stabilize the model's output. However, existing solutions fail to generate fake images that are advantageous for the detection model. Adversarial training [24] helps form robust model parameters but can inadvertently cause model deformations. On the other hand, adversarial purification effectively eliminates perturbations in the input. However, the leading method called DiffPure [21] compromises the semantics of the original input by introducing unnecessary noise.

In this paper, we introduce a detector training framework designed to addres the problem we first raised above. For the purpose, We employ a diffusion model [8] to cleanse the perturbations from the distorted real images, without altering the parameters of the deepfake generator responsible for producing the fake training images. Our approach uses a diffusion model similar to Diff-Pure [21] but we do not conduct a forward process that introduces noise to the input. Instead, we perform solely a reverse process to remove perturbations, rendering purification more effective and efficient. We evaluated the performance of our framework in comparison to DiffPure [21] and adversarially trained StarGAN (StarGAN AT) [24]. The results of our purification process yield L_2 distances comparable to those of existing purification methods. Furthermore, the distribution of deepfake images produced by our method aligns more closely with the original deepfakes compared to existing methods. The contributions of this paper are as follows:

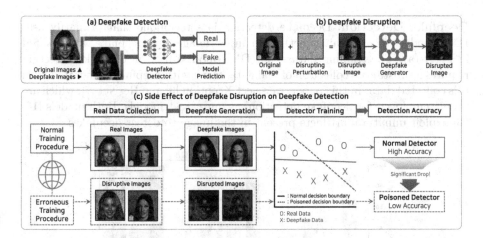

Fig. 1. Background and motivation of this work. (a) Deepfake detector takes a collection of images from the Internet to train models and decides whether an input image is real or fake. (b) Deepfake disruption creates disruptive images by perturbing genuine images to thwart deepfake generation. (c) The coexistence of two defense mechanisms can lead to data poisoning in the training dataset of detectors. If disruptive images are collected from the Internet and used to train the detector, the detection accuracy will be significantly reduced.

- We first raise a great concern that the coexistence of two countermeasures, *detection* and *disruption*, against deepfakes may inevitably cause their conflict at training phase of detection (Sect. 2). To highlight this concern, we empirically demonstrate that the accuracy of detection models drops significantly when their training datasets are poisoned by disrupted images.
- We introduce a robust training method that involves the purification of disruptive perturbations to mitigate data poisoning in deepfake detection models (Sect. 3). By capitalizing on the denoising method DDPM and bypassing the step of adding random noise, our approach decreases both the distortion and execution time of the generated outputs.
- Through comparative analysis with DiffPure and adversarially trained Star-GAN, we demonstrate that our framework is successful in generating real images that result in deepfake images, visually similar to standard fake images. This similarity is comparable to that achieved by existing methods (Sect. 4.2). Furthermore, our method significantly outperforms existing methods in terms of detection accuracy when the training dataset is poisoned (Sect. 4.3).

2   Background and Motivation

2.1   Deepfake Defense Methods

Deepfake Detection. Deepfake detection is a technique that primarily uses DNN models to ascertain whether an input image is a deepfake, as depicted in Fig. 1-(a). The training dataset for DNN models used in deepfake detection requires a substantial collection of real data, along with deepfakes generated from this collected data. In this paper, we select Xception [3] and ResNet [7], which are widely employed for deepfake detection, as our target models. Both models [15, 23] exploit unnatural artifacts present in the image to detect deepfakes.

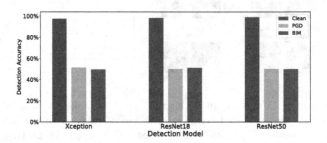

Fig. 2. Dectection accuracy. Deepfake detection models are trained on a clean dataset and a poisoned dataset, respectively. PGD and BIM means adversarial attack methods used for disruption. From a defender's perspective, the percentage of poisoned data is set to 100%, assuming the worst-case scenario.

Disruption. Deepfake disruption introduces a perturbation to the real image, as depicted in Fig. 1-(b), prompting the deepfake generator to produce an image significantly different from the typical deepfake image. Although there are various methods to create perturbations, we focus on the approach that leverages adversarial attacks [24]. Adversarial attacks generate perturbations using the gradient of a deep learning model to deviate the output from the correct result. In this paper, we employ BIM and PGD attacks to generate disrupting perturbations, thereby interrupting deepfake generation. Further details on adversarial attacks can be found in Sect. 6.

2.2   Threat Model

When deepfake detection and disruption methods coexist, the training data poisoning problem occurs, consequently reducing detection accuracy, as illustrated in Fig. 1-(c). Users who employ disruption may upload their perturbed images to the Internet to prevent their images from being exploited for deepfake generation. However, if these disruptive images are inadvertently collected by deepfake detectors while sourcing real data from the Internet, the quality of the training data for detectors suffers. In essence, the training dataset becomes inundated with disruptive images, as opposed to standard deepfake images. As a result, vital information about deepfake images fails to reach the detectors, resulting in a significant decrease in their accuracy. Figure 2 illustrates the detection accuracy drop observed in our small experiments. Note that deepfake detectors perform quite accurately when their training data is comprised of clean real images only, but the detection accuracy severely drops almost by half when training data is constructed with disruptive real images in the worst-case scenario.

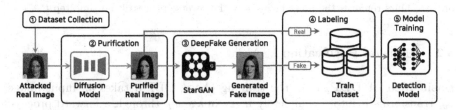

Fig. 3. Overview of our detection model training framework. The disruptive image with disruption perturbation is purified through diffusion model and put into deepfake generator to generate deepfake image. Generated deepfake images are used to train deepfake detection model.

3 System Design

3.1 Overview

Our framework proceeds in a sequence of five steps as shown in Fig. 3: ① data collection, ② purification, ③ deepfake generation, ④ dataset labeling, and ⑤ model training. Our approach has two differences from the traditional training of deepfake detection models in Fig. 1 (c). First, we newly deploy the purification step to address disruptive real images. Second, we discard the disruptive images and only consider the purified images from them for the later steps.

In the ① data collection step, we collect real images, regardless of whether the images are disruptive. Instead, all collected images are then fed into the diffusion model during the ② purification step. The diffusion model outputs new real images from the disruptive images where perturbations are removed. We adopt DDPM [8] as the diffusion model structure. In the ③ deepfake generation step, we feed the output images of the diffusion model into the generative model instead of the collected real images to get the normal fake images. The generative model produces results that are almost similar to the output of the normal real images. We label the purified real images as real and the generated fake images as fake during the ④ dataset labeling step. Finally, in the ⑤ training step, we train the detector using the labeled data (Fig. 4).

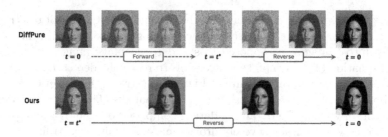

Fig. 4. The difference between our method and DiffPure [21]. DiffPure adds noise to the image in a forward process up to timestep t^* and then removes it in a reverse process. Ours removes the noise using only the reverse process from timestep t^*.

3.2 Diffusion Purification

Basic Idea of DDPM. In the training phase, DDPM takes an input image x_0, transforms it into a completely noisy image x_T through a forward process, and then restores it back to the original image x_0 through a reverse process. The forward process is denoted as $q(x_t \mid x_{t-1})$. The image x_t is generated by combining the preceding image x_{t-1} with noise $\mathbf{I}$ in a ratio of $1 - \beta_t$ to β_t. This process creates a noisy image by introducing noise up to the targeted timestep T, as dictated by t. Here, t is an integer between 0 and T that represents the level of noise in the image.

$$q(x_t \mid x_{t-1}) := \mathcal{N}\left(x_t; \sqrt{1 - \beta_t}x_{t-1}, \beta_t \mathbf{I}\right) \tag{1}$$

The reverse process, denoted as $p_\theta(x_{t-1} \mid x_t)$, essentially reverses the forward process to produce an image x_0' from the noisy image x_T. An image x_{t-1} at timestep $t-1$ is generated using the mean, $\mu\theta(x_t, t)$, and variance, $\Sigma_\theta(x_t, t)$, derived from the image x_t from the previous step.

$$p_\theta(x_{t-1} \mid x_t) := \mathcal{N}(x_{t-1}; \mu_\theta(x_t, t), \Sigma_\theta(x_t, t)) \tag{2}$$

Our Purification Strategy. In our purification method, we only employ the reverse process of DDPM. Given a clean real image x, let x' denote the corresponding disruptive image. We input x' into DDPM, specifying the timestep $t = t^*$ as the starting point of purification, so $x_{t^*} = x'$. In essence, we are assuming that x' is a real image with added little noise, not the complete noise. Our reverse process continues until the timestep reaches $t = 0$ with $x_0 = \hat{x}$ where $\hat{x}$ represents the purified image.

Technical Difference from DiffPure. Our purification step is designed by referring to DiffPure. DiffPure also inputs x' into the diffusion model, but it employs both forward and reverse processes, starting from $t = t_0$ where $x_0 = x'$. The objective of DiffPure is to retain only the generalized knowledge of the

Table 1. Purification performance of defense methods against the disruption. We measured the distance between the StarGAN output from the disruptive image and the normal deepfake image in the input (L_1 and L_2) and feature spaces (FID). Following the previous work [24], we consider the disruption fails when L_2 distance is greater than or equal to 0.05.

Defense Model	PGD			BIM		
	FID	L_1	L_2	FID	L_1	L_2
No Defense	151.6	0.418	0.267	141.62	0.430	0.278
MagNet Reformer [20]	181.8	0.265	0.118	177.7	0.265	0.118
StarGAN AT [24]	33.5	0.080	0.012	34.1	0.081	0.012
DiffPure [21]	30.6	0.072	0.010	31.56	0.073	0.010
Ours	38.3	0.083	0.013	32.3	0.075	0.010

input image, enabling the classification model to correctly classify the image. To accomplish this, DiffPure adds noise to the image during the forward process from $t = 0$ to $t = t^*$, thereby gradually eliminating the local structures of adversarial examples. However, our goal differs in that we do not generalize the image, but restore it precisely to its original form. The more forward process repeats, the more detail in the original image is destroyed. Therefore, we preserve more detail in the original image than DiffPure by removing the forward process.

3.3 Timestep for Purification

DiffPure argues that a substantial amount of noise is needed to remove the local structure, leading them to set the timestep t^* to a relatively large value of 300. However, a larger timestep not only introduces more disruption to the image in both the forward and reverse processes, but it also prolongs the process due to an increased number of iterations. As the magnitude of the disruption perturbation is nearly imperceptible to the human eye, there's no need for a large t^*. Consequently, we choose a smaller timestep value of $t^* = 10$ to enhance efficiency and resilience. In this scenario, the DDPM's timestep t_T is set to 1000.

4 Evaluation

To evaluate the performance of the proposed framework, we formulated two research questions and conducted experiments to answer them. **RQ1** investigates whether normal deepfake images can be generated from disruptive images through purification (Sect. 4.2). **RQ2** verifies whether a training dataset constructed by our purification can uphold the accuracy of the deepfake detector (Sect. 4.3).

4.1   Experimental Settings

Deepfake Dataset and Detection Model. We divide the entire CelebA [18] dataset into three groups. Group A occupies the first 60% of the dataset and is assumed to be the original image dataset initially owned by the defender. All defense methods against disruption are trained with Group A images. Group B occupies the following 30% of the dataset and is used to train the deepfake detection model. We assume that data poisoning based on disruption occurs for this group. Group C occupies the last 10% of the dataset and is used to evaluate the accuracy of detectors. The images in all datasets are cropped to 178×178 and subsequently resized to 128×128. Our baseline deepfake detection models are the Xception [3] model used in FaceForensics++ [23], and the ResNet18 and ResNet50 [7] models used in the disruption perturbation paper [26].

Parameters for Disruption. The disrupting perturbation is generated to make the deepfake image gets closer to a black image, targeting StarGAN [2]. We assume the grey-box disrupter knows the structure and parameters of the Star-GAN, but not those of the defense model. We use a 10-step BIM and a 10-step PGD with $\epsilon = 0.05$ with step size 0.01 for disruption.

Comparison Target Model. Our comparison targets are MagNet reformer [20], adversarially trained StarGAN with PGD (StarGAN AT) [24], and DiffPure [21], a SOTA purification technique using DDPM. All defense methods are trained with the Group A dataset.

Environments. We performed all experiments on a single machine Ubuntu 20.04 environment with two NVIDIA RTX 4090 (24 GB) GPUs.

4.2   Purification Ability for Disruptive Images

From Table 1, we can see that our L_2 distance is lower than the disruption threshold ($L_2 \geq 0.05$), indicating the successful generation of deepfake images. For the PGD, our performance is better than the MagNet reformer and similar to DiffPure and StarGAN AT. Moreover, our method results in the lowest L_2 distance alongside DiffPure for the BIM. Figure 5 illustrates the distribution of deepfake images generated by each defense method against PGD-based disruption. We found that our method is more effective in terms of the distribution of defended images. Our distribution in Fig. 5 (d) closely resembles the distribution of normal deepfake images. This result is better than DiffPure (Fig. 5 (b)) and StarGAN AT (Fig. 5 (c)) whose distributions are located between the distributions of normal real and deepfake images. We also found that our method is faster than DiffPure because of our reverse process alone and fewer timestep. DiffPure took 0.129 s to purify one image, while ours took 0.119 s, which is a 7.75% reduction in defense time over DiffPure.

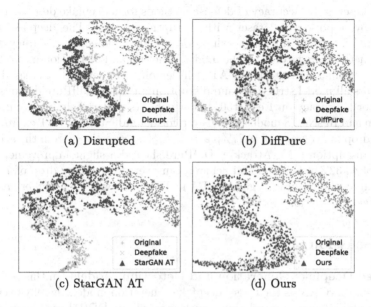

(a) Disrupted   (b) DiffPure

(c) StarGAN AT   (d) Ours

Fig. 5. The distribution of defended deepfake images (in blue) against PGD-based disruption. Image features were extracted from the ResNet18 model. t-SNE was used for visualization. Our method was superior in defense even in the worst case scenario. (Color figure online)

Table 2. Detection accuracy of detectors trained with the poisoned Group B dataset. Normal real and deepfake images in the Group C dataset are used to measure the accuracy.

Defense Model	Xception		ResNet18		ResNet50	
	PGD	BIM	PGD	BIM	PGD	BIM
No Attack	97.48		98.19		99.04	
No Defense	51.56	49.80	50.15	51.31	50.40	50.05
MagNet Reformer [20]	50.05	50.05	50.05	50.10	54.13	49.95
StarGAN AT [24]	50.05	50.05	49.55	50.00	49.95	50.05
DiffPure [21]	53.53	58.97	53.43	53.83	73.39	85.28
Ours	**83.37**	**95.58**	**89.37**	**99.55**	**90.88**	**96.52**

4.3 Accuracy of Detection Models Under the Poisoned Dataset

Table 2 presents the accuracy of defense methods for a deepfake detection model trained by a poisoned dataset with disruptive images. The deepfake detector trained using our approach exhibits the highest detection accuracy among defense methods, regardless of the model structure and disruption method. The MagNet reformer and StarGAN AT still demonstrate severely decreased accuracy across all model structures and disruption methods. DiffPure demonstrates satisfactory accuracy on ResNet50, but it exhibits underwhelming accuracy on Xception and ResNet18 models. MagNet reformer and StarGAN AT exhibited an average drop in accuracy of 48.77%p and 48.87%p respectively from the accuracy without disruption ("No Attack"). DiffPure showed a slight improvement with a drop of 43.32%p. Our method achieved an average accuracy drop of 7.83%p, and notably, the accuracy against BIM in ResNet18 was even higher than the "No Attack" scenario.

5 Discussion

Targeted Deepfake Generation and Detection Models. In this paper, we focused on StarGAN as the target deepfake generation model, thereby excluding other deepfake generation techniques such as faceswap. DDPM used in our purification is not trained for a specific disruption method or target model. Therefore, our method is agnostic to disruption methods or deepfake generation methods. Nevertheless, experimental verification is necessary to confirm our capability. Furthermore, in this paper, the experiments were conducted specifically on spatial-based deepfake detection techniques using a DNN model. Additional experiments are required for other detection methods, including frequency-based and biological-based ones. We leave the extension of our method as future work.

Poisoning Rate in Training Dataset. In this paper, we assumed a worst-case scenario, setting the poisoning rate of the training dataset to 100%. However, in reality, it is challenging to achieve a 100% rate of disrupted data. Furthermore, the attacker's knowledge of the target deepfake generator and the capability of the attacker may be limited in reality. However, from the defender's perspective, it is advisable to evaluate the worst-case scenario to prepare an effective defense method. Therefore, in this paper, we conducted experiments under the fully poisoned training data where the attacker acquires the knowledge of the deepfake generation model.

6 Related Work

Deepfake Generation. Various deepfake generation techniques exist for face generation [13], face conversion [22,31], attribute manipulation [2,27], and expression conversion [9]. Among them, StarGAN [2], a prominent technique for modifying attributes such as gender and age in faces, has been extensively used for evaluating deepfake detection [1,12,17,26] and disruption methods [1,24–26]. Therefore, in this paper, we have chosen StarGAN as the target generator to assess the issues arising when disruption and detection coexist.

Deepfake Detection. Among deepfake detection methods, spatial-based detection identifies visual artifacts in deepfake images [12,23]. Frequency-based detection uncovers artifacts in deepfake images within the frequency domain [1,30]. Biological-signal-based detection analyzes natural biological signals exclusive to real faces [4,10]. Deepfake detection models are predominantly trained on benchmark deepfake datasets such as Celeb-DF [16], FaceForensics++ [23], and UADFV [28]. Given that the real images in these datasets are collected from the Internet, all aforementioned deepfake detection techniques are inevitably susceptible to poisoning if the collected images are disruptive.

Deepfake Disruption. The early works on deepfake disruption [29] leverage adversarial attacks [6,14,19] Ruiz et al. [24] added a disrupting perturbation to the real image along with the gradient of the generative model toward a distorted deepfake image. Some other works utilize perturbation generators which are also generative models to disrupt deepfake generators [11,26]. There is a large chance of the coexistence of deepfake detection and disruption because they operate at different phases of the deepfake lifetime. Wang et al. were concerned that disrupted images can spoof the detection models [26]. Although they also studied the relationship between detection and disruption, we focused more on the unexpected side effect of the disruption on the training of detectors.

Adversarial Purification. Generative models are frequently employed for adversarial purification. MagNet [20], for instance, uses an autoencoder to learn a manifold of normal images. Images situated far from the learned manifold are rejected, and those close to the manifold are purified. DiffPure harnesses a diffusion model for adversarial purification due to its robust performance in image generation and noise reduction [21]. We also utilized DDPM [8], a standard diffusion model. However, unlike previous approaches, we omitted the forward process and used a smaller timestep.

7   Conclusion

Our framework is tailored to address the training data poisoning problem in deepfake detection models, the first of its kind in academia. Using the DDPM [8] denoising model, it minimizes image distortion and cuts defense time by eliminating extra noise introduced by DiffPure [21]. Our approach generates deepfake images that better resemble normal ones compared to those created by DiffPure or StarGAN Adversarial Training [24]. Moreover, our method achieves a 7.75% defense time reduction compared to DiffPure, and when applied to training deepfake detection models, it outperforms StarGAN AT and DiffPure in detection accuracy on Xception [3], ResNet18 [7], and ResNet50 [7] under PGD [19] and BIM [14] disruption attacks, anticipating widespread applicability.

Acknowledgments. This work was supported by the Institute of Information & Communications Technology Planning & Evaluation (IITP) grant funded by the Korea Government (MSIT) (No.RS-2023-00230337) and by the ITRC (Information Technology Research Center) support program (IITP-2023-2020-0-01602).

References

1. Asnani, V., Yin, X., Hassner, T., Liu, S., Liu, X.: Proactive image manipulation detection. In: Proceedings of the CVPR, pp. 15386–15395 (2022)
2. Choi, Y., Choi, M., Kim, M., Ha, J.W., Kim, S., Choo, J.: StarGAN: unified generative adversarial networks for multi-domain image-to-image translation. In: Proceedings of the CVPR, pp. 8789–8797 (2018)
3. Chollet, F.: Xception: deep learning with depthwise separable convolutions. In: Proceedings of the CVPR (2017)
4. Ciftci, U.A., Demir, I., Yin, L.: FakeCatcher: detection of synthetic portrait videos using biological signals. IEEE Trans. Pattern Anal. Mach. Intell. (2020)
5. Goodfellow, I.J., et al.: Generative adversarial networks (2014)
6. Goodfellow, I.J., Shlens, J., Szegedy, C.: Explaining and harnessing adversarial examples. arXiv preprint arXiv:1412.6572 (2014)
7. He, K., Zhang, X., Ren, S., Sun, J.: Deep residual learning for image recognition. In: Proceedings of the CVPR, pp. 770–778 (2016)
8. Ho, J., Jain, A., Abbeel, P.: Denoising diffusion probabilistic models. Adv. Neural. Inf. Process. Syst. **33**, 6840–6851 (2020)
9. Hsu, G.S., Tsai, C.H., Wu, H.Y.: Dual-generator face reenactment. In: Proceedings of the CVPR, pp. 642–650 (2022)
10. Hu, S., Li, Y., Lyu, S.: Exposing GAN-generated faces using inconsistent corneal specular highlights. In: Proceedings of the ICASSP, pp. 2500–2504. IEEE (2021)
11. Huang, Q., Zhang, J., Zhou, W., Zhang, W., Yu, N.: Initiative defense against facial manipulation. In: Proceedings of the AAAI, vol. 35, pp. 1619–1627 (2021)
12. Hulzebosch, N., Ibrahimi, S., Worring, M.: Detecting CNN-generated facial images in real-world scenarios. In: Proceedings of the CVPR Workshops (2020)
13. Karras, T., Laine, S., Aila, T.: A style-based generator architecture for generative adversarial networks. In: Proceedings of the CVPR, pp. 4401–4410 (2019)
14. Lee, K., Kim, J., Chong, S., Shin, J.: Making stochastic neural networks from deterministic ones (2017)
15. Li, Y., Lyu, S.: Exposing deepfake videos by detecting face warping artifacts. arXiv preprint arXiv:1811.00656 (2018)
16. Li, Y., Yang, X., Sun, P., Qi, H., Lyu, S.: Celeb-DF: a large-scale challenging dataset for deepfake forensics. In: Proceedings of the CVPR, pp. 3207–3216 (2020)
17. Liu, B., Yang, F., Bi, X., Xiao, B., Li, W., Gao, X.: Detecting generated images by real images. In: Avidan, S., Brostow, G., Cisse, M., Farinella, G.M., Hassner, T. (eds.) ECCV 2022. LNCS, vol. 13674, pp. 95–110. Springer, Cham (2022). https://doi.org/10.1007/978-3-031-19781-9_6
18. Liu, Z., Luo, P., Wang, X., Tang, X.: Deep learning face attributes in the wild. In: Proceedings OF the ICCV (2015)
19. Madry, A., Makelov, A., Schmidt, L., Tsipras, D., Vladu, A.: Towards deep learning models resistant to adversarial attacks. In: Proceedings of the ICLR (2018)
20. Meng, D., Chen, H.: Magnet: a two-pronged defense against adversarial examples. In: Proceedings of the CCS, pp. 135–147 (2017)

21. Nie, W., Guo, B., Huang, Y., Xiao, C., Vahdat, A., Anandkumar, A.: Diffusion models for adversarial purification. In: Proceedings of the ICML, pp. 16805–16827. PMLR (2022)

22. Nirkin, Y., Keller, Y., Hassner, T.: FSGAN: subject agnostic face swapping and reenactment. In: Proceedings of the ICCV, pp. 7184–7193 (2019)

23. Rossler, A., Cozzolino, D., Verdoliva, L., Riess, C., Thies, J., Nießner, M.: Face-forensics++: learning to detect manipulated facial images. In: Proceedings of the ICCV, pp. 1–11 (2019)

24. Ruiz, N., Bargal, S.A., Sclaroff, S.: Disrupting deepfakes: adversarial attacks against conditional image translation networks and facial manipulation systems. In: Bartoli, A., Fusiello, A. (eds.) ECCV 2020. LNCS, vol. 12538, pp. 236–251. Springer, Cham (2020). https://doi.org/10.1007/978-3-030-66823-5_14

25. Wang, R., Huang, Z., Chen, Z., Liu, L., Chen, J., Wang, L.: Anti-forgery: towards a stealthy and robust deepfake disruption attack via adversarial perceptual-aware perturbations. arXiv preprint arXiv:2206.00477 (2022)

26. Wang, X., Huang, J., Ma, S., Nepal, S., Xu, C.: Deepfake disrupter: the detector of deepfake is my friend. In: Proceedings of the CVPR, pp. 14920–14929 (2022)

27. Xia, W., Yang, Y., Xue, J.H., Wu, B.: TediGAN: text-guided diverse face image generation and manipulation. In: Proceedings of the CVPR, pp. 2256–2265 (2021)

28. Yang, X., Li, Y., Lyu, S.: Exposing deep fakes using inconsistent head poses. In: Proceedings of the ICASSP, pp. 8261–8265. IEEE (2019)

29. Yeh, C.Y., Chen, H.W., Tsai, S.L., Wang, S.D.: Disrupting image-translation-based deepfake algorithms with adversarial attacks. In: Proceedings of the WACV Workshops, pp. 53–62 (2020)

30. Zhang, X., Karaman, S., Chang, S.F.: Detecting and simulating artifacts in GAN fake images. In: Proceedings of the WIFS, pp. 1–6. IEEE (2019)

31. Zhu, Y., Li, Q., Wang, J., Xu, C.Z., Sun, Z.: One shot face swapping on megapixels. In: Proceedings of the CVPR, pp. 4834–4844 (2021)

Multi-class Malware Detection via Deep Graph Convolutional Networks Using TF-IDF-Based Attributed Call Graphs

Irshad Khan and Young-Woo Kwon(✉)

School of Computer Science and Engineering, Kyungpook National University,
Daegu, South Korea
irshad.cs@knu.ac.kr, ywkown@knu.ac.kr
http://sslab.knu.ac.kr

Abstract. The proliferation of malware in the Android ecosystem poses significant security risks and financial losses for enterprises and developers. Malware constantly evolves, exhibiting dynamic behavior and complexity, thus making it challenging to develop robust defense mechanisms. Traditional methods, such as signature-based and battery-monitoring approaches, struggle to detect emerging malware variants effectively. Recent advancements in deep learning have shown promising results in Android malware detection. However, most existing approaches focus on binary classification and need more insights into the model's generality across different types of malware. This study presents a novel approach to address Android malware detection by integrating TF-IDF (Term Frequency-Inverse Document Frequency) features into the call graph structure. By attributing each node in the call graph with TF-IDF-based feature vectors extracted from the opcode sequences of each method using an opcode list, we present a more thorough representation that encapsulates the complex traits of the malware samples. We employ state-of-the-art graph-based deep learning models to classify malware families, including Graph Convolutional Networks (GCN), SAGEConv, Graph Attention Networks (GAT), and Graph Isomorphism Networks (GIN). By incorporating high-level structural information from the call graphs and TF-IDF-based raw features, our approach aims to enhance the accuracy and generality of the malware detection models. We identify an optimal model for the Android malware family classification task through extensive evaluation and comparison of the above-mentioned models. The findings of this study contribute to advancing the field of Android malware detection and provide insights into the effectiveness of graph-based deep learning models for combating evolving malware threats.

Keywords: Malware · TF-IDF · call graph · graph convolutional model

This research was supported by Basic Science Research Program through the National Research Foundation of Korea (NRF) funded by the Ministry of Education (NRF-2021R1I1A3043889) and the Ministry of Science and ICT (No.2021R1A5A1021944).

H. Kim and J. Youn (Eds.): WISA 2023, LNCS 14402, pp. 188–200, 2024.
https://doi.org/10.1007/978-981-99-8024-6_15

1   Introduction

In today's rapidly growing digital landscape, the usage of smartphones has become ubiquitous, with an astounding number of over six billion smartphone users worldwide, as reported by Statista [1]. As the smartphone user base continues to expand at an unprecedented rate, so does the magnitude of valuable and sensitive data generated by these devices. Unfortunately, this proliferation of data also escalates the risk of unauthorized access and data breaches. Malicious actors, often in the form of skilled attackers, exploit vulnerabilities in the system and employ specially crafted malicious applications to gain unauthorized access to users' smartphones. These malicious applications can carry out various unsafe actions, including the theft of personal information such as passwords, text messages, or even private photos. Safeguarding user smartphones against these ever-evolving and pernicious threats has become an arduous task that requires robust defense mechanisms and proactive security measures.

Android is the most popular mobile platform known for its performance and open-source nature. Its user-friendly interface and vast app ecosystem have attracted a large user base. Nevertheless, the popularity of Android has also made it a target for malicious actors, leading to a rapid increase in Android malware. Like other software systems, Android is susceptible to the detrimental effects of malicious applications. According to research, more than three million malicious Android apps were found in 2019 [2]. These statistics emphasize how important it is to create strong defenses against the rising tide of Android malware. While external Android packages (APKs) pose a significant risk, additional sources of malware, such as pre-installed malware and malicious components within software development kits (SDKs), further aggravate the challenge [3]. Recently, several detecting tools have been created to distinguish between trustworthy (i.e., benign) and malicious software applications [4,5]. While binary classification, distinguishing between benign and malicious software, remains the primary focus of malware detection systems, it is increasingly evident that a deeper understanding of the hazards can lead to more effective mitigation strategies.

Manual analysis of Android application security and protection is time-consuming to analyze malicious program patterns and behavior. To overcome this challenge, statistical methods incorporating data mining and machine learning have shown promising results. However, the effectiveness of these methods can be compromised by simple obfuscation techniques that hide the underlying data patterns, making it difficult to distinguish malicious programs. In this context, deep learning techniques have emerged as a powerful tool to strengthen Android malware defenses, outperforming conventional machine learning approaches. These techniques have been successfully employed in various areas, including malware detection, family attribution, and combating adversarial attacks. While the main objective of the Android malware prevention system is binary classification to separate malicious software from benign applications, significant efforts have been dedicated to addressing this fundamental challenge. Notably, Droid-Sec, introduced in the research conducted by Yuan et al. [6], is among the pioneering deep-learning approaches in this field.

Program analysis plays a crucial role by providing valuable insights into the behavior and characteristics of software without executing it. Raw shallow features, such as bytecodes, opcodes, and strings, provide granular information about the inner workings of an application. However, these features also come with certain limitations that need to be considered. For instance, raw shallow features may not capture the higher-level structural characteristics of the program effectively. On the other hand, high-level structural features have been recognized for their higher robustness in application analysis. For example, if a function is renamed, the call graph will still show the calls to that function, even though the name of the function has changed. As a result, researchers utilized graph-based features like Control Flow Graph (CFG) [7], Function Call Graph (FCG) [8], and API Dependency Graph (ADG) [5] to characterize the program. In this context, graph convolutional models are recently proposed for graph-based data structures [9]. The main idea is to update node information by propagating information among the graph nodes.

Low-level features offer detailed information, but they are susceptible to attacks such as code obfuscation, which can hinder their effectiveness. On the other hand, high-level structural information provides more contextual semantics, but alone may not be sufficient to achieve accurate detection, as structural attacks can impact the performance of the model. Our approach addresses this issue by combining both approaches that leverage both low-level and high-level information, which are capable of capturing a comprehensive understanding of malware samples. In the literature, only a few manually selected opcodes are used to provide raw features for node classification. Therefore, in this work, we extract a unique list of opcodes from a dataset of malware samples, allowing for a more comprehensive analysis. Rather than providing a binary feature representation for each opcode, we utilized a TF-IDF feature set derived from the opcodes for each method within the application. Our goal is multi-class classification because detecting malware families in Android applications has received little attention.

This study investigates the effectiveness of graph-based deep learning models for detecting and categorizing Android malware. By integrating TF-IDF features into the call graph structure, we aim to create a comprehensive representation that captures the complex traits of malware samples. Our approach utilizes state-of-the-art graph-based deep learning models to classify malware families. By incorporating high-level structural information from call graphs and low-level information from raw features, our approach aims to enhance the accuracy and generality of the malware detection models. We identify the optimal model for Android malware family classification through extensive evaluation and comparison. This research contributes to providing multi-class Android malware detection, incorporating graph-level (function call graphs) and node-level (TF-IDF of opcodes) information with graph-based deep learning models in combating malware threats effectively.

The rest of the paper is organized as follows. Section 2 provides related work. In Sect. 3, we present our proposed work. Section 4 discusses the results, and Sect. 5 concludes the paper, including future directions.

2   Related Work

In Android malware analysis, three methodologies are commonly used: static, dynamic, and hybrid analysis [3]. Static techniques extract program features without executing the APK, using methods like decompiling and examining call graphs or opcodes [10]. Dynamic analysis observes malware behavior in a controlled environment, while hybrid analysis combines static and dynamic approaches [11]. The hybrid analysis offers comprehensive code coverage and runtime behavior insights but requires advanced computational resources due to its higher complexity.

Conventional anti-malware solutions primarily rely on signature-based detection methods. These methods involve analyzing and comparing malware attack signatures with a predefined list of known signatures [12]. However, these methods have limitations, such as zero-day malware. In contrast, machine-learning-based Android malware methods using static and dynamic analysis performed better when detecting unknown variants of malware [4,13]. In [14], a 15-bit boolean vector derived from the opcode instructions of the method was utilized as a node feature in the Feature Control Graph (FCG) model. To enable binary classification, the authors employed K-mean clustering to extract the k-cluster center, which served as an input to support vector machines and Naive Bayes algorithms. Similarly, McLaughlin et al. [15] employed opcode embedding to train a convolutional neural network (CNN) for classifying malware and benign Android applications. Unlike previous methods that used a limited number of opcodes, this approach employed a larger opcode set consisting of 218 opcodes. Furthermore, the CNN architecture was designed to effectively capture and analyze local spatial features due to its grid-like structure.

These methods showed promising results and provided good solutions to detect the malware. However, graph structures in source code analysis for malware detection provide a robust framework to uncover the code's inherent design and behavior. Incorporating neural graph networks and convolutional graph networks enhances the detection of intricate patterns and dependencies, thereby improving the effectiveness and accuracy of malware detection systems. The exploration of cutting-edge deep learning models and techniques, with a focus on the use of graph convolutional approaches, has recently increased with the goal of developing reliable and robust anti-malware solutions. In [16], authors proposed Grdoid, a graph neural network model that leverages word embedding of API sequences. In MalNet, authors applied graph representation learning approaches on the FCG dataset to compare models, and the GIN achieved higher classification results [17].

3   Proposed Architecture

Our proposed scheme utilizes static analysis techniques to characterize APKs thoroughly and leverage the capabilities of graph convolutional neural networks efficiently for categorical classification. The proposed architecture encompasses multiple stages, which is shown in Fig. 1. The first step is to extract the raw opcodes from the APKs. We obtain a list of 95 opcodes from this extraction, as given in List 1.

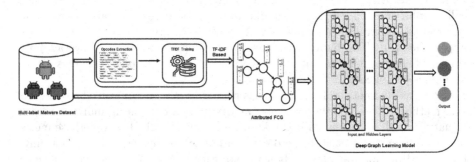

Fig. 1. Android Malware Detection Framework

List. 1: Opcode name list

'move', '-', 'wide', 'iget', 'boolean', 'sub', 'int/2addr', 'div', 'shr', 'long/2addr', 'if', 'lez', 'double/2addr', 'invoke', 'interface', '/', 'range', 'double', 'return', 'object', 'const', 'wide/32', 'aput', 'short', 'float/2addr', 'or', 'and', 'int', 'from16', 'gtz', 'ushr', 'lit8', 'sput', 'char', 'aget', 'super', 'array', 'length', 'eq', 'ne', 'mul', 'instance', 'of', 'string', 'xor', 'long', 'to', 'virtual', 'lit16', 'float', 'shl', 'rem', 'add', 'gt', 'static', 'byte', 'nez', 'monitor', 'enter', 'sget', 'iput', 'rsub', 'result', 'fill', 'data', 'sparse', 'switch', 'gez', 'exit', 'void', 'le', 'cmpl', 'nop', 'goto/16', 'neg', 'goto', 'new', 'payload', 'pack', 'high16', 'direct', 'const/16', 'const/4', 'lt', 'check', 'cast', 'ge', 'class', 'cmp', 'cmpg', 'ltz', 'throw', 'eqz', 'wide/16', 'exception'

In the second step, we extract a feature vector from each class method and create a call graph. The feature vector is derived from the opcodes and serves as the node features for each node in the call graph. This attributed call graph is then fed as an input into graph convolutional models for classification. By leveraging the power of graph convolutional models, we can effectively analyze and classify the given call graph based on the embedded feature vectors derived from the opcodes. The following subsections provide a detailed description of our methodology.

3.1   APK Characterization

We utilize Android packages (APKs) as the input source for our static analysis process. To obtain a comprehensive understanding of the code's structure and behavior, we employ the Androguard tool [10] to extract Function Call Graphs (FCGs) from the Dalvik Executable (dex) code within the APKs. The FCGs capture the relationships between methods in the application, providing valuable insights into the caller-callee interactions. While FCGs offer a high-level overview of the application's structure, they may need to provide more granularity to detect malicious apps accurately. To address this limitation, we enhance the FCGs by attributing the nodes of the extracted graph with node features.

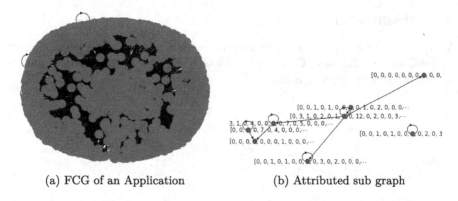

| (a) FCG of an Application | (b) Attributed sub graph |

Fig. 2. (a)Complete Function Call Graph of an Android Application (b) and example of attributed subgraph

For this purpose, we employ a TF-IDF-based approach to enrich the extracted FCGs with informative features. Specifically, we calculate TF-IDF scores for the opcode sequences present in each method of the FCG. By applying TF-IDF, we assign weights to the opcodes based on their frequency within each method and overall importance in the entire FCGs. This process allows us to capture the significance of each opcode in distinguishing between different methods and detecting potentially malicious behavior. The TF-IDF scores serve as feature vectors that are then associated with the corresponding nodes in the FCG. Each node in the graph is attributed with the TF-IDF feature vector, providing valuable contextual information about the opcode usage patterns within the methods. This attribution of TF-IDF-based feature vectors enhances the representation of the FCG, enabling more comprehensive analysis and detection of malicious applications. The attributed FCG now incorporates structural information from the graph and opcode-specific features derived from the TF-IDF analysis.

The TF-IDF method is used to determine the importance of terms in a collection of documents. It considers the frequency of terms within individual documents and across the entire corpus. The TF-IDF value of a term in a document is computed by multiplying its term frequency (TF) by the inverse document frequency (IDF). This method helps identify frequent terms within a document but infrequent across the collection, thus providing valuable insights into the distinguishing characteristics of individual documents [18]. This combined representation empowers subsequent analysis techniques, such as graph convolutional models, to leverage the enriched information for improved classification and detection accuracy [19].

For the comparison purpose, we attributed nodes of the extracted graph with the raw features, i.e., frequency of opcode sequences for each method in the graph [14]. Function call graph and its subgraph snippet with frequency attribute are shown in Fig. 2.

3.2 Classification

We conducted a comparison of four graph convolutional neural networks, namely GraphConv, SAGEConv, GATConv, and GIN, to identify the optimal models for Android malware classification.

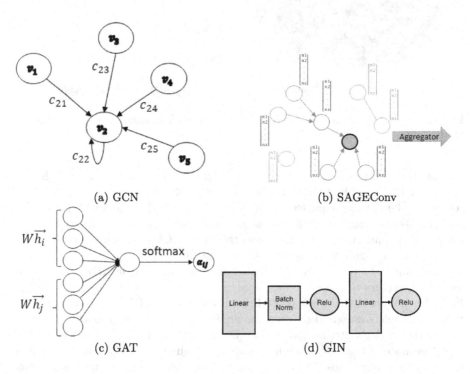

(a) GCN   (b) SAGEConv

(c) GAT   (d) GIN

Fig. 3. Layer architecture of graph convolutional models

GCN: GCN is the most commonly used architecture for graph-based applications [20]. It consists of Graph Convolutional layer and is defined mathematically as follows:

$$h^{l+1} = \sigma \left(b^l + \sum_{j \in N(i)} \frac{1}{c_{ij}} h_j^l W^l \right) \tag{1}$$

where $c_{ij} = \sqrt{|N(i)|} \cdot \sqrt{|N(j)|}$, and $N(i)$ is the set of neighbors of node i, σ is ReLU activation function, and W and b are the weight and bias matrix. The graphical representation of a layer is given in Fig. 3a.

SAGEConv: The main idea of SAGEConv is to sample a set of nodes uniformly, then aggregate the features from the set of neighbors, and graph classification is performed based on aggregation [21]. SAGEConv layer used inductive learning and can be defined as,

$$\begin{aligned} h_{N(i)}^{l+1} &= aggregate \left(\left\{ h_j^{(l)}, \forall j \in N(i) \right\} \right) \\ h_i^{l+1} &= \sigma \left(W^{(l)}.concat \left\{ h_j^{(l)}, h_{N(i)}^{(l+1)} \right\} \right) \\ h_i^{l+1} &= norm(h_i^{l+1}) \end{aligned} \tag{2}$$

Here $W_{(l)}$ is weight, aggregate (mean) combines node representation of neighbor nodes, norm normalizes the node representation, and σ is the ReLU activation function. Figure 3b visualizes the aggregation of SAGEConv layer.

GATConv: The main idea behind the graph attention network is to use more information and give attention to neighbors, which are more important than others [22]. The graph Attention layer is defined as,

$$\begin{aligned} h_i^{l+1} &= \sum_{j \in N(i)} \alpha_{i,j} W^l h_j^l \\ \alpha_{i,j}^l &= softmax(e_{i,j}^l) \\ e_{i,j}^l &= LeakyReLU((W^l h_i^l)^T.(W^l h_i^l)) \end{aligned} \tag{3}$$

here $\alpha_{i,j}$ is the attention score between nodes i and j and W^l is a weight matrix. GATconv is illustrated in Fig. 3c.

GIN: Unlike other GNN models that rely on specific aggregation functions, The GIN aggregator is a learnable aggregation function [23]. The aggregator applies a fully connected layer with a non-linear activation function to the sum of node features in the neighborhood and then combines the updated features with the original node features. GIN exhibits graph isomorphism invariance, generating identical representations for isomorphic graphs. This property enables GIN to capture structural patterns and generalize effectively to unseen graphs. The update rule of GIN for a node is as follows,

$$h_i^{(l+1)} = f_\Theta \left((1 + \epsilon) h_i^{(l)} + aggregate \left(\left\{ h_j^{(l)}, j \in N(i) \right\} \right) \right)$$

The function f_Θ transforms the input using neural network parameters Θ. The term $h_i^{(l)}$ denotes the current representation of node i at layer l. The small constant ϵ controls the influence of the previous representation. The aggregate operation aggregates the representations of neighboring nodes j of node i at layer l. Figure 3d visualizes the aggregation of GIN.

Models Architecture: Each model in our study employed a three-layer architecture. To address the issue of overfitting, we incorporated dropout regularization. The Adam optimizer was utilized for the learning process.

4 Evaluation

4.1 Experimental Setup

For the purpose of analyzing our case scenarios, we used the MalDroid2020 dataset [24]. Adware, Banking Malware, SMS Malware, Mobile Riskware, and Benign APKs are among the five classifications of APKs in the dataset. Inside trustworthy software, adware hides ads. Ads keep popping up and harming the victim's device with this infection. Malware for banking is made to look like a banking program or interface to access the victim's online banking system. By sending malicious SMS to the victim's smartphone, SMS malware obtains data from the target device. Utilizing normal apps, mobile riskware converts them into ransomware or adware. Benign applications, on the other hand, belong to the normal class. We used a balanced dataset of 7000 Android packages for our evaluation. The dataset was carefully selected to ensure an equal representation of each class containing different classes of malicious and benign applications. By maintaining balance, we aim to create a fair and reliable evaluation framework that can accurately assess the performance of our methods and models in distinguishing between each class [25].

4.2 Performance Measures

Precision (Prec:), recall (Rec:), and F1-score (F1:) measurements are used to assess the model performance for each class [26]. Precision measures how many of the correctly predicted positive outcomes. Recall or sensitivity is a measurement of how many positive occurrences of each class, out of all the positive cases in the class, a classifier correctly predicted. F1, which combines recall and precision, is the harmonic mean.

4.3 Results and Discussion

We divided the dataset into train, validate, and test sets, allocating 75%, 5%, and 20% of the data, respectively. The three models were trained using a supervised approach since labels for all classes were available. The test results of the trained models are presented in Table 1. Among the four models, the GIN model achieved the highest overall precision, recall, and F1-score of 89.18, 90.43,

Table 1. Test results of the models

Model	GraphConv			SAGEConv			GATConv			GIN		
Class	Prec:	Rec :	F1:	Prec:	Rec :	F1:	Prec:	Rec :	F1:	Prec:	Rec :	F1:
Adware	62.20	93.95	74.85	87.22	91.58	89.34	91.01	86.51	88.70	87.54	94.47	90.87
Banking	86.66	95.79	91.00	91.58	96.40	93.92	88.05	90.36	89.19	94.15	92.03	93.08
SMS	64.92	60.66	62.72	86.63	86.63	86.63	84.85	88.53	86.65	82.96	91.74	87.13
Riskware	99.35	57.76	73.05	97.45	81.68	88.87	98.20	88.40	93.04	99.07	86.93	92.60
Benign	76.47	83.88	80.00	78.62	86.23	82.25	80.21	87.97	83.91	82.19	86.96	84.51
Overall	77.92	78.41	76.32	88.30	88.50	88.20	88.47	88.35	88.30	89.18	90.43	89.64

and 89.64, respectively. Following closely, the GAT model obtained the second-highest scores of 88.47, 88.35, and 88.30, indicating its strong performance. The SAGEConv model also performed well, with a precision of 88.30, recall of 88.50, and F1-Score of 88.20, showing comparable results to GATConv. In contrast, the GraphConv model exhibited lower performance across all metrics and classes compared to the other three models.

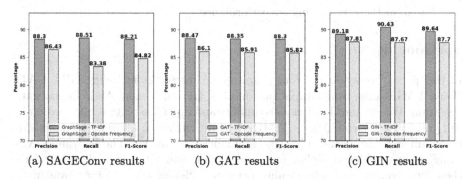

(a) SAGEConv results   (b) GAT results   (c) GIN results

Fig. 4. Comparison of Precision, Recall, and F1-Score opcodes frequency and TFIDF feature set using SAGEConv, GAT, and GIN models

Both GIN and GATConv exhibited strong performance in differentiating riskware samples, achieving F1-scores of 92.60 and 93.04, respectively. This indicates their effectiveness in identifying instances of riskware. On the other hand, the SMS and Benign classes demonstrated lower precision, recall, and F1-score across all models, implying that distinguishing between SMS and benign samples is more arduous, likely due to attacker-obfuscation techniques and graph-based structural attacks. Notably, GIN achieved a higher F1-score of 93.08, specifically for the Banking class. Based on these results, we can rank the models as follows: GIN, GATConv, SAGEConv, and GraphConv. The observed performance differences suggest that GIN, GATConv, and SAGEConv are more adept at handling the intricate challenges presented by the dataset, rendering them suitable choices for the given classification task.

We compared the proposed work results with a baseline feature set (i.e., opcode frequency). We train and test the top three models, GIN, GAT, and SAGEConv, in a similar manner. Comparison is visualized using the performance metrics (precision, recall, and F1-score) for the TF-IDF and opcode frequency feature sets and models given in Fig. 4. Similar to TF-IDF test performance, GIN achieved higher scores of 87.81, 87.67, and 87.70. The GAT model trained on the opcode frequency feature set achieved precision, recall, and F1 scores of 86.10, 85.91, and 85.82, respectively. Similarly, the SAGEConv model trained on the opcode frequency feature set achieved precision, recall, and F1 scores of 86.43, 83.38, and 84.82, respectively. SAGEConv performed slightly better than GAT in precision, while GAT had a slightly higher recall and F1-score.

In terms of feature set, the results indicate that the choice of feature set (TF-IDF or opcode frequency) has a noticeable impact on the performance of the models. The TF-IDF feature set generally yielded higher precision, recall, and F1-score results than the opcode frequency feature set. Additionally, while the scores between the SAGEConv and GAT models are small, SAGEConv tends to perform slightly better on the opcode frequency feature set, whereas GAT shows a slight advantage on the TF-IDF feature set. In summary, the TF-IDF feature set, combined with the GIN or GAT model, could be preferable for the given task based on their overall higher performance.

5   Conclusion

In this paper, we evaluated four graph neural networks including GIN, GAT-Conv, SAGEConv, and GraphConv models for multi-class Android malware detection. We enhanced the models' understanding of the textual information in call graphs by incorporating a TF-IDF feature set, which allowed the models to better differentiate between benign and malicious behavior. The GIN and GAT-Conv models achieved higher precision, recall, and F1 scores, demonstrating their effectiveness in distinguishing between different classes of Android malware. SAGEConv showed competitive performance, particularly in identifying riskware samples. However, GraphConv performed average across all measures and classes. Our study highlights the importance of combining high-level structural features, such as call graphs, with deep neural graph models and TF-IDF features for Android malware detection. Considering both the structural and textual aspects improves classification performance.

References

1. "Smartphones-statistics   and   facts."   https://www.statista.com/topics/840/smartphones/
2. "Mobile   malware   evolution   report."   https://securelist.com/mobile-malware-evolution-2019/96280/
3. Qiu, J., et al.: Data-driven android malware intelligence: a survey. In: Chen, X., Huang, X., Zhang, J. (eds.) ML4CS 2019. LNCS, vol. 11806, pp. 183–202. Springer, Cham (2019). https://doi.org/10.1007/978-3-030-30619-9_14

4. Arp, D., Spreitzenbarth, M., Hubner, M., Gascon, H., Rieck, K., Siemens, C.: DREBIN: effective and explainable detection of android malware in your pocket. In: NDSS, vol. 14, pp. 23–26 (2014)
5. Zhang, M., Duan, Y., Yin, H., Zhao, Z.: Semantics-aware android malware classification using weighted contextual API dependency graphs. In: Proceedings of the 2014 ACM SIGSAC Conference on Computer and Communications Security, pp. 1105–1116 (2014)
6. Yuan, Z., Lu, Y., Wang, Z., Xue, Y.: Droid-sec: deep learning in android malware detection. In: Proceedings of the 2014 ACM Conference on SIGCOMM, pp. 371–372 (2014)
7. Narayanan, A., Meng, G., Yang, L., Liu, J., Chen, L.: Contextual Weisfeiler-Lehman graph kernel for malware detection. In: 2016 International Joint Conference on Neural Networks (IJCNN), pp. 4701–4708. IEEE (2016)
8. Hassen, M., Chan, P.K.: Scalable function call graph-based malware classification. In: Proceedings of the Seventh ACM on Conference on Data and Application Security and Privacy, pp. 239–248 (2017)
9. Xu, K., Li, Y., Deng, R.H., Chen, K.: DeepRefiner: multi-layer android malware detection system applying deep neural networks. In: 2018 IEEE European Symposium on Security and Privacy (EuroS&P), pp. 473–487. IEEE (2018)
10. Androguard. https://androguard.readthedocs.io/en/latest/
11. Tam, K., Fattori, A., Khan, S., Cavallaro, L.: Copperdroid: automatic reconstruction of android malware behaviors. In: NDSS Symposium 2015, pp. 1–15 (2015)
12. Gandotra, E., Bansal, D., Sofat, S.: Malware analysis and classification: a survey. J. Inf. Secur. 2014 (2014)
13. Li, J., Sun, L., Yan, Q., Li, Z., Srisa-An, W., Ye, H.: Significant permission identification for machine-learning-based android malware detection. IEEE Trans. Ind. Inf. **14**(7), 3216–3225 (2018)
14. Liu, Y., Zhang, L., Huang, X.: Using G features to improve the efficiency of function call graph based android malware detection. Wireless Pers. Commun. **103**(4), 2947–2955 (2018)
15. McLaughlin, N., et al.: Deep android malware detection. In: Proceedings of the Seventh ACM on Conference on Data and Application Security and Privacy, pp. 301–308 (2017)
16. Gao, H., Cheng, S., Zhang, W.: GDroid: android malware detection and classification with graph convolutional network. Comput. Secur. **106**, 102264 (2021)
17. Xu, K., Hu, W., Leskovec, J., Jegelka, S.: How powerful are graph neural networks?. arXiv preprint arXiv:1810.00826 (2018)
18. Jing, L.P., Huang, H.K., Shi, H.B.: Improved feature selection approach TFIDF in text mining. In: Proceedings International Conference on Machine Learning and Cybernetics, vol. 2, pp. 944–946. IEEE (2002)
19. Ozogur, G., Erturk, M.A., Gurkas Aydin, Z., Aydin, M.A.: Android malware detection in bytecode level using TF-IDF and XGBoost. Comput. J. bxac198 (2023)
20. Kipf, T.N., Welling, M.: Semi-supervised classification with graph convolutional networks. arXiv preprint arXiv:1609.02907 (2016)
21. Hamilton, W., Ying, Z., Leskovec, J.: Inductive representation learning on large graphs. In: Advances in Neural Information Processing Systems, vol. 30 (2017)
22. Veličković, P., Cucurull, G., Casanova, A., Romero, A., Lio, P., Bengio, Y.: Graph attention networks. arXiv preprint arXiv:1710.10903 (2017)
23. Hu, W., et al.: Strategies for pre-training graph neural networks. arXiv preprint arXiv:1905.12265 (2019)

24. Mahdavifar, S., Kadir, A.F.A., Fatemi, R., Alhadidi, D., Ghorbani, A.: Dynamic android malware category classification using semi-supervised deep learning. In: 2020 IEEE International Conference on Dependable, Autonomic and Secure Computing, International Conference on Pervasive Intelligence and Computing, International Conference on Cloud and Big Data Computing, International Conference on Cyber Science and Technology Congress (DASC/PiCom/CBDCom/CyberSciTech), pp. 515–522. IEEE (2020)

25. Kotsiantis, S., Kanellopoulos, D., Pintelas, P., et al.: Handling imbalanced datasets: a review. GESTS Int. Trans. Comput. Sci. Eng. **30**(1), 25–36 (2006)

26. Goutte, C., Gaussier, E.: A probabilistic interpretation of precision, recall and F-score, with implication for evaluation. In: Losada, D.E., Fernández-Luna, J.M. (eds.) ECIR 2005. LNCS, vol. 3408, pp. 345–359. Springer, Heidelberg (2005). https://doi.org/10.1007/978-3-540-31865-1_25

OCR Meets the Dark Web: Identifying the Content Type Regarding Illegal and Cybercrime

Donghyun Kim[1] , Seungho Jeon[1] , Jiho Shin[2] , and Jung Taek Seo[1]([⊠])

[1] Gachon University, Seongnam-daero, 1342, Seongnam-si, Korea
{202240222,shjeon90,seojt}@gachon.ac.kr
[2] Korean National Police University, Hwangsan-gil, 100-50, Asan-si, Korea
suchme@police.go.kr

Abstract. The dark web provides features such as encryption and routing changes to ensure anonymity and make tracking difficult. Cybercrimes exploit the characteristics to gain revenue by distributing illegal and cybercrime content through the dark web and take a financial benefit as a business strategy. Illegal and cybercrime content includes drug and arms trafficking, counterfeit documents, malware, and the sale of personal information. A text crawling system in dark web has been developed and researched to counter illegal and cybercrime content distribution. However, because traditional text crawler in the dark web collects all text, identifying the exact data type can be difficult if dark web pages serve different types of illegal and cybercrime content. In this paper, we propose a method of using the text embedded within images to accurately identify the types of illegal and cybercrime content on the dark web. We conducted the experiments with a combination of text and texts from both web page and images to accurately identify illegal and cybercrime content types. We collected keywords for the three types of illegal and cybercrime content. The distribution and types of illegal and cybercrime content were identified by calculating whether the collected keywords were included in dark web pages. Through experiments, we confirmed that using text embedded within images improves performance. Our proposed method accurately identified over 90% of dark web pages where drugs were distributed.

Keywords: Dark Web · Crawler · Illegal and Cybercrime Content

1 Introduction

The dark web leverages the Tor network, which ensures anonymity by employing online encryption that renders traffic analysis and Internet Protocol (IP) address tracking infeasible [1]. Initially, the Tor network was utilized by users in many countries with stringent internet regulations to safeguard their privacy [1]. However, malicious parties have started exploiting the anonymity features of the Tor network to disseminate illegal and cybercrime content. Notable illegal and cybercrime contents distributed by these parties encompass malware such as ransomware and botnets, personal information, weapons, drugs, terrorism-related materials, and pornography [2, 3]. By capitalizing on the attributes of the dark web, Cybercrimes adopt illicit content distribution and fee-based models as part of their business strategy [4].

To combat the proliferation of illicit and cybercrime content on the dark web, an investigation into methodologies for effective data harvesting is underway. The primary focus of this endeavor lies in collecting text data from web pages, which comprise a significant segment of illegal and cybercrime content. However, ascertaining the exact nature of the content proves challenging when different forms of data are concurrently from dark web pages. Moreover, procuring ordinary text becomes complex when dark web pages present descriptions of illegal activities, cybercrime content, and vendor information through images [6]. Absent automation in text collection from images, analysts are tasked with scrutinizing these images manually, subsequently determining their legality or affiliation with cybercrime activity. The absence of automated systems inadvertently extends the timeframe for analysis and collection. Consequently, critical data from dark web with limited uptime may evade collection [7].

This paper proposes a method to address the issues mentioned earlier; it integrates both the textual content of dark web pages and the text embedded within images to identify the illegal and cybercrime content disseminated on the dark web. It has been noted that the proportion of image data significantly surpasses that of text in illicit and cybercrime content on dark web pages [8]. Information such as descriptions and tags for image content on the dark web is created by cybercrimes and traders. In addition, they can insert text related to the illegal and cybercrime content they provide to the image. Using such user-generated text can enhance the effectiveness of content type classification [9]. The presence of text embedded within images displayed on the dark web frequently indicates a piece of related information to the illegal and cyber-crime content circulated. Text recognition technology may be used to capture the text within these images. Text recognition technology takes an image file as input and extracts the text embedded in the image. This study utilizes image text recognition technology to extract text from images of illegal and cybercrime content distributed on the dark web. Based on this, we identify illegal and cybercrime content types. An incidental advantage of applying this technology is its ability to circumvent text anti-crawl mechanisms [5, 7]. Furthermore, the image-embedded text may indicate the type of disseminated content in identifying illegal and cybercrime content.

Currently, numerous studies focus on collecting text from dark web pages. However, the utilization of text embedded within images remains limited. Cybercrimes and traders on the dark web continuously adapt their methods to impede the collection of illicit and cybercrime text. This paper proposes a text collection method considering the sophisticated technology employed on the dark web. We implemented a system to identify illegal and cybercrime content types from the collected text, demonstrating its performance. The system addresses the limitations of crawling systems and content type identification systems that solely gather text from dark web pages. This contribution aids analysts in efficiently identifying illegal and cybercrime content types on the dark web, leading to time and cost savings. The key contributions of this paper include the following:

- This paper presents a novel approach to integrate text extracted from dark web pages and text embedded within images, aiming to effectively enhance the identification of illegal and cybercrime content types.
- An implemented system leverages texts from dark web pages and text embedded within images to accurately identify illegal and criminal content types.
- Experimental results demonstrate improved performance when incorporating text from images in conjunction with text from dark web pages, surpassing the performance of methods relying solely on text from dark web pages.

In this paper, Sect. 2 explains related research and background, and Sect. 3 describes how to collect dark web text through text recognition technology to identify illegal and cybercrime content types, Sect. 4 describes experiments, Sect. 5 ends with the conclusion and future research directions.

2 Background and Related Works

2.1 Analysis on Dark Web Content

In the early days of the Internet, privacy was not guaranteed. To address this concern, the United States Naval Research Laboratory developed Onion Routing to ensure privacy [1]. This paved the way for the emergence of the dark web, a platform where illegal and cybercrime content is distributed.

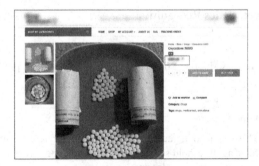

Fig. 1. Dark web drug distribution page

Figure 1 exemplifies the distribution of drugs, illegal and cybercrime content, on the dark web. The Tor network is vital in ensuring anonymity by employing encryption to prevent user tracking [1]. Presently, Cybercrimes exploit these characteristics to trade illicit and cybercrime content, such as drugs, weapons, and counterfeit passports [2, 3]. Ransomware groups like Conti and Lockbit have transitioned from trading illegal and cybercrime content to activities involving encryption disclosure and theft of personal information through the dark web. Additionally, intangible items like Distributed Denial of Service (DDoS) attack services, murder, human trafficking, and financial transactions are traded as specific content [3]. These illegal and cybercrime contents can be classified into market-type sites and sites specializing in distributing specific types of content. Due

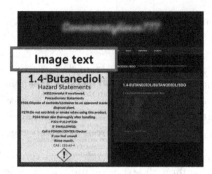

Fig. 2. Examples of text substitution with images on the dark web

to the diversity of text collected when dispersed in a market-like format, there is a risk of misidentifying illegal and cybercrime content types.

Figure 2 demonstrates an example of information dissemination by replacing text with images on the dark web. Typically, illegal and cybercrime content conveys information through text within dark web pages. However, to prevent text collection, alternative formats such as images and Cascading Style Sheets (CSS) are utilized as substitutes for text [5]. Our proposed method also considers cases where text providing important information is replaced with images. The methods we suggest can ensure that no sensitive information is left out in dark web investigations and tracking.

2.2 Optical Characteristics Recognition

Table 1. Description of 6 steps of OCR text recognition process

Step	Description
Image Acquisition	Import images
Pre-Processing	This step is to increase the text recognition rate. It includes spatial image filtering, threshold setting, noise removal, and screw detection/correction steps starting with binarization
Segmentation	Segmentation in the necessary part from the rest of the image includes page division, character division, image size normalization, and morpheme processing
Feature Extraction	Among the vectors representing the points of each character, only feature vectors necessary for improving the efficiency and accuracy of object identification are selected. It includes area specification, Projection histogram features, Distance profile features, Background directional distribution, and the combination of various features steps

(continued)

Table 1. (*continued*)

Step	Description
Classification	This classification step uses the feature vector obtained in the feature extraction step. A Probabilistic Neural Network classifier, Support Vector Machines classifier, and K-Nearest Neighbor classifier can be used
Post Processing	Since the result is not 100% accurate if the text is not in standard language, the accuracy is improved through the Post Processing step

Optical Characteristics Recognition (OCR) is a technology that converts printed documents into machine-readable documents [10]. Table 1 describes the text recognition process of a typical OCR in 6 steps [11]. The user first inputs an image to recognize text. Next, the user can perform pre-processing operations such as converting to binary data, setting thresholds, and removing noise to increase the success rate. Then, a segmentation process is performed to distinguish the text area from the background, and features are extracted from the corresponding region of the image. Finally, classification is accomplished through the extracted features. Performing post-processing is a step to improve precision. Through this process, the text within the image is recognized. When Cybercrimes replace text with images to avoid the automated text collection, analysts can respond through OCR [5].

2.3 Existing Works Related to Dark Web Crawling

Medina, P. B et al. [7] collected text from images by applying Text Spotting techniques to bypass text crawling prevention techniques on the dark web. The selected connectionist Text Proposal Network (CPTN) algorithm was for text detection and used Convolutional Recurrent Neural Network (CRNN) for the text recognition model. The experiment confirmed the performance using the TOIC dataset, and the handwritten text confirmed a slightly better performance than OCR.

Alaidi, A. H. M. et al. [12] implemented a crawling function to collect content from the dark web and a position to classify the collected web pages by using the text mining technique for the collected content. The system proceeds with data crawling and collection, data pre-processing, dataset automatic labeling, classification, and evaluation. Dark web links were collected using search engines such as Ahmai to perform the crawling function. The text mining technique utilized term frequency - inverse document frequency (TF-IDF), support vector classification (SVC), and naïve bayes. Based on this, illegal and cybercrime data was classified into five types. In this study, the text within the image is not included in the subject of the collection.

Jeziorowski, S. et al. [13] proposed a data collection method for tracking cybercrime in a dark web environment where anonymity is guaranteed. This study aims to solve the problem of needing help to obtain open-source information on the dark web through images easily. In image metadata, data such as the image's creator, the date and time of creation, the device's location, and the device's model can be used as cybercrime evidence. In addition, to save resources, they proposed storing images on the dark web as hashes. Through this study, it is possible to identify cybercrime evidence in the dark web market. However, responding to illegal and cybercrime-related text crawling prevention technology is challenging.

Pannu, M. et al. [14] proposed a system for collecting and monitoring illegal and cybercrime content to remove the anonymity of cybercrimes on the dark web. The proposed method comprises a central server, distributed nodes, and clients. The central server performs node management, asset parser, database control, and search management functions. In the case of the data parser, it targets all <href> tags, text in HTML documents, and images that exist on the dark web. The purpose of image collection in the system is to create a histogram through OpenCV, and the text in the image is not included in the subject of the collection.

In the previous study, in the process of illegal and criminal text collection, a study was conducted to classify the text of the dark web page as a target. In addition, a study was conducted to collect text embedded within images to circumvent text crawling prevention techniques. However, the text embedded within images was not used to identify illegal and criminal content types. In this paper, we intend to improve the performance of dark web text crawling and identify illegal and criminal content types by utilizing the text of dark web pages and the text embedded within images in images.

3 Methodology

3.1 Overview

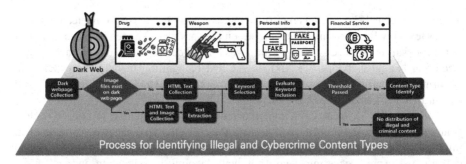

Fig. 3. Illegal and Crime Content Type Identify Process

This section provides an overview of the research methodology. This paper aims to identify illegal and cybercrime content types by collecting text from images on the dark web using OCR. Figure 3 illustrates the sequential steps in collecting dark web pages and identifying illegal and cybercrime content types. The process starts with collecting dark web pages where illegal and cybercrime content is circulated. The collected dark web pages contain both text and images. Extracting text data from dark web pages undergoes no specific processing, while the images are subjected to text extraction to facilitate the identification of illegal and cybercrime content. Specific keywords are collected to identify the presence of illegal and cybercrime content. These keywords are tailored to the type of illegal and cybercrime content. These extracted texts are then analyzed using a keyword inclusion rate based on a predetermined threshold to determine the presence of illegal and cybercrime content. Finally, the process concludes with identifying the specific type of dark web page.

3.2 Collecting the Dark Web Page

This section describes the method for collecting dark web pages containing illegal and cybercrime content. The goal is to identify various types of illegal and cybercrime content circulating on the dark web. To collect these pages, we utilize dark web search engines specifically designed for accessing the dark web [15]. Unlike the search engines used on the Surface Web, they cannot be accessed the Dark Web through traditional means [15]. Users need to have the exact addresses of the dark web pages or rely on dedicated search engines [15]. Users can access dark web pages associated with the desired content by entering relevant keywords into a dark web search engine. In this paper, we collect the addresses of dark web pages by inputting illegal and cybercrime terms into Ahmia.fi a dedicated search engine for the dark web.

3.3 Collecting the Text and Image from the Dark Web Page

This section describes the process of gathering text and images from the addresses of dark web pages obtained using specialized search engines dedicated to the dark web. On the Surface Web, data is presented using the Hypertext Markup Language (HTML) file structure, where tags organize content. Similarly, the dark web employs files with a comparable structure to the Surface Web [16]. To collect text, specific areas or the entire text can be captured by leveraging tags within these web file structures. Images can also be identified and collected by extracting information from the <img> tag, which contains the path to the image.

3.4 Text Extraction

This section describes the methodology for extracting text from image files on dark web pages that distribute illegal and cybercrime content. Various techniques exist for recognizing text embedded within images. In this study, we employ OCR technology to extract text from the images collected from dark web pages. The text extraction process encompasses all images from the dark web pages.

3.5 Keyword Collection

This section describes the method for collecting keywords for identifying various illegal and cybercrime content types. We collect text data from the dark web to conduct our keyword collection process, which follows the method described in Sect. 3.2. We collect keywords that are high frequency of use on dark web pages. During the keyword collect process, we exclude stopwords such as "the, a, an, is, I, my" words commonly used on the surface web, such as "order". Additionally, users can independently collect words and slang as keywords, which are highly pertinent to different types of illegal and cybercrime content. Keyword collection should be done separately by illegal and cybercrime content types.

3.6 Evaluating Keyword Inclusion

This section describes how to identify whether illegal and cybercrime content is circulating and what type of content it is. After collecting text through HTML files of dark web pages and collection through images, it is necessary to identify illegal and cybercrime content types. We need to use keywords associated with each type of illegal and cybercrime content to do this. We calculate the inclusion rate of how many collected keywords are detected in words on dark web pages. The types of illegal and cybercrime content are identified based on the calculation of the inclusion rate.

4 Experiment

4.1 Dataset Description

This section describes the datasets utilized for identifying illegal and cybercrime content types. We employ text-based analysis to identify different types of illegal and cybercrime content. To gather the necessary text data, we initially collect dark web page link that distributes illegal and cybercrime content using the dark web search engine Ahmia.fi. We targeted the four types of dark web pages: drug distribution, arms trafficking, sale of fake document, and financial services. A total of 10 dark web pages are collected for each type.

Following the collection of dark web pages, we gathered the text and images from these HTML pages. In addition, we employed OCR technology to extract text from the images. Specifically, we utilized Google's Cloud Vision API, a machine learning-powered service offering advanced image analysis functionalities [17]. We successfully extracted text from the images through the OCR function provided by the Cloud Vision API. However, it is worth noting that special newline characters sometimes appear within the text when extracting text from images. To address this, we replaced these newline characters with blank spaces, resulting in a dataset that would be utilized for identifying various types of illegal and cybercrime content.

4.2 Setup

This section outlines the preparations to identify the types of content found on dark web pages where illegal and cybercrime activities occur. We have curated a set of keywords classified into four types to facilitate the identification of different types of illegal and cybercrime content. Specifically, for drugs, we included keywords related to the drug type, unit of measurement, and associated symptoms. Regarding weapons, keywords encompassed the gun model name, bullet type, accessory details, and explosive types.

Personal information keywords included passport, identification card, social security number, certificate, license, and corresponding abbreviations.

$$rate = \frac{Keyword\ count}{list\ of\ words\ in\ Dark\ web\ page} \tag{1}$$

Equation 1 presents the formula for determining the keyword inclusion rate of dark web pages. This calculation helps identify the types of illegal and cybercrime content on these pages. In our experiment, a threshold of 5% was set for the keyword inclusion rate on dark web pages. The threshold may be arbitrarily adjusted according to the quality of keywords set for each illegal or cybercrime content. If the threshold is exceeded, it is determined that illegal and cybercrime content related to the keyword is being distributed. We calculate the inclusion of relevant keywords for each content type and identify the type with the highest inclusion rate. The type of illegal and cybercrime content is determined by the type with the highest inclusion rate among the four types. Rate is determined by counting the number of keywords present in the text of a dark web page and dividing it by the total number of words in the page's text. To implement our system, we utilized Python 3.84 and leveraged open libraries and modules such as Beautifulsoup and re.

4.3 Experiment and Results

This section describes an experiment that utilized text on dark web pages and text embedded within images to identify types of illegal and cybercrime content. The experiment tests three methods. When using text only, experiment with text and text embedded within images. Next, experiment using text and text embedded within images, giving text embedded within images more points. We check the performance of illegal and cybercrime content type identification through four methods.

Table 2. Dark Web Illegal and Cybercrime Content Type Identification Test Results

Type	Type Identify by Text only	Type Identify by Text and image text	Type Identify by Text and image text * 3	Type Identify by Text and image text (keyword)
Drug	9/10	9/10	9/10	9/10
Weapon	8/10	9/10	9/10	9/10
Personal Information	10/10	10/10	8/10	10/10

Table 2 shows the results of experiments conducted on three types of illegal and cybercrime content. Among the texts in HTML text and images, using a combination of keywords showed the highest performance. However, the experimental results also revealed poor performance when using all the text within an image together. We confirm that combining all the text within an image is not always the best approach.

Table 3. Result of identifying drug content on the dark web

	Type Identify by Text only	Type Identify by Text and image text	Type Identify by Text and image text * 3	Type Identify by Text and image text (keyword)
Drug 1	**Drug (5.78%)**	**Finance (5.21%)**	**Fail (4.56%)**	**Finance (6.40%)**
Drug 2	Drug (6.78%)	Drug (6.22%)	Drug (5.53%)	Drug (8.23%)
Drug 3	**Drug (19.35%)**	**Drug (7.69%)**	**Drug (5.01%)**	**Drug (28.21%)**
Drug 4	Drug (14.53%)	Drug (10.06%)	Drug (6.36%)	Drug (14.77%)
Drug 5	Drug (10.71%)	Drug (11.26%)	Drug (12.14%)	Drug (13.10%)
Drug 6	Fail (4.83%)	Drug (5.09%)	Drug (5.46%)	Drug (6.54%)
Drug 7	Drug (24.57%)	Drug (23.76%)	Drug (22.28%)	Drug (24.57%)
Drug 8	Drug (6.08%)	Drug (6.2%)	Drug (6.37%)	Drug (7.71%)
Drug 9	Drug (10.69%)	Drug (8.6%)	Drug (6.18%)	Drug (10.55%)
Drug 10	Drug (7.56%)	Drug (6.05%)	Drug (4.6%)	Drug (8.75%)

Table 3 shows a detailed experiment on ten collected drug distribution web pages. Drug 3, part of the collected drug distribution web pages, showcases a case where anti-crawling techniques are applied. In this experiment, there are cases where illegal and cybercrime content distribution is not identified, or the type is misidentified. In cases where there are multiple types, such as marketplaces, or a high percentage of irrelevant content, such as product reviews, the identification process becomes more challenging. A high percentage of other content type text and irrelevant text makes distribution and type identification imprecise. Table 3 presents the results of experiments to identify illegal content types by using a combination of the text embedded within images and text in HTML, considering these issues. We combined the text in the image with the HTML text to identify the content type. As a result, we observed an increase in the coverage ratio, leading to a more accurate identification of related types. However, the coverage ratio showed significant deviations in some cases, making the results less reliable. To address this issue, we performed another experiment, focusing solely on the keywords found within the text of the image. The experiments revealed that using HTML text and specific keywords text in images got better results than using HTML text alone. Notably, we observed a significant increase in the inclusion rate when dealing with dark web pages equipped with anti-crawl technology. The results suggest that using a combination of HTML text and text keywords in images is effective when dealing with anti-crawling dark web pages.

From our experimentation, we checked that using text within an image can be stable and effective when concentrating on the text corresponding to the keyword rather than using all the text within the image. Also, the more sophisticated the keywords used to identify illegal and cybercrimes content, the better the performance.

5 Limitations

In this paper, we confirmed that the performance of identifying illegal and cybercrime types on the dark web could be improved by extracting text using OCR. However, the experiment has the following limitations.

- Keywords used to identify illegal and cybercrime content types do not use common datasets.
- Tested only for keywords of type Illegal and Cybercrime: Drug Trafficking, Arms Trafficking, Personal Information.
- Use only English in type identification experiments, and challenging to identify if the keywords are not elaborate.
- Introducing noise into images to impede OCR in dark web illicit and cybercrime content or the exclusive use of slang by distributors and consumers pose challenges in identifying illegal content.

6 Conclusion and Future Works

Today, Cybercrimes are exploiting their anonymity and untraceability on the dark web. By exploiting these characteristics, various illegal and cybercrime contents such as malicious code, drugs, personal information, and weapons are distributed. A crawling system that collects text has been developed and researched to counter illegal and cybercrime content distribution. Much research has been done on how to collect the dark web. How we process the data we collect on the dark web can contribute to determining whether a crime has occurred. However, it is difficult to identify the exact type when various types of illegal and cybercrime content are circulated, such as in markets on the dark web. In addition, existing developed and researched crawling systems did not consider text prevention techniques. In this paper, to solve these problems, we propose to collect dark web text through OCR and use it to identify illegal and cybercrime content. The system can bypass the dark web's anti-text crawling techniques. Also, text embedded within images allowed us to collect better data than collecting the full text of dark web pages. Our experiments found that using HTM/HTML text data from dark web pages and text embedded within images improves the performance of identifying illegal and cybercrime content types. The experiment confirmed that the performance was favorable when combining HTML and keyword text in images.

In future research, we plan to automate the sophisticated collection of keywords and use it for evidence identification and cybercrime tracking. By doing so, we hope to contribute to law enforcement agencies fighting cybercrime on the dark web.

Acknowledgement. This work was supported by the Nuclear Safety Research Program through the Korea Foundation of Nuclear Safety (KoFONS) using the financial resource granted by the Nuclear Safety and Security Commission (NSSC) of the Republic of Korea (No. 2106058).

References

1. Kaur, S., Randhawa, S.: Dark web: a web of crimes. Wirel. Pers. Commun. **112**, 2131–2158 (2020)

2. He, S., He, Y., Li, M.: Classification of illegal activities on the dark web. In: Proceedings of the 2nd International Conference on Information Science and Systems, Tokyo, Japan, pp. 73–78 (2019)

3. Rawat, R., Rajawat, A.S., Mahor, V., Shaw, R.N., Ghosh, A.: Dark web—onion hidden service discovery and crawling for profiling morphing, unstructured crime and vulnerabilities prediction. In: Mekhilef, S., Favorskaya, M., Pandey, R.K., Shaw, R.N. (eds.) Innovations in Electrical and Electronic Engineering. LNEE, vol. 756, pp. 717–734. Springer, Singapore (2021). https://doi.org/10.1007/978-981-16-0749-3_57

4. Laferrière, D., Décary-Hétu, D.: Examining the uncharted dark web: trust signalling on single vendor shops. Deviant Behav. **44**(1), 37–56 (2023)

5. Turk, K., Pastrana, S., Collier, B.: A tight scrape: methodological approaches to cybercrime research data collection in adversarial environments. In: 2020 IEEE European Symposium on Security and Privacy Workshops (EuroS&PW), Genoa, Italy, pp. 428–437. IEEE (2020)

6. Faizan, M., Khan, R.A.: Exploring and analyzing the dark web: a new alchemy. First Monday (2019)

7. Medina, P.B., Fernández, E.F., Gutiérrez, E.A., Al Nabki, M.W.: Detecting textual information in images from onion domains using text spotting. In: XXXIX Jornadas de Automática: actas, Badajoz, 5–7 de septiembre de 2018, pp. 975–982. Universidad de Extremadura (2018)

8. Dalvi, A., Paranjpe, S., Amale, R., Kurumkar, S., Kazi, F., Bhirud, S.G.: SpyDark: surface and dark web crawler. In: 2021 2nd International Conference on Secure Cyber Computing and Communications (ICSCCC), Jalandhar, India, pp. 45–49. IEEE (2021)

9. Huang, C., Fu, T., Chen, H.: Text-based video content classification for online video-sharing sites. J. Am. Soc. Inform. Sci. Technol. **61**(5), 891–906 (2010)

10. Nguyen, T.T.H., Jatowt, A., Coustaty, M., Doucet, A.: Survey of post-OCR processing approaches. ACM Comput. Surv. (CSUR) **54**(6), 1–37 (2021)

11. Mittal, R., Garg, A.: Text extraction using OCR: a systematic review. In: 2020 Second International Conference on Inventive Research in Computing Applications (ICIRCA), Coimbatore, India, pp. 357–362. IEEE (2020)

12. Alaidi, A.H.M., Roa'a, M., ALRikabi, H.T.S., Aljazaery, I.A., Abbood, S.H.: Dark web illegal activities crawling and classifying using data mining techniques. iJIM **16**(10), 123 (2022)

13. Jeziorowski, S., Ismail, M., Siraj, A.: Towards image-based dark vendor profiling: an analysis of image metadata and image hashing in dark web marketplaces. In: Proceedings of the Sixth International Workshop on Security and Privacy Analytics, New Orleans, LA, USA, pp. 15–22 (2020)

14. Pannu, M., Kay, I., Harris, D.: Using dark web crawler to uncover suspicious and malicious websites. In: Ahram, T.Z., Nicholson, D. (eds.) AHFE 2018. AISC, vol. 782, pp. 108–115. Springer, Cham (2018). https://doi.org/10.1007/978-3-319-94782-2_11

15. Kavallieros, D., Myttas, D., Kermitsis, E., Lissaris, E., Giataganas, G., Darra, E.: Understanding the dark web. In: Akhgar, B., Gercke, M., Vrochidis, S., Gibson, H. (eds.) Dark Web Investigation. SILE, pp. 3–26. Springer, Cham (2021). https://doi.org/10.1007/978-3-030-55343-2_1

16. Bergman, J., Popov, O.B.: Exploring dark web crawlers: a systematic literature review of dark web crawlers and their implementation. IEEE Access (2023)

17. Thammarak, K., Kongkla, P., Sirisathitkul, Y., Intakosum, S.: Comparative analysis of Tesseract and Google Cloud Vision for Thai vehicle registration certificate. Int. J. Electr. Comput. Eng. **12**(2), 1849–1858 (2022)

Enriching Vulnerability Reports Through Automated and Augmented Description Summarization

Hattan Althebeiti(iD) and David Mohaisen(✉)(iD)

University of Central Florida, Orlando, USA
{hattan.althebeiti,mohaisen}@ucf.edu

Abstract. Security incidents and data breaches are increasing rapidly, and only a fraction of them is being reported. Public vulnerability databases, e.g., national vulnerability database (NVD) and common vulnerability and exposure (CVE), have been leading the effort in documenting vulnerabilities and sharing them to aid defenses. Both are known for many issues, including brief vulnerability descriptions. Those descriptions play an important role in communicating the vulnerability information to security analysts in order to develop the appropriate countermeasure. Many resources provide additional information about vulnerabilities, however, they are not utilized to boost public repositories. In this paper, we devise a pipeline to augment vulnerability description through third party reference (hyperlink) scrapping. To normalize the description, we build a natural language summarization pipeline utilizing a pretrained language model that is fine-tuned using labeled instances and evaluate its performance against both human evaluation (golden standard) and computational metrics, showing initial promising results in terms of summary fluency, completeness, correctness, and understanding.

Keywords: Vulnerability · NVD · CVE · Natural Language Processing · Summarization · Sentence Encoder · Transformer

1 Introduction

Vulnerabilities are weaknesses in systems that render them exposed to any threat or exploitation. They are prevalent in software and are constantly being discovered and patched. However, given the rapid development in technologies, discovering a vulnerability and developing a mitigation technique become challenging. Moreover, documenting vulnerabilities and keeping track of their development become cumbersome.

The common vulnerability and exposure CVE managed by MITRE and the National vulnerability database NVD managed by NIST are two key resources for reporting and sharing vulnerabilities. The content of each resource may differ slightly according to [8], but they are mostly synchronized and any update to the CVE should appear eventually in the NVD. However, NVD/CVE descriptions have several shortcomings. For example, the description might be incomplete, outdated or even contain inaccurate information which could delay the development and deployment of patches. In 2017

H. Kim and J. Youn (Eds.): WISA 2023, LNCS 14402, pp. 213–227, 2024.
https://doi.org/10.1007/978-981-99-8024-6_17

Risk Based Security also known as VulbDB reported 7,900 more vulnerabilities than what was reported by CVE [9, 10]. Another concern with the existing framework is that the description provided for vulnerabilities is often incomplete, brief, or does not carry sufficient contextual information [3, 5].

To address some of these gaps, this work focuses on the linguistic aspects of vulnerability description and attempts to improve them by formulating the problem as a summarization task over augmented initial description. We exploit the existence of third party reports associated with vulnerabilities, which include more detailed information about the vulnerabilities that goes beyond the basic description in the CVE. Therefore, we leverage these additional resources employing a natural language processing (NLP) pipeline towards that goal, providing informative summaries that cover more details and perform well on both computational and human metrics.

Contributions. The main contributions of this work are as follows. (1) we present a pipeline that enriches the description of vulnerabilities by considering semantically similar contents from various third party resources (reference URLs). (2) In order to normalize the enriched description and alleviate some of the drawbacks of the augmentation (e.g., redundancy and repetition, largely variable length of description), we build an NLP pipeline that exploits advances in representation, pretrained language models that are fine-tuned using the original (short description) as a label, and generate semantically similar summaries of vulnerabilities. (3) We evaluate the performance of the proposed NLP pipeline on NVD, a popular vulnerability database, with both computational and human metric evaluations.

2   Related Work

Vulnerabilities are constantly being exploited due to the wide spread of malware and viruses along with the improper deployment of countermeasures or missing security updates. Mohaisen et al. [16] proposed AMAL, an automated system to analyze and classify malware based on its behaviour. AMAL is composed of two components AutoMal and MaLabel. AutoMal collect information about malware samples based on their behaviours for monitoring and profiling. On the other hand, MaLabel utilizes the artifacts generated by AutoMal to build a feature vector representation for malware samples. Moreover, MaLabel builds multiple classifiers to classify unlabeled malware samples and to cluster them into separate groups such that each group have malware samples with similar profiles.

Public repositories provide comprehensive information about vulnerabilities, however, they still suffer from quality and consistency issues as demonstrated in previous works [3, 8]. Anwar et al. [3] have identified and quantified multiple quality issues with the NVD and addressed their implications and ramifications. The authors present a method for each matter to remedy the discovered deficiency and improve the NVD. Similarly, Anwar et al. [4] studied the impact of vulnerability disclosure on the stock market and how it affects different industries. They were able to cluster industries into three categories based on the vulnerabilities impact on the vendor's return.

Limited prior works studied different characteristics of vulnerabilities and used NLP based-approach on the task, although NLP has been utilized extensively for other security and privacy applications. Alabduljabbar et al. [1] conducted a comprehensive study to classify privacy policies established by a third party. A pipeline was developed to classify text segments into a high-level category that correspond to the content of that segment. Likewise, Alabduljabbar et al. [2] used NLP to conduct a comparative analysis of privacy policies presented by free and premium content websites. The study highlighted that premium content websites are more transparent in terms of reporting their practices with respect to data collection and tracking.

Dong et al. [8] built VIEM, a system to capture inconsistency between CVE/NVD and third party reports utilizing Named Entity Recognition model (NER) and a Relation Extractor model (RE). The NER is responsible for identifying the name and version of vulnerable software based on their semantics and structure within the description and label each of them accordingly. The RE component utilizes the identified labels and pairs the appropriate software name and version to predict which software is vulnerable.

Other research focused on studying the relationship between CVE and Common Attack Pattern Enumeration and Classification (CAPEC) and if it is possible to trace a CVE description to a particular CAPEC using NLP as in Kanakogi et al. [12]. Similarly, Kanakogi et al. [11] tested a new method for the same task but using Doc2Vec. Wareus and Hell [22] proposed a method to automatically assigns Common Platform Enumeration (CPE) to a CVEs from their description using NLP.

This Work. We propose a pipeline for enriching the vulnerability description, and a pipeline for normalizing description through summarization and associated evaluation.

3   Dataset: Baseline and Data Augmentation

Data Source and Scraping. Our data source is NVD because it is a well-known standard accepted across the globe, in both industry and academia, with many strengths: (1) detailed structured information, including the severity score and publication date, (2) human-readable descriptions, (3) capabilities for reanalysis with updated information, and (4) powerful API for vulnerability information retrieval.

In our data collection, we limit our timeframe to vulnerabilities reported between 2019 and 2021 (inclusive). Based on our analysis, CVEs reported before 2019 do not include sufficient hyperlinks with additional text, which is our main source for augmentation. We list all the vulnerabilities reported in this period, and scrap them. For each vulnerability, we scrap the URLs pointing to the NVD page that hosts a particular vulnerability. As a result, we obtain 35,657 vulnerabilities with their unique URLs. Second, we iterate through every URL various data elements. After retrieving the URL, we scrap the description and the hyperlinks for that vulnerability.

Description Augmentation. To augment the description, we iterate through the scrapped hyperlinks. Each hyperlink directs us to a page hosted by a third party, which could be an official page belonging to the vendor or the developer or an unofficial page; e.g., GitHub issue tracking page. We scrape every paragraph tag in each page separately and apply various preprocessing steps to the extracted paragraph to clean up the text. This preprocessing includes removing web links, special characters, white redundant spaces, phone numbers, and email addresses. We also check the length of the paragraph

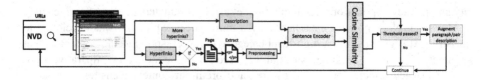

Fig. 1. Data collection pipeline

and ensure it is more than 20 words after preprocessing. We conjecture that paragraphs shorter than 20 words will not contribute to our goal.

After cleaning the text and verifying the length, we use a sentence encoder to encode the semantic for the extracted paragraph and the scrapped description into low dimensional vector representations (more in Sect. 4.1). To determine the similarity between the vectorized representations, we use the cosine similarity which yields a value between -1 and 1. For example, let the vector representation of the extracted paragraph be $\mathbf{v}_p$ and that of the description be $\mathbf{v}_d$, the cosine similarity is defined as:

$$\cos(\mathbf{v}_p, \mathbf{v}_d) = \frac{\vec{v_p} \cdot \vec{v_d}}{||\vec{v_p}|| \; ||\vec{v_d}||} \qquad (1)$$

If $\cos(\mathbf{v}_p, \mathbf{v}_d)$ exceeds a predefined threshold, we add/augment the paragraph as the input text and the description as the summary text. This process is repeated with every paragraph contained within a page. We repeat this step for every hyperlink by extracting the page, associated paragraph tags, applying preprocessing, encoding semantic and measure the similarity with the description. We note that some vulnerabilities may not be added to our dataset; e.g., if the vulnerability did not have any hyperlinks or if its associated hyperlinks did not include any paragraph that meets the predefined threshold. We repeat the process for each URL until we cover all the URLs, upon which dataset is ready to be presented to the model.

Figure 1 shows our pipeline. The choice of a sentence encoder will affect the dataset because the inclusion of a paragraph is based on the similarity score between the vectorized representation of the description and paragraph encoded by the sentence encoder. To enhance our experiments and provide a better insight into different encoders and summarization models, we use two sentence encoder choices: Universal Sentence Encoder (USE) and MPNet sentence encoder. In our analysis, we use the best performing encoder with respect to the end-goal outcome of our summarization task.

Per Fig. 1, the similarity score must exceed a predefined threshold. From our preliminary assessment of the two encoders, we found that USE is more accurate (sensitive) than MPNet in terms of the similarity score representation, meaning that when the description and the paragraph are (semantically) similar to one another, USE produces a higher score than MPNet and vice versa. Considering this insight, we set different threshold for each encoder. Namely, we set the similarity score for USE to be between 0.60 and 0.90, since the encoder is accurate. On the other hand, since MPNet is less accurate (sensitive) than USE, we enforce a more restrictive threshold and set it between

0.70 and 0.90. We excluded paragraphs with a similarity score above 0.90 because we found those paragraphs to be almost identical to the description, thus adding them would not serve the main purpose of enriching the description. Those values were picked as part of our assessment over the two encoders using a small set of vulnerabilities and following the procedure explained above.

Some hyperlinks analysis took extremely long time. Upon examining the content of those pages, we found that they contain a history of the software vulnerability with updates, e.g., over 20,000 paragraph tags in some cases. Moreover, most of them were not considered by the sentence encoder because they do not meet the threshold. As such, we consider the first 100 paragraph tag in each hyperlink to speed up the process. We justify this heuristic by noting that most pages contain the related textual information at the beginning with subsequent paragraphs being reiteration of information that is already mentioned earlier. Finally, to only limit our collection to authentic descriptions, we consider hyperlinks with valid SSL certificate.

Additionally, we curated a third dataset using both and enforcing multiple thresholds on the similarity criterion. For that, we used the same the threshold for the MPNet as before, and relaxed the threshold for USE to 0.50 to relax an imposed restrictive setting by possibly excluding otherwise qualified candidate paragraphs.

Given the differences between the two encoders, we consider a paragraph to be similar if the difference between the two similarity scores is at most 0.20; otherwise we consider them dissimilar and discard the paragraph. Here, we favored the consistency between the two encoding techniques to conceptually alleviate the discrepancy presented from using the

Table 1. Datasets

# CVEs	Encoders	Vuln.
35,657	USE	9,955
	MPNet	8,664
	Both	10,766

two different encoders. Table 1 shows the datasets. In the next section, we elaborate about the encoders in more detail.

4   Methodology and Building Blocks

4.1   Sentence Encoders

Among the multiple tried encoders over multiple CVEs along with their similar paragraphs, we found that the best encoders for our task are the Universal Sentence Encoder (USE) [6] and MPNet sentence encoder [20], which we explain in the following.

Universal Sentence Encoder. Two architectures are proposed for USE. The first is a transformer-based model which uses a transformer architecture to compute context aware representation of the words while preserving words' positions, followed by embeddings used to compute fixed length sentence encoding using element-wise sum at each word position. The downside of this architecture is its time and space complexities, i.e., it takes $O(n^2)$ and is proportional in space to the sentence length. The second architecture is much simpler and uses a Deep Averaging Network (DAN). It computes a sentence initial embedding by averaging words with bi-gram embeddings and passes this embedding through a feed forward network to produce the final embedding. Unlike the transformer architecture, DAN's time complexity is $O(n)$ and its space is constant with respect to the length of the sentence. The trade-off in choosing among those two architectures is between the high accuracy with intensive computation achieved by the transformer architecture versus the efficient inference and computation with a reduced accuracy achieved by the DAN architecture. Given our problem's characteristics, we decided to use the DAN architecture because (1) our data will be scraped, and its length may vary widely, and (2) our data is domain-specific and is limited in its linguistic scope. We conjecture DAN will produce accurate embedding since the vocabulary size is limited (i.e., small). Finally, considering that we have over 35,000 Vulnerabilities, where each has multiple hyperlinks to be scraped, the scalability benefit of DAN outweighs the high accuracy of the transformer-based architecture.

MPNet. The second technique we utilize is MPNet. MPNet is a model that leverages the advantages presented in two famous pretrained models: BERT [7] and XLNET [23]. BERT uses a masked language modeling objective, which masks 15% of the tokens and the model is trained to predict them. The downside of BERT is that it does not consider the dependency between the masked tokens. On the other hand, XLNET retains the autoregressive modeling by presenting permuted language modeling objective in which each token within a sequence considers the permutations of the previous tokens in the sequence but not after it. However, this causes position discrepancy between the pretraining and fine-tuning. MPNet unifies the objectives of the two models by considering dependency among predicted tokens and considering all tokens' positions to solve the position discrepancy. Moreover, MPNet sentence transformer is built by fine-tuning MPNet on 1 billion sentence-pair dataset and uses contrastive learning objective. Given a sentence from the pair, the model tries to predict which other sentence it was paired with. This is done by computing the cosine similarity with every other sentence in the batch and then using the cross-entropy loss with respect to the true pair. In the next section we explain the pipeline for our summarization models.

4.2   Pretrained Models

The goal of this work is to use pretrained models and fine-tune them on our datasets for vulnerability summarization and description enrichment. The pretrained models inherit the architecture of the original transformer [21] with some adjustments to the weights depending on the task it is performing. The transformer itself constitutes of two major components: an encoder and a decoder. The encoder's role is to build a representation for the input sequence that captures the dependencies between tokens in parallel without losing positional information of those tokens. The transformer relies on the attention mechanism to capture interdependency within a sequence, which provides a context-aware representation for each token. The decoder's role is to use the built representation and map it to a probability distribution over the entire vocabulary to predict the next word. Figure 2 shows the pipeline of a the encoder-decoder transformer from the beginning of inputting the raw text to the prediction (decoded into utterances for sequences generation; i.e., summarization).

The original transformer was developed and is intended for machine translation, although generalized to other tasks with remarkable results. We note that most modern pretrained models use a transformer architecture that depends on an encoder only;

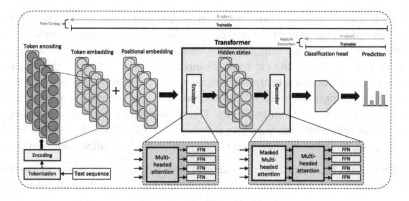

Fig. 2. Our summarization pipeline

e.g., BERT [7], a decoder only; e.g., GPT (Generative Pre-trained Transformer) [17], or both. Each architecture has its own advantages, which allows it to excel in specific tasks. The summarization task, for example, can be modeled as a seq2seq task where the model takes an input (long text) and outputs the summary, which naturally makes a model that constitutes of encoder and decoder ideal for its design. In the NLP literature, the most performant models for summarization are BART [15], T5 [18], and Pegasus [24], with BART and T5 being more widely used. BART is a denoising autoencoder for pretraining seq2seq with an encoder-decoder architecture. The idea of BART is to use a noising function to corrupt the text and train the model to reconstruct the original (uncorrupted) text. In contrast, T5 uses a masked language modelling objective like BERT for training. Instead of masking a token, T5 masks a span of the original text as its corruption strategy. The length of the span does not influence the model performance unless too many tokens are within that span. Moreover, T5 attempts to define a framework for many NLP tasks by adding a prefix that identifies the task it tries to learn. Therefore, one model can support multiple tasks by defining those prefixes in the training data and adding those prefixes to a sample allows the model to predict for the task associated with that prefix.

4.3 Pipeline

Next, we discuss the pipeline depicted in Fig. 2 in more details. The major steps of our pipeline are tokenization of the input text sequence (description), encoding, token embedding, positional embedding, encoding-decoding (utilizing a fine-tuned pretrained language model), and prediction. Those steps are elaborated in the following.

Tokenization. The first step for most models is tokenization, which includes breaking text into individual independent entities and encoding them into numerical representation. Tokenization could be applied at the word or character level. With word tokenization, we will end up with a large vocabulary size that will affect the dimensionality of the word embedding. To address the dimensionality issue, it is common to limit the size to the most common 100,000 words in a corpus and encode all unknown words as <UNK>. However, most words morphemes will be encoded as unknown although they possess very similar meaning to their root. Similarly, character embedding dominant limitation is losing the linguistic structure and considering a text as a stream of characters. A third type is the subword tokenization, which alleviates the drawbacks of the two aforementioned tokenization granularities. Subword tokenization splits rare words into a meaningful unit which helps the model to handle complex words and associate their embedding with similar words. This allows the model to associate singular with plural and relate different morphemes to their root. BART uses Byte-Pair Encoding (BPE) [19] and T5 uses SentencePiece [13, 14] which are both subword tokenizer.

Token Encoding. The tokenized text is transformed into numerical representation using one-hot encoding with a size equal to the vocabulary size; e.g., 20k–200k tokens.

Token Embedding. The token encodings are then projected into lower dimensional space that captures the characteristics of each word in a token embedding. However, for a pretrained model this and the previous step are already done and the token embedding is already computed during the model training. Those two steps are required if we plan to build our own transformer from the bottom-up. In practice, each token will be represented by an id that identifies it with respect to the model.

Each text consists of tokenized words and each token is represented by an input id. To increase the efficiency of the model, we create a batch of multiple text before feeding the text into the transformer. However, to create a batch, we must ensure that all texts have the same size as the longest text in that batch. For that padding is used to pad short text to meet the length requirements by adding id '0' to the text sequence. Moreover, the attention mask informs the model to ignore those padding during encoding by assigning 1 to tokens that are part of the original sequence and 0 for padding. Finally, the batch of texts (with attention masks) is passed to the transformer block. Each model has some reserved ids that are used for a specific purpose.

Positional Embedding. The transformer uses the attention mechanism to capture the contextual interdependence between words. However, this method is oblivious to the words' positions, and we need a way to inject this information into the word embedding. As with tokenizer, each model has its own way of including this information. BART uses the same method used in the original transformer where a simple sinusoidal function is used to create a positional embedding for each token within a sequence. On the other hand, T5 uses a more sophisticated approach, called the Relative Positional Encoding (RPE), which uses a multi-headed attention to encode the relative positions between tokens. The intuition behind RPE stems from the fact that what is most important is the surrounding words rather than its exact position, and that is how RPE computes the positional embedding. The token embedding, and the positional embedding are added together to build the final embedding that will be fed into the transformer.

Transformer. This step consists of an encoder an a decoder. The encoder uses a multi-headed attention to build a representation that captures the contextual interdependence relationship between tokens. The encoder uses several layers of self-attention to compute how much attention should be paid by every token with respect to other tokens to build the final numerical representation. Modern transformers use the scaled dot product attention which utilizes a query, key, and value computed for each token to produce the attention score for every token with respect to other tokens in the sequence. A simple intuition behind applying several attention layers (heads) is that each head may focus on one aspect of attention, while others may capture a different similarity. By concatenating the output of all heads, however, we obtain a more powerful representation that resembles that sequence. The feed forward network receives every token embedding from the multi-headed attention and processes it independently to produce its final embedding which is referred to as the hidden states.

As the encoder outputs a representation of the input sequence, the decoder's objective is to leverage the hidden states to generate the target words. We note that summarization requires text generation to generate the next token in an autoregressive fashion. As such, the generation procedure's objective is to predict the next token given the previous tokens. This can be achieved using the chain rule to factorize the conditional probabilities as

$$P(x^{(t+1)}|x^{(t)}, ..., x^{(1)}) = \prod_{t=1}^{T} P(x^{(t+1)}|x^{(t)}, ..., x^{(1)}) \tag{2}$$

A numerical instability results from the product of the multiple probabilities as they become smaller. Thus, it is common to use the log of the conditional probability to obtain a sum, as

$$\log(P(x^{(t+1)}|x^{(t)}, ..., x^{(1)})) = \sum_{t=1}^{T} \log(P(x^{(t+1)}|x^{(t)}, ..., x^{(1)})) \tag{3}$$

From this objective, there are various methods to select the next token through decoding with two aspects to consider. (1) The decoding method is done iteratively, where the next token is chosen based on the sequence at each time step. (2) It is important to emphasize certain characteristics of the selected word; e.g., in summarization we care about the quality of the decoded sequence, compared to storytelling or open domain conversation where care more about the diversity when generating the next token.

Decoding. In this work, the beam search is used as decoder, since summarization emphasizes factual or real information in the text. This method is parameterized by the number of beams, which defines the number of the most probable next tokens to be considered in the generated sequence and keep track of the associated sequences by extending a partial hypothesis to include the next set of probable tokens to be appended to the sequence until it reaches the end of sequence. The sequences are then ranked based on their log probabilities, and the sequence with the highest probability is chosen. It is important to ensure that at each time step, the decoder is conditioned on the current token and the past output only. This step is crucial to assure the model does not cheat by accessing future tokens. While the transformer architecture is task-independent, the classification head is task-specific, and we use a linear layer that produces a logit followed by a softmax layer to produce a probability distribution for decoding.

Operational Considerations. Transformers are typically deployed in one of two setting. (1) As a feature extractor, where we compute the hidden states for each word embedding, the model parameters are frozen, and we only train the classification head on our task. Training using this method is fast and suitable in the absence of resources to fine tune the whole model. (2) As a fine-tuning setting, where all the model trainable parameters are fine-tuned for our task. This setting requires time and computational resources depending on the model size. In our case we use BART and T5 for fine-tuning and since BART has a smaller number of parameters, its fine-tuning is faster.

5   Evaluations

Statistical Analysis. After assembling the three datasets, we picked the dataset produced by both encoders, given that it is the largest, for statistical analysis (the results with other datasets are omitted for the lack of space). The goal of this analysis is to obtain a better insight over the dataset language characteristics. From this analysis, we found the number of tokens of most augmented descriptions falls below 1000 tokens, in contrast to the original summary which is below 200 tokens for the majority of vulnerabilities. Therefore, we set the threshold for the augmented description and the summary to be 1000 and 250 tokens, respectively, in our pipeline.

We collect the word, character, and sentence count of the augmented and original summary and found a significant difference between them (e.g., (mean, standard deviation) for word, character, and sentence in both cases are: (48, 2086) vs (49, 31), (2939, 12370) vs (279, 186), and (43, 184) vs (7, 5.32). This highlights the need for a summarization to normalize the augmented description.

Next, we perform named entity recognition to understand which entities were presented across the summary because this is our target in the dataset. We found the following frequent named entities: (XSS, 799), (N/AC 523), (IBM X-Force ID, 463), (N/S, 343), (Cisco, 336), (SQL, 334), (Server, 315), (JavaScript, 267), (WordPress, 264), (Jenkins, 240), (IBM, 237), (Firefox, 200), (Java, 187), (VirtualBox, 174), (PHP, 164), (Java SE, 150), and (Android, 148). The common names include organizations, e.g., Cisco and IBM, technologies, e.g., JavaScript, and PHP, or vulnerabilities, e.g., XSS.

We further analyze the most frequent trigram across the dataset. We found that the description trigrams are meaningful, and form the basis for a good summary, in contrast to the augmented text trigrams that, in general, do not present useful information and appear to be uninformative. This might be a result of augmenting repeated content, which highlights certain trigrams based on the frequency. Those initial results highlight the need for an additional summarization step.

Experimental Settings. We fine-tune both models using two different settings. First, We split the dataset with %10 reserved for testing. Then, we split the training set with %10 reserved for validation. Second, based on our preliminary analysis, we set 1000 and 250 tokens as the maximum lengths for augmented descriptions and new summary.

Finally, We set the batch size to 8 and the learning rate to 0.0001 based on various parameters (results omitted for the lack of space). We use beam search as our decoding method, with a beam size of 2. We also fix several parameters: length penalty to 8 (which encourages the model to produce longer summary if it is set to a value higher than 1), and the repetition penalty to 2 (which instructs the model whether to use words that have already been generated or not). Those values are chosen among various values

Table 2. Results after fine-tuning the models using different hyperparameters (**Recall, Precision,** b = number of beams, T = text maximum limit, B = batch size)

Model	R	P	F1	T	b	B
BART	0.51	0.50	0.49	1000	2	8
	0.51	0.46	0.47	1000	5	8
	0.52	**0.52**	**0.51**	500	2	8
	0.53	0.50	0.50	500	5	8
	0.50	0.51	0.49	500	2	4
	0.51	0.49	0.49	500	5	4
T5	0.46	0.50	0.47	500	2	8
	0.47	0.49	0.47	500	5	8
	0.47	**0.52**	**0.48**	500	2	4
	0.47	0.50	0.47	500	5	4

for their best performance, as demonstrated in Table 2. As we stated earlier, we did extensive experimentation on the mixed dataset that uses both encoders and based on its result we experimented with other datasets.

Computational Metrics and Results. ROUGE measures the matching n-gram between the prediction and the target. For our evaluation, we use ROUGE-1, which measures the overlapping unigram, and gives an approximation of the overlap based on individual words. For ROGUE, we use three sub-metrics: recall, precision, and F1 score. The recall measures the number of matching n-gram between our generated summary and the target summary, normalized by the number of words in the target summary. In contrast, the precision normalizes that quantity by the number of words in the generated summary. Finally, F1 score is expressed as:

$$F1-Score = 2 \times \frac{precision \times recall}{precision + recall} \qquad (4)$$

Table 2 shows the ROUGE scores after fine-tuning BART and T5. Multiple experiments have been conducted using different batch sizes, text limit, and number of beams. As we can see in Table 2, when the text limit has shrunk to 500 tokens for the augmented text, all metrics have improved. We also can see that most metrics achieved better score with a smaller number of beams. This is explained by the beam search decoding, as we increase the number of sequences by having a high number of beams, the risk introduced by considering the wrong sequence increases.

Table 3. Models training T_ℓ and validation loss V_ℓ over different batch sizes (B)

Model	T_ℓ	V_ℓ	B
BART	0.42	0.46	8
	0.32	0.46	4
T5	1.96	1.48	8
	2.35	1.46	4

We tested BART with a batch size of 4 and with 500 tokens as the augmented description limit and it outperformed the model trained with 1000 as text limit. It is important to notice that as the number of beams increases, the time it takes the model to generate the summary increases. Considering our initial results from BART and the resources demand for T5 as it is much larger, we decided to train it on text limited to 500 tokens. However, the results did not align with BART. For example, we found that batch size of 4 did better than 8 across all three metrics for T5. Moreover, we see that increasing the number of beams did not help. We point out, however, that the validation loss varies between the two models as shown in the Table 3. This shows that BART did better than T5 during training, which is why BART achieved better scores.

Summary Comparison. We compare the target summary with the model generated summary using the same sentence encoders. We encode both summaries (original and new) using both encoders and measure the similarity between the target and the prediction. We found that most predictions are very close to the target with the mean of the distribution around a similarity of 0.75 (the figures are omitted for the lack of space).

We report the computational metrics in Table 4. Although the mixed dataset had more instances, the models trained on the separate datasets outperformed it. This could be attributed to the restriction we relaxed for the USE encoder, which allows the pipeline to include more paragraphs. Moreover, since the two encoders use different architectures, using them together may have a negative effect on the curated dataset. More experimentation might be needed to find the perfect threshold to use them both.

The models trained using USE dataset outperformed the MPNet dataset. While the USE dataset is larger, we believe the results are better due to USE's accuracy in encoding text semantic. It also prove that USE produces a reliable representation for long text. We reiterate here that we used the DAN architecture for USE which is less accurate than the transformer architecture as we explained in Sect. 4.1. Therefore, using the transformer architecture to build the dataset could generate a more accurate dataset that is likely to outperform the result in Table 4.

Table 4. Results after fine-tuning the models using different single encoder (**P**recision, **R**ecall, b = beams, B = batch)

Model	Encoder	R	P	F1	b	B
BART	USE	0.61	0.60	0.59	2	8
	MPNet	0.55	0.57	0.55	2	8
T5	USE	0.58	0.62	0.59	2	4
	MPNet	0.53	0.59	0.54	2	4

Human Metrics Results. We consider four human metrics: fluency, correctness, completeness, and understanding. All human metrics are graded on a scale between 1–3 in which 3 is the best grade and 1 is the worse in terms of the metric definition.

Fluency measures the grammatical structure of the prediction and how coherent the semantics of the generated summary. The *correctness* measures how accurate the model prediction is in terms of capturing the correct vulnerability details. The *completeness* measures how complete is the generated summary with respect to details in the original summary. The *understanding* measures how easy it is to understand the generated summary. The human evaluation on the generated summary from both models is done over 100 randomly selected samples where the average is reported in Table 5.

After analyzing both models we observed similar behaviors. We found that both models produce a fluent summary with very few exceptions. Similarly, the generated summaries are mostly easy to follow and understand. However, in some cases when the generated summaries are short, they do not convey much meaning and it becomes hard to understand the summaries. In contrast, complete-

Table 5. Human evaluation: Fluency, Completeness, Correctness, and Understanding

Model	F	Cm	Cr	U
BART	2.69	2.15	2.16	2.58
T5	2.72	2.07	2.04	2.57

ness and correctness suffered with both models. We did not anticipate the models to perform well across those metrics because the dataset was not curated for detecting such features. Moreover, the dataset is imbalanced with respect to its features in terms of augmented text length which we believe is the main reason for both models in missing those two metrics. However, when the augmented text is of certain length, those two metrics achieve good results. The human evaluation metrics are averaged and shown in Table 5. We can see that both models are comparable in terms of human metrics when their generated summary is compared against the corresponding target.

Qualitative Results. Both models experienced unpredictable behaviors by repeating some sentences multiple times, or by adding unrelated software to the prediction. Both models also tend to be extractive when the augmented text is of a certain length. For instance, if the text is short (20 words), both models will tend to make up summrization that was learned during training by including vulnerability description such as gain access or code execution, even when none of these were mentioned in augmented text. On the other hand, when the augmented description is too long, the prediction becomes repetitive and hard to understand, although it still covers different portions of the target summary. One possible solution is to ensure a diversity among the augmented sentences and that no sentence is repeated. However, this could be expensive, as it requires checking every new candidate paragraph against all already augmented paragraphs.

6   Conclusion

We leverage publicly available resources to enhance and enrich vulnerabilities description through data augmentation. Our method relies on public databases for collection of text data and pass them through multiple filters to extract relevant text that could contribute to our dataset. We fine-tune two pretrained models that excel in summrization tasks using our curated dataset and report initial and promising result using computational and human metrics. Data curation is a future direction for improving accuracy.

Acknowledgement. This work was supported in part by NRF under grant number 2016K1A1A2912757 and by CyberFlorida's Seed Grant.

References

1. Alabduljabbar, A., Abusnaina, A., Meteriz-Yildiran, Ü., Mohaisen, D.: Automated privacy policy annotation with information highlighting made practical using deep representations. In: Proceedings of the 2021 ACM SIGSAC Conference on Computer and Communications Security, pp. 2378–2380 (2021)

2. Alabduljabbar, A., Mohaisen, D.: Measuring the privacy dimension of free content websites through automated privacy policy analysis and annotation. In: Companion Proceedings of the Web Conference (2022)

3. Anwar, A., Abusnaina, A., Chen, S., Li, F., Mohaisen, D.: Cleaning the NVD: comprehensive quality assessment, improvements, and analyses. CoRR abs/2006.15074 (2020). https://arxiv.org/abs/2006.15074

4. Anwar, A., et al.: Measuring the cost of software vulnerabilities. EAI Endorsed Trans. Secur. Saf. **7**(23), e1–e1 (2020)

5. Anwar, A., Khormali, A., Nyang, D.H., Mohaisen, A.: Understanding the hidden cost of software vulnerabilities: measurements and predictions. In: Beyah, R., Chang, B., Li, Y., Zhu, S. (eds.) SecureComm 2018. LNICST, vol. 254, pp. 377–395. Springer, Cham (2018). https://doi.org/10.1007/978-3-030-01701-9_21

6. Cer, D., et al.: Universal sentence encoder. arXiv preprint arXiv:1803.11175 (2018)

7. Devlin, J., Chang, M.W., Lee, K., Toutanova, K.: BERT: pre-training of deep bidirectional transformers for language understanding. In: 2019 Conference of the North American Chapter of the Association for Computational Linguistics (2018)

8. Dong, Y., Guo, W., Chen, Y., Xing, X., Zhang, Y., Wang, G.: Towards the detection of inconsistencies in public security vulnerability reports. In: 28th USENIX Security Symposium, pp. 869–885 (2019)

9. Help Net Security: Still relying solely on CVE and NVD for vulnerability tracking? Bad idea (2018). https://www.helpnetsecurity.com/2018/02/16/cve-nvd-vulnerability-tracking/

10. Information Security Buzz: Why critical vulnerabilities do not get reported in the CVE/NVD databases and how organisations can mitigate the risks (2018). https://informationsecuritybuzz.com/articles/why-critical-vulnerabilities/

11. Kanakogi, K., et al.: Tracing CAPEC attack patterns from CVE vulnerability information using natural language processing technique. In: 54th Hawaii International Conference on System Sciences (2021)

12. Kanakogi, K., et al.: Tracing CVE vulnerability information to CAPEC attack patterns using natural language processing techniques. Information **12**(8), 298 (2021)

13. Kudo, T.: Subword regularization: improving neural network translation models with multiple subword candidates. arXiv preprint arXiv:1804.10959 (2018)

14. Kudo, T., Richardson, J.: Sentencepiece: a simple and language independent subword tokenizer and detokenizer for neural text processing. arXiv preprint arXiv:1808.06226 (2018)

15. Lewis, M., et al.: BART: denoising sequence-to-sequence pre-training for natural language generation, translation, and comprehension. arXiv preprint arXiv:1910.13461 (2019)

16. Mohaisen, A., Alrawi, O., Mohaisen, M.: AMAL: high-fidelity, behavior-based automated malware analysis and classification. Comput. Secur. **52**, 251–266 (2015)

17. Radford, A., Narasimhan, K., Salimans, T., Sutskever, I.: Improving language understanding by generative pre-training. OpenAI (2018)

18. Raffel, C., et al.: Exploring the limits of transfer learning with a unified text-to-text transformer. arXiv preprint arXiv:1910.10683 (2019)

19. Sennrich, R., Haddow, B., Birch, A.: Neural machine translation of rare words with subword units. In: 54th Annual Meeting of the Association for Computational Linguistics (2015)

20. Song, K., Tan, X., Qin, T., Lu, J., Liu, T.Y.: MPNet: masked and permuted pre-training for language understanding. In: Advances in Neural Information Processing Systems, vol. 33, pp. 16857–16867 (2020)

21. Vaswani, A., et al.: Attention is all you need. In: Advances in Neural Information Processing Systems, vol. 30 (2017)

22. Wåreus, E., Hell, M.: Automated CPE labeling of CVE summaries with machine learning. In: Maurice, C., Bilge, L., Stringhini, G., Neves, N. (eds.) DIMVA 2020. LNCS, vol. 12223, pp. 3–22. Springer, Cham (2020). https://doi.org/10.1007/978-3-030-52683-2_1

23. Yang, Z., Dai, Z., Yang, Y., Carbonell, J., Salakhutdinov, R., Le, Q.V.: XLNet generalized autoregressive pretraining for language understanding (2019). https://arxiv.org/abs/1906.08237. Accessed June 21
24. Zhang, J., Zhao, Y., Saleh, M., Liu, P.: Pegasus: pre-training with extracted gap-sentences for abstractive summarization. In: International Conference on Machine Learning, pp. 11328–11339. PMLR (2020)

Hardware and Software Security

Protecting Kernel Code Integrity with PMP on RISC-V

Seon Ha and Hyungon Moon(✉)

UNIST (Ulsan National Institute of Science and Technology), Ulsan, South Korea
{seonha,hyungon}@unist.ac.kr

Abstract. Kernel code integrity is the foundation of the security of the entire system. Attackers are motivated to compromise the kernel code integrity because it gives them the highest possible privilege on the system, allowing them to take the full control of it. They can perform the attack by either modifying the kernel code directly or tricking the kernel to execute from data pages. Existing kernels and processors are working together to defeat this threat, but their reliance on the page table leaves the attackers leeway to bypass the protection. Existing solutions aiming to tackle this limitation, the reliance on the page table integrity, are either too expensive or require custom hardware. In this paper, we present a software-only design of a kernel code integrity protection mechanism for RISC-V-based systems that implement the Physical Memory Protection (PMP). We show that, despite the lack of direct support for kernel code protection, the kernel and the machine mode firmware can work together to leverage the PMP to defeat the advanced kernel code integrity-compromising attacks by dynamically switching the memory protection policies on user-kernel switches. The performance estimation using our prototype shows that the proposed mechanisms incur moderate ($<24\%$) overhead on system call latencies. The security evaluation using synthetic advanced attacks also demonstrates that the proposed mechanism can effectively prevent the page table-corrupting kernel code injection attacks.

Keywords: Operating System Kernel · Code Integrity · RISC-V

This work was supported by the National Research Foundation of Korea(NRF) grant funded by the Korea government(MSIT) (No. NRF-2022R1F1A1076100) and this work was supported by Institute of Information & communications Technology Planning & Evaluation (IITP) grant funded by the Korea government(MSIT) (No. 2021-0-00724, RISC-V based Secure CPU Architecture Design for Embedded System Malware Detection and Response) and this research was supported by the MSIT(Ministry of Science and ICT), Korea, under the ITRC(Information Technology Research Center) support program(IITP-2023-2021-0-01817) supervised by the IITP(Institute for Information & Communications Technology Planning & Evaluation) and this work was supported by Samsung Electronics Co., Ltd.

H. Kim and J. Youn (Eds.): WISA 2023, LNCS 14402, pp. 231–243, 2024.
https://doi.org/10.1007/978-981-99-8024-6_18

1 Introduction

Operating system kernels, being the most privileged software components in a computer system, are responsible for managing resources and enforcing security protocols. Unfortunately, their inherent complexity makes them vulnerable to malicious manipulation, potentially enabling attackers to breach the system's integrity. At the center of the kernel is its code that specifies how it behaves under varying situations. This makes the integrity of kernel code a key pillar of an operating system's security. Attackers can manipulate the kernel code in multiple ways including the direct modification and data page execution, effectively causing the kernel to execute attacker-written code with the kernel's privilege.

Existing solutions for protecting kernel code integrity either rely on the page table integrity [4,5] or custom hardware [6,7,11]. The importance of the kernel code integrity led to the development and deployment of the dedicated page table attributes as we explain in Sect. 2. Modern kernels are proactively using them to ensure that the kernel will execute only the kernel code while in the privileged mode. Unfortunately, this is only a mitigation not a prevention mechanism in that the protection relies fully on the integrity of the page table. When assuming the attackers exploiting the kernel vulnerabilities, the page tables are not out the range of their corruption. The page tables must remain writable, and the attackers can use such writable mappings to first create counterfeit page table entries and then use them to modify the kernel code or execute data pages. Existing software-based mechanisms aimed to address this problem by mediating all page table updates using a trusted software component, but the approach often comes with substantial performance overheads. This motivated the development of mechanisms using dedicated hardware [6,7,11]. Hardware-based approaches are effective in detecting and preventing kernel code integrity-compromising attacks and efficient in that they do not degrade the software performance significantly. However, the reliance on custom hardware makes them hard to adopt and could accompany hidden cost in energy, power or area.

This paper presents a mechanism in the middle ground between the software-based and hardware-based approaches. The mechanism that we propose in this paper protects the kernel code integrity without relying on the page table. Instead, it uses the Physical Memory Protection (PMP) feature of the RISC-V processor that enables it to specify and enforce access control policies at the physical address level.

The PMP by itself is incapable of protecting the kernel code integrity because it does not have the notion of the kernel code and does not take the current privilege mode into account when enforcing the access control policies. To overcome this challenge, we prepare two concise yet effective sets of access control policies to be used by during in the kernel and user modes, respectively. We find that the sophisticated design of the PMP enables us to specify these two policies without using too many of their configuration registers, which are precious hardware resources, and the kernel can be efficiently hooked to trigger the switches between the two policies, by invoking the machine mode firmware.

The evaluation using our prototype suggests that the proposed mechanism incurs moderate performance overhead on system call latencies. We measure the number and the composition of additional instructions that the kernel and machine mode firmware must execute, and use the result to emulate the implementation to estimate the overhead of the proposed mechanism on the system call latencies. The result shows that the proposed mechanism incurs less than 24% overhead on the system call latencies, making it an acceptable approach for systems that do not have the custom hardware. We also demonstrate that our prototype effectively prevents the advanced attacks from manipulating the kernel code using two synthetic attacks. Our prototype successfully prevented these two attacks that the baseline system fails to even recognize due to its reliance on the page table.

2   Background and Motivation

Operating system kernel is a cornerstone of a computer system's security. The kernel is the most privileged software component in a computer system and it is responsible for managing the system's resources and enforcing the system's security policies. An attacker who takes control of the kernel by any means can manipulate the system in any way they want. The inherent complexity of modern commodity operating system kernels makes them have vulnerabilities that can be exploited by attackers to gain such control of the kernel.

2.1   Kernel Code Integrity

Kernel code integrity is one of the fundamental properties that should be guaranteed to ensure the genuineness of an operating system kernel. An attacker can manipulate the kernel in many different ways, and they often want the manipulation to be persistent, for example, by hooking a system call with an attacker-defined routine. Although it is known that an attacker can craft an in-kernel hook by stitching gadgets [15], it is often desirable to directly manipulate the kernel code to achieve the same goal due to the inherent complexity of the gadget stitching technique. For example, jailbreaks for iOS devices often rely on the manipulation of the kernel code to achieve the goal of escaping the sandbox [12,14,17].

Kernel code injection refers to the manipulation of the kernel code by injecting attacker-defined code into the kernel. Specifically, an attacker can inject a piece of code into the kernel by either directly modifying the kernel code pages or by tricking the kernel to execute the attacker's code from outside the kernel code pages. The latter can be done by corrupting the code pointers in the kernel such as the return address or system call table entries.

2.2   Limitation of Existing Solutions

The importance of kernel code integrity has been recognized for a long time, leading the development and adoption of page table attributes to protect kernel memory such as Privileged eXecute Never (PXN) [9], Supervisor Mode Execution Protection (SMEP) [8]. These attributes enable the operating system kernel to fight against kernel code injection attacks together with the other attributes. Using these, a kernel can set the kernel code pages to be non-writable and privileged-executable, and set the others privileged-non-executable. This can be done, for example, by setting the PXN attribute for all pages except the kernel code pages.

The weakness of this approach is in its reliance on the page tables. The attributes are associated with each virtual page and they are stored in the main memory, which an attacker could corrupt by exploiting kernel vulnerabilities. Write-protecting the pages containing the attributes, or the page table entries, is not an option because the kernel has to repeatedly create and manipulate them during its execution. Note that complete kernel code injection prevention requires the intervention of all page table entries because all page table entries that do not map the kernel code region must be marked as privileged-non-executable. As we show in the evaluation (Sect. 5.2), an attacker can craft a writable mapping to a kernel code page to bypass the write protection and make a data page executable similarly.

Existing solutions that help defeat such advanced attackers manipulating page tables can be classified into two categories. First are the software-based approaches [4,13] that often protect page table entries to ensure the kernel code integrity. They devise a more privileged software layer, similar to the machine mode firmware in our approach, to mediate every single page table update to ensure that no counterfeit page table entries are actually used by the processor to translate virtual addresses and examine the memory accesses. The drawback of these approaches is often in their performance overhead, as we present in Sect. 5. The second is hardware-based approaches [6,7,11] that devise new hardware features tailored for kernel code integrity protection. They all are designed with different assumptions and goals, resulting in differences in design. What they share in common is that they often incur negligible or no performance overhead (i.e., system call latency) because they implement selective permission enforcement at the hardware level. We note that the former, software-based approaches protecting the entire page table, suffers from substantial performance overhead of mediating all page table updates, while the latter requires custom hardware which could come with hidden costs in energy or power as well. This motivated us to devise a novel software-only mechanism tailored for RISC-V systems where we can utilize existing hardware feature that enforces access control at the physical address level.

2.3 RISC-V Physical Memory Protection

RISC-V Physical Memory Protection (PMP) [16] is a hardware feature that is designed to protect the machine mode firmware's memory from the other software components. It specifies a set of configuration register pairs, where each pair specifies a memory region and the access permissions of the region. Its sophisticated design allows to specify nearly arbitrarily sized address ranges, as long as they are size-aligned. One unique characteristic of PMP is that it defines a strict priority between these pairs, i.e., address ranges so that only one pair is matched for each memory access. This is not only implementation-friendly but also allows us to associate permission to non-aligned or even non-contiguous address ranges, as we do in designing the proposed mechanism (Sect. 4.1).

3 Threat Model

We consider attackers who are aiming to take control of an operation system kernel in a victim system by exploiting kernel vulnerabilities. To that end, the attacker may or may not have the power to execute an arbitrary user-level code, and if they can, they can run such code only as a part of a non-root user-level process. The attackers are not assumed to have the capability to implant an arbitrary kernel module. The only way for the attackers to run a piece of their code with the kernel's privilege is to exploit a kernel vulnerability to either compose a gadget chain, modify the kernel code, or trick the kernel to execute from data pages. We assume that the attackers are in fact motivated to arrive at the last stage, the kernel code injection, due to the difficulty in persisting their control only using the gadget chain, as evidenced in the known attacks.

4 Design and Implementation

Overview. The proposed mechanism is composed of two components as Fig. 1 shows. One is two in-kernel hooks that are invoked on every deliberate kernel entry and exit, and the other is the permission switch services residing in the machine mode firmware that switches the PMP entries between the policy for the user mode and the policy for the kernel model.

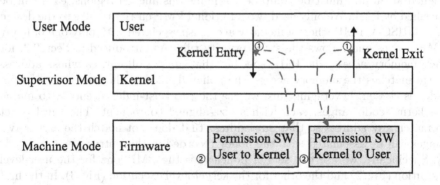

Fig. 1. Overview of the proposed mechanism

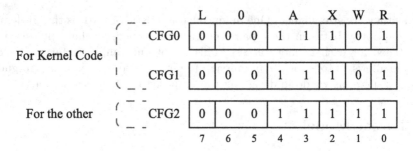

Fig. 2. The permissions for PMP entries while in user mode.

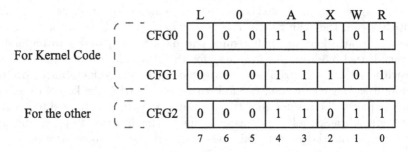

Fig. 3. The permissions for PMP entries while in kernel mode.

4.1 PMP Policies for Locking Kernel Code

Our mechanisms use two additional PMP entries for kernel code page protection. The number of additional PMP entries depends on the number of size-aligned memory regions composing the kernel code page, and it is 2 in our prototype. Despite the fact that the remaining pages other than the kernel code are not aligned at all and must be composed of numerous aligned regions, each can be specified by PMP. We only need two additional PMP entries thanks to the design of the RISC-V PMP where a memory access is associated with only one of many PMP entries and follows the strict priority rule. As introduced in Sect. 2.3, for each memory access, the PMP specifies that among all entries whose address range matches the memory access, the policy defined in the one with the least index is chosen. Leveraging this, we use the two least-indexed entries to match the kernel code ranges, each with a size-aligned component. The third is set to match any address so that any address that does not match the earlier two ranges will be associated with the policy recorded in this entry.

Specifically, we use two sets of policies for the PMP, one for the user-level execution (Fig. 2) and the other for the kernel-level execution (Fig. 3). In the first set, we enable the processor to execute from any physical memory because the data execution prevention for user-level process is the job of the operating system kernel, which can effectively use the page table attributes. The only additional assurance that we provide using PMP is the write protection of the kernel code regions, which is done by clearing the W bit in the first two PMP entries that are applied to any memory access to the kernel code regions. In the second set, we use the same permission attributes for the first two entries where R and X are set. The difference from the first set is in the third entry, where we set R and W but clear X to prevent any execution from the memory regions that are not kernel code regions.

4.2 Hooking Kernel Entries and Exits

The next step for ensuring the kernel code integrity is to switch between the two policies when and only when needed. This requires us to hook all possible kernel entries and exits. Fortunately, modern processors provide a limited entry point of each privileged mode execution for various reasons, often as the form of an exception vector table or exception handler. RISC-V is no exception, and the Linux kernel for RISC-V contains dedicated assembly routines handling low-level context switches for the kernel entry and exit. Moreover, the kernel is already distinguishing which mode the processor was executing in before the exception was raised because it affects how the exception should be handled, and we can take advantage of this to determine whether a particular kernel entry is from the user level or not. Similarly, returning to the user mode also requires the execution of a particular instruction, with a special register set appropriately. We locate this kernel exit point and add our hook to invoke the firmware's permission switch service. In detail, we let the hook deliver the kernel code range information to the permission switch service upon its first invocation so that the service can determine the address range for each PMP entry. Note that we can further harden this procedure to deliver the kernel range during the boot time without significant effort.

Called from these hooks are the permission switch services residing in the machine mode firmware. The kernel for RISC-V already implements a standard routine for invoking the firmware services, so we utilize it to invoke the two new services, each switching from and to the kernel-mode PMP policy. The behavior of the services is straightforward. The service for kernel entry changes the PMP policy to the kernel-mode policy, and the service for kernel exit changes the PMP policy to the user-mode policy. Note that in the current prototype, the machine mode firmware's memory spaces are not strictly protected from the kernel- or user-mode code. This is the limitation of our baseline firmware and can be easily fixed by adding the PMP entries for the firmware memory spaces and the corresponding permission switch services.

5 Evaluation

We evaluate the performance impact and the effectiveness of the proposed mechanism by measuring the system call latencies (Sect. 5.1) and deploying synthetic attacks (Sect. 5.2).

5.1   Performance Overhead

Prototype Implementation. We implement the proposed mechanism by extending the Linux kernel 5.16.0, and the Berkeley Boot Loader (BBL) [1] for RISC-V. We add invocations to the permission switching services in the kernel entries and exits, and implement the services as Supervisor Binary Interface (SBI) calls within the BBL, which also serves as the machine mode firmware.

Experimental Setup. We measure the impact of the proposed mechanism in two steps. First, we obtain the number and the composition of additional instructions that the system (i.e., the kernel and the machine mode firmware) must execute using the default standard instruction set architecture (ISA) simulator, Spike [2]. However, we do not measure the performance impact of the proposed mechanism using Spike because it is a functional simulator. Instead, as the second step, we measure the performance impact using an x86 machine with an Intel Core i7-8086K CPU and 64GB of RAM, running Ubuntu 18.04.3 LTS with Linux kernel 5.5.7. To emulate the performance impact of the proposed mechanism, we add dummy instructions that are similar to the additional instructions for our mechanism in terms of the number of instructions and the composition of the instructions. In particular, the implementation of the proposed mechanism requires the system to execute a substantial number of memory access instructions, which is expected to affect the performance significantly. To correctly emulate this, we ensure that the dummy instructions also include a substantial number of memory access and instructions that are not optimized.

Table 1. The additional instructions that the system must execute to implement the proposed mechanism.

Action	Total	Load	Store	Mode Switch	Jumps	Others
Enter	178	52	43	2	16	65
Exit	149	42	40	2	11	54

Additional Instructions. Table 1 shows the number of additional instructions that the system must execute additionally to implement the proposed mechanism in both parts of the kernel and the machine mode firmware. They each have two mode switches in common, the entering and the exiting the machine mode. They also incorporate many loads and stores due to the context switches, potentially affecting the performance negatively.

Impact on System Call Latency. Table 2 shows the impact of the proposed mechanism on the system call latency and compares the result with the existing

Table 2. The impact of the proposed mechanism on the system call latency.

Benchmark	Baseline (ms)	Proposed (ms)	PrivLock	Kargos	RiskiM	perspicuOS	SecVisor
Simple syscall	0.26	0.32 (1.23×)	1.02×	1.09×	1.00×	1.10×	256.00×
Simple read	0.37	0.44 (1.19×)	0.99×	N/A	N/A	N/A	N/A
Simple write	0.33	0.40 (1.21×)	1.04×	N/A	N/A	N/A	N/A
Simple stat	0.70	0.78 (1.11×)	1.00×	N/A	1.01×	1.01×	N/A
Simple fstat	0.40	0.46 (1.15×)	1.00×	N/A	N/A	N/A	N/A
Simple open/close	1.53	1.73 (1.13×)	0.95×	0.99×	1.01×	1.01×	N/A
Protection fault	0.54	0.61 (1.13×)	1.29×	1.00×	N/A	N/A	110.00×
fork+exit	91.56	90.65 (0.99×)	0.99×	0.99×	N/A	2.80×	N/A
fork+execve	298.11	299.88 (1.01×)	0.99×	0.99×	1.01×	2.60×	N/A

solutions using the results that they reported. We use the LMBench [10] to measure the system call latencies and compare the result with the hardware- and software-based existing solutions, PrivLock [6], Kargos [11], RiskiM [7], perspicuOS [4], and SecVisor [13]. The experimental result shows that the performance impact of the proposed mechanism is not negligible and clearly higher than the two hardware-based solutions, Kargos and RiskiM. However, the overhead is significantly lower than SecVisor thanks to the help of PMP. When compared to perspicuOS, which ensures the page table integrity using its nested kernel, the proposed mechanism slows down the system calls in general while the overhead of perspicuOS is significantly higher on **fork** operations where the kernel substantially modifies the page tables.

5.2   Security Evaluation

To evaluate the correctness and effectiveness of the proposed mechanism and our prototype, we test the prototype using two synthetic attacks. The baseline system that we use write-protects the kernel code pages and makes data pages non-executable, thwarting the direct kernel code modification and data page execution. Nevertheless, the attacker can bypass this kernel-only defense using page tables by crafting counterfeit page table entries in two ways, which we implement to evaluate the effectiveness of the proposed mechanism.

Attack 1: Executing Data Page. The first synthetic attack aims to execute attacker-written code on the data page. An attacker can craft a memory page containing their payload by exploiting kernel vulnerabilities and directing the kernel to execute it by modifying code pointers. To further bypass the kernel's protection using page tables, the attacker also crafts a counterfeit page table entry that maps the data page with a kernel-executable page. The baseline system failed to detect this attack because the kernel relies fully on the attributes in the page table. When the proposed mechanism is enabled, the attack generates a memory access that violates the PMP's policy because the data page where the attacker stores their code is outside the range of the kernel code pages in the physical address, which the attacker cannot change. This leaves the modification of the kernel code the only remaining option for the attacker who aims to perform the kernel code injection.

Attack 2: Corrupting Kernel Code Page. As mentioned earlier, an attacker can neither modify the kernel code pages using genuine page table entries because all code pages are marked as non-writable. The synthetic attack that we implemented bypasses this protection by crafting a counterfeit page table entry, similar to the first attack. As expected, the baseline system is incapable of detecting this attack because the page table entries, which the kernel fully relies on, are compromised. The attack is stopped by the proposed mechanism. When we launch the attack with our prototype enabled, the attack generates writes to the physical pages containing the kernel code, and the pages are marked non-writable by PMP.

5.3   Limitation in Performance Overhead Estimation

In our evaluation, we estimate the performance overhead of the proposed mechanism primarily due to the difficulty in obtaining RISC-V based systems. The estimation itself is likely to be reasonably accurate because the additional latency on the mode switches, which is accompanied by system calls, is affected only by the number of additional instructions and their memory access delays. We strive to make the estimation accurate by considering both the number and the composition of instructions.

The only source that could affect the estimated performance overhead is the fact that PMP policy changes could require Translation Lookaside Buffer (TLB) flushes on some RISC-V based systems. Unlike the permission checks by the MMU, the PMP policy checks must be done after the address translation, potentially increasing either the memory access latency by one cycle or increasing the critical path delay of the memory interface. For this reason, existing open-source processors such as the Rocket [3] core gives an option to locate this PMP policy check at the TLB refill. When handling TLB misses, the page table walker refers both to the page table entry and the corresponding PMP entry to determine the exact attribute that the page table entry will have while stored in the TLB. Consequently, the processor can perform one permission check during the address translation to effectively enforce the two rules, one from the page table and the other from the PMP. If this is how a baseline system implements the PMP, the proposed mechanism must also flush the entire TLB to ensure that all TLB entries are reflecting the correct, appropriate PMP entry. This adds the cost of the full TLB flush to the kernel entry and exits, potentially incurring a substantial performance overhead.

One possible workaround would be possible if the processor uses two translation tables, one for the kernel and the other for the user, strictly prohibiting the use of the user's page table entries in kernel mode. On a system that uses two translation tables strictly, even without TLB flushes, the processor will use the kernel page table entries which are correctly examined with the PMP entries for the kernel mode, and use the user page table entries during in the user mode.

6   Related Work

In this section, we explore various mechanisms established for safeguarding operating system kernels from potential security threats. The protective measures typically involve the use of a hypervisor, security domain, or specific hardware features.

Hypervisor-Based Defenses. Among similar works, SecVisor [13] shares close proximity with our research objectives as it focuses on preserving kernel code integrity. Unlike approaches that introduce dedicated hypervisors or modify hardware, SecVisor provides a lightweight, software-based solution. It ensures that only authorized code can operate in kernel mode for the entire system's lifecycle. Despite its benefits, it incurs a more substantial overhead compared to our system as shown in Sect. 5.

ARM TrustZone-Based Defenses. ARM processors feature a unique support for isolated execution environment called TrustZone, which facilitates the creation of a trusted platform. TrustZone enables the segregation of software resources such that secure subsystems reside within a *Secure World* and all other components exist in a *Normal World*. An instance of a protective solution leveraging this functionality is SPROBES [5], which utilizes TrustZone to maintain kernel code integrity. In particular, SPROBES mediates page table updates using software components in the Secure World to ensure that all page table attributes are set correctly to prevent any kernel code integrity violation.

Hardware-Based Defenses. Hardware-assisted mechanisms can provide additional fortification for kernel integrity. Both Kargos [11] and RiskiM [7] are analogous to our proposed system in their abilities to detect attacks compromising kernel code integrity. They employ hardware monitoring systems to preempt kernel code injection attacks.

Kargos implements external CPU monitoring to identify malicious behaviors. However, a potential issue with this method is the semantic gap problem, where there may be a delay between the actual attack occurrence and when the monitoring system detects it.

RiskiM, another hardware monitoring system, aims to ensure kernel code integrity. They address the semantic gap problem with a novel solution, the Program Execution Monitoring Interface (PEMI), offering a significant advancement in hardware-based kernel defense mechanisms.

7 Conclusion

In this paper, we presented a design of kernel code integrity protection mechanism for RISC-V based systems using existing hardware support. Despite the limitations, the existing PMP can be leveraged to dynamically switch the memory protection policies at the physical address level to effectively prevent the advanced kernel code injection attacks. The performance estimation using our prototype implementation on the Spike simulator and emulation on an x86-based system suggests that the proposed mechanism can be implemented with a reasonable performance overhead. The security evaluation using two synthetic, advanced attacks proves that the proposed mechanism can effectively prevent the advanced kernel code injection attacks. We believe that the proposed mechanism can be a good starting point for future research on the kernel code integrity protection on RISC-V based systems, both motivating the adoption of dedicated hardware support for kernel code protection and the adoption of software-only mechanisms if the expected overhead is acceptable.

References

1. RISC-V proxy kernel and boot loader (2023). https://github.com/riscv-software-src/riscv-pk
2. Spike RISC-V ISA simulator (2023). https://github.com/riscv-software-src/riscv-isa-sim
3. Asanovic, K., et al.: The rocket chip generator. Technical report. UCB/EECS-2016-17, EECS Department, University of California, Berkeley (2016). http://www2.eecs.berkeley.edu/Pubs/TechRpts/2016/EECS-2016-17.html
4. Dautenhahn, N., Kasampalis, T., Dietz, W., Criswell, J., Adve, V.: Nested kernel: an operating system architecture for intra-kernel privilege separation. In: International Conference on Architectural Support for Programming Languages and Operating Systems, ASPLOS 2015, pp. 191–206. Association for Computing Machinery, New York (2015). https://doi.org/10.1145/2694344.2694386
5. Ge, X., Vijayakumar, H., Jaeger, T.: SPROBES: enforcing kernel code integrity on the trustzone architecture. CoRR abs/1410.7747 (2014). http://arxiv.org/abs/1410.7747
6. Ha, S., Yu, M., Moon, H., Lee, J.: Kernel code integrity protection at the physical address level on RISC-V. IEEE Access (2023). https://doi.org/10.1109/ACCESS.2023.3285876
7. Hwang, D., Yang, M., Jeon, S., Lee, Y., Kwon, D., Paek, Y.: RiskiM: toward complete kernel protection with hardware support. In: 2019 Design, Automation Test in Europe Conference Exhibition (DATE), Germany, pp. 740–745. IEEE (2019). https://doi.org/10.23919/DATE.2019.8715277

8. Intel: Intel(r) supervisor mode execution protection (SMEP). https://www.intel.com/content/www/us/en/developer/articles/technical/intel-sdm.html
9. Lee, J.: ARM: support for the PXN CPU feature on ARMV7 (2014). https://patchwork.kernel.org/project/linux-arm-kernel/patch/1414259997-9350-1-git-send-email-js07.lee@gmail.com/
10. McVoy, L., Staelin, C.: LMbench: portable tools for performance analysis. In: USENIX Annual Technical Conference, ATEC 1996, USA, p. 230. USENIX Association (1996)
11. Moon, H., Lee, J., Hwang, D., Jung, S., Seo, J., Paek, Y.: Architectural supports to protect OS kernels from code-injection attacks and their applications. ACM Trans. Des. Autom. Electron. Syst. **23**(1) (2017). https://doi.org/10.1145/3110223
12. SauriklT, L.: Cydia substrate (2022). http://www.cydiasubstrate.com/
13. Seshadri, A., Luk, M., Qu, N., Perrig, A.: SecVisor: a tiny hypervisor to provide lifetime kernel code integrity for commodity OSes. In: ACM SIGOPS Symposium on Operating Systems Principles, SOSP 2007, pp. 335–350. Association for Computing Machinery, New York (2007). https://doi.org/10.1145/1294261.1294294
14. Siguza: KTRR (2018). https://blog.siguza.net/KTRR/
15. Vogl, S., Pfoh, J., Kittel, T., Eckert, C.: Persistent data-only malware: function hooks without code. In: NDSS, USA, pp. 1–16. Internet Society (2014)
16. Waterman, A., Asanovic, K.: The RISC-V Instruction Set Manual Volume II. The RISC-V Foundation (2017). https://riscv.org/wp-content/uploads/2017/05/riscv-privileged-v1.10.pdf
17. xerub: Tick (FPU) tock (IRQ) (2017). https://xerub.github.io/ios/kpp/2017/04/13/tick-tock.html

Exploiting Memory Page Management in KSM for Remote Memory Deduplication Attack

Seungyeon Bae, Taehun Kim, Woomin Lee, and Youngjoo Shin[✉]

School of Cybersecurity, Korea University, Seoul, South Korea
{bsybsy012,taehunk,redcokeb,syoungjoo}@korea.ac.kr

Abstract. In virtualized environments, modern operating systems take advantage of memory deduplication feature to efficiently manage physical memory. However, the adoption of this technique has given rise to memory deduplication attacks that disclose memory pages used by a victim VM. All these attacks rely on the latency of the memory write operation to distinguish deduplicated pages from other pages. While performing such attacks in a cross-VM attack scenario is relatively straightforward, implementing a remote memory deduplication attack is not trivial due to the limitations in issuing memory write requests to the desired physical page on the remote machine. In this paper, we present a novel memory deduplication attack that exploits the memory page management mechanism in Kernel Samepage Merging (KSM). Modern implementation of KSM enforces the maximum number of shared pages for performance reasons. Therefore, if the number of pages with the same content exceeds the maximum page limit, they can refer to different physical pages despite having the same content. We exploit this property by intentionally mapping the maximum number of pages, causing two physical pages with the same content to exist in the physical memory. Unlike the previous work, our attack measures the latency for the memory unmap operation to figure out the victim VM's memory page. This novel type of attack allows an attacker to infer other applications' memory pages, such as the Nginx web server, without relying on the memory write operation.

Keywords: Memory deduplication · Side-channel attack · Linux KSM

1 Introduction

Virtualization technology which is a fundamental component of cloud services has gained widespread adoption owing to its flexibility and scalability. However, the increasing number of tenants utilizing cloud services has resulted in a substantial increase in the data volume that cloud service providers must handle. As a result, memory pages containing duplicate content have become prevalent in physical memory. To address these challenges, various operating systems have introduced memory deduplication techniques, known as page combining in Windows [1], KSM in Linux [2], and TPS (Transparent Page Sharing) in VMWare's

© The Author(s), under exclusive license to Springer Nature Singapore Pte Ltd. 2024
H. Kim and J. Youn (Eds.): WISA 2023, LNCS 14402, pp. 244–256, 2024.
https://doi.org/10.1007/978-981-99-8024-6_19

ESXi [3]. Memory deduplication is a memory-saving technique that merges identical physical pages into a single read-only page through Copy-on-Write (CoW) mapping. However, this technique poses a risk of revealing memory pages used by other virtual machines due to page faults that occur during write access to the merged pages. As a result, side-channel attacks that exploit memory deduplication techniques have recently emerged. These attacks mainly leverage the timing difference between a deduplicated page and a normal page to infer security-sensitive information from other VMs. These attacks exploit timing differences between write accesses to pages merged by memory deduplication techniques to extract sensitive information from other users.

Previous memory deduplication attacks are primarily performed in cross-VM [4–7] and remote attack scenarios [8]. In a cross-VM attack, the attacker can execute local code to create a physical page that will be shared with the victim VM's page, allowing them to perform write access to the deduplicated page. However, in a remote attack, the attacker has no shared resources with the victim and cannot execute local code. There is only one previous work presenting remote attacks that overcame this limitation by using in-memory databases. However, they require a highly constrained attack model due to the assumption of using in-memory databases.

Therefore, the limitation of current memory deduplication attacks in remote environments is that they can only target applications with memory write operation capabilities, such as in-memory databases. To surpass this limitation, this paper exploits the mechanism of limiting the maximum number of deduplicated pages in KSM. The implementation of this mechanism takes place within KSM by utilizing a stable tree structure. Each node in the stable tree has a maximum number of pages that can be deduplicated. If the deduplication limit is not exceeded, the node remains a single node in the stable tree; if the limit is exceeded, it is split into two nodes. The time taken to unmap a single node is shorter than unmapping two nodes.

In this paper, we exploit the timing difference in memory unmapping between those two cases to perform a memory deduplication attack that does not require write access in a cross-VM environment and a remote environment. Specifically, in the remote attack, the sockets used by the Nginx web server to respond to client requests can be exploited to learn the victim's secret information. Unlike previous research, the attack technique proposed in this paper is not limited to specific applications that require write access and can be utilized for a general purpose in remote environments.

The main contributions of our work are as follows:

- We propose a new memory deduplication attack by exploiting the memory page management mechanism in KSM.
- We present a novel type of remote memory deduplication attack without relying on write operation.
- We propose a tool to track merged pages through KSM and to verify the content of merged pages.

The remainder of this paper is structured as follows. In Sect. 2, we provide an introduction to the Linux KSM and a description of memory deduplication attacks that exploit this technique, and present a comparison and analysis of memory deduplication attacks proposed in previous research. In Sect. 3, we describe the building blocks required for the novel memory deduplication attack proposed in this thesis. We then propose a scenario where the proposed attack is performed in a remote environment. Finally, we conclude in Sect. 4.

2 Background

In this section, we provide background on the Linux KSM and a description of memory deduplication attacks that exploit this technique to perform side-channel attacks.

2.1 Memory Deduplication Attack

The memory deduplication attack is a technique that takes advantage of the timing difference in memory write access between deduplicated pages and non-deduplicated pages to extract the memory information of the victim. Unlike non-deduplicated pages, the pages merged through deduplication have a read-only status due to the CoW mechanism, which leads to page faults when attempting to write to them. These page faults introduce latency in the operating system's handling process. An attacker can exploit this latency to carry out an attack.

The memory deduplication attack is performed in three stages as follows:

Step 1. The attacker performs the memory mapping to binary files that are expected to be in the victim's memory.
Step 2. The attacker tries to write to the mapped page.
Step 3. The attacker can determine whether the mapped page has been merged with a page existing in the victim's memory by measuring the delay after writing access to the mapped page.

Previous research on memory deduplication attacks utilizes the CoW mechanism. They cause page faults by attempting to write accesses to pages merged into a single physical read-only page via CoW mapping. To handle these page faults, the operating system copies the merged page, allocates a new physical page, and grants write access. Because of this page fault handling described above, there is a latency incurred in the write access time for merged pages compared to the write access time for random pages. The previous studies utilizing the timing differences in memory write access are as follows. An attacker in a cross-VM environment sharing the same host can perform a memory deduplication attack against a victim's VM by executing local code within his VM [4–6]. Proposed a memory deduplication attack using Java Script executed through a browser in a remote environment that does not share the same host [7]. For the first time in a remote environment that does not share the same host, we

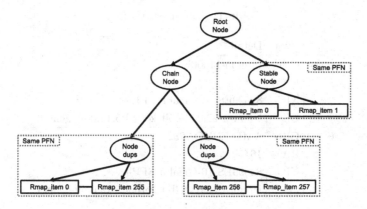

Fig. 1. KSM stable-tree node component that exceeded the maximum deduplication page count limit, resulting in a chain node

proposed a memory deduplication attack through remote write requests on an in-memory DB without local code execution [8].

Previous attacks are limited in that they require the attacker to pinpoint the merged page among the victim's pages and attempt to write to it. This requires the attacker to execute local code or use an application such as a shared resource or in-memory DB to perform write access. To overcome these limitations, this paper proposes a novel memory deduplication attack that performs memory unmapping on deduplicated pages.

2.2 Analyzing the KSM Behavior

Overview of KSM Behavior. KSM is a Linux kernel module that periodically scans anonymous page regions and merges pages with duplicate content into a single physical page. To manage these deduplicated pages, KSM uses two red-black trees. The first of the two trees is the stable tree, which manages the pages merged into a single page by KSM. The stable tree adds one stable node for each deduplicated page it encounters, and these nodes collectively form the stable tree.

When KSM scans pages in an anonymous memory region, it first compares them to the stable tree's internal merged-pages node to see if they are the same, and the comparison process is as follows. First, KSM compares the contents of the physical pages using the memcmp() function to see if they are identical. If the pages are identical, they are merged into a single physical page. If not, a checksum is calculated to determine if it is a new page. If it is a new page, the checksum is updated, and if it is a candidate page that already exists, it is compared to a node in the second tree.

The second tree is the unstable tree, which manages unmerged candidate pages. As KSM scans the pages in the anonymous memory region, it records a 32-bit checksum for each page, checks if it has changed, and excludes pages with

Table 1. Experiment setup

	Type	Detail
server	CPU	Intel i5-11600K
	RAM	16 GB
	NIC	82599ES 10-Gigabit SFP+
	OS	Ubuntu 22.04 64bit kernel 5.15.0-58-generic
client	CPU	AMD EPYC 7282
	RAM	16 GB
	NIC	82599ES 10-Gigabit SFP+
	OS	Ubuntu 20.04 64bit kernel 5.15.0-69-generic

changed checksums from the candidate pages. In this paper, we focus on a stable tree that manages deduplicated pages.

Maximum Page Limit in KSM. The mechanism of limiting the maximum number of deduplicated pages in KSM was introduced to solve the problem of unresponsive virtual machines when many pages were merged into one physical page by KSM. To address this issue, Linux has limited the number of pages that KSM can deduplicate, starting with Linux kernel version 4.4.0-96.119, under the name max_page_sharing [9]. The default setting for max_page_sharing = 256, meaning a maximum of 256 virtual pages can be mapped to a single physical page. If the maximum number of deduplication pages is exceeded, deduplication is performed by mapping virtual pages to new physical pages.

Figure 1 shows the KSM stable tree node component where a chain node is created when more than 256 pages are mapped to a stable node. A chain node is a linked list that manages node dups created by exceeding the maximum number of deduplicated pages. In this Fig. 1 the stable node does not exceed the deduplication page count limit because it has two pages mapped to one physical page. Therefore, the physical pages on the stable node have the same Page Frame Number (PFN). However, because the chain node has 258 pages mapped to it, which exceeds the threshold for deduplication pages, the node dups attached to the chain node have different PFN

3 Remote Memory Deduplication Attack with KSM's Memory Page Management Mechanism

3.1 Building Blocks of the Attack

In this section, we want to generalize and discuss the necessary building blocks to exploit KSM's memory page management for a memory deduplication attack. The attacker targets to exploit KSM's memory page management to disclose secret values stored in memory pages. KSM implements a mechanism to suggest

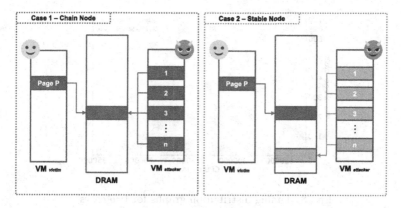

Fig. 2. Comparison of memory layouts based on the content mapped by the $VM_{attacker}$

a maximum number of deduplicated pages to manage merged pages efficiently. The implementation of this mechanism takes place within KSM by utilizing a stable tree structure. Each node in a stable tree can contain up to n duplicate pages, depending on the `max_page_sharing = n` setting. If a node consists of exceeding n pages, KSM splits it into two nodes. And the time taken to unmap a single node is shorter than unmapping two nodes. The attacker utilizes the timing differences occurring during the unmapping of merged pages in a single node and the unmapping of merged pages in two divided nodes to create a side channel Consisting of two building blocks.

The first building block for creating a side channel is to prepare as many pages as n by copying pages P that the attacker expects to exist in the victim's memory. The second building block for creating side channels is a timer to time the memory unmapping performs. In a cross-VM environment, use `RDTSC()`. And in a remote environment, use the hardware timestamp on the network interface card. In this work, we want to show how this technique can be leveraged to leak otherwise inaccessible secrets.

Attack Primitives. In this section, we show that $VM_{attacker}$ can leak VM_{victim}'s memory information on a page-by-page basis in a cross-VM environment using the maximum deduplication page limit mechanism provided by KSM. The experiments in the cross-VM environment can be categorized into successful and unsuccessful attacks based on whether the pages mapped to memory by $VM_{attacker}$ reside on the chain node or the stable node, as shown in Fig. 2. If the page mapped to memory by $VM_{attacker}$ exists on the chain node, it corresponds to Case 1 in Fig. 2. This is a case where the memory deduplication attack on one page of VM_{victim}'s memory is successful.

If the page mapped to memory by $VM_{attacker}$ exists on the stable node, it corresponds to Case 2 in Fig. 2. This is a case where the memory deduplication attack on one page of VM_{victim}'s memory fails. The attack process is as follows.

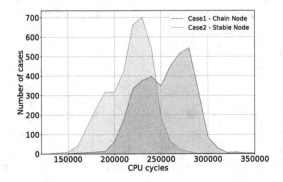

Fig. 3. Timing distribution graphs for two cases

First, the $VM_{attacker}$ prepares a binary file with a size of n pages that can be deduplicated by copying the binary for the P page that is expected to exist in the VM_{victim}'s memory. As a result, in Case 1 of Fig. 2, the n pages mapped to memory in $VM_{attacker}$ are the same as the pages in VM_{victim}'s memory, exceeding KSM's maximum deduplication page limit. Therefore, chain nodes and node dups are created during the deduplication process. Also, in Case 2 of Fig. 2, the n memory-mapped pages in $VM_{attacker}$ are not the same as the pages in VM_{victim}'s memory, so the maximum deduplication page limit of KSM is not exceeded. Therefore, only stable nodes are created during the deduplication process. Based on this deduplication page count limit mechanism, we perform memory unmapping in two cases when the threshold is exceeded and when it is not exceeded and measure the execution time. By exploiting the difference in execution time between these two cases, the attacker can perform a memory deduplication attack without writing access to the pages.

The experiments for each case, the experiment proceeds by repeating step 3 as follows:

Step 1. Memory map the binary file prepared by the $VM_{attacker}$.
Step 2. Wait for deduplication to be performed by KSM.
Step 3. Perform unmapping on the $VM_{attacker}$'s mapped pages and measure the time.

The $VM_{attacker}$'s Memory unmapping is performed at intervals based on how often KSM completes a full scan. With KSM settings of sleep_millisecs = 1,000 and pages_to_scan = 250,000 up to 1 GB of pages can be deduplicated per second. Therefore, with 4 GB of memory allocated to each VM, the scan completes in 8 s. After memory mapping, wait 8 s, the maximum time for a KSM scan, and measure the unmapping and performance time.

Experimental Setup. The cross-VM experimental environment was set up as follows. The *server* uses an i5-11600K processor and Ubuntu 22.04 (kernel 5.15.0-58-generic). The environment hosts two virtual machines, VM_{victim}, and

$VM_{attacker}$, via Linux KVM on a *server*. Table 1 shows the experimental environment for the cross-VM attack.

Threat Model. We consider a cross-VM environment where an attacker VM shares the same host machine with a victim VM. It can be simply achieved by mounting co-location attacks such as Repttack [10]. We also assume that the hypervisor uses KSM for efficient memory management and fully isolates each VM to protect it from the malicious behavior of other VMs. Finally, we assume that the hypervisor and guest OS have no bugs or known vulnerabilities to breach the security boundaries. Hence, there is no way for an attacker VM to learn the victim VM's security-sensitive data through the known vulnerabilities.

Experiment Result. Figure 3 shows the results of the $VM_{attacker}$'s 3,000 iterations of memory mapping and unmapping for each case and the distribution graph of the unmapping time. In the first case, the $VM_{attacker}$'s memory-mapped page and the page containing the VM_{victim}'s secret information are deduplicated. In other words, a chain node is created, and the attack is successful. In the second case, the $VM_{attacker}$'s memory-mapped page and the page containing the VM_{victim}'s secret information are not deduplicated. In other words, a stable node is created, and the attack fails. The execution time of memory unmapping for both cases is measured in CPU cycles.

After the $VM_{attacker}$ repeated the memory unmapping for each case 3,000 times, we found that the number of pages unmapped was the same; however, the execution time varies depending on whether the VM_{victim}'s page is deduplicated or not. By comparing the execution time in each case, we can create a side channel that identifies whether the VM_{victim}'s page is deduplicated or not, which enables the memory deduplication attack. The reason for the overall delay in the first case compared to the second case is expected to be due to the different nodes that are looked up in the process of searching and deleting the page in the KSM stable tree when performing memory unmapping.

3.2   Remote Attack Procedure

Figure 4 shows an attack overview in five steps. The attack procedure is as follows:

Step 1. The *client* prepares a binary file containing the *target page* that is expected to exist in the *server*'s memory and uploads it to the *server*. The configuration of the binary file to be uploaded is shown in Eq. (1).

$$(random\ page - HTTP\ response\ header\ size) + target\ page \times n \quad (1)$$

The *random page* in Equation. (1) is a page with a size of 4,096 KB consisting of random binary values. *HTTP response header size* is the size of the response to the download request. The size of the

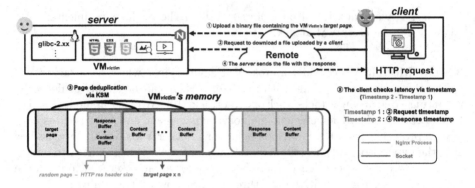

Fig. 4. Remote memory deduplication attack procedure

header may vary depending on the *server*'s configuration, so the *client* needs to check the size of the response header after making an HTTP GET request to the *server*. For later page alignment, subtract *HTTP response header size* from the *random page* and copy the *target page* to form n pages. The Nginx web server running on the *server* uses two buffers to request responses from the *client*. The first buffer records the HTTP response headers that respond to the *client*'s HTTP request. The second buffer records the HTTP content requested by the *client*. Because these two buffers are dynamically allocated with `malloc()`, they are not sorted on a per-page basis, making it challenging to deduplicate pages. However, when the two allocated buffers are merged, written to the socket, and delivered to the *client*, they are aligned on a page-by-page basis. So the *client* can map the desired page by calculating the length of the response header.

Step 2. The *client* requests to download the binary file uploaded to the *server* in Step 1. The *client*'s download request creates a memory mapping of the *client*'s uploaded binary file in the *server*'s memory.

Step 3. The *server*'s OS performs page deduplication.

Step 4. The *server* sends a response for the binary file requested by the *client*.

Step 5. The *client* calculates the elapsed time that the *server* processed the *client*'s download request by taking the difference between the timestamp when the *client* sent the download request and the timestamp in the *server*'s last response.

If the pages of the binary file uploaded by the *client* in Step 3 are deduplicated with the *server*'s target page. The number of deduplicated pages in KSM is exceeded, and chain nodes and node dups are created. This causes the *server*'s Nginx web server to experience latency while processing the download request. The *client* can perform a memory deduplication attack in a remote environment by measuring the latency caused by the presence or absence of this deduplication.

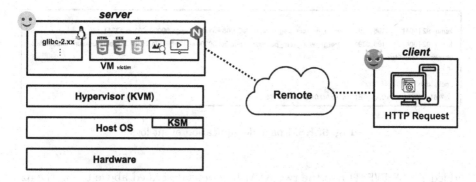

Fig. 5. Threat model for remote memory deduplication attack

Remote Experimental Environment. The experimental setup consists of two machines connected through a local network. Each machine is equipped with a 10-gigabit ethernet supported by an SFP+ direct attach cable. The first machine, referred to as the *server*, uses an i5-11600K processor and runs Ubuntu 22.04 (kernel 5.15.0-58-generic). It also hosts VM_{victim} using Linux KVM. The second machine, referred to as the *client*, uses an AMD EPYC 7282 processor and runs Ubuntu 20.04 (kernel 5.15.0-69-generic).

Remote Threat Model. Figure 5 depicts the threat model for the remote environment. The victim is a VM_{victim} hosted via Linux KVM on a *server* with KSM enabled and it is running an Nginx version 1.22.1 web server that provides file upload and download functionality. The *client* can only make file upload and download requests to the VM_{victim}'s web server, i.e., the *client* and VM_{victim} are in a remote environment with no shared resources.

KSM Deduplication Event Tracing Tool to Verify Remote Memory Deduplication Attack. We utilize the Linux kernel tracepoint [11] to determine if a memory deduplication attack is being performed according to the attack procedure described in Sect. 3.2. Currently, there are no tracepoint in the Linux kernel to trace events that occur in the KSM. Therefore, we will add tracepoint to the KSM. The added tracepoint was then used to implement a tool in this paper that automatically tracks deduplication events for KSM through the TRACE_EVENT() macro [12].

This paper's KSM deduplication event tracing tool focuses on the functions that KSM executes to perform deduplication write_protect_page() and merge_with_ksm_page(). The write_protect_page() function performs the process of changing a page to a read-only page to protect the page being merged from being modified before it is merged. And the merge_with_ksm_page() function merges the KSM page existing in the stable tree with the page with the same content found during the scan once the write_protect_page() function has finished changing the deduplication target page to a read-only page. We

```
...
ksmd- 92 [004] ..... 1196 .389399 : write_protect_page vma 000000005 e31790 c, page 00000000155 a3241, pfn 2759139
ksmd- 92 [004] ..... 1196 .389401 : merge_with_ksm_pageksm page 00000000 e613 e89f pfn 2588124 / oldchecksum 0x9a9fcfe 2
checksum 0x9a9fcfe 2 page pfn 2759139 HVA 0x7f61d4f27000

...
(gdb) x/ 8x 0x7f61d4f27000
0x7f61 d4f27000 : 0xCA 0xFE 0xDE 0xAD 0xCA 0xFE 0xDE 0xAD
```

Fig. 6. KSM page deduplication event logs

added TRACE_EVENT() to the two KSM functions described above to log the 32-bit checksum, PFN (Page Frame Number), and HVA (Host Virtual Address) so that we can track the deduplication target page. Figure 6 is a log output from the KSM Deduplication Event Tracker tool. In the output log, you can see that during the memory scan, KSM identified memory-mapped pages as deduplication targets due to *client* requests for downloads and performed deduplication.

The process of verifying KSM deduplication events is performed in four steps as follows:

Step 1. To protect the pages identified by KSM as deduplication targets during the memory scan, change them to read-only pages via the write_protect_page() function. Print the physical address and PFN to identify the target page.

Step 2. The merge_with_ksm_page() function also outputs the checksum, PFN, and HVA to identify the target page when a page changed to read-only is merged with a KSM page in the stable tree.

Step 3. On the *server*, use GNU Debugger (GDB) to access the VM_{victim}.

Step 4. The HVA accesses the memory-mapped pages in the VM_{victim} and verifies the contents of the deduplicated pages.

The *client* requested to download the page with the string "DEADCAFE" an easily identifiable magic debug value in hexadecimal, confirming that the attack procedure described in Sect. 3.2 is being performed. The above step shows that in a remote environment, a *client* can prepare a content page that is expected to exist in the *server*'s memory, determine whether the page exists, and leak secret information.

4   Conclusion

Existing memory deduplication attacks exploit the CoW mechanism to take advantage of the time difference in execution over in-memory page write accesses. However, in a remote environment, the attacker's ability to attempt to write access to the victim's merged page is limited because the attacker has no resources shared with the victim and cannot execute local code. To overcome these limitations, this paper proposes a new memory deduplication attack that performs memory unmapping and measures the time taken. The memory deduplication attack proposed in this paper exploits the KSM maximum deduplication page count limit mechanism to exploit the performance time difference for memory unmapping. The attack can be conducted in various environments due to the utilization of frequent memory unmapping, a characteristic that frequently occurs in applications, instead of relying on memory write accesses. Furthermore, the proposed attack in this paper suggests that it has the potential to be performed in remote environments as well as in cross-VM environments. However, remote attacks are subject to the constraint that they are vulnerable to network noise. Therefore, when performing memory unmapping on deduplicated pages, it is necessary to amplify the latency to increase the delay.

Acknowledgements. This research was supported by the National Research Foundation of Korea(NRF) grant funded by the Korea government (MSIT) (No. 2023R1A2C2006).

References

1. phstee: Cache and memory manager improvements. Technical report, Microsoft (2022). https://learn.microsoft.com/en-us/windows-server/administration/performance-tuning/subsystem/cache-memory-management/improvements-in-windows-server
2. Arcangeli, A., Eidus, I., Wright, C.: Increasing memory density by using KSM. In: Proceedings of the Linux Symposium, pp. 19–28. Citeseer (2009)
3. VMware vsphere product documentation "memory sharing". Technical report, VMware (2022). https://docs.vmware.com/en/VMware-vSphere/7.0/com.vmware.vsphere.resmgmt.doc/GUID-FEAC3A43-C57E-49A2-8303-B06DBC9054C5.html
4. Suzaki, K., Iijima, K., Yagi, T., Artho, C.: Memory deduplication as a threat to the guest OS. In: Proceedings of the Fourth European Workshop on System Security, EUROSEC 2011. Association for Computing Machinery (2011)
5. Lindemann, J., Fischer, M.: A memory-deduplication side-channel attack to detect applications in co-resident virtual machines. In: SAC 2018, pp. 183–192. Association for Computing Machinery (2018)
6. Kim, T., Kim, T., Shin, Y.: Breaking KASLR using memory deduplication in virtualized environments. Electronics **10**(17) (2021)
7. Gruss, D., Bidner, D., Mangard, S.: Practical memory deduplication attacks in sandboxed Javascript. In: Pernul, G., Ryan, P.Y.A., Weippl, E. (eds.) ESORICS 2015. LNCS, vol. 9326, pp. 108–122. Springer, Cham (2015). https://doi.org/10.1007/978-3-319-24174-6_6
8. Schwarzl, M., Kraft, E., Lipp, M., Gruss, D.: Remote memory-deduplication attacks. In: NDSS 2022 (2022). Network and Distributed System Security Symposium
9. Bader, S.: Ubuntu Linux package, "Linux 4.4.0-96.119 source package in ubuntu". Technical report, Canonical (2017). https://launchpad.net/ubuntu/+source/linux/4.4.0-96.119
10. Fang, C., et al.: REPTTACK: exploiting cloud schedulers to guide co-location attacks. In: NDSS 2021 (2021). Network and Distributed System Security Symposium

11. Rostedt, S.: lwn.net, "using the trace_event() macro (part 1)". Technical report, Eklektix (2010). https://lwn.net/Articles/379903
12. Rostedt, S.: lwn.net, "using the trace_event() macro (part 3)". Technical report, Eklektix (2010). https://lwn.net/Articles/383362

Mutation Methods for Structured Input to Enhance Path Coverage of Fuzzers

Yonggon Park[ID], Youngjoo Ko[ID], and Jong Kim[✉][ID]

Department of Computer Science and Engineering, Pohang University of Science
and Technology (POSTECH), Pohang, South Korea
{nanimdo,y0108009,jkim}@postech.ac.kr

Abstract. Existing mutation methods used in coverage-based grey-box
fuzzing (CGF), such as those employed by AFL and AFL++, can lead
to biased testing for structured inputs. While fuzzing, certain input sections of structured input may receive fewer mutations, resulting in less
testing of the code that handles those sections, which leads to lower path
coverage in those code parts.

In this paper, we propose two mutation methods for the structured
input to address the unbalanced problem and improve path coverage. The
first method, Uniform Mutation, involves conducting additional mutations in input sections that trigger less testing, thereby achieving a more
balanced path coverage across the target program. However, this method
requires prior knowledge of the input format, which reduces its usability
when the format of the target program changes. To overcome the limitation, we propose the second method, Format-agnostic Mutation, which
automatically partitions the input into sections based on coverage feedback. This method redistributes the number of mutations and resizes the
sections to improve path coverage without knowing the input format.

We evaluate the effectiveness of these methods using two real-world
programs (Xpdf and libxml2) and compare them with AFL. The experimental results demonstrate that Uniform and Format-agnostic mutations
(weight and resizing) outperform AFL regarding path coverage exploration.

Keywords: Fuzzing · Mutation · Structured Input · Path Coverage ·
AFL

1 Introduction

Fuzzing can be classified as black-box, white-box, or grey-box, depending on
the level of awareness about the program structure. Grey-box fuzzing methods [5,6,23] employ lightweight instrumentation techniques to gather information about the program. This instrumentation introduces minimal overhead compared to the analysis techniques used in white-box fuzzing [7,9,10]. By leveraging the obtained information, grey-box fuzzing methods can generate inputs

© The Author(s), under exclusive license to Springer Nature Singapore Pte Ltd. 2024
H. Kim and J. Youn (Eds.): WISA 2023, LNCS 14402, pp. 257–268, 2024.
https://doi.org/10.1007/978-981-99-8024-6_20

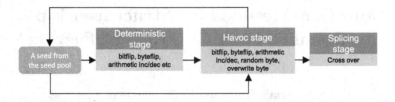

Fig. 1. The mutation method in AFL [23]

that are more effective at triggering bugs than inputs generated by black-box fuzzing [4,8,19].

Coverage-based grey-box fuzzing (CGF) is a widely used technique in the field of grey-box testing for detecting security vulnerabilities in real-world programs. CGF leverages metrics such as path or code coverage, acquired through lightweight instrumentation, to generate test inputs. Its primary objective is to enhance the chances of triggering vulnerabilities that may be present in less frequently executed or unexplored paths within the target program. Typically, CGF involves several key components, including seed selection, power schedule, mutation, execution, and seed evaluation with feedback. Initially, CGF selects a seed from a set of initial inputs and generates multiple test cases by applying mutations to the selected seed. The power schedule then determines the number of test cases created from each seed. Subsequently, CGF executes the program with the generated test cases and collects coverage information. If a test case executes previously unexplored code locations, CGF identifies it as a new seed to explore in the subsequent fuzzing iteration cycle. This iterative process enables CGF to systematically explore different paths of the program and increase the likelihood of uncovering vulnerabilities.

Representative fuzzers, such as AFL, AFL++, and VUzzer, employ the mutation method illustrated in Fig. 1, which involves modifying inputs from the beginning to the end while treating all input parts equally. This mutation process typically employs predetermined bitflips and additions as the modifying operations. The mutation methods employed by these fuzzers generally operate in three stages: deterministic, havoc, and splicing. In the deterministic stage, all input positions are mutated using the predetermined operations. In the havoc stage, positions for mutation are randomly selected from the input. Occasionally, an input is mutated through a crossover operation in the splicing stage. These stages collectively enable the fuzzers to systematically modify inputs and explore different paths, increasing the likelihood of triggering bugs or vulnerabilities in the target program.

However, we have observed that existing mutation methods exhibit a bias towards specific input sections, often neglecting others. This approach may not be optimal for programs that rely on structured inputs, where different input sections dictate the execution of different code segments. For example, consider the case of PDF file inputs, which consist of distinct sections such as the header, data, cross-reference table, and trailer (depicted in Fig. 2). Each section is processed by different code segments within the program, making their comprehensive coverage essential. To evaluate the impact of existing mutation methods on path coverage exploration for PDF inputs, we conducted a 24-hour fuzzing experiment using 30 randomly selected PDF files. The distribution of mutations applied to each section during the fuzzing process is depicted in Fig. 3. The results revealed a significant disparity in the distribution of mutations. Approximately 90% of the mutations were applied to the data section, while the header and cross-reference table sections received less than 3% of the mutations. This observation indicates that the mutation process primarily focused on the larger data section, disregarding smaller sections like the header. Consequently, it fails to consider crucial information about the most effective locations in the input for effective fuzzing. Consequently, certain input parts, such as the header section or less frequently accessed sections, may have fewer mutations, potentially leading to lower path coverage in those areas. This biased mutation approach limits the exploration of specific regions within the input and may hinder the detection of vulnerabilities or bugs associated with those neglected sections.

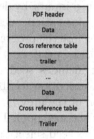

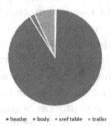

Fig. 2. The structure of PDF file

Fig. 3. Mutation rate of each section of PDF by AFL

We propose two primary mutation methods to address the problem and achieve high path coverage. The first method, Uniform mutation, tackles the issue by introducing additional mutations in input sections that have triggered fewer tests for a particular part of the target program. Its goal is to achieve a more balanced path coverage across the entire program. However, a prerequisite for utilizing this method is prior knowledge of the input format, which may limit its applicability. Furthermore, implementing this method requires extra effort whenever there are changes in the input format or the corresponding part of the target program. To overcome this limitation, we introduce the second method, Format-agnostic mutation. This method automatically divides the input into sections based on feedback obtained from coverage analysis. By partitioning the input, it redistributes the number of mutations and adjusts the sizes of sections to enhance path coverage. The Format-agnostic mutation method eliminates the need for explicit knowledge of the input format and ensures adaptability to changes in the input structure and target program.

The effectiveness of these methods is evaluated by measuring their performance on real-world programs (Xpdf and libxml2) and comparing them with AFL, a popular fuzzer. The evaluation clearly demonstrates that the proposed methods outperform AFL regarding path coverage exploration. This research offers the following key contributions:

- We introduce novel Uniform and Format-agnostic mutation methods.
- We demonstrate the efficiency of the Uniform mutation method in increasing path coverage.
- We effectively partition the input into sections, leading to higher path coverage compared to conventional fuzzers like AFL, while still maintaining usability.

2 Background

2.1 Coverage-Based Grey-Box Fuzzing

Coverage-based grey-box fuzzing has been widely used and detected many vulnerabilities in real-world programs. It generates testing inputs by leveraging lightweight instrumentation that extracts the coverage information, such as path and code coverage. The coverage information helps to explore the program's deep paths and detect bugs and vulnerabilities [1,5,6,11–13,15,21,23].

Grey-box fuzzing follows a typical workflow that includes seed selection, power schedule for energy assignment, seed mutation, execution feedback, and seed evaluation. Allow us to provide a brief description of the grey-box fuzzing workflow: The process begins with selecting a seed from the seed pool. The initial seed pool consists of regular inputs known as seeds. This seed selection process determines which seed from the pool is used to generate test cases, which serve as input for testing the target program. The power schedule plays a crucial role in determining the number of test cases, referred to as energy (E), that will be generated from the selected seed. The fuzzer applies mutation techniques to the seed based on the energy, creating new test cases. The target program executes each test case, which provides feedback during execution. This feedback typically includes coverage information, highlighting which code paths, branches, or functions were traversed. Leveraging this feedback, the fuzzer evaluates the input and identifies cases that increase coverage or exhibit abnormal behaviors. These interesting inputs are considered valuable and are added to the seed pool for further exploration in subsequent iterations. The fuzzing process continues iteratively, generating new test cases, executing them, and evaluating their impact based on the coverage feedback collected. Once all seeds in the seed pool are selected, the fuzzer selects seeds again from the beginning so they can be selected multiple times.

2.2 Mutation Method

We explain the mutation method used in AFL (shown in Fig. 1) because many coverage-based fuzzers have been implemented based on AFL and have adopted

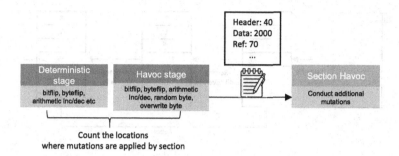

Fig. 4. The workflow of Uniform mutation. The yellow stage, section havoc, is the mutation stage that we newly added. (Color figure online)

a similar mutation method. This method consists of several stages, including deterministic, havoc, and occasionally splicing. Let us delve into each stage:

- **Deterministic stage.** AFL applies predetermined mutation operations to the input data in a systematic manner. These operations are typically performed on every bit or byte of the input. The deterministic stage encompasses mutation operators such as bit flips, byte flips, arithmetic increments/decrements, and other simple transformations.
- **Havoc stage.** In the havoc stage, randomness is introduced into the mutation process. AFL randomly selects positions by offsets within the input data and modifies the bytes or bits at those positions. These modifications can involve altering values, flipping bits, or applying arithmetic operations.
- **Splicing stage.** The splicing stage combines portions of two or more different inputs to generate new test cases. It is important to note that this stage is occasionally conducted.

While most mutations in AFL primarily occur in the deterministic and havoc stages, it is noteworthy that these mutation stages lack information regarding which positions in the input are particularly effective for fuzzing.

3   The Proposed Mutation Methods

3.1   Uniform Mutation

The first proposed mutation method, Uniform mutation, aims to tackle the inequality problem present in existing mutation methods by introducing additional mutations in input sections that have triggered less testing within the target program. Figure 4 illustrates the workflow of Uniform mutation with the newly added component, the section havoc stage. The fuzzer needs prior knowledge of the section structure of the input to facilitate fuzzing with the boundaries and divisions of different sections within the input. The mutation algorithm follows the standard execution of the deterministic and havoc stages. Upon completing the existing mutation stage, the fuzzer keeps track of the number of

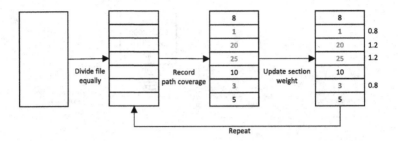

Fig. 5. Format-agnostic mutation with control of weight

mutations performed in each input section during the deterministic and havoc stages. This allows comparing the number of mutations across sections to identify those that have undergone less testing. To address the imbalance problem, we incorporate the section havoc stage into the fuzzer, wherein random positions within the sections requiring additional mutations are selected. Random offsets are chosen like the existing havoc stage, and additional mutations are applied at these positions. By integrating the section havoc stage into the mutation method, Uniform mutation ensures a more equitable distribution of mutations across input sections. This approach helps mitigate coverage imbalances and increases the likelihood of exploring new paths in the target program that have received less testing.

3.2   Format-Agnostic Mutation

The second mutation method, Format-agnostic mutation, aims to increase the usability of the prior Uniform mutation by allowing arbitrary division of the input into sections when there is no prior knowledge of the input format structure. We propose two versions of Format-agnostic mutation, as shown in Figs. 5 and 6.

The first version is the Format-agnostic mutation with weight, depicted in Fig. 5. This method divides the input into sections with equal size and weight, which might be not consistent with the actual section structure. Subsequently, it applies existing mutation methods to each section, according to the weight given to each section. Throughout this process, the fuzzer keeps track of the number of discovered paths for each section, serving it as a measure of path coverage. Based on this information, the fuzzer calculates a distinct weight for each section. The weight calculation is adjustable and determines the weight ratio using the following heuristic: Sections in the top one-third of path coverage receive a weight increase of 20%, while sections in the bottom one-third experience a weight decrease of 20%. We repeated above process 10 times, to form more precise and useful section information. In Fig. 5, the blue part corresponds to the top one-third, indicating a weight increase, while the red part corresponds to the bottom one-third, reflecting a weight decrease.

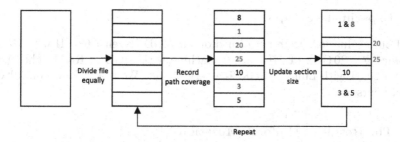

Fig. 6. Format-agnostic mutation with control of section size

The second version is the Format-agnostic mutation with resized sections, illustrated in Fig. 6. Similar to the previous version, it evenly divides the input into sections and applies existing mutation methods to each section. Each section's path coverage is evaluated like the Format-agnostic mutation with weight approach. Sections within the top one-third of path coverage undergo resizing by dividing them in half. Conversely, sections within the bottom one-third of path coverage are merged with adjacent sections exhibiting low path coverage. Following the resizing of sections, the fuzzer once again proceeds with the mutation algorithm, targeting the resized sections. In Fig. 6, the blue sections, which have discovered 20 and 25 paths, are divided, while the red sections, with only one and three paths, are merged with neighboring low-coverage sections.

4   Evaluation

Prototypes of the Uniform mutation and two versions of the Format-agnostic mutation (weight and resizing sections) are implemented on AFL as part of our research. The experiments are conducted using Xpdf and libxml2 as the target programs. The performance of the Uniform and Format-agnostic mutation methods was compared to that of AFL. The primary focus of the evaluation was to assess the path coverage achieved by each method. Our evaluation aims to address the following research questions:

RQ1. Does the Uniform mutation approach, which targets input sections with knowing the input structure, enhance the coverage exploration capabilities of fuzzing?

RQ2. Can we attain high path coverage by automatically dividing the input into sections without knowing the input structure?

By conducting comprehensive experiments and analyzing the results, we provide insightful answers to these research questions, shedding light on the benefits and potential of the Uniform and Format-agnostic mutation methods in improving coverage exploration during fuzzing.

4.1   Experiment Setup

All of our evaluations were performed on an AMD Ryzen 7 6800H with Radeon Graphics @ 3.20 GHz (4 MB cache) machine with 8 GB of RAM. The O.S. is Ubuntu 20.04 with Linux 5.15.0-72-generic 64-bit. We tested Xpdf and libxml2 for six hours.

4.2   The Result of Uniform Mutation

Table 1 shows the number of paths found by AFL and the Uniform mutation method. The experiment was conducted multiple times (five times) on the Xpdf benchmark for six hours to ensure fairness. The average results showed that the Uniform mutation method explored 9.64% more paths than AFL.

Table 1. The # of paths found by AFL and Uniform mutation on Xpdf.

Test Number	AFL (path)	Uniform (path)
#1	4011	4769
#2	4705	4754
#3	4083	4744
#4	4745	4722
#5	4052	4689
Avg	4319.2	4735.6

AFL's performance demonstrates inconsistency, whereas the Uniform mutation method consistently produces stable results. This inconsistency in AFL's performance can be attributed to the imbalance of mutations. AFL mutates the input by flipping all positions in the input one by one (deterministic stage) or randomly selecting positions with offsets to modify bytes or bits (havoc stage) without considering the input section. As a result, the code handling each input section is not tested with an equal chance. In contrast, the Uniform mutation method achieves stable results and higher path coverage by focusing on the exploration of smaller sections (such as the header and the cross-ref) based on the input section format. By uniformly applying mutations based on the input sections, this method achieves enhanced coverage and maintains stable fuzzing performance across multiple experimental attempts. These results clearly demonstrate the advantages of the Uniform mutation method over AFL in terms of path coverage and stability in fuzzing performance.

4.3   The Result of Format-Agnostic Mutation

Table 2 displays the path coverage results obtained from AFL, Uniform mutation, and the Format-agnostic mutations (weight and resize strategies) on the Xpdf benchmark. The experiment was repeated five times, with each run lasting six hours. On average, the Format-agnostic mutations (weight and resize strategies) revealed 7.0% and 6.4% more paths, respectively, compared to AFL. However, they still exhibited lower path coverage when compared to the Uniform mutation method, which has prior knowledge of the input format. These findings highlight that while the format-agnostic mutations achieved some improvements in path coverage compared to AFL, the Uniform mutation approach, benefiting from its understanding of the input format, outperformed the other methods by achieving higher path coverage.

Table 2. The # of paths found by AFL and Format-agnostic mutation on Xpdf.

Test Number	AFL	Uniform mutation	Format-agnostic (weight)	Format-agnostic (resize)
#1	4011	4769	4660	4665
#2	4705	4754	4654	4517
#3	4083	4744	4659	4525
#4	4745	4722	4567	4629
#5	4052	4689	4559	4647
Avg	4319.2	4735.6	4619.8	4596.6

The Format-agnostic mutation method is proposed as a solution for cases where prior knowledge of the input structure is unavailable. We observed that this method effectively divides the input into sections, resulting in only a slight difference in performance compared to the Uniform mutation method. When comparing the two versions (weight and resize strategies) of the Format-agnostic mutation method applied to the PDF input, the weight strategy shows similar performance to the resize strategy. This can be attributed to the PDF input's simple section structure, which aligns well with the divided sections determined by the Format-agnostic mutation method. Furthermore, since there is a separate code segment in the target program that handles each section of the PDF input, conducting additional mutations on sections with low weight, as facilitated by the weight strategy, contributes to exploring paths associated with the specific code segment.

Table 3 provides a detailed overview of the path coverage results of AFL and the Format-agnostic mutations (weight and resize strategies) on the libxml2 benchmark. The experiment was repeated five times, with each run lasting six hours. In the evaluation of AFL and Format-agnostic mutations for the libxml2 benchmark, which employs XML format inputs—a more intricate structure than PDF, the Uniform mutation method was not applied due to the complexity of XML syntax, including the presence of user-defined tags and attributes. On average, the Format-agnostic mutations (weight and resize strategies) achieved 101% and 105.4% higher path coverage, respectively, compared to AFL. These results highlight the effectiveness of the Format-agnostic mutation method in exploring path coverage by partitioning the input and applying varying numbers of mutations to each section, even for inputs with complex formats like XML. Notably, the resize strategy outperformed the weight strategy in the case of XML. This can be attributed to the densely sized sections present in XML inputs, and the resizing strategy adeptly divides the input to accommodate these dense sections, thereby contributing to improved path coverage.

Table 3. The # of paths found by AFL and Format-agnostic mutation on libxml2.

Test Number	AFL	Format-agnostic (weight)	Format-agnostic (resize)
#1	1533	3447	3150
#2	1697	3249	3654
#3	2073	3686	3556
#4	1519	3219	3434
#5	1593	3314	3490
Avg	1683	3383	3456.8

Overall, the results demonstrate that the Uniform and Format-agnostic mutation methods offer significant advantages over AFL regarding path coverage. The Uniform mutation method, leveraging its prior knowledge of the input format structure, outperforms the other methods in achieving higher path coverage. However, the Format-agnostic mutation methods also exhibit notable path coverage by dynamically partitioning the input into sections based on coverage feedback, even without prior knowledge of the input format structure, regardless of its structure complexity. This highlights their effectiveness in adapting to different input scenarios and achieving satisfactory path coverage.

5   Related Work

Mutation-Based Fuzzing. Mutation-based fuzzing has been proposed to generate inputs by randomly modifying valid inputs. Some studies leverage heuristics to guide mutation. AFL [23], Angora [2], CollAFL [6], and Mopt [11] utilize coverage for the guidance, and MemFuzz [3] and MemLock [18] leverage memory access and memory usage. Mutation-based fuzzing shows high speed to generate inputs but, it is less effective for programs that use structured inputs. For example, fuzzers like Angora [2] and Qsym [22] rely on program context (e.g., branches), not the file context, there may still exist codes that are less tested for a given time.

Structured Input Fuzzing. Several approaches have been proposed to perform mutations based on grammar or specification to generate structured inputs. Squirrel [24], Superion [17], SD-Gen [14] leverage the AST based on input specifications and the grammar to generate the valid inputs. On the other hand, JANUS [20] and AFLTurbo [16] apply mutations on the metadata dimension intensively. They focus only on a specific segment of the structured input rather than the overall input segments.

6   Conclusion

In this paper, we have tackled the bias issue present in existing mutation methods utilized in coverage-based grey-box fuzzing. We introduced new mutation methods for structured input, namely Uniform and Format-agnostic. The Uniform mutation method addresses the bias by conducting additional mutations on the input sections that invoke less testing for the code segments in the target program responsible for handling those corresponding input sections. This method ensures more balanced path coverage across the target program. On the other hand, the Format-agnostic mutation method automatically divides the input into sections based on coverage feedback. Then it adjusts the number of mutations or section sizes according to the adopted strategy. Unlike the Uniform mutation method, the Format-agnostic mutation method does not rely on explicit format knowledge, making it more versatile for inputs with complex structures.

To evaluate the effectiveness of our proposed methods, we conducted experiments using two real-world programs (Xpdf and libxml2) and compared the results with AFL. The experimental outcomes demonstrated that our approaches surpassed AFL regarding path coverage exploration. The Uniform mutation method consistently achieved stable results with higher path coverage compared to AFL. Meanwhile, the Format-agnostic mutation method effectively partitioned the input into sections and successfully explored paths within target programs even when dealing with inputs featuring complex structural formats. Our proposed approaches effectively address the bias problem inherent in existing mutation methods, leading to improved path coverage while maintaining usability.

Acknowledgements. This research was supported by the MSIT (Ministry of Science and ICT), Korea, under the ITRC (Information Technology Research Center) support program (IITP-2023-2018-0-01441) supervised by the IITP (Institute for Information & Communications Technology Planning & Evaluation).

References

1. Böhme, M., Pham, V.T., Roychoudhury, A.: Coverage-based greybox fuzzing as Markov chain. IEEE Trans. Softw. Eng. **45**(5), 489–506 (2017)
2. Chen, P., Chen, H.: Angora: efficient fuzzing by principled search. In: 2018 IEEE Symposium on Security and Privacy (SP), pp. 711–725. IEEE (2018)
3. Coppik, N., Schwahn, O., Suri, N.: MemFuzz: using memory accesses to guide fuzzing. In: 2019 12th IEEE Conference on Software Testing, Validation and Verification (ICST), pp. 48–58. IEEE (2019)
4. Fan, R., Chang, Y.: Machine learning for black-box fuzzing of network protocols. In: Qing, S., Mitchell, C., Chen, L., Liu, D. (eds.) ICICS 2017. LNCS, vol. 10631, pp. 621–632. Springer, Cham (2018). https://doi.org/10.1007/978-3-319-89500-0_53
5. Fioraldi, A., Maier, D., Eißfeldt, H., Heuse, M.: {AFL++}: combining incremental steps of fuzzing research. In: 14th USENIX Workshop on Offensive Technologies (WOOT 2020) (2020)

6. Gan, S., et al.: CollAFL: path sensitive fuzzing. In: 2018 IEEE Symposium on Security and Privacy (SP), pp. 679–696. IEEE (2018)
7. Ganesh, V., Leek, T., Rinard, M.: Taint-based directed whitebox fuzzing. In: 2009 IEEE 31st International Conference on Software Engineering, pp. 474–484. IEEE (2009)
8. Gascon, H., Wressnegger, C., Yamaguchi, F., Arp, D., Rieck, K.: PULSAR: stateful black-box fuzzing of proprietary network protocols. In: Thuraisingham, B., Wang, X.F., Yegneswaran, V. (eds.) SecureComm 2015. LNICST, vol. 164, pp. 330–347. Springer, Cham (2015). https://doi.org/10.1007/978-3-319-28865-9_18
9. Godefroid, P., Kiezun, A., Levin, M.Y.: Grammar-based whitebox fuzzing. In: Proceedings of the 29th ACM SIGPLAN Conference on Programming Language Design and Implementation, pp. 206–215 (2008)
10. Godefroid, P., Levin, M.Y., Molnar, D.: Sage: whitebox fuzzing for security testing. Commun. ACM 55(3), 40–44 (2012)
11. Lyu, C., et al.: MOPT: optimized mutation scheduling for fuzzers. In: 28th USENIX Security Symposium (USENIX Security 2019), pp. 1949–1966 (2019)
12. Peng, H., Shoshitaishvili, Y., Payer, M.: T-fuzz: fuzzing by program transformation. In: 2018 IEEE Symposium on Security and Privacy (SP), pp. 697–710. IEEE (2018)
13. Rawat, S., Jain, V., Kumar, A., Cojocar, L., Giuffrida, C., Bos, H.: Vuzzer: application-aware evolutionary fuzzing. In: NDSS, vol. 17, pp. 1–14 (2017)
14. Sargsyan, S., Kurmangaleev, S., Mehrabyan, M., Mishechkin, M., Ghukasyan, T., Asryan, S.: Grammar-based fuzzing. In: 2018 Ivannikov Memorial Workshop (IVMEM), pp. 32–35. IEEE (2018)
15. Serebryany, K.: {OSS-Fuzz}-Google's continuous fuzzing service for open source software (2017)
16. Sun, L., Li, X., Qu, H., Zhang, X.: AFLTurbo: speed up path discovery for grey-box fuzzing. In: 2020 IEEE 31st International Symposium on Software Reliability Engineering (ISSRE), pp. 81–91. IEEE (2020)
17. Wang, J., Chen, B., Wei, L., Liu, Y.: Superion: grammar-aware greybox fuzzing. In: 2019 IEEE/ACM 41st International Conference on Software Engineering (ICSE), pp. 724–735. IEEE (2019)
18. Wen, C., et al.: MemLock: memory usage guided fuzzing. In: Proceedings of the ACM/IEEE 42nd International Conference on Software Engineering, pp. 765–777 (2020)
19. Woo, M., Cha, S.K., Gottlieb, S., Brumley, D.: Scheduling black-box mutational fuzzing. In: Proceedings of the 2013 ACM SIGSAC Conference on Computer & Communications Security, pp. 511–522 (2013)
20. Xu, W., Moon, H., Kashyap, S., Tseng, P.N., Kim, T.: Fuzzing file systems via two-dimensional input space exploration. In: 2019 IEEE Symposium on Security and Privacy (SP), pp. 818–834. IEEE (2019)
21. Yue, T., et al.: {EcoFuzz}: adaptive {Energy-Saving} greybox fuzzing as a variant of the adversarial {Multi-Armed} bandit. In: 29th USENIX Security Symposium (USENIX Security 2020), pp. 2307–2324 (2020)
22. Yun, I., Lee, S., Xu, M., Jang, Y., Kim, T.: {QSYM}: a practical concolic execution engine tailored for hybrid fuzzing. In: 27th USENIX Security Symposium (USENIX Security 2018), pp. 745–761 (2018)
23. Zalewski, M.: American fuzzy lop (2020). https://lcamtuf.coredump.cx/afl/
24. Zhong, R., Chen, Y., Hu, H., Zhang, H., Lee, W., Wu, D.: SQUIRREL: testing database management systems with language validity and coverage feedback. In: Proceedings of the 2020 ACM SIGSAC Conference on Computer and Communications Security, pp. 955–970 (2020)

Improved Differential-Linear Cryptanalysis of Reduced Rounds of ChaCha

Ryo Watanabe, Nasratullah Ghafoori$^{(\boxtimes)}$ [ID], and Atsuko Miyaji [ID]

Osaka University, 2-1 Yamadaoka, Suita-shi, Osaka, Japan
{watanabe,ghafoori}@cy2sec.comm.eng.osaka-u.ac.jp,
miyaji@comm.eng.osaka-u.ac.jp

Abstract. ChaCha is a stream cipher introduced by Daniel Bernstein as a variant of Salsa20. Since the release of ChaCha, it has received the attention of many researchers as it has been widely deployed. In this study, we derive a new linear approximation for ChaCha with a higher probability bias. In addition, we found a combination of input/output differences corresponding to a new linear relationship. Furthermore, we proved that the proposed bias can be used to attack 7-round ChaCha with a reduced computational complexity from $2^{221.95}$ to $2^{120.9}$.

Keywords: symmetric-key cryptography · stream ciphers · ChaCha · differential linear analysis

1 Introduction

Symmetric key cryptography is widely used in the modern computing era. It ensures secure information exchange. ChaCha [5] is a stream cipher based on ARX. It's important to assess its security due to its deployment, especially in TLS and DTLS protocols [5,16]. While ChaCha is generally resilient against attacks, it shows some weakness in the first few rounds against Differential and Differential Linear Cryptanalysis, making those the primary attack methods. Aumasson [1] proposed a significant cryptanalysis method to attack ChaCha. One of the notable research studies in this area is based on the notion of *probabilistic neutral bits* (PNBs). Aumasson divides secret key bits into two subsets, significant key bits "m" and non-significant key bits "n" which is the fundamental idea behind PNB (Probabilistic Neutral Bits). Aumasson reported attacks on ChaCha7 and ChaCha6 with the complexity of 2^{248}, and 2^{139} respectively. Almost all subsequent attacks on the mentioned ciphers improved Aumasson's method. In 2012, Zhenqing Shi [21] introduced the concept called (column and row) chaining distinguishers. Shi published attack on ChaCha7 with complexity of $2^{246.5}$ and ChaCha6 with complexity of 2^{136}. In due course, Maitra [17] presented the chosen IV attack on Salsa20 and ChaCha. Maitra reported attacks on ChaCha7 with the complexity of 2^{239}. Following that, Choudhuri [7] introduced the differential linear adversary model on Salsa20 and ChaCha. Choudhuri reported report biases for 4/4.5/5 rounds of ChaCha. The proposed attack

H. Kim and J. Youn (Eds.): WISA 2023, LNCS 14402, pp. 269–281, 2024.
https://doi.org/10.1007/978-981-99-8024-6_21

resulted in ChaCha7 with 2^{233} operations. Later, in 2017 Dey [13] studied the proposed technique to construct a PNB set. The author reported attacks on ChaCha7 with a $2^{235.2}$ complexity. In 2020 Coutinho [8] improved the method introduced by Choudhuri and provided new linear approximations that increase the efficiency of attack on ChaCha stream cipher. Coutinho introduced an attack on ChaCha7 with $2^{231.9}$ operation and 2^{50} data complexity. In 2020 Beierle [2] improved the framework of differential-linear attacks with a special focus on ARX ciphers and attacked ChaCha7 with $2^{230.86}$ operations and $2^{48.83}$ data complexity. Miyashita [19] in 2021 worked on PNB-focused differential cryptanalysis on ChaCha7 and introduced an attack with a time complexity of $2^{231.63}$. Dey [12] presented Revamped Differential-Linear Cryptanalysis on ChaCha7 with $2^{221.95}$ operations. Zhongfeng [20] in 2022 reported improved differential-linear distinguisher for ChaCha4. In 2022, **Coutinho** [10] introduced a 2^{214} operation differential-linear attack on ChaCha7. In 2023, Dey [11] introduced attack with $2^{99.48}$ operations attack on ChaCha6. Later in 2022, Ghafoori [14] and Miyaji comprehensively analyzed the neutrality measure of Salsa20 keybits and proposed an attack with a complexity of $2^{144.75}$. In 2023, Bellini1 [4] presented a key recovery attack on chaCha7 and a distinguisher on ChaCha7.5 with complexity of $2^{206.8}$ and $2^{251.54}$ respectively. In this study, we present an analysis of the differential linear attack on ChaCha7. First, we show a new linear approximation for ChaCha by combining existing linear approximations. The computational complexity of the existing studies is listed in Table 1. Table 2 describes the notation used in the following sections and its meaning.

2   Preliminary

ChaCha stream cipher consists of the following three steps to generate a keystream block of 16 words, where each word size is 32 bits:

Step 1. To generate 512 bits key stream, ChaCha initial state matrix $X^{(0)}$ of order 4×4 is initialized from a 256-bit secret key $k = (k_0, k_1, \ldots, k_7)$, a 96-bit nonce $v = (v_0, v_1, v_2)$, a 32-bit block counter t_0, and four 32-bit constants $c = (c_0, c_1, c_2, c_3)$, such as $c_0 = 0x61707865$, $c_1 = 0x3320646e$, $c_2 = 0x79622d32$, and $c_3 = 0x6b206574$. After initialization, we obtain the following initial state matrix:

$$
X^{(0)} = \begin{pmatrix} x_0^{(0)} & x_1^{(0)} & x_2^{(0)} & x_3^{(0)} \\ x_4^{(0)} & x_5^{(0)} & x_6^{(0)} & x_7^{(0)} \\ x_8^{(0)} & x_9^{(0)} & x_{10}^{(0)} & x_{11}^{(0)} \\ x_{12}^{(0)} & x_{13}^{(0)} & x_{14}^{(0)} & x_{15}^{(0)} \end{pmatrix} = \begin{pmatrix} c_0 & c_1 & c_2 & c_3 \\ k_0 & k_1 & k_2 & k_3 \\ k_4 & k_5 & k_6 & k_7 \\ t_0 & v_0 & v_1 & v_2 \end{pmatrix}.
$$

Step 2. The round function of ChaCha comprises four simultaneous computations of the quarterround function. According to the procedure, a vector

Table 1. Comparison of analysis results of existing studies and this study for ChaCha

Attack Type	Target Rounds	Time Complexity	Data Complexity	Reference
Distinguisher	4	2^6	2^6	[7]
Distinguisher	5	2^{16}	2^{16}	[7]
Key Recovery	6	2^{139}	2^{30}	[1]
Key Recovery	6	$2^{127.5}$	$2^{37.5}$	[7]
Key Recovery	6	$2^{77.4}$	2^{58}	[3]
Distinguisher	6	2^{116}	2^{116}	[7]
Distinguisher	6	2^{51}	2^{51}	[9]
Key Recovery	7	2^{248}	2^{27}	[1]
Key Recovery	7	$2^{237.7}$	2^{96}	[7]
Key Recovery	7	$2^{230.86}$	$2^{48.8}$	[3]
Key Recovery	7	$2^{221.95}$	$2^{48.83}$	[12]
Key Recovery	7	$2^{221.95}$	$2^{48.83}$	[12]
Distinguisher	7	2^{224}	2^{224}	[9]
Distinguisher	7	2^{214}	2^{214}	[10]
Key Recovery	7	$2^{206.8}$	$2^{110.81}$	[4]
Distinguisher	7.5	$2^{251.54}$	$2^{251.54}$	[4]
Distinguisher	7	$2^{120.9}$	$2^{120.9}$	This work

$(x_a^{(r)}, x_b^{(r)}, x_c^{(r)}, x_d^{(r)})$ in the internal state matrix $X^{(r)}$ is updated by sequentially computing the following:

$$
\begin{cases}
x_{a'}^{(r)} = x_a^{(r)} + x_b^{(r)} & x_a^{(r+1)} = x_{a'}^{(r)} + x_{b''}^{(r)} \\
x_{d'}^{(r)} = x_d^{(r)} \oplus x_{a'}^{(r)} & x_{d'''}^{(r)} = x_{d''}^{(r)} \oplus x_a^{(r+1)} \\
x_{d''}^{(r)} = x_{d'}^{(r)} \lll 16 & x_d^{(r+1)} = x_{d'''}^{(r)} \lll 8 \\
x_{c'}^{(r)} = x_c^{(r)} + x_{d''}^{(r)} & x_c^{(r+1)} = x_{c'}^{(r)} + x_d^{(r+1)} \\
x_{b'}^{(r)} = x_b^{(r)} \oplus x_{c'}^{(r)} & x_{b'''}^{(r)} = x_{b''}^{(r)} \oplus x_c^{(r+1)} \\
x_{b''}^{(r)} = x_{b'}^{(r)} \lll 12 & x_b^{(r+1)} = x_{b'''}^{(r)} \lll 7
\end{cases}
\tag{1}
$$

The symbols "$+$", "$\oplus$", and "$\lll$" represent wordwise modular addition, bitwise XOR, and bitwise left rotation, respectively. For odd-numbered rounds, which are called columnrounds, the quarterround function is applied to the following four column vectors: $(x_0^{(r)}, x_4^{(r)}, x_8^{(r)}, x_{12}^{(r)})$, $(x_1^{(r)}, x_5^{(r)}, x_9^{(r)}, x_{13}^{(r)})$, $(x_2^{(r)}, x_6^{(r)}, x_{10}^{(r)}, x_{14}^{(r)})$, and $(x_3^{(r)}, x_7^{(r)}, x_{11}^{(r)}, x_{15}^{(r)})$. For even-numbered rounds, which are called diagonalrounds, the quarterround function is applied to the following four diagonal vectors: $(x_0^{(r)}, x_5^{(r)}, x_{10}^{(r)}, x_{15}^{(r)})$, $(x_1^{(r)}, x_6^{(r)}, x_{11}^{(r)}, x_{12}^{(r)})$, $(x_2^{(r)}, x_7^{(r)}, x_8^{(r)}, x_{13}^{(r)})$, and $(x_3^{(r)}, x_4^{(r)}, x_9^{(r)}, x_{14}^{(r)})$.

Table 2. Notation in this paper

Notation	Description
X	The ChaCha matrix of 4×4 with 16 words of 32 bit each
$X^{(0)}$	The initial state matrix of ChaCha
$X'^{(0)}$	The associate matrix with a single bit difference at $x_{i,j}$ position
$X^{(R)}$	The matrix after ChaCha R rounds
$X^{(r)}$	The matrix after ChaCha r rounds where $R > r$ (internal round)
$x_i^{(R)}$	The ith word of state matrix $X^{(R)}$
$x_{i,j}^{(R)}$	The jth bit of ith word of matrix $X^{(R)}$
$x + y$	The word-wise addition of word x and y modulo 2^{32}
$x \oplus y$	Bit-wise XOR operation of the word x and y
$x \lll n$	The left rotation of word x by n bits
Δx	The XOR difference of word x and x' defined as $\Delta x = x \oplus x'$
$\varepsilon_e, \varepsilon_l$	The forward bias and linear correlation of ChaCha respectively

Step 3. A 512-bit keystream block is computed as $Z = X^{(0)} + X^{(R)}$, where R is the final round. The original version of ChaCha has $R = 20$ rounds, and the ChaCha20/R denotes the reduced-round version of ChaCha.

3   Differential-Linear Cryptanalysis

In this section, we explain Differential-Linear Cryptanalysis as the adversary model of this paper. Differential analysis was proposed by Eli Biham et al. [6] in 1990, Linear Cryptanalysis was introduced by Matsui [18]. Langford [15] introduced the idea of Differential-Linear Cryptanalysis. Let E represent the cipher, we write $E = E2 \cdot E1$ covering the l and m round of cipher respectively. We apply differential cryptanalysis on sub cipher $E1$. Let $X^{(0)}$ be the initial state and we introduce an input difference $\mathcal{ID}$ denoted as $\Delta X^{(0)}$ in $X^{(0)}$ and get output difference $\mathcal{OD}$ denoted as $\Delta X^{(m)}$ after m rounds $X^{(m)}$. Next, we apply Linear Cryptanalysis on $E2$ sub cipher. We use Γ_m and Γ_{out} to obtain a linear approximation of the remaining l round of the cipher E. This adversary model covers the $m + l$ round of the cipher E. We use the differential linear distinguisher of $m + l$ to attack cipher E with higher efficiency. Let $\Delta X^{(r)} = X^{(r)} \oplus X'^{(r)}$ be the differential of matrices $X^{(r)}$ and $X'^{(r)}$, and $\Delta_i^{(0)}[j] = x_i^{(0)}[j] \oplus x_i'^{(0)}[j]$ be the difference of individual words at j-th word of i-th bit after r internal rounds. Let $\mathcal{J}$ be the set of bits and σ and σ' be the linear combination of bits in the set $\mathcal{J}$. Precisely, $\sigma = \left(\bigoplus_{(i,[j]) \in \mathcal{J}} x_{i,[j]}^{(r)} \right)$ and $\sigma' = \left(\bigoplus_{(i,[j]) \in \mathcal{J}} x_{i,[j]}'^{(r)} \right)$, let $\Delta X = \left(\bigoplus_{(i,[j]) \in \mathcal{J}} \Delta x_{i,[j]}^{(r)} \right)$ be the linear combination of σ and σ'. The differential bias ϵ_d is computed as $Pr\left[\Delta\sigma = 0 | \Delta X^{(0)}\right] = \frac{1}{2}(1 + \epsilon_d)$. We can use linear cryptanalysis to move forward and get new relationships between the initial state and the state after the target round $R > r$. Let $\rho = \left(\bigoplus_{(i,[j]) \in \mathcal{J}} x_{i,[j]}^{(R)} \right)$ and $\rho' = \left(\bigoplus_{(i,[j]) \in \mathcal{J}} x_{i,[j]}'^{(R)} \right)$. Let $\Delta\rho = \left(\bigoplus_{(i,[j]) \in \mathcal{J}} \Delta x_{i,[j]}^{(R)} \right)$ be the linear combination of ρ and ρ'. $Pr\left[\sigma = \rho \right] = \frac{1}{2}(1 + \epsilon_L)$ where ϵ_L denotes the linear correlation. The differential linear correlation is computed as the $Pr\left[\Delta\rho = 0 | \Delta X^{(0)} \right] = \frac{1}{2}(1 + \epsilon_d \cdot \epsilon_L^2)$ where $\epsilon_d \cdot \epsilon_L^2$ denote the differential linear bias. The distinguisher complexity is computed as $\mathcal{O}\left(\frac{1}{\epsilon_d^2 \cdot \epsilon_L^4} \right)$. Typically, a minimum of $\mathcal{O}\left(\frac{1}{pq^2} \right)$ samples is needed to discern between two events, with one event having a probability of p and the other event having a substantially smaller probability of q. For the proof one may refer to [7].

Lemma 1 *(Lemma 3 of [7]). Let*

$$\Delta A^{(m)} = \Delta x_{\alpha,0}^{(m)} \oplus \Delta x_{\beta,7}^{(m)} \oplus \Delta x_{\beta,19}^{(m)} \oplus \Delta x_{\gamma,12}^{(m)} \oplus \Delta x_{\delta,0}^{(m)},$$

$$\Delta B^{(m)} = \Delta x_{\beta,19}^{(m)} \oplus \Delta x_{\gamma,0}^{(m)} \oplus \Delta x_{\gamma,12}^{(m)} \oplus \Delta x_{\delta,0}^{(m)},$$

$$\Delta C^{(m)} = \Delta x_{\delta,0}^{(m)} \oplus \Delta x_{\gamma,7}^{(m)} \oplus \Delta x_{\delta,8}^{(m)} \oplus \Delta x_{\alpha,0}^{(m)}, and$$

$$\Delta D^{(m)} = \Delta x_{\delta,24}^{(m)} \oplus \Delta x_{\alpha,16}^{(m)} \oplus \Delta x_{\alpha,0}^{(m)} \oplus \Delta x_{\gamma,0}^{(m)} \oplus \Delta x_{\beta,7}^{(m)}.$$

Then, the following equations for four biases hold:

$$\left| \epsilon_{(A^{(m)})} \right| = \left| \epsilon_{(x_\alpha^{(m-1)}{}_{[0]})} \right|, \left| \epsilon_{(B^{(m)})} \right| = \left| \epsilon_{(x_\beta^{(m-1)}{}_{[0]})} \right|, \left| \epsilon_{(C^{(m)})} \right| = \left| \epsilon_{(x_\gamma^{(m-1)}{}_{[0]})} \right|, and \left| \epsilon_{(D^{(m)})} \right|$$

$$= \left| \epsilon_{(x_\delta^{(m-1)}{}_{[0]})} \right|.$$

where these relations are divided into two cases depending on m,

1. *If m is odd number:*

$$(\alpha, \beta, \gamma, \delta) \in \{(0,4,8,12), (1,5,9,13), (2,6,10,14), (3,7,11,15)\},$$

2. *If m is even number:*

$$(\alpha, \beta, \gamma, \delta) \in \{(0,5,10,15), (1,6,11,12), (2,7,8,13), (3,4,9,14)\}.$$

Lemma 2 *(Lemma 9 of [7]). For a single input bit in $m-1$ rounds and multiple output bits in m rounds, the following relationship holds.*

$$x_{b,i}^{(m-1)} = x_{b,i+19}^{(m)} \oplus x_{c,i+12}^{(m)} \oplus x_{d,i}^{(m)} \oplus x_{c,i}^{(m)} \oplus x_{d,i-1}^{(m)}, \quad w.p. \frac{1}{2}\left(1 + \frac{1}{2}\right),$$

$$x_{a,i}^{(m-1)} = x_{a,i}^{(m)} \oplus x_{b,i+7}^{(m)} \oplus x_{b,i+19}^{(m)} \oplus x_{c,i+12}^{(m)} \oplus x_{d,i}^{(m)} \oplus x_{b,i+18}^{(m)} \oplus x_{c,i+11}^{(m)} \oplus x_{d,i-2}^{(m)} \oplus x_{d,i+6}^{(m)},$$

$$w.p. \frac{1}{2}\left(1 + \frac{1}{2^4}\right),$$

$$x_{c,i}^{(m-1)} = x_{d,i}^{(m)} \oplus x_{c,i}^{(m)} \oplus x_{d,i+8}^{(m)} \oplus x_{a,i}^{(m)} \oplus x_{a,i-1}^{(m)} \oplus x_{d,i+7}^{(m)} \oplus x_{d,i-1}^{(m)}, \quad w.p. \frac{1}{2}\left(1 + \frac{1}{2^2}\right),$$

$$x_{d,i}^{(m-1)} = x_{d,i+24}^{(m)} \oplus x_{a,i+16}^{(m)} \oplus x_{a,i}^{(m)} \oplus x_{c,i}^{(m)} \oplus x_{b,i+7}^{(m)} \oplus x_{c,i-1}^{(m)} \oplus x_{b,i+6}^{(m)}, \quad w.p. \frac{1}{2}\left(1 + \frac{1}{2}\right).$$

Coutinho et al. [9] proposed an improved linear approximation with a larger bias, using the results of [7].

$$\mathcal{L}_{a,i}^{(m)} = x_{a,i}^{(m)} \oplus x_{b,i+7}^{(m)} \oplus x_{b,i+19}^{(m)} \oplus x_{c,i+12}^{(m)} \oplus x_{d,i}^{(m)}$$
$$\mathcal{L}_{b,i}^{(m)} = x_{b,i+19}^{(m)} \oplus x_{c,i}^{(m)} \oplus x_{c,i+12}^{(m)} \oplus x_{d,i}^{(m)}$$
$$\mathcal{L}_{c,i}^{(m)} = x_{a,i}^{(m)} \oplus x_{c,i}^{(m)} \oplus x_{d,i}^{(m)} \oplus x_{d,i+8}^{(m)}$$
$$\mathcal{L}_{d,i}^{(m)} = x_{a,i}^{(m)} \oplus x_{a,i+16}^{(m)} \oplus x_{b,i+7}^{(m)} \oplus x_{c,i}^{(m)} \oplus x_{d,i+24}^{(m)}$$

Lemma 3 *(Lemma 6 of* [9]*). For $i > 0$,*

$$x_{a,i}^{(m-1)} = \mathcal{L}_{a,i}^{(m)} \oplus x_{b,i+6}^{(m)} \oplus x_{b,i+18}^{(m)} \oplus x_{c,i+11}^{(m)} \oplus x_{d,i-1}^{(m)}$$

is satisfied with probability $\frac{1}{2}\left(1 + \frac{1}{2^3}\right)$.

Lemma 4 *(Lemma 7 of* [9]*). Linear approximation between two input bits in $m - 1$ rounds and multiple output bits in m rounds $x_{\lambda,i}^{(m-1)} \oplus x_{\lambda,i-1}^{(m-1)} = \mathcal{L}_{\lambda,i}^{(m)} \oplus \mathcal{L}_{\lambda,i-1}^{(m)}$ is satisfied with probability $\frac{1}{2}\left(1 + \frac{1}{2^\sigma}\right)$, where $(\lambda, \sigma) \in \{(a,3), (b,1), (c,2), (d,1)\}$ for $i > 0$.*

Lemma 5 *(Eq. 19 and 25 in Lemma 9 of* [9] *respectively). The following linear approximations between multiple input bits of $m - 1$ rounds and multiple output bits of m rounds hold with the following probability.*

$$x_{b,i}^{(m-1)} \oplus x_{c,i}^{(m-1)} = \mathcal{L}_{b,i}^{(m)} \oplus \mathcal{L}_{c,i}^{(m)} \oplus x_{a,i-1}^{(m)} \oplus x_{d,i+7}^{(m)} \quad w.p. \frac{1}{2}\left(1 + \frac{1}{2}\right) \text{ for } i > 0, \quad (2)$$

$$x_{a,i-1}^{(m-1)} \oplus x_{a,i}^{(m-1)} \oplus x_{c,i}^{(m-1)} = \mathcal{L}_{a,i-1}^{(m)} \oplus \mathcal{L}_{a,i}^{(m)} \oplus \mathcal{L}_{c,i}^{(m)} \oplus x_{d,i-2}^{(m)} \oplus x_{a,i-1}^{(m)} \oplus x_{d,i+7}^{(m)}$$
$$w.p. \frac{1}{2}\left(1 + \frac{1}{2^4}\right) \text{ for } i > 1. \quad (3)$$

4   Improved Differential-Linear Analysis on ChaCha

This section presents our approach which greatly reduced the ChaCha 7 computational complexity in Differential-Linear analysis.

4.1   Our Strategy

The Differential-Linear Cryptanalysis bias is computed as $Pr\left[\Delta\rho = 0|\Delta X^{(0)}\right] = \frac{1}{2}(1 + \epsilon_d \cdot \epsilon_L^2)$. The linear bias is crucial for reducing the overall attack complexity. To get a higher bias, we focused on two strategies: First, improving the linear component bias by reducing the number of rounds. Specifically, we focus on four rounds for the differential part and three rounds for the linear part. Second, we focus on a single bit active bit in linear approximation. Adopting this approach helped us to reduce the distinguisher for ChaCha7.

4.2   Linear Part

In this section, we introduce a new linear approximation.

Lemma 6. *The following linear approximation holds between a single bit in the 4th round and multiple bits in the 6th round.*

$$x_{3,0}^{(4)} = x_0^{(6)}[0,16] \oplus x_1^{(6)}[11,12] \oplus x_{3,0}^{(6)} \oplus x_4^{(6)}[7,19] \oplus x_{5,7}^{(6)} \oplus x_7^{(6)}[6,26] \oplus x_8^{(6)}[7,31]$$

$$\oplus\, x_{9,12}^{(6)} \oplus x_{10,0}^{(6)} \oplus x_{11,12}^{(6)} \oplus x_{12}^{(6)}[11,12,19,20] \oplus x_{13}^{(6)}[6,7,18,19] \oplus x_{14,0}^{(6)} \oplus x_{15,24}^{(6)}$$

$$w.p.\frac{1}{2}\left(1+\frac{1}{2^4}\right).$$

Proof. Applying Lemma 1 to the input bit $x_{3,0}^{(4)}$, we obtain the following linear approximation,

$$x_{3,0}^{(4)} = x_{3,0}^{(5)} \oplus x_{7,7}^{(5)} \oplus x_{7,19}^{(5)} \oplus x_{11,12}^{(5)} \oplus x_{15,0}^{(5)} \quad w.p.1.$$

Furthermore, for each bit on the right-hand side of this equation, we apply Lemma 2 as follows:

$$x_{3,0}^{(5)} = x_{3,0}^{(6)} \oplus x_{4,7}^{(6)} \oplus x_{4,19}^{(6)} \oplus x_{9,12}^{(6)} \oplus x_{14,0}^{(6)} \quad w.p.1 \quad (Lemma\ 1),$$

$$x_{15,0}^{(5)} = x_{0,0}^{(6)} \oplus x_{0,16}^{(6)} \oplus x_{5,7}^{(6)} \oplus x_{10,0}^{(6)} \oplus x_{15,24}^{(6)} \quad w.p.1 \quad (Lemma\ 1),$$

$$x_{7,7}^{(5)} = x_{7,26}^{(6)} \oplus x_{8,7}^{(6)} \oplus x_{8,19}^{(6)} \oplus x_{13,7}^{(6)} \oplus x_{13,6}^{(6)} \quad w.p.\frac{1}{2}\left(1+\frac{1}{2}\right) \quad (Lemma\ 2),$$

$$x_{7,19}^{(5)} = x_{7,6}^{(6)} \oplus x_{8,19}^{(6)} \oplus x_{8,31}^{(6)} \oplus x_{13,19}^{(6)} \oplus x_{13,18}^{(6)} \quad w.p.\frac{1}{2}\left(1+\frac{1}{2}\right) \quad (Lemma\ 2),$$

$$x_{11,12}^{(5)} = x_{1,12}^{(6)} \oplus x_{11,12}^{(6)} \oplus x_{12,12}^{(6)} \oplus x_{12,20}^{(6)} \oplus x_{1,11}^{(6)} \quad \oplus x_{12,19}^{(6)} \oplus x_{12,11}^{(6)} \quad w.p.\frac{1}{2}\left(1+\frac{1}{2^2}\right) \quad (4)$$

Then, Lemma 6 follows by combining the above equations. The bias is expressed as the product of each biases in each equation. In addition, we will show Lemma 7 that extends the number of rounds between the input and output of Lemma 6.

Lemma 7. *The following linear approximation holds between a single bit in the 4th round and multiple bits in the 7th round.*

$$x_{3,0}^{(4)} = x_0^{(7)}[0,3,4,6,7,11,12,16,19,20,27,28,30,31] \oplus x_1^{(7)}[2,3,6,7,18,19,22,23]$$

$$\oplus\, x_{2,16}^{(7)} \oplus x_3^{(7)}[0,8,11,12,24] \oplus x_4^{(7)}[2,3,6,7,18,22,23,27]$$

$$\oplus\, x_5^{(7)}[13,14,18,19,25,30,31] \oplus x_{6,7}^{(7)} \oplus x_7^{(7)}[7,13,19,25,30,31] \oplus x_8^{(7)}[11,19,20,27,28]$$

$$\oplus\, x_9^{(7)}[6,12,18,23,24] \oplus x_{11}^{(7)}[18,23,24,26] \oplus x_{12}^{(7)}[0,3,4,6,7,11,12,14,16,18,19,30,31]$$

$$\oplus\, x_{13}^{(7)}[6,7,19,20,30,31] \oplus x_{14}^{(7)}[0,8,24] \oplus x_{15}^{(7)}[0,5,6,11,12,16,19,20,25,26]$$

$$w.p.\frac{1}{2}\left(1+\frac{1}{2^{25}}\right).$$

Proof. The formula expansion for rounds 4 through 6 is the same as in Lemma 6. The expansion from round 6 to round 7 is done by dividing the right-hand side of the Lemma 6 into four groups and expanding each of them as follows.

G1: $x_0^{(6)}[0, 16], x_4^{(6)}[7, 19], x_8^{(6)}[7, 31], x_{12}^{(6)}[11, 12, 19, 20]$

G2: $x_1^{(6)}[11, 12], x_{5,7}^{(6)}, x_{9,12}^{(6)}, x_{13}^{(6)}[6, 7, 18, 19]$

G3: $x_{10,0}^{(6)}, x_{14,0}^{(6)}$

G4: $x_{3,0}^{(6)}, x_7^{(6)}[6, 26], x_{11,12}^{(6)}, x_{15,24}^{(6)}$

Thereafter, each group will expand to 7 rounds. For G1, the equation is expanded as follows.

$$x_{0,0}^{(6)} = x_{0,0}^{(7)} \oplus x_4^{(7)}[7, 19] \oplus x_{8,12}^{(7)} \oplus x_{12,0}^{(7)} \quad w.p.1 \quad (Lemma\ 1),$$

$$x_{4,7}^{(6)} \oplus x_{8,7}^{(6)} = x_0^{(7)}[6, 7] \oplus x_{4,26}^{(7)} \oplus x_{8,19}^{(7)} \oplus x_{12}^{(7)}[14, 15] \quad w.p.\frac{1}{2}\left(1 + \frac{1}{2}\right) \quad (Eq.\ (2)),$$

$$x_{12,11}^{(6)} \oplus x_{12,12}^{(6)} = x_0^{(7)}[11, 12, 27, 28] \oplus x_4^{(7)}[18, 19] \oplus x_8^{(7)}[11, 12] \oplus x_{12}^{(7)}[3, 4]$$
$$w.p.\frac{1}{2}\left(1 + \frac{1}{2}\right) \quad (Lemma\ 4),$$

$$x_{12,19}^{(6)} \oplus x_{12,20}^{(6)} = x_0^{(7)}[3, 4, 19, 20] \oplus x_4^{(7)}[26, 27] \oplus x_8^{(7)}[19, 20] \oplus x_{12}^{(7)}[11, 12]$$
$$w.p.\frac{1}{2}\left(1 + \frac{1}{2}\right) \quad (Lemma\ 4),$$

$$x_{0,16}^{(6)} = x_{0,16}^{(7)} \oplus x_4^{(7)}[2, 3, 22, 23] \oplus x_8^{(7)}[27, 28] \oplus x_{12}^{(7)}[15, 16]$$
$$w.p.\frac{1}{2}\left(1 + \frac{1}{2^3}\right) \quad (Lemma\ 3),$$

$$x_{4,19}^{(6)} = x_{4,6}^{(7)} \oplus x_8^{(7)}[19, 31] \oplus x_{12}^{(7)}[18, 19] \quad w.p.\frac{1}{2}\left(1 + \frac{1}{2}\right) \quad (Lemma\ 2),$$

$$x_{8,31}^{(6)} = x_0^{(7)}[30, 31] \oplus x_{8,31}^{(7)} \oplus x_{12}^{(7)}[6, 7, 30, 31] \quad w.p.\frac{1}{2}\left(1 + \frac{1}{2^2}\right) \quad (Lemma\ 2).$$

Therefore, we get

$$x_0^{(6)}[0, 16] \oplus x_4^{(6)}[7, 19] \oplus x_8^{(6)}[7, 31] \oplus x_{12}^{(6)}[11, 12, 19, 20]$$
$$= x_0^{(7)}[0, 3, 4, 6, 7, 11, 12, 16, 19, 20, 27, 28, 30, 31]$$
$$\oplus x_4^{(7)}[2, 3, 6, 7, 18, 22, 23, 27] \oplus x_8^{(7)}[11, 19, 20, 27, 28]$$
$$\oplus x_{12}^{(7)}[0, 3, 4, 6, 7, 11, 12, 14, 16, 18, 19, 30, 31]$$
$$w.p.\frac{1}{2}\left(1 + \frac{1}{2^9}\right). \tag{5}$$

For G2, the equation is expanded as follows.

$$x_{1,11}^{(6)} \oplus x_{1,12}^{(6)} \oplus x_{9,12}^{(6)} = x_5^{(7)}[18,19,30,31] \oplus x_9^{(7)}[12,23,24] \oplus x_{13}^{(7)}[10,11,19,20]$$

$$w.p.\frac{1}{2}\left(1+\frac{1}{2^4}\right) \quad (Eq.~(3)),$$

$$x_{13,6}^{(6)} \oplus x_{13,7}^{(6)} = x_1^{(7)}[6,7,22,23] \oplus x_5^{(7)}[13,14] \oplus x_9^{(7)}[6,7] \oplus x_{13}^{(7)}[30,31]$$

$$w.p.\frac{1}{2}\left(1+\frac{1}{2}\right) \quad (Lemma~4),$$

$$x_{13,18}^{(6)} \oplus x_{13,19}^{(6)} = x_1^{(7)}[2,3,18,19] \oplus x_5^{(7)}[25,26] \oplus x_9^{(7)}[18,19] \oplus x_{13}^{(7)}[10,11]$$

$$w.p.\frac{1}{2}\left(1+\frac{1}{2}\right) \quad (Lemma~4),$$

$$x_{5,7}^{(6)} = x_{5,26}^{(7)} \oplus x_9^{(7)}[7,19] \oplus x_{13}^{(7)}[6,7] \quad w.p.\frac{1}{2}\left(1+\frac{1}{2}\right) \quad (Lemma~2).$$

$$(6)$$

As a result, we obtain.

$$x_1^{(6)}[11,12] \oplus x_{5,7}^{(6)} \oplus x_{9,12}^{(6)} \oplus x_{13}^{(6)}[6,7,18,19] = x_1^{(7)}[2,3,6,718,19,22,23]$$

$$\oplus x_5^{(7)}[13,14,18,19,25,30,31]$$

$$\oplus x_9^{(7)}[6,12,18,23,24] \oplus x_{13}^{(7)}[6,7,19,20,30,31] \quad w.p.\frac{1}{2}\left(1+\frac{1}{2^7}\right)$$

$$(7)$$

For G3, the equation is expanded as follows.

$$x_{10,0}^{(6)} = x_{2,0}^{(7)} \oplus x_{10,0}^{(7)} \oplus x_{14}^{(7)}[0,8] \quad w.p.1 \quad (Lemma~1),$$

$$x_{14,0}^{(6)} = x_2^{(7)}[0,16] \oplus x_{6,7}^{(7)} \oplus x_{10,0}^{(7)} \oplus x_{14,24}^{(7)} \quad w.p.1 \quad (Lemma~1).$$

Therefore, we get

$$x_{10,0}^{(6)} \oplus x_{14,0}^{(6)} = x_{2,16}^{(7)} \oplus x_{6,7}^{(7)} \oplus x_{14}^{(7)}[0,8,24] \quad w.p.1. \quad (8)$$

For G4, each equation is expanded as follows.

$$x_{3,0}^{(6)} = x_{3,0}^{(7)} \oplus x_7^{(7)}[7,19] \oplus x_{11,12}^{(7)} \oplus x_{15,0}^{(7)} \quad w.p.1 \quad (Lemma~1),$$

$$x_{7,6}^{(6)} = x_{7,25}^{(7)} \oplus x_{11}^{(7)}[6,18] \oplus x_{15}^{(7)}[5,6] \quad w.p.\frac{1}{2}\left(1+\frac{1}{2}\right) \quad (Lemma~2),$$

$$x_{7,26}^{(6)} = x_{7,13}^{(7)} \oplus x_{11}^{(7)}[6,26] \oplus x_{15}^{(7)}[25,26] \quad w.p.\frac{1}{2}\left(1+\frac{1}{2}\right) \quad (Lemma~2),$$

$$x_{11,12}^{(6)} = x_3^{(7)}[11,12] \oplus x_{11,12}^{(7)} \oplus x_{15}^{(7)}[11,12,19,20] \quad w.p.\frac{1}{2}\left(1+\frac{1}{2^2}\right) \quad (Lemma~2),$$

$$x_{15,24}^{(6)} = x_3^{(7)}[8,24] \oplus x_7^{(7)}[30,31] \oplus x_{11}^{(7)}[23,24] \oplus x_{15,16}^{(7)} \quad w.p.\frac{1}{2}\left(1+\frac{1}{2}\right) \quad (Lemma~2).$$

Consequently, we obtain.

$$x_{3,0}^{(6)} \oplus x_7^{(6)}[6,26] \oplus x_{11,12}^{(6)} \oplus x_{15,24}^{(6)} = x_3^{(7)}[0,8,11,12,24]$$
$$\oplus x_7^{(7)}[7,13,19,25,30,31] \oplus x_{11}^{(7)}[18,23,24,26] \tag{9}$$
$$\oplus x_{15}^{(7)}[0,5,6,11,12,16,19,20,25,26] \quad w.p. \frac{1}{2}\left(1+\frac{1}{2^5}\right).$$

From the above Eqs. (5), (7), (8), (9) and Lemma 6, we get Lemma 7. The bias of this linear approximation, $2^{-(4+9+7+0+5)=2^{-25}}$, immediately follows.

4.3   Differential Part

In this section, we focus on the differential part. We aim to find input differentials $\mathcal{ID}$ position that results in a higher bias at $\mathcal{OD}$. The $\mathcal{ID}$ candidates are x_{12}, x_{13}, x_{14}, x_{15} with 128 possible positions. We selected $(12,0)$ as the $\mathcal{ID}$ position to investigate the differential bias. To calculate the bias[1], we ran the experiment with a total complexity of 2^{40}, involving 2^{10} key trials and 2^{30} samples of IVs. The median bias was computed based on the 2^{10} key trials.

$$Pr\left(\Delta x_{3,0}^{(4)} | \Delta x_{12,0}^{(0)}\right) = 0.00002, \quad \epsilon_d = 2^{-15.6}.$$

Considering the median bias, $2^{32.2}$ samples are enough to distinguish between two events.

4.4   Computational Complexity

We use the results in Subsects. 4.2 and 4.3 to compute the computational complexity of the attack using our analysis. First, we conducted the following experiments on the bias of Lemma 6.

Computational Result 1. *Experiments with a linear approximation of the Lemma 6 for 2^{30} random samples yielded the probabilities as $\epsilon_{L_0} = 2^{-3.5849}$. Next, we conduct the following experiments on the bias of the Lemma 7.*

Computational Result 2. *We experimented with a linear approximation of Lemma 7 on a random sample of 2^{30}. We experiment separately with Eqs. (5), (7), (8), and (9), which are linear approximations of each group within Lemma 7. Letting each bias be ϵ_{L_1}, ϵ_{L_2}, ϵ_{L_3}, and ϵ_{L_4}, we obtain $\epsilon_{L_1} = 2^{-7.5979}, \epsilon_{L_2} = 2^{-6.6622}, \epsilon_{L_3} = 1, \quad \epsilon_{L_4} = 2^{-4.5855}.$*

The computational complexity of Differential-Linear analysis for ChaCha is obtained by $\mathcal{O}\left(\frac{1}{\epsilon_d^2 \epsilon_L^4}\right)$. Now, since $\epsilon_d = 2^{-15.6}$ and ϵ_L is $\epsilon_L = \epsilon_{L_0}\epsilon_{L_1}\epsilon_{L_2}\epsilon_{L_3}\epsilon_{L_4} = 2^{-(3.5849+7.5979+6.6622+0+4.5855)} = 2^{-22.4304}$. We get $\epsilon_d \epsilon_L^2 = 2^{-60.4}$. Therefore, the computational complexity of the analysis in this study is $2^{120.9}$.

---

[1] We conducted the differential bias experiment on an Intel(R) Xeon(R) CPU E7-4830 v4 @ 2.00GHz machine with Ubuntu 21.0 OS. In addition, we used the Maximum Length Sequence Random Number Generator.

Table 3. Number of rounds for the differential and linear part in this study and in [9].

	differential part	linear part
[9]	3	4
this work	4	3

Table 4. ID/OD of the differential part in this study and in [9].

	ID	OD
[9]	$\Delta x_{14,6}^{(0)}$	$\Delta x_{3,0}^{(3)} \oplus \Delta x_{4,0}^{(3)}$
this work	$\Delta x_{12,0}^{(0)}$	$\Delta x_{3,0}^{(4)}$

5   A Comparative Analysis of Our Research Findings and Existing Studies

In this section, our results are compared with the existing study [9]. The number of rounds for the differential part and the linear part were as shown in Table 3. In this study, we adopted a form with one more round of the differential part and one less round of the linear part than the one used in [9]. The $\mathcal{ID}$ and $\mathcal{OD}$ in the differential part are as shown in Table 4. The bias in Differential-Linear analysis can be increased by setting the output differential to 2 bits, as in [9]. In fact, in [9], the 3-round OD is expanded to a 5-round linear approximation as in Eq. (10).

$$x_{3,0}^{(3)} \oplus x_{4,0}^{(3)} = x_{1,0}^{(5)} \oplus x_{3,0}^{(5)} \oplus x_{4,26}^{(5)} \oplus x_{7,7}^{(5)} \oplus x_{7,19}^{(5)} \oplus x_{8,7}^{(5)} \oplus x_{8,19}^{(5)} \oplus x_{9,0}^{(5)} \oplus x_{11,12}^{(5)}$$
$$\oplus x_{12,6}^{(5)} \oplus x_{12,7}^{(5)} \oplus x_{13,0}^{(5)} \oplus x_{13,8}^{(5)} \oplus x_{15,0}^{(5)} \quad w.p. \frac{1}{2}\left(1 + \frac{1}{2}\right).$$

(10)

On the other hand, differential analysis with multiple bits of $\mathcal{OD}$ may result in a smaller bias than when the $\mathcal{OD}$ is a single bit (Table 5).

Table 5. Bias of each part in this study and in the [9]

	ϵ_d	ϵ_L
[9]	$2^{-11.02}$	$2^{-111.86}$
this work	$2^{-15.6}$	$2^{-22.4304}$

6   Conclusion

In this study, we used Differential-Linear Cryptanalysis to attack the 7-round ChaCha, significantly reducing computational complexity. Our new linear approximation from 4 to 7 rounds was experimentally confirmed, along with biases.

Acknowledgement. This work is partially supported by JSPS KAKENHI Grant Number JP21H03443 and SECOM Science and Technology Foundation.

References

1. Aumasson, J.-P., Fischer, S., Khazaei, S., Meier, W., Rechberger, C.: New features of Latin dances: analysis of Salsa, ChaCha, and Rumba. In: Nyberg, K. (ed.) FSE 2008. LNCS, vol. 5086, pp. 470–488. Springer, Heidelberg (2008). https://doi.org/10.1007/978-3-540-71039-4_30
2. Beierle, C., Broll, M., Canale, F., David, N., Flórez-Gutiérrez, A., Leander, G., Naya-Plasencia, M., Todo, Y.: Improved differential-linear attacks with applications to ARX ciphers. J. Cryptol. **35**(4), 29 (2022). https://doi.org/10.1007/s00145-022-09437-z
3. Beierle, C., Leander, G., Todo, Y.: Improved differential-linear attacks with applications to ARX ciphers. In: Micciancio, D., Ristenpart, T. (eds.) CRYPTO 2020, Part III. LNCS, vol. 12172, pp. 329–358. Springer, Cham (2020). https://doi.org/10.1007/978-3-030-56877-1_12
4. Bellini, E., Gerault, D., Grados, J., Makarim, R.H., Peyrin, T.: Boosting differential-linear cryptanalysis of ChaCha7 with MILP. ToSC **2023**(2), 189–223 (2023)
5. Bernstein, D.J.: ChaCha, a variant of Salsa20. In: Workshop Record of SASC, pp. 1–6 (2008)
6. Biham, E., Shamir, A.: Differential cryptanalysis of DES-like cryptosystems. J. Cryptol. **4**(1), 3–72 (1991). https://doi.org/10.1007/BF00630563
7. Choudhuri, A.R., Maitra, S.: Significantly improved multi-bit differentials for reduced round salsa and ChaCha. IACR Trans. Symmetric Cryptol. **2016**(2), 261–287 (2016)
8. Coutinho, M., Neto, T.: New multi-bit differentials to improve attacks against ChaCha. IACR Cryptology ePrint Archive 2020/350 (2020)
9. Coutinho, M., Souza Neto, T.C.: Improved linear approximations to ARX ciphers and attacks against ChaCha. In: Canteaut, A., Standaert, F.-X. (eds.) EUROCRYPT 2021, Part I. LNCS, vol. 12696, pp. 711–740. Springer, Cham (2021). https://doi.org/10.1007/978-3-030-77870-5_25
10. Coutinho, M., Passos, I., Grados Vásquez, J.C., de Mendonça, F.L., de Sousa Jr, R.T., Borges, F.: Latin dances reloaded: improved cryptanalysis against salsa and ChaCha, and the proposal of Forró. In: Agrawal, S., Lin, D. (eds.) ASIACRYPT 2022, Part I. LNCS, vol. 13791, pp. 256–286. Springer, Cham (2023). https://doi.org/10.1007/978-3-031-22963-3_9
11. Dey, S., Garai, H.K., Maitra, S.: Cryptanalysis of reduced round ChaCha-new attack and deeper analysis. Cryptology ePrint Archive (2023)
12. Dey, S., Garai, H.K., Sarkar, S., Sharma, N.K.: Revamped differential-linear cryptanalysis on reduced round ChaCha. In: Dunkelman, O., Dziembowski, S. (eds.) EUROCRYPT 2022, Part III. LNCS, vol. 13277, pp. 86–114. Springer, Cham (2022). https://doi.org/10.1007/978-3-031-07082-2_4
13. Dey, S., Sarkar, S.: Improved analysis for reduced round Salsa and ChaCha. Discrete Appl. Math. **227**, 58–69 (2017)
14. Ghafoori, N., Miyaji, A.: Differential cryptanalysis of Salsa20 based on comprehensive analysis of PNBs. In: Su, C., Gritzalis, D., Piuri, V. (eds.) ISPEC 2022. LNCS, vol. 13620, pp. 520–536. Springer, Cham (2022). https://doi.org/10.1007/978-3-031-21280-2_29

15. Langford, S.K., Hellman, M.E.: Differential-linear cryptanalysis. In: Desmedt, Y.G. (ed.) CRYPTO 1994. LNCS, vol. 839, pp. 17–25. Springer, Heidelberg (1994). https://doi.org/10.1007/3-540-48658-5_3
16. Langley, A., Chang, W., Mavrogiannopoulos, N., Strombergson, J., Josefsson, S.: ChaCha20-Poly1305 cipher suites for transport layer security (TLS). Technical report (2016)
17. Maitra, S.: Chosen IV cryptanalysis on reduced round ChaCha and Salsa. Discrete Appl. Math. **208**, 88–97 (2016)
18. Matsui, M.: Linear cryptanalysis method for DES cipher. In: Helleseth, T. (ed.) EUROCRYPT 1993. LNCS, vol. 765, pp. 386–397. Springer, Heidelberg (1994). https://doi.org/10.1007/3-540-48285-7_33
19. Miyashita, S., Ito, R., Miyaji, A.: PNB-focused differential cryptanalysis of ChaCha stream cipher. Cryptology ePrint Archive, Report 2021/1537 (2021). https://ia.cr/2021/1537
20. Niu, Z., Sun, S., Liu, Y., Li, C.: Rotational differential-linear distinguishers of ARX ciphers with arbitrary output linear masks. In: Dodis, Y., Shrimpton, T. (eds.) CRYPTO 2022, Part I. LNCS, vol. 13507, pp. 3–32. Springer, Cham (2022). https://doi.org/10.1007/978-3-031-15802-5_1
21. Shi, Z., Zhang, B., Feng, D., Wu, W.: Improved key recovery attacks on reduced-round Salsa20 and ChaCha. In: Kwon, T., Lee, M.-K., Kwon, D. (eds.) ICISC 2012. LNCS, vol. 7839, pp. 337–351. Springer, Heidelberg (2013). https://doi.org/10.1007/978-3-642-37682-5_24

SP-Fuzz: Fuzzing Soft PLC
with Semi-automated Harness Synthesis

Seungho Jeon(iD) and Jung Taek Seo$^{(\boxtimes)}$ (iD)

Gachon University, Seongnam-daero 1342, Seongnam-si, Republic of Korea
{shjeon90,seojt}@gachon.ac.kr

Abstract. A programmable logic controller (PLC) is an essential component to automatically control field devices in the industrial control system (ICS). Before the PLC is deployed in the field, vulnerabilities should be removed in advance by sufficiently testing the runtime. However, commercial soft PLCs have a closed-source ecosystem, and it is difficult to find vulnerabilities using fuzzing due to the non-stop operational characteristics. To address this problem, several studies have been presented for testing the soft PLCs with a fuzz harness, a small code snippet replicating the target. Unfortunately, most of them are not clearly show how to synthesize the harness and rely on extreme reverse engineering. In this paper, we propose SP-Fuzz, a toolkit for fuzzing soft PLCs by overcoming these challenges. SP-Fuzz provides a semi-automated method to create a fuzz harness based on collecting context information during the execution of PLC runtime. The fuzzer uncovers potential vulnerabilities by testing synthesized harnesses without directly testing the PLC runtime. In an evaluation with known vulnerabilities, SP-Fuzz successfully synthesized the harness and reproduced the vulnerabilities.

Keywords: Soft PLC · Fuzzing · Dynamic tracking · Harness generation

1 Introduction

A programmable logic controller (PLC) is an essential component that automatically controls industrial control systems (ICS) processes. PLCs are largely divided into hard PLCs [1] and soft PLCs [2]. Hard PLCs provide high reliability for process control by using dedicated hardware to execute the control logic and strictly adhering to cycle times for instruction execution. On the other hand, soft PLCs use a runtime implemented as software to execute the control logic. Also, a real-time operating system (RTOS) is adopted to ensure response time for process control. Soft PLCs are used even though they provide lower reliability than hard PLCs because they are cost-effective and, in some cases, the runtime can be customized.

Soft PLC is structurally similar to a general embedded system equipped with an operating system, and PLC runtime operates as a single program. Therefore, if an attacker exploits a runtime's vulnerability, the assets related to the PLC will be significantly affected. Therefore, security vulnerabilities should be removed in advance by sufficiently testing the runtime before the PLC is deployed in the field [3].

Fuzzing is a popular security testing method. The target program is executed with ill-formed input values randomly generated by the fuzzer, and the fuzzer observes the testing results [4]. Although fuzzing is a lightweight and scalable testing method, there are some challenges to testing the PLC runtime. 1) Fuzzer quickly and repeatedly tests a target. However, fuzz testing is difficult to efficiently test the PLC runtime because the PLC runtime continuously executes the control logic without termination. 2) PLC runtime includes various functionalities such as control logic execution, command sending-and-receiving, and scheduling. Testing all the functionalities simultaneously can make it difficult to reproduce the crash, even if the fuzzer found one. 3) Most modern fuzzers use the target's source code to conduct coverage-guided fuzzing. However, soft PLCs are mostly commercial products, making securing source codes challenging.

We focus on the first two of the presented challenges. A popular method to solve them is to write a harness (or fuzz driver) and use it for fuzzing [5–7]. A harness is a small piece of code that implements a simplified implementation of the target's functionality. However, most of the studies on automating the harness writing target open-source projects, so they are not suitable for testing soft PLCs [6, 7]. WINNIE [5] presented a method for automatically synthesizing harnesses for closed source programs, but it is aimed at the Windows environment, so it cannot be applied to soft PLCs that are generally based on Linux. Some studies have been presented to test the soft PLCs with the harness and successfully discovered the vulnerabilities [8, 9].

In this paper, we overcome the above challenges and propose a testing framework, SP-Fuzz, for the runtime of soft PLCs. SP-Fuzz consists of two major components: A semi-automated harness generator and a fuzzer. In order to create a reliable harness reflecting the semantics of the PLC runtime, the runtime tracer executes the PLC runtime. It collects various information, such as invoked functions and their arguments. Based on information collected through runtime tracer and reverse engineering, a harness is manually synthesized by rebuilding the PLC runtime's control and data flow. Finally, the fuzzer runs the generated harness to find bugs or potential vulnerabilities. Several evaluations were conducted to evaluate the SP-Fuzz. Through a comparative study, we confirmed that SP-Fuzz is more suitable for PLC runtime testing than existing fuzzers. Next, unit tests were run on several simple library functions, and SP-Fuzz successfully found bugs in all functions. We conducted a case study with previously reported CVEs for evaluating the effectiveness of SP-Fuzz. SP-Fuzz successfully synthesized the harnesses and reproduces the vulnerabilities. The contributions of this paper are as follows.

- We implemented a runtime tracer working on ARM processor to collect context information during the execution of soft PLC.
- We wrote a fuzz harness using information collected through the runtime tracer and reverse engineering.
- We implemented SP-Fuzz, a toolkit that semi-automates the above process. In addition, through evaluation with known vulnerabilities, it was shown that SP-Fuzz reveals its effectiveness for security testing for soft PLCs.

The remainder of this paper is organized as follows. Section 2 presents studies related to fuzzing for soft PLCs. In Sect. 3, we describe the architecture of a typical soft PLC. Section 4 describes the details of the proposed SP-Fuzz, and Sect. 5 comprehensively evaluates the performance of the SP-Fuzz. Finally, we discuss some limitations of SP-Fuzz in Sect. 6 and summarize this paper in Sect. 7.

2 Related Research

American fuzzy lop (AFL) is one of the most successful coverage-guided fuzzers and has been adopted in various studies [4, 10, 11]. AFL inserts instruments into the target program's source code while compiling it and receives coverage information about the test case during testing. By utilizing test cases with high coverage in the next fuzzing loop, AFL can test the target effectively. This grey-box fuzzing strategy is adopted by various modern fuzzers [12, 13]. Fuzz testing is applied to testing devices used in ICS, including PLC.

Although the grey-box fuzzing reveals its efficiency, most commercial software has a closed-source ecosystem. So, fuzzers cannot insert the instruments into the source code. To overcome this limitation, the fuzz harness can be adopted to efficiently test the closed-source programs [5]. The fuzz harness is synthesized based on the contextual information of the target, then fuzzers run the harness to find vulnerabilities, instead of directly run the target.

Recently, above strategy has been employed to test devices in ICS environment. IFFSET presented various toolsets for fuzzing the PLC runtime using the QEMU emulator [8]. However, IFFSET showed its inefficiency in the fuzzing process because the instrument could not be used during the fuzzing process. ICSFuzz, a follow-up study of IFFSET, implemented an instrument using a binary patch to overcome this limitation [9]. ICSFuzz measures code coverage and enables more efficient fuzz testing. Both IFFSET and ICSFuzz have succeeded in finding crashes in the PLC runtime but rely solely on reverse engineering the harness writing.

3 Preliminary

The soft PLC's software stack consists of several layers: hardware layer, operating system layer, library layer, PLC runtime layer, and service layer. The hardware layer consists of several components, but the most important components are the processor and the input/output ports. Soft PLC products generally use ARM-based processors and general-purpose input/output ports (GPIOs). With these hardware specifications, the soft PLC uses a Linux-based RTOS to ensure a fast response time. Common Linux binaries and services such as coreutils operate on the OS, and various libraries are included. The soft PLC provides libraries to implement functions as a PLC, and the functions provided by these libraries are used to write PLC runtime and control logic. Most PLC runtimes running on Linux-based RTOS are in the ELF-formatted file and provide various services such as driving control logic and interacting with users. A service (or task) in the PLC runtime usually operates as a thread. The control logic written in structure text or ladder diagram is called an application, and the main task executes this application. Web server task supports web-based monitoring service for PLC. In addition, it provides communication-related primitives or OPC-UA-related functions.

4 Fuzzing Soft PLC with Harness

4.1 Overview

Figure 1 shows an overview of SP-Fuzz. SP-Fuzz consists of two parts: a semi-automated harness generator (Sect. 4.2) and a fuzzer (Sect. 4.3). The harness generator selects one of the tasks running in PLC runtime as a target. We introduce a dynamic execution tracer to collect context information during the execution of a target task. Then, we reconstruct the control-and-data flow of the target task by combining the information from the execution tracer and reverse engineering. Based on the reconstructed control-and-data flow, we manually write the harness. Finally, the synthesized harness is tested by the fuzzer, and if a crash is found during this process, it is reported along with the test case that caused the crash.

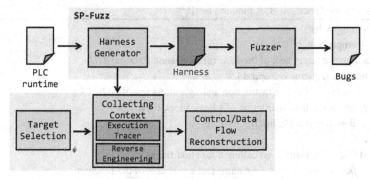

Fig. 1. Overview of SP-Fuzz.

4.2 Semi-automated Harness Generator

The semi-automated harness synthesis proceeds in three stages: target selection, collecting context, and control-and-data flow reconstruction. In this section, we describe each step-in detail.

Target Selection. We select the test target among the running tasks of the PLC runtime. The selection of the fuzzing target is largely composed of two steps. First, it identifies both the thread names and thread ids (TID) of all tasks running as threads in the PLC runtime. This includes the main task, web server, or communication service, as described in Sect. 3. Second, we choose a fuzzing target from among the identified tasks. At this time, the fuzzing target should be able to receive user input. User input includes network and file inputs. We can identify the tasks that allows these inputs through the brief reverse engineering of the PLC runtime. In this way, the crash found by fuzzing the harness can be reproduced in the actual PLC runtime.

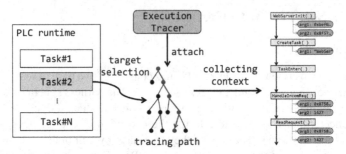

Fig. 2. Collecting context with the execution tracer.

Algorithm 1. Algorithm for collecting dynamic context using execution tracer.

Inputs: *PID* of PLC runtime, *TID* of the task to be traced.
Outputs: A basic block list B, A function list Π.

1	B ← empty list;
2	Π ← empty list;
3	attach to the target task of the PLC runtime using *PID* and *TID*;
4	**While** not *stopping criteria* **do**
5	*addr, inst* ← get one instruction and its address specified by PC;
6	**If** *inst* is the first instruction of a basic block **then**
7	B ← B ∪ {(*addr, inst*)};
8	**end**
9	**If** *inst* is the instruction calling a function **then**
10	*fname, args* ← parse the name and arguments of the function;
11	Π ← Π ∪ {(*addr, inst, fname, args*)};
12	**end**
13	PC ← calculate the next PC;
14	**end**

Collecting Context. Once the target task to be fuzzed is selected, the context information for this task should be gathered. We utilize dynamic analysis to gather this context information. Typically, dynamic taint analysis [14, 15] can be used for this purpose. However, the PLC runtime runs on ARM architecture and lacks reliable taint analysis tools in the ARM environment. Therefore, we implemented a dynamic analysis tool, an execution tracer, using a debugging technique [16]. The execution tracer collects information about executed instructions, the order of functions called, function arguments, and return addresses from target tasks (see Fig. 2). In a program implemented in the C language, function arguments can be largely values, pointers, and structures (or a combination of them). We use the ARM architecture's calling convention [17] to identify function arguments. Then, we determine the type of each function argument. For functions in the PLC library, application programming interfaces (APIs) specifications provided by the manufacturer can be adopted to find the type of arguments. Otherwise, if a function not included in the PLC APIs is observed, the type is inferred according to the following rules. First, if an argument has a value other than an address, it is simply considered a value. Second, if the argument's value is included in a valid address space, the argument is identified as a pointer type. In the case of pointer-type arguments, they are again classified into simple values, arrays/delimiters, and strings.

Algorithm 1 is an algorithm that collects context information during execution from target tasks in PLC runtime using the execution tracer. This algorithm takes the process ID (*PID*) of the PLC runtime and the target task's thread ID (*TID*). The execution tracer attaches to a PLC runtime process/task based on this information. Then, this algorithm repeatedly performs the following process for every instruction until the target task is terminated or context collection is stopped. First, the tracer gets the instruction *inst* and the address *addr* pointed to by the current PC register. If *inst* is the first instruction of a basic block, it is recorded in the list B of the executed basic block. Next, we check if *inst* is an instruction that calls a function, and if so, we parse the name *fname* of the called function and its arguments *args*. The aforementioned method is used to identify the argument list. The identified *fname* and *args* are kept in the list Π of functions called with *addr* and inst. When context collection ends, this algorithm returns B and Π.

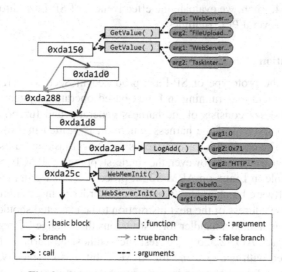

Fig. 3. Reconstructing the control-and-data flow.

Control-and-Data Flow Reconstruction. The execution tracer makes it easy to collect context information during the execution of a target task. However, since only executed control flows can be observed, information, such as unexecuted branches, is easy to miss. Therefore, when the execution path and called function are specified using the execution tracer, the correct control flow is restored through reverse engineering. In this process, branch statements or loop statements are imported into the control flow, and to reduce the complexity of the harness to be synthesized, we made branches not observed by the execution tracer end with normal termination (e.g., exit(0)). Once the control flow is restored, data flow is restored using function arguments collected by the execution tracer. Also, by identifying variables and arguments affected by external input, we can specify where to deliver the test cases generated by the fuzzer. Figure 3 is an example of a control-and-data flow reconstructed through the above process[1]. Finally, we manually write the harness using the reconstructed control and data flow.

4.3 Fuzzing the Harness

SP-Fuzz tests the PLC runtime using the harness generated in the previous step. Most modern fuzzers have adopted the grey-box fuzzing strategy, inserting instruments while compiling the source code. However, obviously, we cannot obtain the source code of the PLC runtime because we have to test the off-the-shelf PLC runtime. So, instead of a grey-box fuzzing strategy, we test the harness in a black-box setting. If SP-Fuzz finds a crash while testing the harness, it reports the crash along with a test case.

5   Evaluation

In this section, we describe the implementation details and experimental setup of SP-Fuzz proposed in Sect. 4. Then, we evaluate the effectiveness of SP-Fuzz through published vulnerabilities for several PLC runtimes.

5.1   Implementation

We implemented the prototype of SP-Fuzz proposed in Sect. 4. Currently, SP-Fuzz can only test PLC runtimes running in Linux-based operating systems on ARM 32-bit processors. SP-Fuzz consists of the harness generator and fuzzer. The execution tracer, the core component of the harness generator, is written in 1.6K lines of code (LoC) in C code. The execution tracer attaches to a target task and uses ptrace [16] to trace all executed instructions. However, the single-stepping (PTRACE_SINGLESTEP) option is unavailable in Linux on ARM 32-bit processors, so we implemented single-stepping using software breakpoints. In addition, in order to insert a breakpoint at the correct location, the address of the next instruction to be executed should be accurately predicted. We implemented a handler for instructions that change PC registers.

Next, we adopted AFL-2.52b [4] to test the synthesized harness. Note that AFL should be compiled with gcc or clang for ARM 32-bit. Also, typically, AFL receives coverage information by inserting an instrument while compiling the source code of the target program using afl-gcc. However, since the source code for the off-the-shelf PLC runtime is unavailable, and the use of afl-gcc is limited in the ARM 32-bit environment, we run AFM in dumb mode instead of grey-box fuzzing.

Last but not least, we developed a simple framework that makes it easy to write harness from contextual information gathered through execution tracers and reverse engineering. This framework was implemented inspired by LLVM [18]'s libFuzzer [19]. In other words, if we simply write a function(test_one_input)[2] that takes the test case from the fuzzer and passes it to the code to be tested, the harness program is compiled by the framework.

---

[1] Figure 3 shows the simplified control and data flow of one part of the PLC runtime. The function names and arguments used in this figure are slightly different from those used in actual PLC runtime.

[2] This simple function is designed to do the same thing as libFuzzer's LLVMFuzzerTestOneInput.

5.2 Experimental Setup

In this experiment, we adopted WAGO PFC100 as the testing target to verify the effectiveness of SP-Fuzz. The WAGO PFC100 is one of the popular soft PLCs equipped with the PLC Runtime developed by Codesys (hereafter Codesys Runtime). We can connect to WAGO PLC through protocols like SSH, but Codesys runtime testing is difficult because there is no compiler, debugger, or fuzzer in the PLC's firmware. Therefore, we evaluated the performance of SP-Fuzz by importing Codesys runtime binaries and related shared libraries on Raspbian, an operating system using an ARM 32-bit processor. In addition, for easy configuration of the experimental environment, a lower versioned Codesys runtime was adopted for evaluation.

5.3 Comparative Study

We conducted a comparative study between the fuzzers on the following four key features for closed-source PLC runtimes (see Table 1). 'Coverage feedback' indicates whether the fuzzer receives coverage information from the target during fuzzing campaign. 'Harness automation' checks fully or partially automating harness synthesis. 'Native run' means testing without the aid of an emulator like QEMU. 'ARM base' indicates whether the ARM-based process can be tested. As a result of comparative analysis, AFL and WINNIE are not suitable for testing PLC runtimes in terms of processor architecture or harness synthesis. IFFSET and ICSFuzz originally target programs on soft PLCs. However, IFFSET is difficult to efficiently do fuzzing the PLC runtimes. ICSFuzz is not scalable because it relies purely on human efforts for harness synthesis. In contrast, SP-Fuzz has features other than coverage feedback, so its efficiency is somewhat lower, but it has higher scalability than ICSFuzz.

Table 1. Comparison between the fuzzers for closed-source PLC runtimes.

Fuzzer	Coverage feedback	Harness automation	Native run	ARM base
AFL	X	X	O	O
WINNIE	O	O	O	X
IFFSET	X	X	X	O
ICSFuzz	O	X	O	O
SP-Fuzz	X	O	O	O

5.4 Unit Test

We performed unit tests on several library functions used in the Codesys runtime. SP-Fuzz observes the execution flow of Codesys runtime and synthesizes harnesses based on contextual information at the time library functions are called. Table 2 shows the unit test results for the four functions. The Codesys runtime often uses these functions to take external inputs. We run each harness for an hour, and SP-Fuzz successfully found crashes for all functions. All crashes were related to a buffer overflow. However, since the Codesys runtime strictly limits the values assigned to the parameters of these functions, the discovered crashes are difficult to reproduce in the Codesys runtime.

Table 2. Fuzzing results for library functions.

Function	Description	Crashes[3]
SysSockRecv	Receiving data through TCP communication	1
SysSockSend	Sending data through TCP communication	1
SysComRead	Reading data from the given file descriptor	1
SysComWrite	Writing data to the given file descriptor	1

5.5 Case Study

We conducted a case study using several known vulnerabilities (CVEs) to evaluate the effectiveness of SP-Fuzz. The CVEs used in this evaluation were selected as related to memory corruption bugs that are easy for fuzzer to find. In addition, one relatively simple vulnerability and one complex vulnerability were each selected. Based on these criteria, we conducted a case study on CVE-2020-7052 [20] and CVE-2020-10245 [21].

5.5.1 CVE-2020-7052

Listing 1. Fuzz harness snippet for CVE-2020-7052.

```
1    // filename is the path to test case generated by fuzzer
2    // base_addr is the base address of shared library
3    int test_one_input (const char* filename, void* base_addr) {
4        int buffer_size, max_channels, tmp;
5        char *ptr1, *ptr2;
6        // read one testcase from filename
7        // skip the code getting the address of functions
8        SettgGetIntValue(..., &buffer_size);
9        SettgGetIntValue(..., &max_channels);
10       if (max_channels <= 0) exit(0);
11       else tmp = 2* max_channels;
12       // skip the complicated code
13       ptr1 = SysMemAllocData(...);
14       ptr2 = SysMemAllocData(...);
15       if (ptr1 == NULL || ptr2 == NULL) abort();
16   }
```

---

[3] We deduplicated the discovered crashes.

Listing 1 is a code snippet of the harness created through the context information that SP-Fuzz's harness generator collects from CmpChannelServer, which manages communication channels among Codesys runtime components. Originally, CmpChannelServer reads the values of BufferSize and MaxChannels in signed integer type from the configuration file using the SettgGetValue function. This harness assigns fuzzer-generated values to these variables instead of reading them from a configuration file. These variables intervene in dynamically allocating heap memory through a complex operation process. If a large positive number is assigned to BufferSize or MaxChannels, or a value, which becomes a negative value by multiplying an appropriate integer due to integer overflow, is assigned, the SemMemAllocData function may fail to allocate heap memory, causing a bug. This bug leads to a denial-of-service vulnerability and was reported as CVE-2020-7052 [20].

5.5.2 CVE-2020-10245

Listing 2. Fuzz harness snippet for CmpWebServer regarding CVE-2020-10245.

```
1     // filename is the path to z
2     // base_addr is the base address of shared library
3     int test_one_input (const char* filename, void* base_addr) {
4         // read one testcase from filename
5         // skip the code getting the address of functions
6         // set payload for WEB_CLIENT_OPENCONNECTION
7         WebServerHandler();
8         // set payload for WEB_CLIENT_RUN_SERVICE
9         WebServerHandler();
10        // skip writing data to allocated memory
11    }
```

Listing 2 is the harness of the code that CmpWebServer processes HTTP packets. CmpWebServer is a web server of Codesys runtime and serves as a web-based human-machine interface (HMI) and some kind of representational state transfer (REST) API server. WebServerHandler parses request (inputs) in a specific format to perform designated functions. Instead of listening for HTTP requests, this harness passes fuzzer-generated test cases as input to WebServerHandler. First, this harness passes the WEB_CLIENT_OPENCONNECTION message to open a connection and requests the memory size to be allocated dynamically. Then, the WEB_CLIENT_RUN_SERVICE message is passed, and the heap chunk is allocated. The heap chunk size for allocating memory is the heap size requested with the WEB_CLIENT_OPENCONNECTION message plus a small integer. This triggers an integer overflow bug, so very little memory could be allocated despite requesting a large heap chunk. When writing data to the allocated memory, a heap-based buffer overflow occurs. This vulnerability was reported as CVE-2020-10245 [21], and several similar vulnerabilities have been reported.

6 Limitations

Despite the competitive performance of SP-Fuzz shown by the series of experiments, there are still some limitations:

- The biggest challenge in implementing the tracer is to handle system calls. Most system calls in Linux work intuitively like ordinal library functions, but some system calls are not intuitive. These system calls have side effects on the memory, which makes it difficult to collect the exact execution context.
- Many parts have been automated to synthesize the harnesses for fuzzing off-the-shelf PLC runtime, but the harnesses are still written manually. This is because there is no effective means to lift the low-level instructions collected by the tracer into a high-level language such as C. The lifting functionality of tools like Ghidra or IDA pro can help in part to overcome this limitation.
- Currently, SP-Fuzz writes only the path observed by the execution tracer as harnesses. This enables testing of only a very narrow area of the PLC runtime. To deal with this, we can expand the call-graph by automatically exploring the binary around the observed path.
- Currently, SP-Fuzz adopts a black-box fuzzing strategy, so the instrument cannot be used. Accordingly, testing is inefficient because coverage information cannot be utilized during the fuzzing process.

7 Conclusion

In this paper, we proposed SP-Fuzz to test the runtime of soft PLC. SP-Fuzz consists of the harness generator and fuzzer. The harness generator targets one of the PLC runtime's tasks, observes the execution path and context, and synthesizes the harness. AFL tests the generated harness. We verified the effectiveness of SP-Fuzz using Codesys runtime, and as a result of a series of experiments, SP-Fuzz showed competitive performance. Especially, with the known vulnerabilities, SP-Fuzz successfully synthesized the harnesses from the PLC runtime and found the vulnerabilities. With this SP-Fuzz's such capability, we can report the vulnerabilities found in the test before deploying the soft PLC in the field or use other security devices to filter out input values that cause the vulnerabilities. By doing this, the ICS system can be operated more safely. Also, we discussed some limitations of SP-Fuzz. Finally, although Codesys runtime was used to evaluate SP-Fuzz in this paper, the proposed fuzzing process can be sufficiently applied to other soft PLCs with similar software stacks to Codesys runtime.

Acknowledgement. This work was supported by Institute of Information & communications Technology Planning & Evaluation (IITP) grant funded by the Korea government (MSIT) (No. 2021-0-00493, 5G Massive Next Generation Cyber Attack Deception Technology Development).

References

1. SIEMENS. https://www.siemens.com/global/en.html. Accessed 22 May 2023

2. CODESYS GmbH. https://www.codesys.com/. Accessed 22 May 2023
3. Bytes, A., et al.: FieldFuzz: stateful fuzzing of proprietary industrial controllers using injected ghosts. arXiv:2204.13499 (2022)
4. Zalewski, M.: American fuzzy lop. https://lcamtuf.coredump.cx/afl/. Accessed 22 May 2023
5. Jung, J., Tong, S., Hu, H., Lim, J., Jin, Y., Kim, T.: WINNIE: fuzzing windows applications with harness synthesis and fast cloning. In: Proceedings of the 2021 Network and Distributed System Security Symposium (2021)
6. Babić, D., et al.: FUDGE: fuzz driver generation at scale. In: Proceedings of the 2019 27th ACM Joint Meeting on European Software Engineering Conference and Symposium on the Foundations of Software Engineering (2019)
7. Ispoglou, K.K., Austin, D., Mohan, V., Payer, M.: FuzzGen: automatic fuzzer generation. In: Proceedings on the 29th USENIX Security Symposium (2020)
8. Tychalas, D., Maniatakos, M.: IFFSET: in-field fuzzing of industrial control systems using system emulation. In: 2020 Design, Automation & Test in Europe Conference & Exhibition (2020)
9. Tychalas, D., Benkraouda, H., Maniatakos, M.: ICSFuzz: manipulating I/Os and repurposing binary code to enable instrumented fuzzing in ICS control applications. In: USENIX Security Symposium (2021)
10. Böhme, M., Pham, V.-T., Roychoudhury, A.: Coverage-based greybox fuzzing as Markov chain. In: Proceedings of the 2016 ACM SIGSAC Conference on Computer and Communications Security (2016)
11. Jeon, S., Moon, J.: Dr.PathFinder: hybrid fuzzing with deep reinforcement concolic execution toward deeper path-first search. Neural Comput. Appl. **34**, 10731–10750 (2022). https://doi.org/10.1007/s00521-022-07008-8
12. honggfuzz. https://honggfuzz.dev/. Accessed 22 May 2023
13. OSS-Fuzz. https://google.github.io/oss-fuzz/. Accessed 22 May 2023
14. Luk, C.-K., et al.: Pin: building customized program analysis tools with dynamic instrumentation. ACM SIGPLAN Not. **40**(6), 190–200 (2005)
15. Nethercote, N., Seward, J.: Valgrind: a framework for heavyweight dynamic binary instrumentation. ACM SIGPLAN Not. **42**(6), 89–100 (2007)
16. Ptrace(2)-Linux manual page. https://man7.org/linux/man-pages/man2/ptrace.2.html. Accessed 22 May 2023
17. ARM developer: ARM Cortex-A Series Programmer's Guide for ARMv7-A. https://developer.arm.com/documentation/den0013/d/Application-Binary-Interfaces/Procedure-Call-Standard. Accessed 22 May 2023
18. Lattner, C., Adve, V.: LLVM: a compilation framework for lifelong program analysis & transformation. In: International Symposium on Code Generation and Optimization (GGO) (2004)
19. libFuzzer. https://llvm.org/docs/LibFuzzer.html. Accessed 22 May 2023
20. CVE-2020-7052. https://cve.mitre.org/cgi-bin/cvename.cgi?name=CVE-2020-7052. Accessed 22 May 2023
21. CVE-2020-10245. https://cve.mitre.org/cgi-bin/cvename.cgi?name=CVE-2020-10245. Accessed 22 May 2023

Post-Quantum Cryptography
and Quantum Cryptanalysis

Quantum Circuit Designs of Point Doubling Operation for Binary Elliptic Curves

Harashta Tatimma Larasati[ID] and Howon Kim[✉][ID]

School of Computer Science and Engineering, Pusan National University, Busan
609735, Republic of Korea
howonkim@pusan.ac.kr

Abstract. In the past years, research on Shor's algorithm for solving the
elliptic curve discrete logarithm problem (Shor's ECDLP) as the basis
for cracking elliptic curve-based cryptosystems (ECC) has started to gar-
ner significant interest. To achieve this, existing works put their focus on
quantum point addition subroutines to realize the double scalar multiplication circuit essential to Shor's ECDLP. In contrast, the quantum
point doubling subroutines have often been overlooked. In this paper,
we bridge this gap by investigating the quantum point doubling operation to be used for the stricter assumption of Shor's algorithm, i.e.,
when doubling a point should also be taken into consideration. In particular, we analyze the challenges on implementing the circuit and provide
the probable solution. Subsequently, we design and optimize the corresponding quantum circuit, then analyze the high-level quantum resource
cost. Additionally, we discuss the implications of our findings, including
the concerns for its integration with point addition for a complete double scalar multiplication circuit and the potential opportunities resulting
from its implementation. Our work lays the foundation for advancing the
evaluation of Shor's ECDLP.

Keywords: Elliptic curve discrete logarithm problem · Point
doubling · Quantum circuit · Quantum cryptanalysis · Shor's algorithm

1 Introduction

Over the decade, there has been a growing interest in Shor's algorithm for solving the elliptic curve discrete logarithm problem (i.e., Shor's ECDLP) [17,18].

This research was supported by the MSIT (Ministry of Science and ICT), Korea, under
the Convergence security core talent training business (Pusan National University)
support program (IITP-2023-2022-0-01201) supervised by the IITP (Institute for Information & Communications Technology Planning & Evaluation), and by the Institute
for Information & Communications Technology Planning & Evaluation (IITP) grant
funded by the Korean Government (MSIT) (No. 2019-0-00033, Study on Quantum
Security Evaluation of Cryptography based on Computational Quantum Complexity,
50%).

Acknowledged to render existing elliptic curve-based cryptosystems (ECC) breakable in polynomial time [16], this algorithm has the potential to accomplish its objective of cracking existing public-key cryptography (PKC) sooner than its more popular counterpart, i.e., Shor's factoring algorithm for cracking RSA, due to its lower quantum resource requirement for the same security level [9,14]. In particular, the advantage of lower key size in ECC is—ironically—the reason why it becomes in graver danger in the presence of a quantum computer, considering the current development of quantum computing that is still in the early stage, which often favors the number of qubits as the most essential metric.

To date, several works have discussed how to concretely realize Shor's ECDLP for quantum cryptanalysis purposes [1,3,5,11,16], with heavily-referenced state-of-the-art works [1,5,16] primarily assessing the implementation for the superconducting qubits architecture as arguably the most prominent quantum hardware platform. Starting from the works by Roetteler et al. [16] and perfected by Haner et al. [5], which both consider prime curves implementation, the landscape then extends to binary elliptic curves through the work by Banegas et al. [1].

All those advancements are based on the pioneering efforts of Proos and Zalka [14], one of the earliest works to translate the high-level Shor's ECDLP algorithm into the description of their possible quantum circuit derivation. Over time, their paper has established itself as the standard reference for subsequent papers that aims to optimize the quantum circuit implementation of Shor's ECDLP, which has been made easier for testing, verification, and concretely estimating the quantum resource requirement by leveraging reversible circuit and quantum computing simulators emerging in the past decade (e.g., RevKit, LIQ$U i |\rangle$, and the more recent ProjectQ, Qiskit, Microsoft QDK/Azure Quantum, and Q-Crypton).

From our observation, these papers preserve the scope provided by Proos and Zalka [14]. That is, for cracking ECC via Shor's ECDLP, the rule can be simplified by considering only the generic case (i.e., for points $P+R$ where $P, R \neq O$, and $P \neq \pm R$) for the elliptic curve group operation [14]. In other words, to achieve the desired *double scalar multiplication* as the essential component (see Fig. 1), computation will be done solely by a series of *point addition* operations. Meanwhile, the complementing subroutine to perform a more special case where $P = R$, namely the *point doubling* operation, is set aside. The authors of [14] argued that the expected loss of fidelity from its absence would still be negligible, which was also agreed upon by succeeding papers, e.g., [8].

Nevertheless, when considering the stricter assumption where the occurrence of $P = R$ is more probable during computation and minimum fidelity loss is expected from the design, the point doubling will also hold considerable significance. In this case, exploring the point doubling operation, including its quantum circuit construction and the analysis of its quantum resource, will be very beneficial and insightful for a more complete resource estimation of Shor's ECDLP.

In this study, we examine the point doubling operation as required for the less relaxed case of Shor's ECDLP, i.e., when the points to be computed happen to be the same two points. To the best of our knowledge, this subject, including the corresponding quantum circuit implementation, has so far been absent in state-of-the-art works in quantum cryptanalysis. For this initial work, we focus

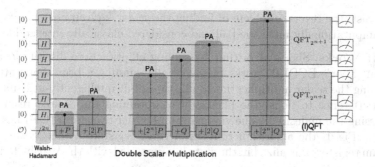

Fig. 1. Quantum circuit of Shor's algorithm for solving the elliptic curve discrete logarithm problem (ECDLP). Figures adapted from [10,16].

on point doubling circuit for binary elliptic curves, whose inherent characteristics make it simpler for tinkering and constructing the operation compared to the prime curves counterpart. To highlight our contributions, we start by analyzing the point-doubling formula and identifying the challenges in its construction with their possible solution. Subsequently, we design the quantum circuits for elliptic curve point doubling to suit several scenarios and analyze its quantum resource cost in a high-level view. Furthermore, we also provide a more detailed discussion of the aspects related to prime curves and the concerns when incorporating the circuit for use in Shor's algorithm.

The contribution of this paper can be summarized as follows:

– We examine the elliptic curve point doubling operation, which is rarely explored in literature. In particular, we discuss the challenges, analyze the formula and the implementation possibility of point doubling circuits for binary elliptic curves.
– We design the corresponding quantum circuit, incorporate several optimization and address the uncomputation, then analyze the high-level quantum resource cost of the circuit.
– We provide an in-depth discussion of our findings and other aspects relevant to point doubling, the concerns when incorporating the circuit with point addition for a complete double scalar multiplication circuit, as well as the open possibilities arising from point doubling implementation.

2 Preliminaries

2.1 Shor's ECDLP

The security of elliptic curve cryptography (ECC) is based on the hardness of the elliptic curve discrete logarithm problem (ECDLP). In this problem, given two points P and Q on an elliptic curve of order r, it is easy to compute the point multiplication $Q = kP$ when the scalar k and the base point P are known.

In contrast, the reverse problem of finding the scalar k given both points P and Q is computationally intensive [16] and considered classically intractable.

How It Works. Shor's algorithm for solving elliptic curve discrete logarithm problem (Shor's ECDLP) works by essentially running a brute-force attack of computing the scalar multiplication of all states, but intelligently utilizing quantum interference to boost the likelihood of obtaining the desired result while suppressing the undesired value via quantum Fourier transform (QFT). As illustrated in Fig. 1, the algorithm consists of three registers with two $n + 1$-sized quantum registers initialized in the state $|0\rangle$ appended with the Walsh-Hadamard (i.e., Hadamard gate on each qubit), which yields the state $\frac{1}{2^{n+1}} \sum_{k,l=0}^{2^{n+1}-1} k, l$. Subsequently, conditional to the state of the register containing k or l, the corresponding multiple of points P and Q are added to the third register of size $2n$ (also called as the *accumulator*) via the double scalar multiplication circuit, performing the mapping as in Eq. 1 [16],

$$\frac{1}{2^{n+1}} \sum_{k,l=0}^{2^{n+1}-1} k, l \mapsto \sum_{k,l=0}^{2^{n+1}-1} k, l \, |[k] P + [l] Q\rangle \tag{1}$$

before appending QFT and measuring the result of the first and second registers. Finally, classical post-processing is performed, which theoretically can yield the sought value with high probability. Consequently, this algorithm enables an adversary with a large-scale, full-fledged quantum computer to obtain the value of k by running the algorithm a few times.

Quantum Scalar Multiplication Circuit. In existing works, as previously shown in Fig. 1, the quantum double scalar multiplication circuit comprises solely of (controlled) point addition subroutines and simplifies the operation by making the added point fixed. However, the use of point addition alone does not cover the case when the appended points and the existing state in the accumulator register are the exact same point, therefore may yield incorrect result when doubling the points [14]. Even though the fidelity loss from this is argued to be small, the stricter case will require the point-doubling circuit as well, which helps to provide a more complete quantum resource analysis for Shor's ECDLP.

2.2 Binary Elliptic Curves in the Quantum Realm

From a quantum cryptanalysis perspective, an ordinary binary elliptic curve is often considered instead of other stronger variants such as supersingular [1]. Here, we first describe the theoretical concept of binary elliptic curves. The Weierstrass equation for an ordinary binary elliptic curve is described in Eq. 2,

$$y^2 + xy = x^3 + ax^2 + b \tag{2}$$

where $a \in \mathbb{F}_2$ and $b \in \mathbb{F}^*_{2^m}$ (the extension field). Then, the points on this elliptic curve, $P = (x, y) \in \mathbb{F}_{2^m}^2$, form a set of points that can be computed under the elliptic curve group law [1] comprising *point addition* and *point doubling* operations. In particular, point addition, e.g., $P_1 + P_2 = P_3$, with $P_1 = (x_1, y_1)$, $P_2 = (x_2, y_2) \neq \pm P_1$, and $P_3 = (x_3, y_3)$, can be computed by following Eqs. 3–5.

$$x_3 = \lambda^2 + \lambda + x_1 + x_2 + a \tag{3}$$

$$y_3 = \lambda(x_1 + x_3) + x_3 + y_1 \tag{4}$$

$$\lambda = \frac{y_1 + y_2}{x_1 + x_2} \tag{5}$$

Meanwhile, the point doubling calculation is as shown in Eqs. 6 to 8 [6,13].

$$x_3 = \lambda^2 + \lambda + a = {x_1}^2 + \frac{b}{{x_1}^2} \tag{6}$$

$$y_3 = {x_1}^2 + (\lambda + 1)x_3 \tag{7}$$

$$\lambda = x_1 + y_1/x_1 \tag{8}$$

Constructing the Quantum Circuit. From the group law formula above, the corresponding quantum circuit can be composed[1]. Regarding the quantum point addition circuit, the recent concrete construction is by Banegas et al. [1], which is presented in Fig. 2. As inferred from the figure, the circuit requires three registers of size n in which two serve as input/output registers and one as a clean ancilla register, plus one qubit serving as the control—which in the full scheme of Shor's ECDLP circuit will be associated with the qubit in the upper registers (the ones appended by Walsh-Hadamard). Additionally, the circuit utilizes two multiplications (M), two divisions (D), and two squaring (S)—all of which are conditionally controlled, linked to the control qubit and other associated register—and several (controlled) additions and addition by a constant.

Quantum Resource Cost. Regarding the exact resource count, however, it will greatly depend on the underlying subroutines since the aforementioned circuit is still a high-level architecture that will be broken down into its finer-grained components. For instance, choosing to use between two different inversion techniques: greatest common divisor (GCD) [1] or Fermat's Little Theorem (FLT) [1,10,19] for the division subroutines, or between Schoolbook [21] and Karatsuba multiplication [2,7,15,20] will yield quite different performance metrics, including in terms of the total number of qubits (i.e., qubit count or circuit width), circuit depth (i.e., the longest path for the quantum operations to run on the quantum hardware, gate count (i.e., the total number of quantum gates), as well as the more specific terms like Toffoli depth and Toffoli count [4,22].

---

[1] All classical computation can be simulated on a quantum computer by reversible gates, e.g., Toffoli (the most common), Fredkin, or Barenco gates [23]. However, how to efficiently perform the operation is a whole different topic pursued by researchers.

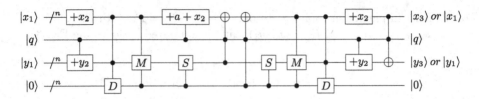

Fig. 2. Point addition circuit for binary elliptic curves by Banegas et al. [1].

3   Quantum Circuit Designs of Point Doubling Operation for Binary Elliptic Curves

In this section, we start by elaborating on the challenges in constructing point-doubling operations. Furthermore, we provide three circuits for point doubling to suit different design considerations.

3.1   Challenges on Quantum Point Doubling Construction

Before going into detail about the point-doubling circuit itself, it would be better to start with the differences between point addition and point doubling from the quantum perspective that we are able to identify. Constructing a point-doubling circuit poses relatively more difficulties than a point-addition circuit. Firstly, to implement point addition, previous works [14] proposed simplification by making one of the two points constant, which is added conditionally depending on the state of the control qubit (i.e., the state of each qubit after being appended by Hadamard gates in the upper registers, see Fig. 1).

With this, the point to be added (i.e., $P_2(x_2, y_2)$) is appended conditionally as a constant; hence can be pre-set and precomputed classically. Furthermore, by making the point a constant, the uncomputation process can be performed with ease since the added point can be immediately subtracted or uncomputed as soon as they are no longer needed in the calculation, making it practical and more efficient. Secondly, as mentioned in [14] and then elaborated in [16], looking further at the point addition formulas (Eqs. 3 to 5), the value of λ in point addition has a direct, clear relation with both x_1 and x_3, as well as y_1 and y_3. That is, x_3 can be obtained from appending x_2 and λ to x_1 (with other relevant operations to yield Eq. 3), and similarly, y_3 can be obtained from appending y_1 and λ to y_1 (with other relevant operations to yield Eq. 4). Here, we say that the initial state of x_1 and y_1 can be "consumed" to obtain the final desired computation. Then, by intelligently arranging the circuit, we can straightforwardly transform the initial state (x_1, y_1) to the subsequent state (x_3, y_3). As a result, an efficient computation (and uncomputation) can be achieved, and a clear reversibility relationship can be maintained.

On the other hand, the construction of point doubling is relatively trickier. Examining the point doubling formula in Eqs. 6 to 8, to obtain x_3 from x_1 and y_3 from y_1 is not as straightforward. The term x_1 does not directly evolve into x_3, and similarly for y_1 and y_3. In detail, as inferred from Eq. 6, obtaining x_3

from x_1 requires "copying" x_1 to be squared and then appended (i.e., $x_1^2 + \frac{b}{x_1^2}$), while obtaining it from λ does not require any form of x_1. Hence, we say that it does not "consume" the initial state, and similarly for y_3 as obtaining it does not make use of y_1 at all. As a consequence, the initial value of y_1 may need to be preserved in the circuit as it can not be erased, hence requiring a placeholder (such as an ancilla register) to hold its value. Moreover, due to both input points being quantum and the operations being conditionally dependent on the state of a controlled qubit q, many of the operations will ultimately require "elevation": CNOT becomes CCNOT (controlled-controlled NOT gate a.k.a. Toffoli gate), CCNOT becomes CCCNOT (triple/multi-controlled Toffoli gate), and so on, in which these complex operations leads to higher resource requirement. As a result, it becomes a challenge to devise an efficient design for the quantum circuit implementation.

3.2 Proposed Quantum Circuits

Despite the challenges, there are still opportunities from the point-doubling formula that we can leverage to implement the circuit rather efficiently. We observe that there exists an indirect relation that can be taken advantage of. In particular, notice that x_1 has a direct relation to y_3, while y_1 has a direct relation to x_3. By utilizing this correlation, it is possible to transform x_1 and y_1 into y_3 and x_3, respectively. Thereby, a relatively efficient circuit can still be obtained, albeit with a "twisted" input-output relation (i.e., where x_1 maps to y_3 and y_1 maps to x_3 instead of the aligned mapping of x_1 to x_3 and y_1 to y_3).

Fundamentally, there is no requirement for the input and the output to be aligned. However, considering the conditional nature of the computation (i.e., if the control qubit q is in the state zero, the doubling does not occur and the value remains as x_1 instead of being transformed into y_3) and the fact that the circuit will be integrated with point addition to fit a larger scheme of scalar multiplication, a direct alignment will be helpful for clarity of the operations, which can be done simply by appending (controlled) swap gates.

Nevertheless, as previously described, the construction of point doubling may necessitate more space (i.e., ancilla registers) than that of point addition. While the latter, as proposed by Banegas et al. [1], requires one ancilla register used as a placeholder for division operation (see Fig. 2), two auxiliary registers will be required for performing point doubling. Below, we provide three schemes of point-doubling circuits to suit different implementation preferences.

The proposed circuits for performing point doubling are illustrated in Fig. 3. These circuits consist of two n-sized input/output registers, a control qubit q, and two n-sized ancilla registers to store intermediate results. Additionally, the readers may notice the presence of triple-controlled gates (i.e., in the last division subroutine of Fig. 3c and the first multiplication subroutine of all circuits) absent from the point addition counterpart. This is required to maintain a correct relation for the point doubling equations as in Eqs. 6 to 8.

The state change corresponding to these circuits is presented in Table 1. In detail, the complete steps (up to line 15) are for the third scenario (Fig. 3c), while

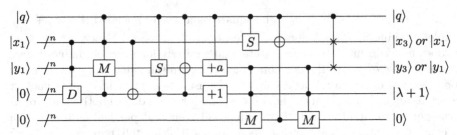

(a) Proposed point doubling circuit, with clearing one ancilla register

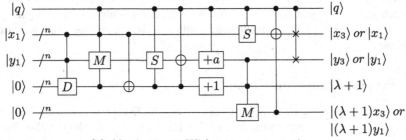

(b) Alternative 1: Without uncomputation

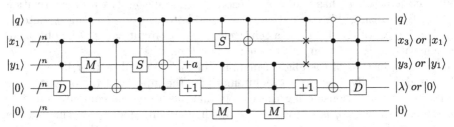

(c) Alternative 2: Fully uncompute when $q = 0$, otherwise leaving one ancilla as λ

Fig. 3. Our proposed point doubling circuits for binary elliptic curves: (a) balanced version that clears one ancilla register, and two alternatives of (b) without uncomputation for lower depth and lower gate count, and (c) full uncomputation when control qubit $q = 0$, and with a garbage ancilla in state λ when $q = 1$.

the second scenario (Fig. 3b) and the first scenario (Fig. 3a) terminate at lines 10 and 12, respectively. It is important to highlight that our proposal focuses on the high-level structure of the circuit arrangement, whereas the underlying field operations and subroutines (e.g., multiplication, squaring) may employ existing techniques such as Schoolbook or Karatsuba multiplication as proposed in [1,7, 15], with necessary adjustments made to accommodate the required number of qubits on each construction.

In the first circuit (Fig. 3a), we propose a balanced approach that strikes a tradeoff between the number of operations and the need to clear the ancillas. While this construction involves a relatively smaller number of operations, it requires an additional multiplication circuit for performing uncomputation upon

Table 1. Point Doubling State Change

Step	$q = 1$	$q = 0$
1	$anc_1 = \frac{y_1}{x_1}$	$anc_1 = \frac{y_1}{x_1}$
2	$y = 0$	$y = y_1$
3	$anc_1 = \frac{y_1}{x_1} + x_1 = \lambda$	$anc_1 = \frac{y_1}{x_1} + x_1 = \lambda$
4	$y = \lambda^2$	$y = y_1$
5	$y = \lambda^2 + \lambda$	$y = y_1$
6	$y = \lambda^2 + \lambda + a = x_3$	$y = y_1$
7	$anc_1 = \lambda + 1$	$anc_1 = \lambda + 1$
8	$anc_2 = (\lambda + 1)x_3$	$anc_2 = (\lambda + 1)y_1$
9	$x = x_1{}^2$	$x = x_1$
10	$x = x_1{}^2 + (\lambda + 1)x_3 = y_3$	$x = x_1$
11	$anc_2 = 0$	$anc_2 = 0$
12	$swap : x = x_3, y = y_3$	$none : x = x_1, y = y_1$
13	$anc_1 = (\lambda + 1) - 1 = \lambda$	$anc_1 = \lambda$
14	$anc_1 = \lambda$	$anc_1 = \lambda - x_1 = \frac{y_1}{x_1}$
15	$anc_1 = \lambda$	$anc_1 = 0$

one of the ancilla registers. As a result, we obtain one clean ancilla register that can be used for subsequent computations, and one dirty (i.e., does not revert to its initial state after use) ancilla register in the state $(\lambda + 1)$. This is our favored version because we can secure one clean register with relatively minimal effort.

Alternatively, if circuit depth and gate count take precedence over qubit count, the more suitable circuit would be as illustrated in Fig. 3b. Here, the circuit only performs the expected point doubling operation without considering any uncomputation for ancilla registers. This minimizes depth and the number of subroutines, but we are left with two dirty ancilla registers.

Regarding the third case, our initial goal was to clear all ancilla registers. However, we have not found a more efficient method to fully uncompute them for all possible states of the control qubit ($|0\rangle$ or $|1\rangle$). A complete uncomputation can be achieved when $q = 0$, but the state of λ remains a dirty ancilla when $q = 1$. Note that λ from the previous state (i.e., $x_1 + \frac{y_1}{x_1}$) may not be in the same value as λ in the subsequent operation (i.e., $x_3 + \frac{y_3}{x_3}$); due to this potential differences in value, we should not uncompute it by utilizing x_3 and y_3 when $q = 1$. Had it been the same, it would allow us to obtain two perfectly-uncomputed, clean ancilla registers. This can be done by appending another controlled multiplication circuit and Toffoli gate targeting that ancilla register.

Nevertheless, this third construction is still useful; Evidently, at the time when $q = 0$ indicates that the point doubling does not occur—meaning that most likely a point addition is taking place. This register can be temporarily repurposed using a clever arrangement to substitute the ancilla register in the point addition circuit (i.e., the one for performing division operation in Fig. 2).

The uncomputation itself can be performed by appending a series of Toffoli gates, a multi-controlled and negative-controlled division operation, and an addition by a constant. This circuit serves as a beneficial alternative construction when circuit width or qubit utilization is the most prioritized quantum resource.

The high-level resource cost of the proposed circuits can be summarized as follows. Compared to point addition, point doubling construction employs one more ancilla register and significantly more controlled and multi-controlled operations. In detail, for the first scenario (balanced), a total of one division, three multiplications (including multi-controlled version), two squarings (one multi-controlled), one controlled swap (i.e., Fredkin gate), as well as several (controlled and multi-controlled) additions are employed, with one clean ancilla registers and one dirty ancilla register. For the second scenario, one less multiplication is utilized, with the tradeoff of having both ancilla registers dirty. Next, regarding the last alternative of having two clean ancilla registers when the control qubit state is zero, it requires additional subroutines of one negative-control Toffoli series (elevated control from CNOT gates for addition operation), one negative multi-controlled division, and one addition by a constant. Note that we do not elaborate further on the exact resource since the presence of multi-controlled operations requires a more complex circuit decomposition. Nevertheless, we plan to investigate it further on a quantum simulator in our future work to obtain a more concrete resource estimation.

4   Discussions and Limitations

In this study, we delve into the topic of elliptic curve point doubling circuits, which has yet to be further examined in the literature. After presenting the design and description of our approach in the previous section, we now provide discussions related to the broader implications of our proposal.

Transforming to Prime Curves. We begin our study from the binary elliptic curves, which are relatively simpler than prime curves. In the case of prime curves, the quantum circuit will be more complicated because it cannot make use of the simplicity of field operation in binary curves. For instance, an addition in the prime fields requires a full adder, whereas binary fields only necessitate one Toffoli gate for each bit. Additionally, FLT-based inversion, which is comparable in performance to GCD-based inversion in quantum binary elliptic curves, has also not been considered to date for its use on prime curves due to the high resource requirements. Similarly, squaring operations are favorable in the binary case due to their relatively efficient construction (i.e., by leveraging a simple LUP decomposition), which are not applicable to prime curves. Even though there is an advantage in prime curves in terms of intuitive verification due to their nature of resembling decimal calculation, it requires more space and operations that are arguably more complicated and resource-intensive.

Relation to Scalar Multiplication. To realize a quantum elliptic curve scalar multiplication, existing methods rely upon a series of point addition circuits as the sole components. Therefore, the computation is in the form of

$Q = kP = P + P + \ldots + P$ for k times. Considering a more general implementation without limiting its use to Shor's algorithm, performing scalar multiplication by incorporating point doubling alongside point addition can potentially reduce the depth of the circuit and the number of operations. Moreover, the availability of designs for both point addition and point doubling opens up the opportunity to explore various classical elliptic curve point/scalar multiplication (ECPM) techniques (e.g., signed digit method, M-ary method) to be explored in the quantum realm in search of more efficient circuits.

For Use in Shor's ECDLP. In order to create a more theoretically accurate and complete Shor's ECDLP circuit, point doubling will need to be integrated into the existing double scalar multiplication (that currently consists entirely of point addition subroutines) to cover the cases when the doubling of points occurs. Note that for this algorithm, the input comes from the Walsh-Hadamard so that the circuit is expected to cater computation for all possible cases (i.e., any combination of zero and one within the circuit). More importantly, the constant value k is unknown. For this reason, a more thorough conditional mechanism is required to control whether point doubling or point addition is in effect during the certain computation phase, resulting in more complex multi-control operations on the circuit. Additionally, in scenarios where both points of interest are quantum values, a checking mechanism within the circuit will need to be employed to determine whether both values are identical. Note that for the specific use in Shor's ECDLP, both point addition and point doubling will be incorporated to cover all cases, and other implementation requirements (e.g., unique representation for history independence [5], uncomputing garbage outputs to prevent unwanted interference [12]) may need to be taken into account, which are interesting research problems.

Limitations. Even though this paper has provided an initial step to delve into point doubling, there are still various aspects requiring further investigation. This includes how to correctly integrate it with the point addition circuit and whether the previous assumptions taken for Shor's ECDLP regarding the double scalar multiplication still stand in this case, which we will explore in the future.

5 Conclusions and Future Work

In this study, we have examined the point-doubling operation for binary elliptic curves, which are required in the stricter case of Shor's algorithm. We began by analyzing the point doubling formula, identifying the inherent challenges in its construction, and presenting a possible solution. Subsequently, we designed quantum circuits for elliptic curve point doubling to cater to different scenarios, which shows the need for one more ancilla register compared to point addition, and while they may be comparable in terms of the number of subroutines, more complex multi-controlled operations are required than that of point addition. In addition, we provide a more in-depth discussion of the implications and concerns in incorporating the circuit into Shor's algorithm. To obtain a more detailed resource estimation for point doubling and complete double scalar multiplication for Shor's algorithm, we plan to construct the circuit in the existing quantum computing simulators and run the resource analysis as our future work.

References

1. Banegas, G., Bernstein, D.J., van Hoof, I., Lange, T.: Concrete quantum cryptanalysis of binary elliptic curves. IACR Trans. Cryptogr. Hardw. Embed. Syst. **2021**(1), 451–472 (2021)
2. Gidney, C.: Asymptotically efficient quantum Karatsuba multiplication. arXiv preprint arXiv:1904.07356 (2019)
3. Gouzien, É., Ruiz, D., Régent, F.M.L., Guillaud, J., Sangouard, N.: Computing 256-bit elliptic curve logarithm in 9 hours with 126133 cat qubits. arXiv preprint arXiv:2302.06639 (2023)
4. Gyongyosi, L., Imre, S.: Circuit depth reduction for gate-model quantum computers. Sci. Rep. **10**(1), 11229 (2020)
5. Häner, T., Jaques, S., Naehrig, M., Roetteler, M., Soeken, M.: Improved quantum circuits for elliptic curve discrete logarithms. In: Ding, J., Tillich, J.-P. (eds.) PQCrypto 2020. LNCS, vol. 12100, pp. 425–444. Springer, Cham (2020). https://doi.org/10.1007/978-3-030-44223-1_23
6. Hankerson, D., Menezes, A.J., Vanstone, S.: Guide to Elliptic Curve Cryptography. Springer, New York (2006). https://doi.org/10.1007/b97644
7. Jang, K., Kim, W., Lim, S., Kang, Y., Yang, Y., Seo, H.: Optimized implementation of quantum binary field multiplication with toffoli depth one. In: You, I., Youn, T.Y. (eds.) WISA 2022. LNCS, vol. 13720, pp. 251–264. Springer, Cham (2023). https://doi.org/10.1007/978-3-031-25659-2_18
8. Kaye, P.: Optimized quantum implementation of elliptic curve arithmetic over binary fields. Quantum Inf. Comput. **5**(6), 474–491 (2005)
9. Kirsch, Z., Chow, M.: Quantum computing: the risk to existing encryption methods (2015). http://www.cs.tufts.edu/comp/116/archive/fall2015/zkirsch.pdf
10. Larasati, H.T., Putranto, D.S.C., Wardhani, R.W., Park, J., Kim, H.: Depth optimization of FLT-based quantum inversion circuit. IEEE Access **11**, 54910–54927 (2023)
11. Liu, J., Wang, H., Ma, Z., Duan, Q., Fei, Y., Meng, X.: Quantum circuit optimization for solving discrete logarithm of binary elliptic curves obeying the nearest-neighbor constrained. Entropy **24**(7), 955 (2022)
12. Orts, F., Ortega, G., Combarro, E.F., Garzón, E.M.: A review on reversible quantum adders. J. Netw. Comput. Appl. **170**, 102810 (2020)
13. Pornin, T.: Efficient and complete formulas for binary curves. Cryptology ePrint Archive (2022)
14. Proos, J., Zalka, C.: Shor's discrete logarithm quantum algorithm for elliptic curves. arXiv preprint quant-ph/0301141 (2003)
15. Putranto, D.S.C., Wardhani, R.W., Larasati, H.T., Ji, J., Kim, H.: Depth-optimization of quantum cryptanalysis on binary elliptic curves. IEEE Access **11**, 45083–45097 (2023)
16. Roetteler, M., Naehrig, M., Svore, K.M., Lauter, K.: Quantum resource estimates for computing elliptic curve discrete logarithms. In: Takagi, T., Peyrin, T. (eds.) ASIACRYPT 2017. LNCS, vol. 10625, pp. 241–270. Springer, Cham (2017). https://doi.org/10.1007/978-3-319-70697-9_9

17. Shor, P.W.: Algorithms for quantum computation: discrete logarithms and factoring. In: Proceedings of the 35th Annual Symposium on Foundations of Computer Science, pp. 124–134. IEEE (1994)
18. Shor, P.W.: Polynomial-time algorithms for prime factorization and discrete logarithms on a quantum computer. SIAM Rev. **41**(2), 303–332 (1999)
19. Taguchi, R., Takayasu, A.: Concrete quantum cryptanalysis of binary elliptic curves via addition chain. In: Rosulek, M. (ed.) CT-RSA 2023. LNCS, vol. 13871, pp. 57–83. Springer, Cham (2023). https://doi.org/10.1007/978-3-031-30872-7_3
20. Van Hoof, I.: Space-efficient quantum multiplication of polynomials for binary finite fields with sub-quadratic Toffoli gate count. arXiv preprint arXiv:1910.02849 (2019)
21. Vedral, V., Barenco, A., Ekert, A.: Quantum networks for elementary arithmetic operations. Phys. Rev. A **54**(1), 147 (1996)
22. Whaley, B., Karasik, R.: Circuits, randomized computation, deferred measurements (2007). https://inst.eecs.berkeley.edu/~cs191/fa07/lectures/lecture9_fa07.pdf
23. Williams, C.P.: Explorations in Quantum Computing. Springer, London (2010). https://doi.org/10.1007/978-1-84628-887-6

PQ-DPoL: An Efficient Post-Quantum Blockchain Consensus Algorithm

Wonwoong Kim[1], Yeajun Kang[1], Hyunji Kim[2], Kyungbae Jang[1],
and Hwajeong Seo[3(✉)]

[1] Department of IT Convergence Engineering, Hansung University,
Seoul 02876, South Korea
[2] Department of Information Computer Engineering, Hansung University,
Seoul 02876, South Korea
[3] Department of Convergence Security, Hansung University,
Seoul 02876, South Korea
hwajeong84@gmail.com

Abstract. The advancement of quantum computers and the potential polynomial-time solution of Elliptic Curve Cryptography (ECC) using the Shor algorithm pose a significant threat to blockchain security.

This paper presents an efficient quantum-secure blockchain with our novel consensus algorithm. We integrate a post-quantum signature scheme into the transaction signing and verification process of our blockchain, ensuring its resistance against quantum attacks. Concretely, we adopt the `Dilithium` signature scheme, which is one of the selected algorithms in the NIST Post-Quantum Cryptography (PQC) standardization.

Not surprisingly, the incorporation of a post-quantum signature scheme leads to a reduction in the number of Transactions Per Second (TPS) processed by our blockchain. To mitigate this performance degradation, we introduce a new consensus algorithm that effectively combines the Proof of Luck (PoL) mechanism with a delegated approach.

We strive to build an efficient and secure blockchain for the post-quantum era by benchmarking our blockchain, adjusting the security parameters of `Dilithium`, and refining the components of the consensus algorithm.

Keywords: Consensus Algorithm · Blockchain · Post-Quantum Security · Dilithium · TEE

1 Introduction

The ECC-based signature scheme is commonly adopted in blockchains for transaction signing and verification, thanks to its efficiency. However, the following two factors prompt us to consider replacing ECC with PQC:

1. Shor's algorithm [1] efficiently models discrete logarithm problems on elliptic curves and provides polynomial-time solutions.

© The Author(s), under exclusive license to Springer Nature Singapore Pte Ltd. 2024
H. Kim and J. Youn (Eds.): WISA 2023, LNCS 14402, pp. 310–323, 2024.
https://doi.org/10.1007/978-981-99-8024-6_24

2. The emergence of quantum computers capable of running Shor's algorithm is anticipated in the near future.

Grover's algorithm [2] also poses a threat to the security of hash functions by reducing the search complexity by a square root. However, there is an off-the-shelf countermeasure that increases the output size of hash functions. Furthermore, due to the significant quantum circuit depth required by Grover's algorithm [3–5], launching attacks becomes more challenging compared to Shor's algorithm [6]. For these reasons, we focus on the threat posed by Shor's algorithm rather than Grover's algorithm throughout this paper.

To achieve a quantum-secure blockchain, it is crucial to adopt signature schemes that are resistant to quantum attacks, such as those posed by Shor's algorithm. However, it is widely recognized that post-quantum cryptography faces performance-related challenges, including large signature sizes and slow signing/verification speeds. These challenges are particularly significant for blockchain applications due to the nature of their consensus algorithm.

Inspired by this concern, we propose Post-Quantum Delegated Proof of Luck (PQ-DPoL), an efficient and quantum-secure blockchain consensus algorithm. PQ-DPoL utilizes the post-quantum signature scheme `Dilithium` [7], which is one of the recently standardized signature schemes in NIST's PQC standardization[1].

It is important to note that utilizing post-quantum signatures in a blockchain will inevitably lead to performance degradation. To address this issue, we introduce a novel combination of consensus primitives: Proof of Luck (PoL) with a delegated approach.

Our Contribution

This paper makes several contributions, which can be summarized as follows:

1. **Post-quantum Blockchain with PQC Scheme.** After carefully considering our blockchain components, including the targeted device and consensus algorithm, we adopt the `Dilithium` PQC scheme. This decision ensures the security of our blockchain against potential quantum attacks.
2. **New Consensus Algorithm for an Efficient Blockchain.** For the first time, we present the DPoL consensus algorithm, which combines PoL with a delegated approach. DPoL algorithm enhances block generation speed by simplifying the consensus process within a TEE. With the implementation of DPoL algorithm, we achieve satisfactory performance even when utilizing a PQC scheme.
3. **Diversifying Configurations and Benchmarks.** We provide various benchmarks to ensure compatibility and optimal performance in different environments as we build our blockchain with various options (such as adjusting the number of nodes or security parameters of `Dilithium`).

---

[1] https://csrc.nist.gov/Projects/post-quantum-cryptography/selected-algorithms-2022.

2   Preliminaries

2.1   Blockchain Consensus Algorithm

Blockchain is a distributed ledger technology in which nodes within a network communicate in a Peer-to-Peer (P2P) to share ledger. Blockchain is a decentralized method in which nodes each own a ledger. Therefore, nodes directly create blocks and verify transactions.

The consensus algorithm is used by nodes on the blockchain to ensure data integrity through specific procedures and to make the same decision. Each consensus algorithm has a block producer and validator. The block producer creates a block containing transactions and sends it to a validator. Validators verify that the header of a block is valid. Also, the validator performs verification by checking the signature of the transaction contained in the block. There are many types of consensus algorithms. Representatively, there are Proof of Work (PoW) used in Bitcoin and Proof of Stake (PoS) used in Ethereum. There is also Delegated Proof of Stake (DPoS), which adds delegation to PoS. In addition to this, there are Proof of Luck (PoL) and Proof of Elapsed Time (PoET) based on TEE.

In PoW, a node must perform mining to become a block producer. However, PoW has a limitation in that it consumes excessive energy during the mining process. PoS can solve the power consumption problem of PoW [8]. In PoS, nodes with sufficient stake become block producers. However, this causes a problem of the rich getting richer and the poor getting poorer, as nodes without stakes cannot create blocks.

DPoS is a consensus algorithm based on PoS [9]. In DPoS, delegates are elected through voting. These delegates perform the PoS consensus algorithm among themselves. As a result, TPS is improved, and the problem of PoS can be overcome. However, if the number of delegates is small compared to the size of the network, centralization issues can arise.

In PoET, the node that completes its assigned wait time first becomes the block producer [10]. Verification can be performed at high speed because it verifies whether the waiting time has actually been achieved through TEE. PoET provides equal opportunities to all nodes. Also, it does not cause the computing resource consumption problem that occurs in PoW.

2.2   Evaluation Metrics for Blockchain Performance

Blockchain has various elements such as network structure and consensus algorithm. Because of this, it is not easy to evaluate the performance of a blockchain using a single metric. For fair evaluation, several works have been conducted on the evaluation of blockchain performance [11,12]. Representative metrics that are mainly used include TPS and latency. In addition, there are other metrics: block verification time, decentralized level, and power consumption.

These metrics are affected by various factors of the blockchain (e.g., block size, the number of nodes and digital signature algorithm). This section describes these evaluation metrics of blockchain.

TPS. TPS means how many transactions can be processed in one second. In other words, it is the number of transactions that can be confirmed in one second. TPS is the most common metric of blockchain performance currently used and represents the speed of the blockchain. Many recent blockchains are being designed in a structure that can achieve high TPS. However, TPS should not be used as the only evaluation metric of a blockchain. If TPS is improved without considering other evaluation metrics, TPS may increase, but problems (e.g. lower scalability of the blockchain) may occur. Bitcoin, the most famous cryptocurrency, has 7 TPS, Ethereum has 20 TPS, and EOS has 3000 TPS. However, since EOS is close to a centralized system. Therefore, the decentralization characteristic of blockchain is not satisfied.

Latency. Latency is the time it takes from the time a transaction appears on the network until it is verified. If the latency is high, it means that a lot of time is required to process one transaction. Therefore, high latency causes performance degradation of the blockchain. Bitcoin's latency is 10 min, which is very large, and Ethereum's is 0.22 min. Also, Ripple, which aims for low latency, has a latency of about 4 s.

2.3 CRYSTALS-DILITHIUM

CRYSTALS-DILITHIUM[2] is a post-quantum cryptography selected by NIST as an algorithm to be standardized. Dilithium is a lattice-based cipher based on the Shortest Vector Problem (SVP). The SVP problem is that it is difficult to find the vector closest to an arbitrary position on the lattice in polynomial time (even on quantum computers).

Table 1 presents the sizes of Dilithium public keys and signatures (in bytes), Dilithium is divided into Dilithium-2,3,5 depending on the level of security. The size of Dilithium public key ranges from 1,312 to 2,592 bytes, private key ranges from 2,528 to 4,864 bytes, and the size of the signature ranges from 2,420 to 4,595 bytes. Compared to other PQCs, Dilithium has larger key and signature sizes but offers faster computational speed [13].

Table 1. Details of Dilithium.

Scheme	NIST level	Public key	Private key	Signature
Dilithium-2	2	1,312	2,528	2,420
Dilithium-3	3	1,952	4,000	3,293
Dilithium-5	5	2,592	4,864	4,595

---

[2] https://pq-crystals.org/index.shtml.

2.4   Trusted Execution Environment

TEE (Trusted Execution Environment) means the security area of the main processor. The security area ensures that code and data inside the processor can be protected in terms of confidentiality and integrity. There are various unique techniques for this. For example, Trusted Time, Monotonic Counter, Random Number Generation, and Attestation are representative. Representative platforms of TEE include Intel SGX, ARM TrustZone, RISC-V MultiZone, and AMD SEE.

Trusted Time. TEE provides PRTC (Protected Real-Time Clock) based timer for trusted time service [14]. This Trusted Time Service can be used to measure the elapsed time since reading the previous timer. Timer Source Epoch can be used to detect discontinuities between Read Time points. Discontinuity means that the PRTC has been reset due to an event such as a battery replacement, or the timer has been paired with a different PRTC due to an unexpected event such as a software attack. In this case, the user MUST NOT trust the calculated period between the two Timer Readings and handle the error condition appropriately. It can be used through $sgx\_get\_trusted\_time()$, a library API function of the Intel SGX SDK.

Monotonic Counter. Users can use a monotonic counter with ID, which is a unique identifier [14]. The user can create a monotonic counter through the Intel SGX SDK, increase the value, read or delete the value.

Attestation. There are cases in which different TEEs must cooperate for various reasons such as communication. At this time, a function to prove each other's reliability is provided, which is called Attestation. Attestation is divided into local attestation and remote attestation. If two TEE areas exist on the same CPU, verification is possible through local attestation, and if they exist on different CPUs, verification must be performed through remote attestation.

Random Number Generation. TEE can generate a random value from an Intel on-chip hardware random number generator seeded by an on-chip entropy source through a command called RDRAND.

3   PQ-DPoL

This section presents various methodologies gathered to construct our PQ-DPoL, an efficient post-quantum blockchain consensus algorithm.

Before presenting our methodologies, we provide the following remarks on the key aspects/considerations for post-quantum blockchain:

- **Key Sizes** When considering the use of Internet of Things (IoT) devices for blockchain, it is advisable to adopt PQC (Post-Quantum Cryptography) with small public and private keys.
- **Signature Size** Blockchain transactions involve user signatures. To increase the number of transactions that can be included in a block, it is recommended to adopt PQC with small signature sizes.
- **Execution Speed** PQC scheme should process a large number of transactions per second, allowing for high-speed blockchain operation.
- **Computational Complexity** While fast execution is desirable, it is important to consider the computational complexity. A PQC scheme may execute quickly on certain hardware but be slower on others, so a balance needs to be struck between computational complexity, execution time, and supported hardware devices.
- **Power Consumption** Power consumption is a concern for energy-intensive blockchains like Bitcoin. Factors such as hardware, communication transactions, and security schemes contribute to energy usage. Therefore, PQC schemes should aim for efficient energy consumption.

3.1   Post-Quantum Blockchain Using Dilithium

The Dilithium scheme provides the advantage of faster signing and verification speeds compared to many other PQC signature schemes. However, this advantage comes at the cost of large key and signature sizes (PQC schemes often involve this trade-off).

As noted earlier (Sect. 3), when considering IoT devices, it is recommended to use PQC schemes with small key sizes for blockchain. However, the devices targeted for our blockchain are CPUs that support TEE for the PoL consensus algorithm. This indicates that our blockchain is capable of accommodating PQC with large key sizes. Thus, the large key sizes of Dilithium do not present any issues for our blockchain, and we can benefit from its fast signing and verification speeds. In this regard, Dilithium is well-suited for our blockchain.

However, the large signature size of Dilithium leads to an increased transaction size. Consequently, the capacity for including transactions in a block is reduced, resulting in lower TPS.

In Sect. 3.3, we will present how to increase the lowered TPS using the proposed consensus algorithm, DPoL.

3.2   Construction of Trusted Execution Environment

In this work, the system is designed based on Intel SGX, one of the TEEs. TEE enforces correct operation of an algorithm or critical operation process. Representatively, in order to vote for delegation or to be elected as a delegate who can be qualified to create a block, a random value generation process through TEE is required. A monotonic counter is used to prevent concurrent invocation or a remote attestation to verify operation. Also, the Trusted Time Service (TTS) provides a reliable verification method for whether a certain amount of waiting time has been passed.

For these reasons, TEE is required to participate in the blockchain network. In addition, even if we have a large number of CPUs with TEEs, malicious actions such as controlling the network with the majority of TEEs in the network are close to impossible due to the price of TEEs.

However, in our current implementation, the actual TEE is not used and is implemented in the form of an interface. Measuring performance by applying real TEE remains a follow-up study. The details of the functions of the TEE used are as follows.

Trusted Time. TEE has a reliable time service. This allows reliable elapsed time measurements. Set the time at which the consensus algorithm starts through TEE as *round time*. *Sleep* for as much time as round time to let the time pass. After that, it verifies the block of this round and whether the time passed as much as round time.

Through this process, nodes have a deterministic block verification time, so that block creation time can be synchronized without additional operation. Because sleep is busy-wait, other work is available during this time, so time and energy are not wasted. Also, if another luckier chain is broadcasted while busy waiting, it can be changed to that chain. In NS-3[3], this function can be provided by giving the Delay of Schedule as much as round time.

After verifying the block of the previous round, it is verified whether the round time has passed during the verification process. Through this process, nodes have a deterministic block verification time, so that block creation time can be synchronized without additional operation. By doing busy-wait, sleep is performed during the round time, and other tasks are possible during this time, so time and energy are not wasted.

Monotonic Counter. A malicious user may try to gain an unfair advantage by running an algorithm concurrently on a single CPU. If the value of TEE monotonic counter is increased every time, concurrent invocation can be prevented. To do this, the monotonic counter value is stored at the time of starting the algorithm. After that, it is compared with the value of the monotonic counter when verifying the block. If the two monotonic counter values are different, it means that the algorithm was executed in parallel on the same CPU. In this case, the monotonic counter verification fails and the node cannot create a block.

Remote Attestation. Algorithm 1 shows the remote attestation function.

REMOTE ATTESTATION is the process of generating a *proof*, a value that nodes can verify with each other. Proof is used as a record of whether an algorithm or data has been manipulated. Because of attestation, the operation process and data in TEE cannot be manipulated.

---

[3] https://www.nsnam.org/.

Algorithm 1. Remote Attestation.
_____
1: **function** REMOTEATTESTATION(*nonce, luck*)
2:     *input* ← *nonce* ‖ *luck*
3:     *proof* ← BASE58-ENCODING(*input*)
4:     **return** *proof*
5: **end function**
_____

Proof is a value generated by BASE58-ENCODING the concatenated data of *nonce*, which is a hash value of the block header to be generated, and *luck*, which is a random value generated through RDRAND of TEE. It is included in the block and broadcast at the end of the consensus algorithm process. The node extracts the nonce and luck by BASE58-DECODING the proof contained in the broadcast block. Through the extracted data, it is verified whether the value of proof has been tampered with or whether it is a value generated from the correct nonce and luck.

As a result, it is possible to prove that no block or transaction has been manipulated. It also allows nodes to communicate with each other even if they do not have a trust relationship.

Random Number Generation. TEE can produce reliable random numbers, which an attacker cannot influence. A reliable random value is generated using RDRAND of Intel SGX and used as the luck value in the algorithm. This luck value is used as a value for voting or when deciding who will be the block generator in the consensus algorithm. The node with the block with the highest luck value is selected as the block producer.

3.3   Proof of Luck with Delegated Approach

PQ-DPoL, a post-quantum consensus algorithm proposed in this work, consists of *a delegation phase* and *a consensus phase*. Figure 1 shows the overview of PQ-DPoL.

In the delegation phase, the delegated node to be the delegate is selected through the voting of all nodes in the blockchain. In the consensus phase, delegated nodes take turns generating blocks. Here, the transactions included in the generated block include the signature and public key of Dilithium. Finally, after delegated nodes verify the block, the verified block is added to the chain.

Delegation. Figure 2 shows the *delegation phase* of PQ-DPoL. The details of the delegation process are as follows:

1. **Random Number Generation** Each node generates a random number. This random number is used as a vote value.
2. **Vote** Each node broadcasts a voting transaction. A voting transaction contains a random number (vote) and the signature and public key of Dilithium.

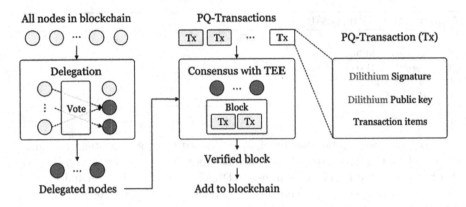

Fig. 1. Overview of PQ-DPoL.

3. **Verification** Each node receives voting transactions of other nodes and verifies the voting transaction with `Dilithium`. If the signature verification succeeds, the voting transaction is considered valid, indicating a valid vote. If the signature verification fails, it means that the transaction has been manipulated (i.e., the vote is invalid).

4. **Delegation** The number of votes received is summed up. The top n nodes with the most votes are then selected as delegated nodes.

Since we apply `Dilithium`, the TPS decreases because of the large signature size, leading to fewer transactions that can be included in one block. However, in the delegation approach, only some nodes in the blockchain perform consensus. In other words, since the number of nodes participating in the consensus is reduced, the time taken for all nodes to verify is reduced. As a result, the time required for consensus is reduced.

Thanks to the delegation phase we overcome the degraded TPS due to `Dilithium`. Further, there is the advantage of improving scalability [15], which is another important factor of blockchain.

Consensus with TEE. Figure 3 shows the consensus phase of PQ-DPoL. The details of the consensus process are as follows:

1. **Block Generation** In order to generate a block, the integrity of the block must be verified. Also, PoL verifies that *round time* has passed and that the monotonic counter has not changed. If the current time is greater than round time + consensus start time, then round time has passed. And, if the monotonic counter set based on the TEE and the current monotonic counter called in the consensus process are not the same, verification is failed. After verification is completed, *luck* (random number) is generated using TEE, and *proof* is generated in the REMOTE ATTESTATION process. Finally, the block is broadcast to other delegated nodes.

1. Each node generates a random number

2. Vote : Broadcast a random number

3. Verifies the voting transaction (Dilithium)

4. Select delegated nodes (with the most votes).

Fig. 2. Delegation phase of PQ-DPoL.

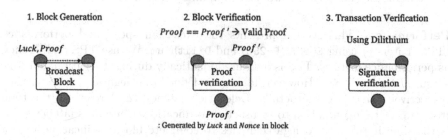

1. Block Generation

2. Block Verification
Proof == Proof' → Valid Proof

3. Transaction Verification
Using Dilithium

Luck, Proof

Broadcast Block

Proof'

Proof verification

Signature verification

Proof'
: Generated by *Luck* and *Nonce* in block

Fig. 3. Consensus phase of PQ-DPoL.

2. **Block Verification** In the block verification process, verification of nonce, the previous hash, and proof are performed. It must be verified that the Nonce generated by hashing the header of the block to be created is the same as the nonce extracted from proof (note that the nonce is the hash of the header of the current block). This process ensures the integrity of nonce.

To verify the proof, the proof contained in the received block is compared with the *proof'* (new proof) generated in the consensus process. Here, proof' is a string encoded after concatenating luck and nonce of the block. In other words, it means verifying that the received proof is actually created from luck and nonce. Finally, the block verification process is completed by comparing the previous hash with the previous hash included in the block to be generated.

3. **Transaction Verification**

Finally, verification for the transactions contained in the block must be performed. Delegated nodes verify the signature of transactions included in the received block. In this process, as mentioned in the delegation phase (Sect. 3.3), the signature verification process using Dilithium is performed.

In this way, TEE-based verification is performed in the consensus phase. In other words, this consensus phase is a process of verifying the values of the elements included in the block (such as luck, nonce, and proof) to ensure that a legitimate block is generated. As noted earlier, the number of transactions included in a block can be decreased due to Dilithium for transaction verification. However, since only delegated nodes participate in consensus, the consensus time can be reduced. Thus, by using post-quantum lightweight consensus, we can ensure security while mitigating the decrease in TPS due to the large signature size.

4 Benchmark

4.1 Environment and Evaluation Metrics

Environment. C++ language and an Intel i5-8295U CPU with 16GB RAM on Ubuntu 20.04.6 LTS are used in our experiment. To build an environment close to a real blockchain network, we use NS-3, an open-source network simulator.

Performance. This section presents the execution speed and performance (TPS, Latency) using ECDSA (P-256) and Dilithium. We use TPS and latency as performance metrics. TPS is measured identically during delegation and consensus (TPS_D, TPS_C). However, latency is defined in delegation and consensus respectively. Here are the details. Delegation latency (L_D) refers to the time from transaction generation to transaction verification. Consensus latency (L_C) is the time it takes for delegated nodes to complete block verification after a block containing a transaction is generated. We measure TPS_D, TPS_C, L_D, and L_C depending on the size of the blockchain network (the number of nodes is represented by 2^n) and the type of Dilithium applied.

Table 2. Execution speed comparison of ECDSA (P-256) and Dilithium.

Algorithm	Key Gen	Sig Gen	Sig Verify
ECDSA (P-256)	0.000400	0.000670	0.000350
Dilithium-2	0.000027	0.000100	0.000026
Dilithium-3	0.000047	0.000160	0.000043
Dilithium-5	0.000073	0.000200	0.000065

block size: 25 KB, unit: second, $n = 1$

- **Execution speed comparison of ECDSA and Dilithium** Table 2 shows the performance of the signature scheme in the blockchain network. Key generation time, signature generation time, and signature verification time of ECDSA and Dilithium-2/3/5 are measured. Dilithium is faster than ECDSA. However, when the block size is 25KB, the number of transactions included in one block is 100 and 6/4/3 in ECDSA and Dilithium-2/3/5, respectively. This is because Dilithium has a large key size and signature size as described in Sect. 2.3.

Table 3. TPS of DPoL.

n	1	2	3	4	5	6	7
ECDSA	713.5797	122.5398	29.8184	6.9522	0.9468	0.2341	0.1030
Dilithium-2	88.8721	21.0373	5.1244	1.2515	0.3302	0.0776	0.0171
Dilithium-3	48.4901	11.7897	2.8879	0.7128	0.1815	0.0446	0.0104
Dilithium-5	30.8097	7.4470	1.8600	0.4526	0.1203	0.0291	0.0066

block size: 25 KB, unit: second

- **TPS** Despite the faster signing speed, the performance of Dilithium in terms of TPS is relatively low compared to ECDSA due to the large size of Dilithium. As a result, the time is delayed because more transactions are included in the block to which ECDSA is applied, but the TPS is measured higher due to a large number of transactions.

Table 4. Latency of DPoL.

n	1	2	3	4	5	6	7
ECDSA	0.1401	0.8160	3.3536	14.3838	105.6131	427.1180	970.0098
Dilithium-2	0.0675	0.2852	1.1708	4.7940	18.1667	77.2573	350.8609
Dilithium-3	0.0824	0.3392	1.3850	5.6116	22.0333	89.5175	383.3946
Dilithium-5	0.0973	0.4028	1.6128	6.6277	24.9267	103.0436	454.1221

block size: 25 KB, unit: second

- **Latency** It is observed that the TPS decreases as the number of nodes increases (see Tables 3 and 4). Due to the limitations of the hardware environment, the performance when the number of nodes is 512 can not be measured, but based on the previous measurement results, it can be assumed that the TPS will decrease. Thus, the delegate is applied to solve the problem related to the size of Dilithium and the decrease in TPS as the number of nodes increases. The delegated performance measurement result is the same as Tables 3 and 4. By reducing the number of nodes with a delegated approach, the time required for consensus is decreased (i.e., TPS increases).

5   Conclusion

In this work, we gather multiple contributions, including a post-quantum signature scheme and a novel consensus algorithm, to construct an efficient quantum-secure blockchain. Additionally, we make a detailed attempt to ensure compatibility and optimal performance for diverse environments.

In summary of our experimental results, the TPS of DPoL applied with Dillithium is lower than that of ECDSA (since larger key and signature sizes). To improve the degraded performance, we propose DPoL, a new consensus algorithm that combines PoL and a delegation approach. Certainly, when employing Dillithium as the signature scheme in DPoL, although its performance may be lower than that of ECDSA, it still provides reasonable performance.

Finding/Adopting various methods to improve TPS can be considered for the future works. It would be advisable to replace various PQC signature schemes and conduct comparative analyses with other consensus algorithms.

Acknowledgements. This work was supported by Institute for Information & communications Technology Promotion (IITP) grant funded by the Korea government (MSIT) (No. 2018-0-00264, Research on Blockchain Security Technology for IoT Services, 50%) and this work was supported by Institute of Information & communications Technology Planning & Evaluation (IITP) grant funded by the Korea government (MSIT) (No. 2022-0-00627, Development of Lightweight BIoT technology for Highly Constrained Devices, 50%).

References

1. Shor, P.W.: Polynomial-time algorithms for prime factorization and discrete logarithms on a quantum computer. SIAM Rev. **41**(2), 303–332 (1999)
2. Grover, L.K.: A fast quantum mechanical algorithm for database search. In: Proceedings of the Twenty-Eighth Annual ACM Symposium on Theory of Computing, pp. 212–219 (1996)
3. Amy, M., Di Matteo, O., Gheorghiu, V., Mosca, M., Parent, A., Schanck, J.: Estimating the cost of generic quantum pre-image attacks on SHA-2 and SHA-3. In: Avanzi, R., Heys, H. (eds.) SAC 2016. LNCS, vol. 10532, pp. 317–337. Springer, Cham (2017). https://doi.org/10.1007/978-3-319-69453-5_18
4. Lee, J., Lee, S., Lee, Y.-S., Choi, D.: T-depth reduction method for efficient SHA-256 quantum circuit construction. IET Inf. Secur. **17**(1), 46–65 (2023)
5. Lee, W.-K., Jang, K., Song, G., Kim, H., Hwang, S.O., Seo, H.: Efficient implementation of lightweight hash functions on GPU and quantum computers for IoT applications. IEEE Access **10**, 59661–59674 (2022)
6. NIST: Submission requirements and evaluation criteria for the post-quantum cryptography standardization process (2016). https://csrc.nist.gov/CSRC/media/Projects/Post-Quantum-Cryptography/documents/call-for-proposals-final-dec-2016.pdf
7. Ducas, L., et al.: Crystals-dilithium: a lattice-based digital signature scheme. IACR Trans. Cryptogr. Hardw. Embedded Syst. **2018**, 238–268 (2018)
8. Wood, G., et al.: Ethereum: a secure decentralised generalised transaction ledger. Ethereum Project Yellow Paper **151**(2014), 1–32 (2014)
9. Yang, F., Zhou, W., Wu, Q., Long, R., Xiong, N.N., Zhou, M.: Delegated proof of stake with downgrade: a secure and efficient blockchain consensus algorithm with downgrade mechanism. IEEE Access **7**, 118541–118555 (2019)
10. Chen, L., Xu, L., Shah, N., Gao, Z., Lu, Y., Shi, W.: On security analysis of proof-of-elapsed-time (PoET). In: Spirakis, P., Tsigas, P. (eds.) SSS 2017. LNCS, vol. 10616, pp. 282–297. Springer, Cham (2017). https://doi.org/10.1007/978-3-319-69084-1_19

11. Bamakan, S.M.H., Motavali, A., Bondarti, A.B.: A survey of blockchain consensus algorithms performance evaluation criteria. Expert Syst. Appl. **154**, 113385 (2020)
12. Salimitari, M., Chatterjee, M.: A survey on consensus protocols in blockchain for IoT networks. arXiv preprint arXiv:1809.05613 (2018)
13. Raavi, M., Chandramouli, P., Wuthier, S., Zhou, X., Chang, S.-Y.: Performance characterization of post-quantum digital certificates. In: 2021 International Conference on Computer Communications and Networks (ICCCN), pp. 1–9. IEEE (2021)
14. Cen, S., Zhang, B.: Trusted time and monotonic counters with intel software guard extensions platform services. https://software.intel.com/sites/default/files/managed/1b/a2/Intel-SGX-Platform-Services.pdf (2017)
15. Sanka, A.I., Cheung, R.C.: A systematic review of blockchain scalability: issues, solutions, analysis and future research. J. Netw. Comput. Appl. **195**, 103232 (2021)

Efficient Implementation of the Classic McEliece on ARMv8 Processors

Minjoo Sim[1], Hyeokdong Kwon[1], Siwoo Eum[1], Gyeongju Song[1], Minwoo Lee[2], and Hwajeong Seo[2(✉)]

[1] Department of Information Computer Engineering, Hansung University, Seoul 02876, South Korea
[2] Department of Convergence Security, Hansung University, Seoul 02876, South Korea
hwajeong84@gmail.com

Abstract. Classic McEliece is a Code-based Key Encapsulation Mechanisms (KEM) and one of the candidate algorithms in the NIST PQC competition. Based on the McEliece cryptosystem developed in 1978, this system relies on the Niederreiter variant of McEliece. It consists of three phases: Key Generation, Encapsulation, and Decapsulation. In this paper, we propose an optimized implementation of the internal multiplication operations of Classic McEliece on the ARMv8 processor. We utilize parallel computing techniques using vector registers and vector instructions of the ARMv8 processor. We specifically focus on optimizing the multiplication operation, which is a major contributor to the overall execution time of the Classic McEliece algorithm, by leveraging the commutative property and implementing an parallelization technique. As a result, our approach achieves a maximum performance improvement of 2.82× compared to the reference implementation in the multiplication operation.

Keywords: 64-bit ARMv8 Processors · Classic McEliece · Post-quantum Cryptography · Parallel implementation · KEM · Software implementation

1 Introduction

Due to the rapid advancement of quantum computers, conventional modern Cryptography algorithms are facing threats. In preparation for this, efforts are underway to transition existing modern Cryptography algorithms into quantum-resistant Cryptography before the practical realization of quantum computers. Recognizing the need for robust Cryptography solutions, the National Institute of Standards and Technology (NIST) initiated the Post-Quantum Cryptography (PQC) Competition in 2017. The objective of this competition is to identify and standardize quantum-resistant Cryptography algorithms [1]. As part of the NIST PQC standards, CRYSTALS-KYBER [2], CRYSTALS-DILITHIUM [3], SPHINCS+ [4], and FALCON [5] have been selected. Optimal implementation research for the algorithm selected as a NIST PQC standard is being actively conducted on ARMv8 [6–11]. Classic McEliece was selected as one of the Round 4 candidate algorithms [12]. Classic McEliece is a code-based key encapsulation mechanisms. The basic structure is based on the McEliece [13] cryptosystem in 1978, and its stability has been verified through long-term research. In addition, the German Federal Office for Information Security recommends Classic McEliece as long-term security along with FrodoKEM. In this paper, we propose an efficient implementation of Classic McEliece on a 64-bit ARMv8 processor.

The remainder of this paper is structured as follows. The Sect. 2 describes the Classic McEliece, the target 64-bit ARMv8 processor, and related works. The Sect. 3 describes the proposed method. The Sect. 4 shows a performance comparison. Finally, the Sect. 5 describes the conclusion of this document and future work.

1.1 Contribution

-Multiplication with Parallel Operations of the Classic McEliece on ARMv8 Processors. We propose an efficient parallel multiplication implementation using Classic McEliece's parallel operation on ARMv8 processors. The implementation utilizes 128-bit vector registers of the ARMv8 architecture and NEON vector instructions. Our proposed parallel multiplication leverages the commutative property of XOR operation to rearrange internal operations, enabling simultaneous computation of four values within the internal structure. As a result, we observed a maximum performance improvement of approximately 2.82× compared to the reference code (C code) provided by PQ-Clean project [14].

-First Implementation of the Classic McEliece Multiplier on 64-Bit ARMv8 Processors Using Vector Registers. To the best of our knowledge, this paper presents the first implementation of the Classic McEliece multiplier utilizing vector registers supported by 64-bit ARM processors. We believe that our work can serve as a valuable resource for researchers to assess the performance of the Classic McEliece algorithm.

2   Preliminaries

2.1   Classic McEliece

Classic McEliece is designed to combine the advantages of McEliece and Niederreiter. The existing McEliece uses a Generator Matrix (G) for the public key, whereas Classic McEliece uses the Parity Check Matrix (H) used as the public key in Niederreiter. Classic McEliece is designed with a simple matrix multiplication process for Encapsulation and Decapsulation, allowing for fast computation. It also has the advantage of having a shorter Ciphertext compared to the existing Ciphertext. On the other hand, the length of the public key is very long and the key generation process takes a long time. The length of the public key is 256 KB to 1.3 MB, using it difficult to use on low-end devices with small memory space. Classic McEliece parameters are shown in Table 1.

Table 1. Parameters of Classic McEliece; **m** is log_2q (q is the size of the field used); **n** is length of code, and **t** is the sizes of guaranteed error-correction capability;

Algorithm	m	n	t	security level	Public key	Secret key
Mceliece 348864	12	3,488	64	1	261,120	6,492
Mceliece 460896	13	4,608	96	3	524,160	13,608
Mceliece 6688128	13	6,688	128	5	1,044,992	13,932
Mceliece 6960119	13	6,960	119	5	1,047,319	13,948
Mceliece 8192128	13	8,192	128	5	1,357,824	14,120

Classic McEliece algorithm can be divided into three processes: a key generation process, an encryption process (Encapsulation), and a decryption process (Decapsulation).

- **Key Generation** In the Key Generation process, first, g(x) of degree t required for Goppa code generation and L called a support set are generated. Generate H (parity check matrix) using g(x) and L. The generated H is converted to binary form and converted to systematic form by performing Gaussian elimination. That is, it is converted to the form $H = (I_{n-k}|T)$, and after removing I_{n-k} (Identity Matrix), the remaining **T** matrix is used as a public key. The private key consists of **g(x)** and **L**, which are used to generate the Goppa code, and a randomly generated **s**. In conclusion, the public key is **T** and the private keys are **g(x)**, **L**, and **s**.
- **Encapsulation** In the Encapsulation process, a random vector (e) with weight t is first generated. A syndrome (C_0) is generated using the generated e and the public key (T). It uses the value of e and the number 2 to generate a hash value (C_1 = Hash(2, e)) and combines the two values ($C = C_0|C_1$) to finally produce the ciphertext (C). Finally, for the session key, the hash value of the number 1, e, C will be the session key (K = Hash(1, e, C)).
- **Decapsulation** In the Decapsulation process, Decapsulation is performed using the delivered value of C and the owned private key. The value of e (error matrix) can be obtained by performing syndrome decoding with the syndrome (C_0) included in C (ciphertext) and the private key. It is determined whether there is an error by comparing the hash value with the number 2 in front of the e value obtained through syndrome decoding and the C_1 value included in the transmitted C (ciphertext). If the two values are the same, the hash value of the numbers 1, e, and C is computed to obtain the session key.

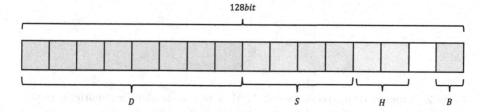

Fig. 1. Register packing of vector registers.

2.2 ARMv8 Processor

ARM is an ISA (Instruction Set Architecture) high-performance embedded processor. ARMv8-A supports both 32-bit AArch32 and 64-bit AArch64 architectures for backward compatibility. ARMv8-A provides 31 64-bit general-purpose registers from $x0$ to $x30$ and 32 128-bit vector registers from $v0$ to $v31$. In this case, the general purpose registers can also be used as 32-bit registers from $w0$ to $w30$. The vector registers can be processed by dividing stored values into specific units. There are four types of units supported: byte (8-bit), half word (16-bit), single word (32-bit), and double word (64-bit). Figure 1 shows register packing of vector registers. A vector instructions (called ASIMD or NEON) is used for the vector register to perform parallel operation. Table 2 shows that instruction lists for proposed implementations [15].

2.3 Related Works

Becker et al. implemented an optimization for Barrett multiplication using the 64-bit ARM Cortex-A NEON vector instruction [7]. They are the combination of Montgomery multiplication and Barrett reduction resulting in Barrett multiplication which allows particularly efficient modular one-known-factor multiplication using the NEON vector instructions. And proposed novel techniques combined with fast two-unknown-factor Montgomery multiplication, Barrett reduction sequences, and interleaved multi-stage butterflies result in significantly faster code. As a result, in the Saber, NTTs are far superior to Toom-Cook multiplication on the ARMv8-A architecture, outrunning the matrix-to-vector polynomial multiplication by 2.0×. On the Apple M1, the matrix-vector products run 2.1× and 1.9× faster for Kyber and Saber respectively.

Sanal et al. implemented CRYSTAL-Kyber encryption on 64-bit ARM Cortex-A and Apple A12 processors [8]. They improved the performance of noise sampling, Number Theoretic Transform (NTT), and symmetric function implementations based on an AES accelerator. As the result, the proposed Kyber512 implementation on ARM64 improved the previous work by 1.72×, 1.88×, and 2.29× for key generation, encapsulation, and decapsulation, respectively. And, the proposed Kyber512-90 s implementation (using AES accelerator) is improved by 8.57×, 6.94×, and 8.26× for key generation, encapsulation, and decapsulation, respectively.

Table 2. Summarized instruction set of ARMv8 for Classic McEliece multiplier implementation; **Xd, Vd**: destination register (general, vector), **Xn, Vn, Vm**: source register (general, vector, vector), **Vt**: transferred vector register.

asm	Operands	Description	Operation
ADD	Vd.T, Vn.T, Vm.T	Add	Vd ← Vn + Vm
AND	Vd.T, Vn.T, Vm.T	Bitwise AND	Vd ← Vn & Vm
EOR	Vd.T, Vn.T, Vm.T	Bitwise Exclusive OR	Vd ← Vn ⊕ Vm
LD1	Vt.T, [Xn]	Load multiple single-element structures	Vt ← [Xn]
LD1R	Vt.T, [Xn]	Load single 1-element structure and replicate to all lanes (of one register).	Vt.T ← [Xn]
MOV	Xd, #imm	Move (immediate)	Xd ← #imm
MOV	Vd.T, Vn.T	Move (vector)	Vd ← Vn
MOV	Vd.Ts[index1], Vn.Ts[index2]	Move vector element to another vector element	Vd ← Vn
MOVI	Vt.T, #imm	Move immediate (vector)	Vt ← #imm
MUL	Xd, Xn, Xm	Multiply	Xd ← Xn × Xm
RET	{Xn}	Return from subroutine	Return
SHL	Vd.T, Vn.T, #shift	Shift Left immediate (vector)	Vd ← Vn << #shift
SRI	Vd.T, Vn.T, #shift	Shift Right and immediate (vector)	Vd ← Vn >>#shift
ST1	Vt.T, [Xn]	Store multiple single-element structures from one, two, three, or four registers	[Xn] ← Vt
SUB	Xd, Xn, #imm	Subtract immediate	Xd ← Xn - #imm
REV32	Vd.T, Vn.T	Reverse elements in 32-bit words	Vd ← Vn of Reverse
CBNZ	Wt, Label	Compare and Branch on Nonzero	Go to Label
CBZ	Wt, Label	Compare and Branch on Zero	Go to Label
ZIP1	Vd.T, Vn.T, Vm.T	Zip vectors primary	Vd ← Vn[even], Vm[even] Vd ← Vn[odd], Vm[odd]
UZP1	Vd.T, Vn.T, Vm.T	Unzip vectors primary	Vd ← Vn[even], Vm[even] Vd ← Vn[odd], Vm[odd]

Kwon et al. implemented the Rainbow signature schemes on 64-bit ARM Cortex-A processor [16]. Rainbow signature is based on the multivariate-based public key signature. They proposed a technique using a look-up table, in which the result of 4×4 multiplication is pre-computed. The techniques used parallel operation of vector registers and vector instructions. As a result, the proposed multiplier by using look-up table performances improvement was improved previous work by maximum of 167.2×.

Kwon et al. implemented the FrodoKEM on 64-bit ARM Cortex-A processor [17]. FrodoKEM is Public-key Encryption and Key-establishment Algorithms, which is selected NIST PQC Round 3 alternate candidates. They proposed the parallel matrix-multiplication and built-in AES accelerator for AES encryption. They applied these techniques to the FrodoKEM640 scheme, utilizing vector registers and vector instructions. And the implementation with all of proposed techniques was improved previous C implementation by maximum of 10.22×.

3 Proposed Method

3.1 Multiplication on $\mathbb{F}_{2^m}$

In Classic McEliece, Multiplication is performed on the extended binary finite-filed $\mathbb{F}_{2^m}$. The expensive operations on public keys are multiplication and inversion on finite-field. Therefore, in this paper, optimization of multiplication on $\mathbb{F}_{2^m}$ is performed (m is 12 or 13). In the specification, $\mathbb{F}_{2^{12}}$ consists of $\mathbb{F}_2[x]/(x^{12} + x^3 + 1)$ and $\mathbb{F}_{2^{13}}$ consists of $\mathbb{F}_2[x]/(x^{13} + x^4 + x^3 + x + 1)$ [18].

Multiplication on $\mathbb{F}_{2^m}$ proceeds as follows. Multiplication is performed on two m-bit values. At this time, since the multiplication result may be out of the range of $\mathbb{F}_{2^m}$, the multiplication is completed on $\mathbb{F}_{2^m}$ by performing modular reduction on the multiplication result value.

To ensure accurate multiplication of two 16-bit values, it is necessary to apply a masking operation using 32-bit variables. By masking the 16-bit variables, multiplication can be performed accurately. Subsequently, the resulting 16-bit values are obtained by unmasking the computed values. Figure 2 is the masking and unmasking operations performed for the multiplication operation in Classic McEliece. After masking four 16-bit with four 32-bit, multiplication is performed. After the multiplication operation is completed, the multiplication result is unmasked again and 4 values of 16 bits are returned.

Algorithm 1 is an optimization implementation code for multiplication on $\mathbb{F}_{2^m}$. Load four 16 bits into one vector register. At this time, four 16-bit values are loaded into each of two vector registers. The having the same value four 16-bit value is loaded into one vector register (v0) and four different 16-bit values are loaded into another vector register (v1)in lines 5–6. Lines 7–8 are performed a masking operation is applied to the four 16-bit values received as input. This masking process ensures that the variables are appropriately extended to 32 bits. Lines 9–26 perform multiplication operations. Lines 27–37 perform the multiplication operations, reduction operations are performed to obtain the desired

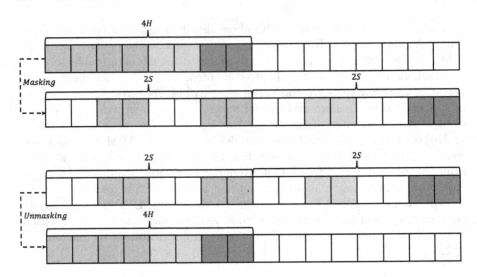

Fig. 2. Masking and Unmasking (In Classic McEliece)

results. Line 38 performs unmasking on the multiplication result. Lines 39–41 call the result of the previous multiplication operation, perform the multiplication operation and xor operation as above, and store the result of the multiplication operation in x0. Lines 42–43 return to Line 4 to Label if the value of x8 is not 0, and repeat the operation until the value of x8 becomes 0. Lines 44–48 When the value of x8 becomes 0, the value of x9 is subtracted by one. The address value of x2, which is loaded into v1, and the address value of x0, where the operation result is stored, are moved appropriately. Move the address value of x1 loaded into v0 by 16 bits. The above operations are repeated until the value of x9 becomes 0.

3.2   Multiplication on $\mathbb{F}_{2^{13t}}$

The commutative property, also known as the exchange law, states that the order of operands in a mathematical operation can be interchanged without affecting the result (e.g. a * b = b * a). In other words, for any given operation, the outcome remains the same regardless of the order in which the operands are arranged. Based on the commutative property, which holds for the XOR operation as well, we can utilize it to rearrange the order of existing operations. This allows us to interchange the operands involved in XOR operations without affecting the final result. Therefore, we performed operations by modifying the order of multiplication operations by utilizing these properties.

Figure 3 represents the original order of multiplication operations performed. The existing multiplication operations follow a sequential process for performing 16-bit multiplication, as illustrated in Fig. 3(a). Once the operations depicted in Fig. 3(a) are completed, the multiplication computations proceed in the order presented in Fig. 3(b).

Algorithm 1. In Classic McEliece-348864, 16-bit value multiplication operation;(x0 : Result of Multiplication Operation, x1, x2 : Input of Multiplication Operation)

```
 1: mov x9, #64                      24: and.16b v8, v1, v5
 2: loop_i:                          25: mul.4s v8, v0, v8
 3: mov x8, #64                      26: eor.16b v6, v6, v8

 4: loop_j:                              //Reduction
 5: ld1R {v0.4h}, [x1]               27: and.16b v9, v6, v14
 6: ld1 {v1.4h}, [x2], #8            28: sri.4s v10, v9, #9
                                     29: eor.16b v6, v6, v10
    //masking                        30: sri.4s v10, v9, #12
 7: zip1.8h v0, v0, v3               31: eor.16b v6, v6, v10
 8: zip1.8h v1, v1, v3
                                     32: and.16b v9, v6, v15
    //Multiplication                 33: sri.4s v10, v9, #9
 9: and.16b v8, v1, v4               34: eor.16b v6, v6, v10
10: mul.4s v6, v8, v0                35: sri.4s v10, v9, #12
                                     36: eor.16b v6, v6, v10
11: shl.4s v5, v4, #1
12: and.16b v8, v1, v5               37: and.16b v6, v6, v11
13: mul.4s v8, v0, v8
14: eor.16b v6, v6, v8                   //unmasking
                                     38: uzp1.8h v6, v6, v7
15: shl.4s v5, v4, #2
16: and.16b v8, v1, v5               39: ld1.4h {v2}, [x0]
17: mul.4s v8, v0, v8                40: eor.16b v2, v2, v6
18: eor.16b v6, v6, v8
                                     41: st1.4h {v2}, [x0], #8
     :
     :                               42: add x8, x8, #-4
                                     43: cbnz x8, loop_j
19: shl.4s v5, v4, #10
20: and.16b v8, v1, v5               44: add x0, x0, #-126
21: mul.4s v8, v0, v8                45: add x2, x2, #-128
22: eor.16b v6, v6, v8               46: add x1, x1, #2

23: shl.4s v5, v4, 11                47: add x9, x9, #-1
                                     48: cbnz x9, loop_i
```

Figure 4 shows the sequence of the proposed multiplication operation using four 16-bit loaded vector registers. To leverage the commutative property of the XOR operation, the paper adopts a modified approach as illustrated in Fig. 4. The results of the multiplication operations, denoted as (a), (b), (c), and (d) in Fig. 4, are stored in each registers designated as temp. Since the XOR operation is commutative, the order of the values does not impact the final result,

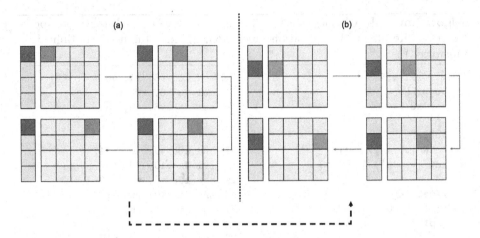

Fig. 3. Order of existing multiplication operations.

allowing for efficient parallel loading and processing. By adopting this strategy, the paper maximizes the utilization of parallel operations and takes advantage of the commutative property of XOR operation, resulting in improved efficiency in the multiplication process.

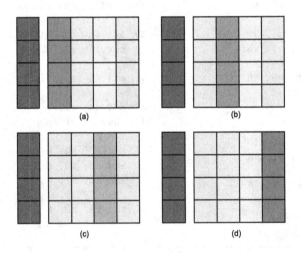

Fig. 4. Order of new multiplication operations.

Algorithm 2 is part of the optimization implementation code for multiplication on $\mathbb{F}_{2^{13t}}$. Lines 4–7 perform operations corresponding to (a), (b), (c), and (d) in Fig. 4 respectively. Lines 8–23 are operations that store the values calculated through Lines 4–7. Address values are directly calculated for each of them, and the address values are moved and stored. Lines 24–26 perform the operation by adding the direct address value appropriately, and the operation of Lines 4–25 is performed until the value of x9 becomes 0. Lines 35–59 are stored using the st1 v2.h[n] because they need to store values for three 16-bit values (n: 0 to 2).

Algorithm 2. In Classic McEliece-348864, 16-bit value multiplication on $\mathbb{F}_{2^{13}t}$ operation.

1: mov x9, #15	30: 4_byte_gf_mul_1781
2: add x0, x0, #246	31: 4_byte_gf_mul_373
3: loop:	32: add x0, x0, #-110
4: 4_byte_gf_mul_877	33: ld1.4h {v2}, [x0]
5: 4_byte_gf_mul_2888	34: eor.16b v2, v2, v20
6: 4_byte_gf_mul_1781	
7: 4_byte_gf_mul_373	35: st1 v2.h[0], [x0], #2
	36: st1 v2.h[1], [x0], #2
8: add x0, x0, #-110	37: st1 v2.h[2], [x0]
9: ld1.4h {v2}, [x0]	38: add x0, x0, #-4
10: eor.16b v2, v2, v20	
11: st1.4h {v2}, [x0]	39: add x0, x0, #-4
	40: ld1.4h {v2}, [x0]
12: add x0, x0, #-4	41: eor.16b v2, v2, v21
13: ld1.4h {v2}, [x0]	
14: eor.16b v2, v2, v21	42: st1 v2.h[0], [x0], #2
15: st1.4h {v2}, [x0]	43: st1 v2.h[1], [x0], #2
	44: st1 v2.h[2], [x0]
16: add x0, x0, #-4	45: add x0, x0, #-4
17: ld1.4h {v2}, [x0]	
18: eor.16b v2, v2, v22	46: add x0, x0, #-4
19: st1.4h {v2}, [x0]	47: ld1.4h {v2}, [x0]
	48: eor.16b v2, v2, v22
20: add x0, x0, #-10	
21: ld1.4h {v2}, [x0]	49: st1 v2.h[0], [x0], #2
22: eor.16b v2, v2, v23	50: st1 v2.h[1], [x0], #2
23: st1.4h v2, [x0]	51: st1 v2.h[2], [x0]
	52: add x0, x0, #-4
24: add x0, x0, #120	
	53: add x0, x0, #-10
25: add x9, x9, #-1	54: ld1.4h {v2}, [x0]
26: cbnz x9, loop	55: eor.16b v2, v2, v23
	56: st1 v2.h[0], [x0], #2
27: add x0, x0, #2	57: st1 v2.h[1], [x0], #2
	58: st1 v2.h[2], [x0]
28: 4_byte_gf_mul_877	59: add x0, x0, #-4
29: 4_byte_gf_mul_2888	

Algorithm 3 is one of the macros used by Algorithm 2. So, Algorithm 1 Therefore, multiplication operation is possible in the same way as Algorithm 1. However, Algorithm 3 performs a load for four 16 bits and performs one masking process over one whole. Because, the other multiplication is a 32-bit constant value, enter the value directly through Line 2 and use it for operation.

Algorithm 3. In Classic McEliece-348864, multiplication $\mathbb{F}_{2^{13}}$ macro for 16-bit value multiplication for $\mathbb{F}_{2^{13}t}$.

```
.macro 4_byte_gf_mul_877              16: mul.4s v8, v0, v8
1: ld1 {v0.4h}, [x0]                  17: eor.16b v6, v6, v8
2: mov.8h v1, v12
                                      18: shl.4s v5, v4, 11
   //masking                         19: and.16b v8, v1, v5
3: zip1.8h v0, v0, v3                 20: mul.4s v8, v0, v8
                                      21: eor.16b v6, v6, v8
   //Multiplication
4: and.16b v8, v1, v4
5: mul.4s v6, v8, v0                  22: and.16b v9, v6, v14
                                      23: sri.4s v10, v9, #9
                                      24: eor.16b v6, v6, v10
6: shl.4s v5, v4, #1                  25: sri.4s v10, v9, #12
7: and.16b v8, v1, v5                 26: eor.16b v6, v6, v10
8: mul.4s v8, v0, v8
9: eor.16b v6, v6, v8                 27: and.16b v9, v6, v15
                                      28: sri.4s v10, v9, #9
10: shl.4s v5, v4, #2                 29: eor.16b v6, v6, v10
11: and.16b v8, v1, v5                30: sri.4s v10, v9, #12
12: mul.4s v8, v0, v8                 31: eor.16b v6, v6, v10
13: eor.16b v6, v6, v8
                                      32: and.16b v6, v6, v11
   ⋮
                                         //unmasking
                                      33: uzp1.8h v20, v6, v7
14: shl.4s v5, v4, #10                .endm
15: and.16b v8, v1, v5
```

---

4 Evaluation

In this section, we evaluate the proposed implementation and reference C implementation (PQ-Clean project reference code in C language) [14]. Since the previous work did not conduct a separate performance evaluation of the multiplier, so it was not included in the performance evaluation [19].

The implementation were developed through the Xcode 14.3 framework and carried out through the Xcode IDE. The implementation were evaluated on a MacBook Pro 13 with the Apple M1 chip that can be clocked up to 3.2 GHz.

Table 3. Evaluation results of multiplier on ARMv8 processors (Apple M1 chip); (cc : Clock Cycle).

Scheme		PQ-Clean	This Work
Classic McEliece 348864	ms	4,294	5,429
	cc	13,740	17,372
Classic McEliece 460896	ms	40,579	14,563
	cc	129,852	46,601
Classic McEliece 6699128	ms	71,185	25,343
	cc	227,792	81,097
Classic McEliece 6960119	ms	61,690	21,972
	cc	197,408	70,310
Classic McEliece 819212	ms	71,193	25,222
	cc	227,817	80,710

Therefore, we measured the operation time by repeating the 1,000,000 times and compiled using the compile option -O2 (i.e. faster). Performance evaluation is given in Table 3. The performance of the implementation of Multiplier optimization using vector registers performed in Classic Mceliece 348864 is 0.79× times lower than [14]. The performance of the implementation of Multiplier optimization using vector registers performed in Classic Mceliece 46089 is 2.79× times higher than [14]. The performance of the implementation of Multiplier optimization using vector registers performed in Classic Mceliece 6699128 is 2.80× times higher than [14]. The performance of the implementation of Multiplier optimization using vector registers performed in Classic Mceliece 6960119 is 2.81× times higher than [14]. The performance of the implementation of Multiplier optimization using vector registers performed in Classic Mceliece 819212 is 2.82× times higher than [14].

According to the performance evaluation, the experimental results verified that the utilization of the proposed method led to a significant performance enhancement of up to 2.82× compared to the reference implementation.

5 Conclusion

In this paper, a parallel multiplication implementation technique for Classic McEliece 348864 was introduced. The proposed method utilizes vector registers and vector instructions of the ARMv8 processor. The proposed parallel multiplication operation efficiently computes multiplication in a parallel manner by exploiting the commutative law and rearranging the order of internal operations. As a result, the proposed method significantly improves the efficiency of the multiplication operation in terms of speed and performance. The performance evaluation results achieve that the proposed multiplication technique achieves a speed improvement of 2.82× compared to the PQ-Clean reference implementation.

Acknowledgements. This work was supported by Institute for Information & communications Technology Promotion (IITP) grant funded by the Korea government (MSIT) (No. 2018-0-00264, Research on Blockchain Security Technology for IoT Services, 50%) and this work was supported by Institute of Information & communications Technology Planning & Evaluation (IITP) grant funded by the Korea government (MSIT) (No. 2022-0-00627, Development of Lightweight BIoT technology for Highly Constrained Devices, 50%).

References

1. NIST PQC project. https://csrc.nist.gov/Projects/post-quantum-cryptography. Accessed 29 July 2022
2. Avanzi, R., et al.: CRYSTALS-Kyber algorithm specifications and supporting documentation. NIST PQC Round **2**(4), 1–43 (2019)
3. Ducas, L., et al.: Crystals-Dilithium: a lattice-based digital signature scheme. IACR Trans. Cryptogr. Hardw. Embedded Syst.ms **2018**, 238–268 (2018)
4. Bernstein, D.J., Hülsing, A., Kölbl, S., Niederhagen, R., Rijneveld, J., Schwabe, P.: The SPHINCS+ signature framework. In: Proceedings of the 2019 ACM SIGSAC Conference on Computer and Communications Security, pp. 2129–2146 (2019)
5. Fouque, P.-A., et al.: Falcon: Fast-Fourier lattice-based compact signatures over NTRU. Submiss. NIST's Post-quantum Cryptogr. Stand. Process **36**(5), 1–75 (2018)
6. Kim, Y., Song, J., Seo, S.C.: Accelerating falcon on ARMv8. IEEE Access **10**, 44446–44460 (2022)
7. Becker, H., Hwang, V., Kannwischer, M.J., Yang, B.-Y., Yang, S.-Y.: Neon NTT: faster Dilithium, Kyber, and Saber on Cortex-A72 and Apple M1. Cryptology ePrint Archive (2021)
8. Sanal, P., Karagoz, E., Seo, H., Azarderakhsh, R., Mozaffari-Kermani, M.: Kyber on ARM64: compact implementations of Kyber on 64-Bit ARM cortex-A processors. In: Garcia-Alfaro, J., Li, S., Poovendran, R., Debar, H., Yung, M. (eds.) SecureComm 2021. LNICST, vol. 399, pp. 424–440. Springer, Cham (2021). https://doi.org/10.1007/978-3-030-90022-9_23
9. Kim, Y., Song, J., Youn, T.-Y., Seo, S.C.: Crystals-Dilithium on ARMv8. Secur. Commun. Netw. **2022**, 1–12 (2022)
10. Kölbl, S.: Putting wings on SPHINCS. In: Lange, T., Steinwandt, R. (eds.) PQCrypto 2018. LNCS, vol. 10786, pp. 205–226. Springer, Cham (2018). https://doi.org/10.1007/978-3-319-79063-3_10
11. Becker, H., Kannwischer, M.J.: Hybrid scalar/vector implementations of Keccak and SPHINCS+ on AArch64. Cryptology ePrint Archive (2022)
12. Bernstein, D.J., et al.: Classic McEliece: conservative code-based cryptography. NIST Submissions (2017)
13. McEliece, R.J.: A public-key cryptosystem based on algebraic. Coding Thv **4244**, 114–116 (1978)
14. PQClean project. https://github.com/PQClean/PQClean. Accessed 29 July 2022
15. Armv8-A instruction set architecture. https://developer.arm.com/documentation/den0024/a/An-Introduction-to-the-ARMv8-Instruction-Sets. Accessed 07 June 2023
16. Kwon, H., Kim, H., Sim, M., Lee, W.-K., Seo, H.: Look-up the rainbow: efficient table-based parallel implementation of rainbow signature on 64-bit ARMv8 processors. Cryptology ePrint Archive (2021)

17. Kwon, H., et al.: ARMing-sword: scabbard on ARM. In: You, I., Youn, T.Y. (eds.) Information Security Applications. LNCS, vol. 13720, pp. 237–250. Springer, Cham (2022). https://doi.org/10.1007/978-3-031-25659-2_17
18. Chen, M.-S., Chou, T.: Classic McEliece on the ARM cortex-M4. IACR Trans. Cryptogr. Hardw. Embedded Syst. **2021**, 125–148 (2021)
19. Sim, M., Eum, S., Kwon, H., Kim, H., Seo, H.: Optimized implementation of encapsulation and decapsulation of Classic McEliece on ARMv8. Cryptology ePrint Archive (2022)

Evaluating KpqC Algorithm Submissions: Balanced and Clean Benchmarking Approach

Hyeokdong Kwon[1] , Minjoo Sim[1] , Gyeongju Song[1] , Minwoo Lee[2] ,
and Hwajeong Seo[2(✉)]

[1] Department of Information Computer Engineering, Hansung University,
Seoul 02876, South Korea
[2] Department of Convergence Security, Hansung University,
Seoul 02876, South Korea
hwajeong84@gmail.com

Abstract. In 2022, a Korean domestic Post Quantum Cryptography contest called KpqC held, and the standard for Post Quantum Cryptography is set to be selected in 2024. In Round 1 of this competition, 16 algorithms have advanced and are competing. Algorithms submitted to KpqC introduce their performance, but direct performance comparison is difficult because all algorithms were measured in different environments. In this paper, we present the benchmark results of all KpqC algorithms in a single environment. To benchmark the algorithms, we removed the external library dependency of each algorithm. By removing dependencies, performance deviations due to external libraries can be eliminated, and source codes that can conveniently operate the KpqC algorithm can be provided to users who have difficulty setting up the environment.

Keywords: Benchmark · Cryptography Implementation · KpqC ·
Post Quantum Cryptography · Standardization

1 Introduction

Quantum computers, first proposed by physicist Richard Feynman in 1981 [1], gradually began to materialize with the introduction of quantum algorithms by Professor David Deutsch in 1985 [2]. Quantum computers can execute quantum algorithms, which pose a significant threat to modern cryptosystems. One example is Grover's algorithm, an algorithm designed to locate specific data among n unsorted data entries [3]. A classical computer would require a brute force search of at most $O(2^n)$ attempts. However, Grover's algorithm reduces the search time to a maximum of $O(2^{n/2})$. This effectively halves the security of symmetric key algorithms and hash functions. Another powerful quantum algorithm is the Shor algorithm, which efficiently performs prime factorization [4]. The Shor algorithm can break public key algorithms such as RSA and ECC in polynomial time. While symmetric key algorithms can temporarily mitigate the threat posed by quantum

© The Author(s), under exclusive license to Springer Nature Singapore Pte Ltd. 2024
H. Kim and J. Youn (Eds.): WISA 2023, LNCS 14402, pp. 338–348, 2024.
https://doi.org/10.1007/978-981-99-8024-6_26

computers by doubling the key length, public key algorithms lack such defenses. To address this issue, NIST initiated a Post Quantum Cryptography competition to foster the development, standardization, and distribution of Post Quantum Cryptography [5]. Similarly, a Post Quantum Cryptography contest was held in Korea, marking the beginning of the process to select a Korean standard. In this paper, we eliminate the dependencies of the algorithms submitted to the KpqC competition and present benchmark results in a standardized environment.

1.1 Contributions

- **Benchmark results in common development environments.** All algorithms in KpqC Round 1 come with detailed white papers that include performance measurements. The provided benchmarks, prepared by the development teams, are highly reliable. However, a challenge arises from the fact that the benchmark environments in the white papers differ. Therefore, conducting the benchmark in an environment with sufficient resources can provide advantageous results. To address this, we conducted a collective benchmark of all algorithms in a standardized environment, enabling a fair performance comparison among the algorithms.
- **Enhancing accessibility by eliminating working dependencies.** Many of the KpqC candidate algorithms rely on external libraries for their implementation. These dependencies offer significant benefits by providing pre-existing modules for algorithm implementation, eliminating the need for separate implementation. However, from the perspective of downloading and using the source code, the absence of these dependencies can create complexity and hinder code operation. This issue is particularly challenging for novice users who may struggle with setting up the development environment. To address this, our focus was on removing the dependencies associated with the algorithms. This approach offers two key advantages.

  Firstly, it enables immediate use of the source code without the need to set up the environment. By distributing the source code in a runnable state, even users unfamiliar with environment setup can easily operate the code. This greatly enhances the accessibility of the source code and attracts a broader user base.

  Secondly, it ensures a fair benchmarking process. While most libraries used are likely to be the same, discrepancies can still arise due to differences in library versions during environment setup. By eliminating external library dependencies and replacing the necessary modules with identical source code, we can provide more accurate and equitable benchmark results.

The rest of the paper is structured as follows. Section 2 provides an overview of the Post Quantum Cryptography contest and the specific details of KpqC. Additionally, we introduce the PQClean project, which served as the inspiration for the research discussed in this paper. In Sect. 3, we detail the methodology employed to benchmark the KpqC algorithms and present the obtained benchmark results. Finally, Sect. 4 concludes the paper by summarizing the key findings and discussing potential directions for future research.

2   Related Works

2.1   NIST Standardization of Post Quantum Cryptography

The significance of Post Quantum Cryptography (PQC) has emerged as a means to ensure secure communication in the age of quantum computers. The United States National Institute of Standards and Technology (NIST) initiated the PQC Standardization Contest in 2016. In 2022, standard algorithms were selected, and Round 4 was conducted to determine additional standards [6]. Following the standard selection process, CRYSTALS-Kyber [7] was chosen as the Key Encapsulation Mechanism (KEM). In the Digital Signature category, the selected algorithms include CRYSTALS-Dilithium [8], Falcon [9], and SPHINCS+ [10]. Round 4 is currently underway to select additional standards for the KEM category, with BIKE [11], Classic McEliece [12], and HQC [13] competing. Although SIKE [14] advanced to Round 4, it subsequently withdrew from the contest due to the discovery of a security vulnerability [15].

2.2   KpqC: Korea's Post Quantum Cryptography Standardization

KpqC, the domestic contest for standardizing Post Quantum Cryptography in Korea, took place at the end of 2021 [16]. The timeline of the KpqC competition is presented in Table 1. The results of Round 1 were announced at the end of 2022, with 16 algorithms passing the evaluation. Subsequently, the Round 2 results will be announced in December 2023, and the final standard will be selected in September 2024. KpqC has defined four evaluation criteria for assessing the algorithms.

The first criterion is safety. Algorithms must demonstrate their security and provide proof of their safety. It is crucial for these algorithms to ensure security not only on quantum computers but also on classical computers.

The second criterion is efficiency. The computational resources required to execute the algorithm should be reasonable, and the computation time should not be excessively long. Some algorithms may have a probability of decryption or verification failure due to their structure, but this failure probability should not hinder their practical use.

The third criterion is usability. The implemented algorithm should be capable of operating in various environments, ensuring its usability across different systems.

The final criterion is originality. The proposed algorithm should possess a creative and innovative structure, showcasing novel approaches in the field of Post Quantum Cryptography.

In Kpqc Round 1, a total of 7 algorithms were chosen in the Key Encapsulation Mechanism (KEM) category, and 9 algorithms were selected in the Digital Signature category. The specific algorithms that passed the evaluation can be found in Table 2. Notably, among the selected algorithms, the Lattice-based algorithms demonstrate strong performance. This observation aligns with the NIST PQC standard, where three out of the four selected standards are also Lattice-based algorithms.

Table 1. Timeline of KpqC competetion.

Phase	Date
Announcement of holding KpqC	2021. 11
Deadline for submitting candidate algorithms	2022. 10
Announcement of Round 1 Results	2022. 12
Scheduled date for announcement of Round 2 results	2023. 9
Scheduled date of announcement of standard selection	2024. 09

Table 2. KpqC Round 1 candidate algorithms.

Scheme	PKE/KEM	Digital Signature
Code-based	IPCC [17]	Enhanced pqsigRM [18]
	Layered-ROLLO [19]	
	PALOMA [20]	
	REDOG [21]	
Lattice-based		GCKSign [22]
	NTRU+ [23]	HAETAE [24]
	SMAUG [25]	NCC-Sign [26]
	TiGER [27]	Peregrine [28]
		SOLMAE [29]
Multivariate Quadratic-based	–	MQ-Sign [30]
Hash-based	–	FIBS [31]
Zero knowledge-based	–	AIMer [32]

2.3   PQClean

A significant number of NIST's Post Quantum Cryptography algorithms rely on external libraries. Utilizing pre-existing implementations rather than building modules from scratch is more efficient in cryptographic algorithm implementation, resulting in the creation of dependencies on external libraries. While dependencies are convenient during development, they can pose inconvenience when using the implemented source code as the development environment must be set up accordingly. To address this issue, PQClean, a library introduced in [33], focuses on removing these dependencies to enable easy operation of Post Quantum Cryptography (PQC).

PQClean not only aims to make source code operation more convenient by eliminating library dependencies but also places emphasis on improving the overall quality of the source code. To achieve this, PQClean conducted approximately 30 implementation checklists. These checklists included verifying adherence to the C standard, ensuring consistency in compilation rules, minimizing Makefiles, and confirming the consistency of integer data. As a result, PQClean not only facilitates the convenient operation of source code by removing library dependencies but also provides clean source code for higher quality implementation.

Another advantage of PQClean is its ease of portability to other platforms or frameworks, as it does not form dependencies. For instance, pqm4 is a library that collectively executes NIST PQC on ARM Cortex-M4 and provides benchmark results [34]. This showcases the versatility and compatibility of PQClean in various computing environments.

3 KPQClean: Clean Benchmark on KpqC

Building upon the inspiration of PQClean, we undertook the KPQClean project for the KpqC competition. The initial phase involved working with a total of 16 candidate algorithms from KpqC Round 1. To present the results, we focused on removing external dependencies for each algorithm and conducting benchmarking.

The project proceeded in a systematic manner, starting with the removal of libraries and subsequently addressing the Makefile rules and benchmarking. During the library removal process, we carefully examined the dependencies present in each code. Most KpqC algorithms rely on OpenSSL [35] and utilize OpenSSL's AES for random number generation. To eliminate these dependencies, the code sections that made external library calls were removed. Consequently, the externally implemented algorithms can no longer be used in their original form. To ensure the operation of these algorithms, we directly integrated the source code that implements the algorithms. For instance, the AES algorithm requires the utilization of CTR-DRBG. We ported the AES code used by PQClean, making necessary modifications to the internal structure to ensure seamless functionality. This approach enables the development of code that operates independently by eliminating external library dependencies.

The next step involved writing a unified Makefile. Most KpqC candidate algorithms offer convenient compilation using gcc by providing compilation rules in the Makefile. However, variations in compilation rules across different algorithms can lead to discrepancies in performance measurements. To address this, we made efforts to create a standardized Makefile with consistent rules, thereby ensuring fair and comparable benchmarking results.

Lastly, the benchmarking process was conducted. A dedicated source code for benchmarking was prepared, compiled, and executed. The benchmarking environment resembled the specifications outlined in Table 3. The two devices use a Ryzen processor and an Intel processor, respectively, and the rest of the device specifications are almost identical. To obtain the measurements, each algorithm underwent 10,000 iterations, and the median number of clock cycles required for operation was calculated for each round. We applied -O2 as an optimization level option. However, most of the KpqC algorithms performed performance measurements on -O3. Therefore, -O3 performance was additionally measured to reflect the developer's intention.

Table 4 presents the benchmark results for the Key Encapsulation Mechanism (KEM) algorithms. Among the KEM candidates, SMAUG performed the best in the Keygen operation, NTRU+ excelled in Encapsulation, and PALOMA show-cased the best performance in Decapsulation. However, it is worth noting that IPCC-1's Encapsulation measurement exhibited excessively slow performance, leading to the exclusion of its measurement as an error value. As a result, it was temporarily excluded from the benchmark.

One KEM algorithm REDOG, was temporarily excluded from the bench-marking process. REDOG presented a unique case as it was implemented in pure Python while all algorithm analyses were based on the C language. Consequently, REDOG was excluded from the benchmarking process as it deviated from the performance standards used for other algorithms.

Table 3. Benchmark environment.

	Environment 1	Environment 2
CPU	Ryzen 7 4800H	Intel i5-8259U
GPU	RTX 3060	Coffee Lake GT3e
RAM	16 GB	16 GB
OS	Ubuntu 22.04	Ubuntu 22.04
Compiler	gcc 11.3.0	gcc 11.3.0
Optimization level	-O2, -O3	-O2, -O3
Editor	Visual Studio Code	Visual Studio Code

Table 5 presents the benchmark results for the Digital Signature candidate algorithms. The performance measurements were conducted in the same bench-marking environment as the Key Encapsulation Mechanism (KEM) algorithms.

In the Digital Signature category, AIMer demonstrated excellent performance in the Keygen operation, while Peregrine showcased exceptional performance in Sign and Verification. However, accurate measurements for FIBS could not be obtained due to incomplete calculations, rendering its measurement inconclusive.

In common, the operation on the Intel processor tends to be somewhat faster than the operation on the Ryzen processor. This is because the Intel processor used in the experiment had better performance than the Ryzen processor. Also, for many algorithms, the performance difference between the -O2 and -O3 options is not noticeable. This is because each algorithm is well optimized and no further optimization is performed at the compiler level. Some algorithms perform better with the -O3 option. In this case, it can be said that the algorithms have a point where optimization is possible.

Table 4. Benchmark result of KpqC KEM Round 1 Candidates. (Unit: clock cycles (algorithm speed), Strikethrough: Lack of consistency in benchmarks, [A]: AVX applied.)

	Environment 1 -O2			Environment 2 -O2		
Algorithm	Keygen	Encapsulation	Decapsulation	Keygen	Encapsulation	Decapsulation
IPCC-1	14,362,627	~~164,892,550~~	2,484,981	13,792,887	~~159,126,051~~	1,196,157
IPCC-3	14,170,647	898,710	2,619,570	13,754,219	870,059	1,235,991
IPCC-4	14,209,594	1,075,059	2,904,524	13,754,687	1,050,451	1,318,173
NTRU+-576[A]	208,742	111,998	128,093	186,944	105,686	120,194
NTRU+-768[A]	279,386	148,480	181,250	246,616	139,310	166,938
NTRU+-864[A]	304,819	179,858	224,953	270,494	160,789	200,702
NTRU+-1152[A]	444,744	223,619	278,690	698,490	202,678	257,114
PALOMA-128	125,800,419	510,922	35,496	118,204,341	499,914	39,724
PALOMA-192	125,360,779	514,228	34,220	118,310,371	499,302	38,846
PALOMA-256	125,294,065	510,284	34,713	118,366,206	503,814	43,174
SMAUG-128	171,477	154,483	178,205	158,149	164,598	196,470
SMAUG-192	250,096	229,999	277,298	244,736	225,490	272,132
SMAUG-256	479,138	385,178	438,364	435,790	411,917	465,572
TiGER-128	273,470	466,755	628,778	163,856	209,168	311,924
TiGER-192	288,550	518,491	674,192	171,578	214,126	312,702
TiGER-256	536,152	~~1,088,747~~	~~1,477,318~~	444,558	433,462	673,105
	Environment 1 -O3			Environment 2 -O3		
IPCC-1	13,940,097	~~160,111,204~~	~~16,360,164~~	12,643,392	~~145,233,220~~	1,159,273
IPCC-3	13,996,024	926,492	2,512,836	12,795,377	874,663	1,206,585
IPCC-4	13,989,832	1,106,031	2,714,531	13,078,917	1,037,485	1,310,503
NTRU+-576[A]	202,652	110,026	121,742	177,748	102,296	111,820
NTRU+-768[A]	270,512	146,566	174,435	239,546	137,135	161,970
NTRU+-864[A]	297,192	168,113	204,537	260,672	153,481	186,386
NTRU+-1152[A]	435,305	222,459	266,626	568,556	201,226	246,050
PALOMA-128	122,325,408	498,365	34,307	108,402,198	459,846	40,838
PALOMA-192	122,290,738	503,266	34,278	108,206,652	460,374	40,688
PALOMA-256	122,321,957	497,959	34,249	108,216,713	459,880	40,886
SMAUG-128	72,790	57,246	50,460	63,020	49,324	39,196
SMAUG-192	105,966	82,940	80,475	92,658	69,739	67,691
SMAUG-256	158,021	139,925	135,749	135,202	122,766	115,096
TiGER-128	65,482	48,749	51,214	62,490	45,398	53,248
TiGER-192	69,426	63,510	57,739	66,512	60,238	58,572
TiGER-256	81,316	87,551	93,090	78,772	82,776	89,902
Layered ROLLO I-128[A]	285,940	83,346	788,104	203,181	66,529	558,503
Layered ROLLO I-192[A]	320,958	136,503	518,491	227,813	102,758	671,605
Layered ROLLO I-256[A]	687,721	201,913	1,014,203	375,056	136,052	1,245,346

Table 5. Benchmark result of KpqC Digital Signature Round 1 Candidates. (Unit: clock cycles (algorithm speed), $_o$: original(NCCSign) $_c$: conserparam (NCCSign), Strikethrough: Lack of consistency in benchmarks, ^{A}: AVX applied.)

Algorithm	Environment 1 -O2			Environment 2 -O2		
	Keygen	Sign	Verification	Keygen	Sign	Verification
AIMer-I	145,058	3,912,361	3,669,834	145,566	3,691,256	3,713,173
AIMer-III	296,496	8,001,274	7,550,063	274,358	7,771,108	7,366,672
AIMer-V	710,442	18,068,276	17,415,022	790,456	18,394,069	17,662,359
GCKSign-II	179,771	601,707	176,987	171,176	640,093	167,116
GCKSign-III	186,673	649,049	183,367	173,252	698,964	168,824
GCKSign-V	252,822	917,415	277,733	248,629	945,815	273,631
HAETAE-II	798,312	4,605,461	147,494	700,875	4,173,002	142,584
HAETAE-III	~~1,533,941~~	~~11,474,155~~	257,926	~~1,352,577~~	10,615,663	250,534
HAETAE-V	846,713	3,902,298	305,428	752,413	3,418,728	311,986
MQSign-72/46	94,788,559	516,954	1,461,281	87,038,447	509,630	1,377,392
MQSign-112/72	488,913,828	1,493,703	5,211,909	448,271,119	1,472,032	4,808,216
MQSign-148/96	1,488,480,956	3,162,943	12,036,827	1,326,638,494	3,128,536	11,091,036
NCCSign-I$_o^A$	2,650,542	10,404,301	5,232,079	2,296,351	15,914,954	4,519,308
NCCSign-III$_o^A$	4,477,513	17,657,839	8,867,243	4,009,717	16,015,734	7,996,462
NCCSign-V$_o^A$	7,240,343	64,377,767	14,358,074	6,561,582	26,019,063	13,005,536
NCCSign-I$_c^A$	1,869,079	23,762,252	3,681,057	1,704,190	27,083,021	3,344,228
NCCSign-III$_c^A$	3,655,334	~~39,587,190~~	7,241,808	3,271,119	~~65,455,745~~	6,533,931
NCCSign-V$_c^A$	6,263,739	179,281,596	12,418,902	5,723,169	39,565,842	6,533,931
Peregrine-512	12,401,256	329,933	37,294	12,073,005	295,128	33,114
Peregrine-1024	39,405,505	709,848	80,243	38,493,479	640,132	71,246
Enhanced pqsigRM-612	6,013,112,315	7,210,560	2,223,401	4,961,556,899	7,505,040	2,125,125
Enhanced pqsigRM-613	58,238,108,879	1,864,512	1,053,034	74,021,054,015	2,113,913	1,126,131
SOLMAE-512^A	23,848,774	378,392	43,935	22,494,902	351,311	64,526
SOLMAE-1024^A	55,350,546	760,380	141,375	52,388,360	706,028	152,984
	Environment 1 -O3			Environment 2 -O3		
AIMer-I	145,986	3,878,272	3,672,923	133,130	3,960,345	3,747,101
AIMer-III	296,032	8,087,462	7,678,098	272,484	8,440,184	7,968,982
AIMer-V	713,922	17,983,857	17,361,691	643,253	17,998,305	17,373,174
GCKSign-II	164,836	537,675	159,674	175,993	597,712	172,893
GCKSign-III	166,199	581,189	161,646	183,987	698,941	179,608
GCKSign-V	231,797	895,549	279,009	238,884	928,251	262,868
HAETAE-II	688,083	3,429,265	131,805	672,901	3,334,242	126,972
HAETAE-III	~~1,329,157~~	~~8,734,670~~	228,578	~~1,291,292~~	~~8,261,232~~	227,780
HAETAE-V	723,318	2,790,612	272,542	719,708	2,627,334	270,600
MQSign-72/46	39,040,917	311,112	512,227	38,474,591	298,952	533,676
MQSign-112/72	115,942,827	669,465	1,143,296	117,049,542	650,928	1,120,124
MQSign-148/96	235,289,035	1,186,622	1,943,667	236,124,011	1,165,706	1,897,664
NCCSign-I$_o^A$	2,619,295	10,301,902	5,171,686	2,317,555	13,776,448	4,568,006
NCCSign-III$_o^A$	4,379,261	~~86,475,041~~	8,685,877	3,981,551	~~83,521,123~~	7,935,382
NCCSign-V$_o^A$	7,178,921	42,637,366	14,245,148	6,333,006	25,183,392	12,555,623
NCCSign-I$_c^A$	1,843,356	~~50,520,712~~	3,636,803	1,666,543	16,352,341	3,248,162
NCCSign-III$_c^A$	3,618,997	21,416,384	7,170,903	3,141,974	34,454,252	6,234,249
NCCSign-V$_c^A$	6,149,059	151,973,282	12,196,791	5,613,303	167,158,023	11,155,020
Peregrine-512	11,953,307	253,402	25,462	11,783,005	260,328	26,262
Peregrine-1024	38,366,232	535,920	53,621	38,493,479	551,168	55,654
Enhanced pqsigRM-612	6,139,551,981	4,610,319	2,278,806	4,702,612,115	4,732,706	2,064,731
Enhanced pqsigRM-613	54,994,439,928	714,647	225,577	71,111,088,778	923,513	417,658
SOLMAE-512^A	23,053,028	349,566	40,513	22,627,042	332,848	64,838
SOLMAE-1024^A	53,966,332	698,581	135,256	53,245,753	668,103	149,168

346   H. Kwon et al.

4 Conclusion

This paper presents a benchmarking effort conducted on the candidate algorithms of KpqC Round 1. To facilitate the benchmarking process, the KPQClean library was developed and is currently available on GitHub[1]. The primary objective of the KPQClean library is to remove dependencies in the KpqC candidate algorithms and provide benchmark results in a standardized environment. However, there are a few limitations that need to be addressed.

Firstly, there are algorithms that have not yet been measured or evaluated. While this issue exists, the goal is to address these gaps and provide benchmark results for all the algorithms. Efforts are ongoing to resolve these outstanding matters.

The second limitation involves the removal of remaining dependencies. Currently, KPQClean focuses on eliminating external library dependencies, but there are other dependencies such as dynamic allocation that still need to be addressed. The aim is to eliminate all dependencies to ensure a fully self-contained library.

Lastly, it is important to rectify any anomalies or unusual values in the measurement results to ensure that they align with normal benchmarking standards. While most algorithms exhibit consistent trends in their measurements, some algorithms may demonstrate anomalies that result in extremely slow performance. These issues will be addressed to provide accurate and reliable benchmark results. This is likely due to limitations of the benchmark method. To measure the performance of the algorithm, many iterations were performed and the median value of the values was used. During this process, the equipment may perform other calculations, and performance may deteriorate due to heat generation. Therefore, we devise a more sophisticated benchmark method.

The KPQClean project is an ongoing endeavor closely aligned with the KpqC Competition. The project aims to present benchmark results in a unified environment while also providing a more convenient PQC library. This endeavor seeks to generate increased interest among researchers and students in the field of KpqC, offering a comfortable and conducive environment for further study and exploration.

References

1. Feynman, R.P.: Simulating physics with computers. In: Feynman and Computation, pp. 133–153. CRC Press (2018)
2. Deutsch, D.: Quantum theory, the Church–Turing principle and the universal quantum computer. Proc. Roy. Soc. Lond. A Math. Phys. Sci. **400**(1818), 97–117 (1985)
3. Grover, L.K.: A fast quantum mechanical algorithm for database search. In: Proceedings of the Twenty-Eighth Annual ACM Symposium on Theory of Computing, pp. 212–219 (1996)
4. Shor, P.W.: Polynomial-time algorithms for prime factorization and discrete logarithms on a quantum computer. SIAM Rev. **41**(2), 303–332 (1999)

---

[1] https://github.com/kpqc-cryptocraft/KPQClean.

5. Jang, K.-B., Seo, H.-J.: Quantum computer and standardization trend of NIST post-quantum cryptography. In: Proceedings of the Korea Information Processing Society Conference, pp. 129–132. Korea Information Processing Society (2019)
6. NIST, Round 4 submissions - post-quantum cryptography: CSRC (2022)
7. Avanzi, R., et al.: CRYSTALS-Kyber algorithm specifications and supporting documentation. NIST PQC Round 2(4), 1–43 (2019)
8. Lyubashevsky, V., et al.: Crystals-dilithium. In: Algorithm Specifications and Supporting Documentation (2020)
9. Prest, T., et al.: Falcon. In: Post-Quantum Cryptography Project of NIST (2020)
10. Bernstein, D.J., Hülsing, A., Kölbl, S., Niederhagen, R., Rijneveld, J., Schwabe, P.: The SPHINCS$^+$ signature framework. In: Proceedings of the 2019 ACM SIGSAC Conference on Computer and Communications Security, pp. 2129–2146 (2019)
11. Aragon, N., et al.: BIKE: bit flipping key encapsulation (2017)
12. Albrecht, M.R., et al.: Classic McEliece. Technical report, National Institute of Standards and Technology (2020)
13. Melchor, C.A., et al.: HQC: hamming quasi-cyclic. In: NIST Post-Quantum Standardization, 3rd Round (2021)
14. Azarderakhsh, R., et al.: Supersingular isogeny key encapsulation. Submission to the NIST Post-Quantum Standardization Project, vol. 152, pp. 154–155 (2017)
15. Castryck, W., Decru, T.: An efficient key recovery attack on SIDH. Cryptology ePrint Archive, Paper 2022/975 (2022). https://eprint.iacr.org/2022/975
16. K. team: KpqC competition round 1 (2023). https://kpqc.or.kr/competition.html. Accessed 07 Apr 2023
17. Ryu, J., Kim, Y., Yoon, S., Kang, J.-S., Yeom, Y.: IPCC-improved perfect code cryptosystems (2022)
18. Cho, J., No, J.-S., Lee, Y., Koo, Z., Kim, Y.-S.: Enhanced pqsigRM: code-based digital signature scheme with short signature and fast verification for post-quantum cryptography. Cryptology ePrint Archive (2022)
19. Kim, C., Kim, Y.-S., No, J.-S.: Layered ROLLO-I: faster rank-metric code-based KEM using ideal LRPC codes. Cryptology ePrint Archive (2022)
20. Kim, D.-C., Jeon, C.-Y., Kim, Y., Kim, M.: PALOMA: binary separable Goppa-based KEM. In: Esser, A., Santini, P. (eds.) CBCrypto 2023. LNCS, vol. 14311, pp. 144–173. Springer, Cham (2022). https://doi.org/10.1007/978-3-031-46495-9_8
21. Kim, J.-L., et al.: REDOG and its performance analysis. Cryptology ePrint Archive (2022)
22. Woo, J., Lee, K., Park, J.H.: GCKSign: simple and efficient signatures from generalized compact knapsacks. Cryptology ePrint Archive (2022)
23. Kim, J., Park, J.H.: NTRU+: compact construction of NTRU using simple encoding method. Cryptology ePrint Archive (2022)
24. Cheon, J.H., et al.: HAETAE: hyperball bimodal module rejection signature scheme (2023)
25. Cheon, J.H., et al.: SMAUG: the key exchange algorithm based on module-LWE and module-LWR (2023)
26. Shim, K.-A., Kim, J., An, Y.: NCC-Sign: a new lattice-based signature scheme using non-cyclotomic polynomials (2023)
27. Park, S., Jung, C.-G., Park, A., Choi, J., Kang, H.: TiGER: tiny bandwidth key encapsulation mechanism for easy miGration based on RLWE (R). Cryptology ePrint Archive (2022)
28. Seo, E.-Y., Kim, Y.-S., Lee, J.-W., No, J.-S.: Peregrine: toward fastest FALCON based on GPV framework. Cryptology ePrint Archive (2022)

29. Kim, K., et al.: SOLMAE algorithm specifications (2022)
30. Shim, K.-A., Kim, J., An, Y.: MQ-Sign: a new post-quantum signature scheme based on multivariate quadratic equations: shorter and faster (2022)
31. Kim, S., Lee, Y., Yoon, K.: FIBS: fast isogeny based digital signature (2022)
32. Kim, S., et al.: The AIMer signature scheme (2023)
33. Kannwischer, M.J., Schwabe, P., Stebila, D., Wiggers, T.: Improving software quality in cryptography standardization projects. In: 2022 IEEE European Symposium on Security and Privacy Workshops (EuroS&PW), pp. 19–30. IEEE (2022)
34. Kannwischer, M.J., Rijneveld, J., Schwabe, P., Stoffelen, K.: pqm4: testing and benchmarking NIST PQC on ARM Cortex-M4 (2019)
35. Viega, J., Messier, M., Chandra, P.: Network Security with openSSL: Cryptography for Secure Communications. O'Reilly Media, Inc. (2002)

Author Index

Printed in the United States
by Baker & Taylor Publisher Services

Printed in the United States
by Baker & Taylor Publisher Services